THE ESSENTIAL EURIPIDES
Dancing in Dark Times

THE ESSENTIAL EURIPIDES
Dancing in Dark Times

Robert Emmet Meagher

BOLCHAZY-CARDUCCI PUBLISHERS, INC.
WAUCONDA, ILLINOIS

Printed in the United States of America
by United Graphics.
Cover and text design by Anne May.
Cover Drawing by Elizabeth Neave.

Mortal Vision: The Wisdom of Euripides
Originally published by St. Martin's Press, 1989.

Euripides, *Helen*
University of Massachusetts Press, 1986.
Published here with permission.

ISBN 0-86516-513-0
Published by
BOLCHAZY-CARDUCCI PUBLISHERS, INC.
1000 Brown Street, Unit 101, Wauconda, Illinois 60084 USA
WWW.BOLCHAZY.COM

Library of Congress Cataloging-in-Publication Data

Euripides.
  [Selections. English. 2002]
  The essential Euripides : dancing in dark times / [compiled by] Robert Emmet Meagher.
    p. cm.
  Includes two previously published essays by Meagher.
  Contents: Mortal vision : the wisdom of Euripides / Robert Emmet Meagher —
Hekabe / Euripides — Helen / Euripides — Iphigenia at Aulis / Euripides —
Iphigenia in Tauris / Euripides — Bacchae / Euripides — Revel and revelation : the
poetics of Euripides / Robert Emmet Meagher.
  ISBN 0-86516-513-0 (pbk. : alk. paper)
    1. Euripides—Translations into English. 2. Euripides—Criticism and interpreta-
tion. 3. Helen of Troy (Greek mythology)—Drama. 4. Hecuba (Legendary
character)—Drama. 5. Pentheus (Greek mythology)—Drama. 6. Dionysus (Greek
deity)—Drama. 7. Mythology, Greek, in literature. 8. Trojan War—Drama. 9.
Bacchantes—Drama. 10. Tragedy. I. Meagher, Robert E. II. Title.

PA3975 .A2 2002b
882'.01—dc21

2002016336

The good and decent man,
even if he lives in some distant place,
and even though I never set eyes on him,
I count as a friend.
EURIPIDES

for

Lou Bolchazy

O man of Shuruppak, son of Ubar-Tutu,
demolish the house, and build a boat!
Abandon wealth, and seek survival!
Spurn property, save life.
Take on board the boat all living things' seed!
GILGAMESH

Wer nicht von dreitausend Jahren
Sich weiss Rechenschaft zu geben,
Bleib' im Dunkeln unerfahren,
Mag von Tag zu Tag leben.
GOETHE

TABLE OF CONTENTS

◇◇◇◇◇◇◇◇◇◇◇◇◇

◇◇◇◇◇◇◇◇

PREFACE
⬦⬦⬦⬦⬦

This volume is the work of exactly twenty years, roughly a third of my life. Not a very long time. Or so it seems. Remember how Jacob, after laboring seven years for the hand of Rachel, said those years seemed to him as several days. Gladly, he took on seven more. And, at the end, he at last had Rachel's hand. Twenty years are a blink of the eye when the prize is not the hand but the essence of Euripides. In truth, however, the title of this volume is deceptive. The "Essential Euripides" indicates more honestly the aspiration than the accomplishment of these bound pages. What they may offer instead is the scent of the man, enough to track him to his lair, enough to begin to read his mind and his heart. Enough, I hope, to fuel another seven year's labor.

Why Euripides? Beyond his secure place in the curriculum and on stage, he tells the truth. He acknowledges the darkness and defies it. I have in mind three rows of seemingly subdued seniors in a matinee production of *Hekabe,* who suddenly sat forward in their seats and found voice when Hekabe threw out these words to them: "you politicians, panderers—you pretend to focus the energies of a people and do no more than unleash your own greed. I loathe you all. I don't want to know you." "You can say that again," one of them added. Then there was an auditorium in Tennessee at an all-girls high school, when a blatantly captive audience of adolescents was confronted for the first time with the incinerating rage of Klytemnestra over her powerlessness to protect her own daughter from insane violence. "You go girl," they called out. And, a moment later, one girl behind me said to another in astonishment, "Shit. I didn't know it would be like this." Truth is a force, not a fact. It lies in the plays of Euripides waiting to be released. And when it is, it comes as a surprise.

Why Euripides? I suppose it comes down to companionship, something we all seek on some level. "You have noticed," teaches the Ogala holy man Black Elk, "that the truth comes into the world with two faces. One is sad with suffering, and the other laughs; but it is the same face, laughing or weeping. When people are already in despair, maybe the laughing face is better for them; and when they feel too good and are too sure

of being safe, maybe the weeping face is better for them to see."
This is precisely what we find in the plays of Euripides, the
human face. Nothing is more challenging or more reassuring.
We can well imagine him, as Kazantzakis imagined Alexis Zorba,
lifting his hands and shouting to the sky:

> What can you do to me, Almighty? You can do
> nothing to me except kill me. Well, kill me! I've
> vented my spleen, I've said all I wanted to say; I've
> had time to dance... and I don't need you anymore.

Euripides lived in dark times. Who doesn't? Take Vedran
Smailovic, only in his thirties and principal cellist for the
Sarajevo Opera. It is May 27, 1992. He looks out his window
and sees an artillery shell slam into a line of his neighbors
standing out in front of one of the few bakeries in Sarajevo
whose walls are still intact and doors open. The blast is blinding.
When Smailovic opens his eyes twenty-two are dead and
many more pray they were. The carnage is indescribable.
His response is to go to his closet, to don his full concert
attire, and—cello in hand—to walk directly to the crater
made by the hellish explosion. There, seated on a camp stool,
he leans his cello against his shoulder and plays with all his
heart, a full concert, as the shelling continues around him.
And every day after, he did the same thing. "It is difficult,"
Euripides wrote 2,400 years ago as if we would ever need to
be reminded, "to overestimate the prevailing chaos among
things human and divine." With the same provocation as
Smailovic, though with admittedly less personal risk,
Euripides too, in the theater of Dionysos, played amidst ruin,
danced in the heart of darkness. Whether we understand it
or not, if we crave such courage, or at least word of it,
Euripides provides a luminous line of victims who refuse to
concede long after they have lost.

A few words about myself might help to explain the shape
of this book. I stumbled on Euripides not in the academy but
in the theater, where he and perhaps I truly belong. I was at
the time a Visiting Professor of Philosophy of Religion in the
Faculty of Divinity, Trinity College, Dublin. And I was, so far
as everyone imagined, doing research. But that was only a guess
on their part, as my door was mostly closed. In fact, I was writing
plays and doing not a stitch of research. They were my first
plays, as playwriting was something I had "saved up" until I

found myself in the right place at the right time. A year of "research" in Dublin provided both. Well, as they say, one thing led to another. Unexpected interest in one of my plays led Michael Cacoyannis graciously to invite me to his home in Athens, where he was absorbed in creating his own eloquent translation of the *Bakkhai* for production that fall on Broadway. When he realized that I knew Greek, he brought me into his current endeavor, which led to days of pouring over his work, in the midst of which he made a comment which I took as a command: "You should really do this yourself." So I did.

I quickly learned, however, that to translate a Greek play, I would have to know more than Greek. I was working in an aquarium, when where I needed to be was in the open sea. So I began studying all things ancient, for which I would need not one but many lives. It remains a work in progress. Most days I know more than I did the day before. What I grasped early on, however, was that Euripides wrote plays and that the test of a translation is on the stage, not on the desk. I had as much to learn from actors as I did from academics; so I tried to spend as much time in rehearsal as I did in research.

The Essential Euripides is a hopefully heady distillate from these past twenty years of translating, directing, and teaching Euripides. Each of its ingredients has seen print elsewhere, and all of the plays have seen multiple productions. Revision is an ongoing reality and necessity with them all. Although each has been adapted here to a common format, in the course of which some minor revisions have been made, each retains its own original style and character. This includes various approaches to transliteration, integral to the tone and rhythm of each effort, which I trust will not be disconcerting to the reader.

Perhaps a few further words on orthographic consistency are in order here. To begin with, there is simply no one agreed upon scheme for writing Greek words, including proper names, using our Latin alphabet. Even the Greek government employs a variety of schemes in its official documents and publications. Look up any Greek island, city or mountain range on three different maps, and you are likely to find three different spellings for each. The reasons for this are complex; but it comes down to several immovable facts: the characters of any alphabet record not only the look of letters but their sound as well; the sounds of any language are in constant flux; and the two languages at issue here—Greek and English—look different, sound different, and have decidedly different histories. Most notorious Greek names have long since been both Latinized and Anglicized before they reach our eyes and ears; so *Odusseus* often comes down to us as Ulysses and *Athenai* as Athens; and, pronounced by the Royal Shakespeare Company, names like Iphigeneia and Clytaemestra sound a good deal more like contagious diseases than ancient Greek royalty. In short, for any one proper name in Greek there is a palate of possible English equivalents. Which one the translator chooses often depends on the whether the text is intended to be seen or heard, and by whom, whether archaism and strangeness are to be sought after or avoided, and so on. Such considerations have always seemed to me more pressing and worthy than the mantle of consistency.

In "Mortal Vision" I endeavor to strike the core of what I take to be Euripides' abiding concerns: war, the plight of women, and the awful mystery of the gods. The five plays selected for inclusion here embody those concerns as fully and powerfully as any in the Euripidean repertoire. Finally, in "Revel and Revelation," I look back at Euripides' consummate masterwork, the *Bakkhai*, as a definitive response to the ancient quip that Athenian drama has little or nothing to do with Dionysos. Nothing could be further from the truth.

My intellectual, artistic, and personal debts incurred across these twenty years are beyond accounting much less payment. I will focus here on the termini. None of this would have happened without Michael Cacoyannis, whose belief in me and daunting example and generous support set me on my way and have kept me going. Nor would this culminating work be possible without Dr. Lou Bolchazy, whose lifelong commitment to preserving the wisdom of the ancients remains childlike in its fervor and immovable in its determination. Then there is the inimitable Dr. Laurie Haight Keenan, editor extraordinaire, whose exceptional acuity is accompanied by irrepressible goodwill. Finally, all along there has been the day to day, the greatest gift of all, and Betsy with whom the many years have seemed as days. My profound thanks to all.

ROBERT EMMET MEAGHER
Hampshire College

MORTAL VISION

THE WISDOM OF EURIPIDES

BIBLIOGRAPHICAL PREFACE

All of the Euripidean passages cited in this essay have one of the following three textual sources: the *Euripidis Fabulae* in the Oxford Classical Texts for all citations from Euripides' extant plays; the *Tragicorum Graecorum Fragmenta* edited by A. Nauck for all citations from Euripidean fragments, except for the one citation from the *Melanippe,* which is from volume one of *Greek Literary Papyri,* edited by D.L.Page in the Loeb series. All translations in this volume are my own. All centuries and specific dates cited in this volume are presumed to be B.C.E. unless otherwise noted.

In my endeavor to contextualize the plays of Euripides, needless to say I have drawn upon a wide range of primary sources, which at the same time represent an ancient bibliography for the further study of Euripides. If I were to draw this focus even more tightly and to select a handful of ancient sources particularly critical to the understanding of Euripides, there would be no surprises on my list: Homer (the well from which all the poets drank), Aeschylus, Sophocles, and Aristophanes (Euripides' closest colleagues), and Thucydides (the most lucid chronicler of his times). Under the rubric of secondary sources, the absence of footnotes in this volume does not mean that I am without debt. Nothing could be further from the truth, which is that my scholarly debts are too extensive to tally, much less to settle here. Scholarly footnotes, like heavy armor, are suited to doing battle but need not be strapped in place every time thinkers share their thoughts. The trappings worn by scholars all too often outweigh the scholars themselves, just as, in their writings, gloss all too often overshadows text. It is my hope that the reader will find in the absence of footnotes a less impeded path to the original texts and to the power they contain.

TABLE OF DATES

◇◇◇◇◇◇◇◇

The titles of the extant plays of Euripides appear in capital letters.
Symbols: ca.=around, <= before; >=after.

ca.534   Tragic contests established in Athens.

ca.498   Aeschylus first competes in the tragic contests.

490   Battle of Marathon.

ca.484   Birth of Euripides.

480   Battle of Salamis.

468   Sophocles first competes in the tragic contests.

456   Death of Aeschylus.

455   Euripides first competes in the tragic contests.

?<440   [RHESUS—authorship debated].

438   ALCESTIS wins second prize.

431   Beginning of Peloponnesian War; MEDEA.

430   Murder of Peloponnesian delegates without trial,
         perhaps reflected in the *Children of Heracles;*
         outbreak of plague in Athens.

?ca.429 CHILDREN OF HERACLES.

428   HIPPOLYTUS wins first prize.

427   Executions of citizens and razing of Plataea.

425   Further unspeakable savagery at Corcyra.

?ca.425 ANDROMACHE.

<423   HECUBA; with CYCLOPS?

424   Thebes refuses to allow the burial of Athenian dead
         after the battle of Delium, perhaps reflected in the
         Suppliant Women. At the age of sixty, Euripides
         presumably completes his military service.

?ca.424 HERACLES.

?ca.423 SUPPLIANT WOMEN.

423 One-year armistice.

412 Peace of Nicias.

415 Annihilation of Melos.

416 TROJAN WOMEN wins second prize; mutiliation of herms; launching of Sicilian expedition; Athenians stressing their Ionianism, perhaps reflected in the *Ion*.

?413 ELECTRA.

413 Spartans occupy Decelea; Athenian debacle in Sicily.

?<412 IPHIGENEIA IN TAURIS.

?<412 ION.

412 HELEN.

411 Oligarchic coup in Athens overthrown. *Lysistrata* and *Thesmophoriazousae* of Aristophanes.

?409 PHOENICIAN WOMEN.

408 ORESTES.

408 Euripides leaves Athens.

406 Death of Euripides.

404 BACCHAE and IPHIGENEIA AT AULIS win first prize.

404 Surrender of Athens.

INTRODUCTION
◇◇◇◇◇◇◇◇◇

Hannah Arendt prefaced her book on *Men in Dark Times* [NY: Harcourt, Brace & World, 1955] with the conviction that "even in the darkest of times we have the right to expect some illumination, and... such illumination may well come from the uncertain, flickering, and often weak light that some men and women, in their lives and works, will kindle under almost all circumstances and shed over the time span that was given them on earth... [and that] eyes so used to darkness as ours will hardly be able to tell whether their light was the light of a candle or that of a blazing sun." The very same conviction underlies this essay; for Euripides wrote in times as dark as our own and shed light not only for his but for all time. Some would say that his was the light of a candle, while others would liken it to a blazing sun. Either way, and more to the point, once kindled it has never gone out.

Euripides, as a poet-playwright of the past, is known, however, only through the voice preserved in his works; and the light he kindles burns within us as we listen to his words. Now, if I were to reveal at once the crystalline core of this essay by stating it as one simple claim, it would be that the prophetic clarity and intensity of Euripides' voice resound in his plays essentially undiminished by time. And if this claim, once stated, were in itself either evident or persuasive, my work would be abruptly concluded. The complication giving warrant to this essay lies in the necessary reciprocity of any revelation or the fact that without ears to hear, neither falling trees nor timeless works of art can successfully resound. And hearing an ancient voice presents a unique challenge to most modern ears.

It is not as if Euripides requires the condescension of contemporary adaptation. His lords need not wear ministerial pin-striped suits nor do his warriors need goose-step their way across the stage to make their meanings for us. Still less does Euripidean drama require companion lectures or program notes telling the audience what the play they are about to see or have just seen would say to them if it were still able. Such remedial interpretation is best described in Susan Sontag's words as "the compliment mediocrity pays to genius." With a theatrically vital translation and a production equal to the text,

Euripides sings his own song and silences those who would presume to speak on his behalf. Such occasions, however, are rare; their rarity being no reflection on Euripides.

This essay, however, addresses itself primarily to those who would read Euripides' plays, rather than to those who would stage or witness stage productions of them. Apart from the numerical superiority of readers, there is the fact that credible theatrical productions of ancient drama are the fruit not of improvisation but of understanding. If the director and his or her cast know and feel why they are saying what they are saying and doing what they are doing, then the audience will know and feel with them. Such is the magic of theatre. In the theatre, understanding is contagious; but so is confusion. Directors and actors, like anyone else, begin by reading a text; and reading implies a certain remove from the immediacy of theatre. Reading is an inward act, more akin to thinking than to sensing; and thinking about Euripidean drama is, before it is anything else, thinking. Theatre, on the other hand, even a theatre of ideas, outreaches thought with an ease which often angers intellectuals. No wonder that criticism has been called the intellect's revenge on art. Beyond revenge, however, there is a place for thinking about art, particularly when the art is ancient drama, which most often finds its enactment only in the solitary imagination of a reader. The reader must eventually design, direct, and act out in a theatre of thought the otherwise inert text grasped in the hands or lying open on the desk; and such collaboration with the author in the reincarnation of a once and future drama requires intense reflection. This essay may be seen as one sustained series of reflections preliminary to the reading of Euripides, preliminary, that is, to the imaginative raising of the written text into dramatic life in the theatre of the imagination, wherein Euripides will speak for himself.

Although the inwardly theatrical reading of Euripides must be regarded as secondary to the actually staged production of Euripides, reading Euripides in private is no necessarily suspect endeavor. In fact, there are solid grounds for saying that Euripides consciously wrote for his readers as well as for his theatre audiences. The first such reader to be named is the god of the theatre, Dionysus himself, who, in the opening scene of Aristophanes' comedy, the *Frogs,* says he has been reading Euripides' *Andromeda* while on board a ship. [We may note here that, according to common practice, Dionysus, although reading alone, would have been reading aloud, a practice to be commended to any reader of Euripides.] To continue, later in the same comedy, the chorus warns that Euripides' audience come armed with their own papyrus copies of his scripts. However broad the comic license taken by Aristophanes in these instances, it is clear that even in the late fifth century Euripides had his readers and that something about Euripidean drama was perceived as inviting private reflection as well as public performance. What that something was will be explored later in some detail; but for now it may suffice to say that Euripides reflected in his work the birth of popular literacy in Athens as well as an accompanying wave of speculative and critical thinking quite foreign and threatening to long-enthroned traditions, religious, artistic, and political. There can be little doubt that much of what he had to say was quite unwelcome, if not unintelligible, to a large part of his audience. It could be argued that he could not afford to be fully understood and so masked his meanings in an irony which allowed his plays to be read either from right to left or from left to right, politically speaking, thereby shielding his words from his foes while entrusting them to his friends, wherever and whenever either might be found. As a revolutionary, fixated on the present yet essentially belonging to the future, Euripides counted on the substantiality of the written text to hold his meaning and to await its time of full disclosure.

In saying that this essay is addressed primarily to those who would read Euripides' plays, I have thus far underscored the notion of reading as distinct from stage production; but equal emphasis is due the notion of the original texts, as opposed to the mountains of gloss encircling even the most slighted of his plays. There is no denying the vantages gained by scaling the heights of Euripidean scholarship or any of the surrounding peaks. However, the simple fact remains that Euripides is to be found first and finally in his own words. If Euripides was concerned to say anything at all to faces and souls knew he himself would never encounter, he must have left it somewhere in his work. After all, it is in each instance the text alone that endures and not its performance, still less its author—a fact we would scarcely assume lost on Euripides. Consequently, any reading of Euripides which is to be hopeful of understanding must trust that Euripides' meanings are present and accessible to its queries.

This trust in the possibility of more or less direct communication between the reader and Euripides mediated solely by the text, or to be both more precise and more offensive to modern methodological sensibilities, the possibility of authentic communion of the reader and Euripides in the text, underlies this essay. Such trust must, however, be sobered at once by the admission that this communion is to be the fruit of labor, not of grace, much less of negligence. To say that Euripides' meanings are present and accessible is not to say that they are obvious; and to say that communication is possible is not to say with any certainty that it has actually occurred in any particular instance. Finally, it seems reasonable at such a remove to expect that bold strokes will stand out over subtleties, and that contours will be read with greater confidence than fineries. In any event, it would be unfortunate to miss or mistake the former for the latter.

The obstacles to reading the mind of Euripides are many. Like any playwright, he speaks through his characters, which is to say that he speaks with many and diverse voices, the question always remaining: which voice, if any, is his? The moral and political span of his characters could not conceivably describe the sympathies or commitments of any one man; rather, they represent a spectrum stretching, as it were, from heaven to hell. As Aristotle reports, Sophocles pointed to this same dilemma when he commented that Euripides wrote of people as they were, while he, Sophocles, wrote of people as they ought to be. Tutored by this comment, we might approach Sophocles' characters, at least his central heroic figures, with some assurance that they embody Sophocles' conceptions of excellence. With the same comment in mind, we might well despair of hearing the voice of Euripides above the cacophony of his characters. It is no wonder that Euripides' readers and audiences across the centuries have held him in such divergent repute, as political or apolitical, as radical or reactionary, as a rationalist or an irrationalist, as a feminist or a misogynist, a philosopher or a phony. What we know of how Euripides' plays were originally received or subsequently regarded provides no more than opinions as unprivileged as our own regarding how Euripides himself regarded his plays and the lives and words unfolded within them. Finally, we are left with the plays themselves and our confidence that Euripides wrote them with communication in mind. "It is only shallow people," wrote Oscar

Wilde, "who do not judge by appearances. The mystery of the world is the visible not the invisible." The same might be said of the lesser mystery of Euripides. Look to the text, and he will appear eventually.

A useful parallel might be drawn between the elusiveness of Euripides and the elusiveness of his younger friend, Socrates. In the *Dialogues* of Plato, we encounter a Socrates who mostly engages in what may be described as experiments. He follows the lines of others' thinking to see and to point out where they lead, without unilaterally offering his own convictions. This is not to say, however, that Socrates remains silent or neutral to the end. His experiments are at the same time contests in which there are winners and losers. In one or other Socratic manner, interlocutors who have pursued false opinions are refuted; and we are surely not misguided in searching such refutations for at least traces of Socrates' and perhaps even Plato's own thoughts on the matter. Similarly, Euripides allows his characters their own ways, as perverse as they might be; but they do not evade judgement. Consider Polymestor in the *Hecuba*. If we were to imagine for a moment that Euripides were commending the character of Polymestor even as he created him, we would measure the playwright to be a very low sort and surely no friend of women. Polymestor is, however, refuted with a vengeance. After being laid bare by Hecuba's lashing words, he is made to stand before Agamemnon and to receive his unequivocal due. Borrowing an image from the prophet Isaiah, if ever there were a cup crafted for destruction by its own potter, it is Polymestor. Admittedly, not everywhere is Euripides' voice so recognizable, his own verdict so vocal. And even when it is, it is often ignored. Even Polymestor's villainry has been and will again be used against his poet-maker in a curious application of collective guilt, as if ink runs as thick as blood. More problematically, Euripides is at times enigmatically silent, even in the face of atrocities. In such moments, the search for his true mind is not to be called off, however; for silence can be as eloquent as any words.

The dilemma I have just described raises a challenge that no one who would read Greek tragedy can evade, least of all a reader of Euripides. As will soon be seen in some detail, morality was the incessant preoccupation of the ancient tragedians of Athens; and morality requires not only the encountering of good and evil but the delineation and judgement of them.

We cannot pretend to know what a play says or means unless we know how we are intended by the author to regard the words and actions it presents to our eyes and ears. To say this is not to eschew all complexity and ambiguity, demanding melodrama or nothing. It is simply to recognize the moral seriousness of the work we confront and the task we undertake in reading Greek tragedy. We are surely not required to match Goethe's singular reverence for Euripides when he asked, "have all the nations of the world since his day produced a single dramatist worthy of handing him his sandals?" Nonetheless, such esteem from high places might well sober efforts from lower places to dismiss or to tame his wild genius.

This essay will focus on the ethical vision and voice of Euripides, because it is my conviction that there lies the core of his concerns, the point of fission. As stated above, this essay will comprise a series of reflections preliminary to a dramatic reading of Euripides in the theatre of one's own imagination. These reflections will not constitute sustained critical commentaries on any, much less all, of his plays. In an essay as modest as this one addressing a corpus as conspicuously manifold as the Euripidean one, there is little place for a rehearsing of the plot-lines of one drama after another, without which focused critical commentary would be deprived of context. If, on the other hand, I were to assume the reader's familiarity with the full Euripidean corpus, I would direct this essay exclusively towards the classical scholar, which is far from my intent. Instead, what I propose to do is to provide what might be called a conceptual setting for the inwardly theatrical reading of Euripides.

The limitations on stage settings in the ancient theatre of Dionysus were, by our standards, severe. Generally speaking, there were only two possibilities, the palace set and the country set, each with a single central door, two side entrances, and a roof; and a playwright was not allowed to change from one set to another in the course of a drama. Every Euripidean drama was thus played out against one of these two sets. Quite apart from and prior to the physical set, however, there lay what may be called a conceptual set, an ordered arrangement of categories, metaphysical and political, which, like chromosomal threads, carry and dictate the essential thought-structure of the grander, more evident organism eventually born in the open air of the orchestra. What I do not have in mind here are story-patterns or generic plot formulas which have been critically examined in considerable detail and with genuine insight in the vast literature on Euripides. The patterns or structures I would disclose lie on a deeper, more expansive level. But before we make our descent to this infra-structure of his work, we turn to Euripides himself; for it is best that he not be a stranger to us as we consider his work.

CHAPTER ONE
◇◇◇◇◇◇
EURIPIDES

Ancient biographies, like any others, can be no more reliable than their sources and may, of course, be a good deal less reliable. Regretably, neither the ancient biographies of Euripides nor their sources inspire confidence. If Thucydides, committed as he was to some reasonable interrogation of hearsay and to some genuine accountability for factual accuracy, had chosen to mention Euripides, we might perhaps be in a position now to sketch more than the contours of the playwright's life. Instead, we are left mostly with legend, the presentation and assessment of which would cast very little light on our subject. A stalemate, however, in the sphere of Euripides' life, need not frustrate our endeavor to enter and to understand his work; for the boldest lines of Euripides' identity are known to us and they are all we need.

We have no good reason to doubt the Parian Marble, carved roughly a century and a half after Euripides' death and citing the year 484 as the year of his birth. This is surely more plausible than the legend which would have the three great tragedians fatefully intersect each others' lives at the Battle of Salamis in the year 480: Aeschylus by fighting with the Athenian forces, Sophocles by dancing in the boys' victory chorus, and Euripides by emerging from his mother's womb. Such luminous synchronicity makes perfect poetic history; but poetic history is no more acceptable as history than is poetic justice acceptable as justice. However, a meticulous sorting out of legends and sources is too lengthy a project for our present purposes, so we must satisfy ourselves for now with reasonable assurances and approximations. With this is mind, we may say that Euripides was born in Attica in 484 and died in Macedon in 406, after emigrating to the court of Archelaus, where he likely shared the eminent company of Zeuxis the painter, Agathon the tragedian, Timotheus the musician, and possibly even Thucydides the historian. Any account of his motives for quitting Athens for Macedon must be conjectured from his plays, from which one could with some confidence conjure the image of a man in despair, holding up to the people of Athens, only thinly masked, their own imminent ruin and inward rot.

How far from the mind of Euripides and that of his audience could Athens have been when, in 408, in the *Orestes,* he presented the house of Agamemnon sick beyond cure and aflame with malice?

Between the years 484 and 406, apart from his endeavors as a playwright, very little is known of Euripides' activities. We may assume that he received a traditional Athenian education, that he participated to some extent in civic life and in the myriad religious festivals strung like beads on the year's cycle, and that he served his compulsory forty years of availability for active duty in the army. What is most important to realize is that Athenian playwrights neither enjoyed nor claimed exemption from the active demands of Athenian citizenship, which we would likely measure quite excessive. Even if the traditions depicting Euripides as an unsociable recluse—ensconced in a cave overlooking the Bay of Salamis, alone with his library and his pen—were in large part accurate, the truth would remain that he must have known the savagery of war, the elemental madness of the mob, the intoxication of empire, and the abysmal despair of defeat far more intimately than most modern poets know the political realities impinging on or informing their work.

Those traditions which would have us believe that Euripides was scorned by the populace and hounded by his critics into exile must be set alongside the more solid facts that we have no certain evidence of his having ever been refused a chorus, that apart from Aeschlylus and Sophocles we know of no fifth-century poet so recognized and rewarded with praise, that his indictment for impiety must have been either defeated or withdrawn in a period when other equally eminent figures were not similarly spared. In addition we might consider the story told by Plutarch of how the mere recitation of lines from Euripides bought the freedom of captive Athenian warriors, otherwise rotting to death in a Sicilian quarry, or the tribute reportedly paid to Euripides by the aged Sophocles, bringing on his chorus robed in black to mourn the death of his younger colleague, or the legend claiming that the Athenian people begged the Macedonians for the return of Euripides' bones. Finally, whatever Euripides' status in the Athenian theatre and polity during the fifth century, he was soon without rival, enjoying a preeminence reflected in the number of his plays preserved in whole or in fragments, compared to those of his once more favored rivals.

Euripides' career as a playwright began in the year 455 with the production of the trilogy including the *Peliades* and ended with the posthumous production of his *Alkmaion in Corinth, Iphigeneia at Aulis,* and *Bacchae,* after 406. The last Athenian production of his work over which he himself presided was in 408, when he presented the *Orestes*. Altogether he seems to have had twenty-two productions in the City Dionysia, the yearly theatrical festival held each spring in Athens, which would account for the sixty-six tragedies known with certainty to be from Euripides' pen and surviving either in whole or in part to this day. If we exclude the *Alcestis* from the formal category of tragedy, the more or less fully extant tragedies of indisputedly Euripidean authorship number sixteen, all from the second half of his career and all but one falling within the war years, the years of bitter internecine conflict between Athens and Sparta. The issues surrounding the composition and dating of the Euripidean canon are too complex and too peripheral to our present purposes to admit of exploration here. May it suffice to say that a quite credible case for the texts, fragmentary or whole, and their dates employed in this book could but won't be made here. In sum, it may be argued that Euripides was one of the three competing tragedians in the City Dionysia approximately every five years early in his career, every three years during his middle years; and every year toward the end of his career, often in direct competition with his senior rival, Sophocles, and with revivals of the late Aeschylus' established "classics."

However thick the mist of doubt over most of Euripides' personal characteristics, there are certain essential elements of his identity which we cannot afford to overlook, as self-evident as they may seem to be. Truisms often contain the sturdiest truths. I wish to group these essential elements under three epithets: Athenian, Scholar, and Playwright; for Euripides was undeniably all of these; and in saying this we are already saying a great deal of significance. Examining the nature of this significance is the task assigned to the remainder of this chapter.

EURIPIDES THE ATHENIAN

To be an Athenian citizen, Euripides had first of all to be Greek, born of Greek blood and reared in the Greek tongue; and this fact bears some preliminary consideration. All too often in classical studies, "the Greeks," at least those of the classical period, are studied in splendid isolation from those non-Greek peoples whom the classical Greeks themselves were wont to lump under the heading of "barbarians." In what might be seen as an alliance of academic parochialism and ancient racism, the extent of mutual influence among ancient East Mediterranean peoples is often all but ignored. Even the Egyptians, who by virtue of sheer topography were uniquely insulated from foreign military invasion and cultural intrusion, have seldom been handled by scholars as hermetically as have the Greeks. Increasingly, however, scholars have come to recognize the extensive mythological, ritual, iconographical, architectural, artistic, linguistic, literary, commercial, and military influences of Egypt, the Near East, and even India on Greece long before and during the period relevant to this book. Firstly, this recognition permits us to trespass stingily-drawn borders marking off those materials of legitimate interpretative relevance to Euripidean studies; and, secondly, this recognition challenges us to a deeper understanding of the chauvinism so endemic to ancient Greece and Athens and so apparently offensive to Euripides. Our own sorties across these borders will soon be in evidence; but for now the second matter, that of ancient Greek chauvinism, is of more immediate concern.

Euripides lived in a time of already established and ever-developing pan-Hellenic consciousness. What this means in simplest terms is that the word "Greek" was, in practice, felt to designate something essential, specific, and enduring. Although there was some recognition of a humanity common to all men, humanity in the flesh was too uneven and diverse and humanity in the mind too abstract to challenge the more concrete and exalted reality of being "Greek." Central among the roots of this consciousness are surely the Homeric and Hesiodic poems, which synthesized and articulated Greek religion, virtue, and pride, as well as the Olympic, Delphic, and Isthmian pan-Hellenic festivals. Of all the catalysts of nationalism, however, paranoia is perhaps the most effective, at least if Hobbes is correct in saying that fear is the magisterial passion. The constant threat and the twice-repelled reality of barbarian invasion, once in 490 and again in 480, minted the meaning of Greek nationalism current in Euripides' era and reflected nowhere so brazenly and pathetically as in his last play, the *Iphigeneia at Aulis,* where the name of "Hellas" is repeated so often as to become a refrain, a spell-casting incantation bemusing the callow soul of Iphigeneia, who imagines herself the "savior of Greece" and willingly gives her body and soul to what is no more than a consciously fabricated abstraction, a cynical construct made by her own father who has no illusions that "Hellas" is anything more than a euphemism for the certifiably deranged mob which he leads to plunder. It is Euripides' last word on patriotism.

Levi-Strauss, for one, has pointed out how most peoples whom we are inclined to call "primitive" designate themselves as "the True Ones," "the Good Ones," or simply, "the Human Beings," and assign to the rest of men one or other name denying their humanity. This practice, however, is scarcely confined to so-called "primitives." More "advanced" peoples, such as the classical Greeks or ourselves, are more likely to dissemble than to disavow such arrogance. It is usually our methods rather than our morals which are more advanced. Thus the Greeks employed all the sophisticated tools of comparative and philosophical anthropology to develop and to support a theory of Hellenic supremacy, i.e. of Greeks as the master race. Whether as an element of fate or as an accident of climate, Greek solidarity and superiority was a common unarguable assumption in the fifth century and ready at hand to justify aggressive war, colonization, and slavery.

Euripides, however, was an Athenian Greek, which hones a sharper edge on what has been said thus far. Whatever its comparative insignificance in Bronze Age Greece, Athens emerged from the archaic period into the classical period, and more specifically into the fifth century, as a military power rivalled only by Sparta and as a cultural center simply without rival in the Greek world. As pan-Hellenic consciousness developed, which is to say as Greek-speaking peoples came to think of themselves as Greeks and of the territories, they inhabited as Greece, then the emergence of its center, its capital city, might seem inevitable. Inevitably or not, in the years following the Persian Wars Athens laid claim to the full title and prerogatives of Greece's capital city; and, however compromised by failure was its claim to that title in the fifth century, Athens has surely achieved it posthumously in the mind of posterity. For Athens and classical Greece are all but synonymous categories in the minds of most people inclined to think at all about such things. This is an equivalency, however, which we must learn to unthink if we are to understand Euripides and his times.

What we are calling Greece and speaking of as if it were a nation began as a make-shift confederacy of city-states hastily formed to confront the massive military might of Persia and its empire. After the trousered barbarian hordes had twice been repelled from Greek soil, Athens argued that the alliances so hastily and provisionally formed under pressure of invasion should be formalized and bolstered so as to provide for the lasting security of Greece against future threats from its enemies. Understating the part played by Sparta as well as by chance in their victories and overstating the admittedly critical part played by itself, Athens crowned itself the "Savior of Hellas," and proceeded to form a new confederation centered in and administered from Athens. In short, Athens presented itself as the first city among its equals; but soon enough the monster emerged and its true designs clicked into place. The confederacy became an empire, peers became subjects, and Greece became a euphemism for the sphere of Athenian hegemony. Appropriately enough, this devolution from a consortium of friends to an empire of subjects is mirrored in Menelaus' account of Agamemnon's rise to primacy in the *Iphigeneia at Aulis;* and we may be hearing an echo of Euripides' own rage at Athens in the words of Menelaus thrown at the pathetically compromised Agamemnon: "I indict you first for those ways in which you first proved yourself perverse."[349] Athens's coup, however, was soon challenged by Sparta, itself only slightly less attracted to empire. The result was civil war with Greek unity sliced every which way as both Athens and Sparta seduced and strangled individual city-states into taking sides. Like the sons of Oedipus in the *Phoenician Women,* Athens and Sparta, rivals for a single rule, each pursued one of twin evils and created a two-headed madness.

The "Savior of Hellas," in short, became "the tyrant city"; and like all tyrants its fall from grace was followed by its fall from power. "Mortal man plays the fool when he wastes cities, desecrates temples, and leaves desolate the holy places of the dead. His own ruin is not far off." [*Trojan Women,* 95–97] The same is easily said, blown large as it were, for cities. It is not difficult to say from Euripides' plays which fall, the moral or the military, he found more painful to witness. We may be allowed to hear Euripides' own sentiments echoed in these words from the *Phoenician Women:* "it would seem that one's homeland is of all things the dearest. Yes, there are no words to describe how dear it is." [406–407] Indeed, in Euripides' earlier extant plays, such as the *Medea,* the *Children of Heracles,* and the *Suppliant Women,* there may be evidence of how dearly Euripides once held his native Athens; for the image of Athens in those plays is of a "holy, inviolate land" [*Medea,* 825–826], a land where freedom, wisdom, and harmony flourish, a land always ready to defend the weak and the wronged. These early portraits of Athens, however, soon bore little resemblance to the tyrant city; and Euripides' later portrayals of his city were as ragged and ruthless as the reality demanded.

The story of Athens's precarious rise to power and its fall therefrom is told nowhere with such poignancy as in Thucydides' history of *The Peloponnesian War,* which work could well be listed among the ancient tragedies, despite the scale of its stage, the multiplicity of its characters, and the absence of poetic diction. It presents the tragedy of Athens, which offers perhaps the most shattering peripeteia in ancient history, the tragic reversal of Athens's fortunes from its Periclean splendor to its Sicilian devastation, and does so by underscoring the gulf that existed between Athens's words and deeds, a gulf opening nowhere more abysmally than between the words of promise pronounced by Pericles over the casualties of the war's first year and the debacle consummated in the quarries of Sicily. This chasm between Athenian rhetoric and reality, possibility and outcome, words and deeds, was witnessed daily by Athenians, like Euripides and Thucydides, possessing sufficient insight and integrity to read their times with perception. Finally, we will see that it is precisely this contemporary tragedy of Athens, unmasked in Thucydides, that is so thinly masked in myth by Euripides in so many of his plays.

In sum, to be an Athenian in the second half of the fifth century was to live and to be complicit in a city at war, a shameless, wasteful war of aggression. It was to watch one's homeland take on all of the distortions of monstrous bad faith, to listen as words changed their meanings to suit otherwise unspeakable wrongs, to be sick not only with the plague bacillus that ravaged Athens in the first years of the war but to be sick as well with the even more unsparing human plague that was the war itself.

However deeply the war marked, or rather scarred, Athens in the Euripidean period, war does not alone tell the story. The shadow cast by war could not eclipse and may in fact have partly provoked what has been called the Athenian "Enlightenment," a period of turbulent questioning, re-evaluation, and discovery.

This was the age of the Sophists, an uneasily defined collage of freethinkers, who despite their reputation for itineracy mostly made their home in Athens. Their widely divergent teachings are not readily synthesized; for they were never a school or a church with any commitment to consensus or to a common doctrine. Generally, however, we may say that they promoted free, empirical inquiry and found an adaptable, humanistic viewpoint to be the most revealing one. They were no friends of the traditional poets, Homer first among them, whom they found to be at best deceived and at worst deceitful, particularly with respect to the gods and their Olympian morals, or lack thereof. Central to their concerns were education, ethics, and theology, concerns which they shared with Euripides.

The fifth-century "Enlightenment" was hardly created by or confined to the Sophists, however. Scientific and philosophical speculation, which had begun long before the fifth century and which in some instances had originated outside of Greece, converged in Athens and came to fruition there. Foundational, as well, to the upheaval of this time was the emergence of popular literacy, which conspired with and supported the contemporary freethinkers in breaking forever the spell of Homer and of traditional oral education. The profound link between literacy and individual freedom is by now a datum of political experience. The acquisition of literacy, it is well known, brings not only a new skill but a new frame of mind. And in fifth-century Athens that new frame of mind meant, for one, the emergence of an autonomous individuality quite foreign to archaic Greece. Antique notions of retribution, inherited guilt, pollution, and predestination were called into question; and new theories of compassion, forgiveness, altruism, intentionality, and free will were forged. New theologies as well as imported cults responded to and generated the longing and hope for personal salvation, just as confidence in the cosmos collapsed. Human reason and its moral affirmations came to be seen by many not as an always imperfect confession of the flawless divine order but as a humane, even defiant, alternative to the callous indifference of the given order of things. Nature and law formed no longer an uncontested unity. Clearly, however, there can be no full chronicling here of the intellectual and political uprisings of the fifth century. May it suffice for now to say that Euripides was in the middle of them.

Finally, there is perhaps no more telling indication of the depth of questioning in fifth century Athens than the fact that it reached even to the institution of slavery, both those slaves captured in battle or purchased in the market and the slaves which Greek law and custom made of all women. It is in the theatre of Euripides that we hear the first indication that there may be something unnatural in chattel slavery; and it is equally clear from his plays that every aspect of women's relationship to men and to male society is under radical review. In this and in numerous other respects, Euripidean drama holds an unmerciful mirror to the face of Athens in the fifth century. Like the acceptance of bold and brilliant pigment on the sublimely blanched sculptures of ancient Athens, so the acceptance of radical turbulence and controversy in the ancient theatre of Euripides may demand that we shatter and recast more familiar conceptions of ancient tragedy and of its mother-city, conceptions more compatible with Aeschylus, Sophocles, and Aristotle.

EURIPIDES THE SCHOLAR

The epithet "scholar" may seem to be an unlikely one for Euripides; and it is used here, admittedly, for lack of something better. To denote the qualities which I have in mind to discuss now under this heading, others have preferred "philosopher" or "thinker" or "Sophist" or even "bookworm," all of which seem at least a shade further from the mark than "scholar," provided that we rid our minds of any formally academic associations with the word; for whatever Euripides was, he was not a schoolman or an academician.

Reference has already been made to the emergence of popular literacy in the late fifth-century. The claim has also been made that literacy brings with it a new frame of mind and freedom of thought. These elements and more, as we shall see, figure centrally in the theatre of Euripides and form the cluster of qualities towards which the name of "scholar" imperfectly gestures.

Tradition suggests that Euripides possessed a personal library of extraordinary size for his day; and his plays give ample evidence of a mind both traditionally learned and immediately engaged in the most current intellectual debates. Interestingly, he wrote not only for readers but also about readers; for written texts play a decisive role in several of his extant dramas. For example, in the surviving second rendering of the *Hippolytus*, it is in a note penned by the suicidal Phaedra that Hippolytus is falsely charged with attempted seduction; and the written word, in this instance, receives credence over Hippolytus' spoken protestations of his own innocence. Death's silence is, it seems, not final; and Theseus prefers to find the truth in what he reads rather than in what he hears. The written word proves equally ineradicable and deadly in the *Iphigeneia at Aulis;* for it is the first fatal letter to Clytemnestra which Agamemnon is attempting the re-draft as the play opens. But neither the original draft of the letter nor the fate of Iphigeneia which it deceivingly prescribes admits of revision. The written word unwittingly effects a brighter event in the *Iphigeneia in Tauris,* however, wherein Euripides constructs the most lengthy and elaborate recognition scene in Greek tragedy around a letter dictated by the illiterate Iphigeneia to one of her more learned and less fortunate victims. In short, literacy—the reading and writing of texts—is thematically explicit and crucial, uniquely so, in Euripidean drama.

More significant, however, than the literal presence of the act and artefacts of literacy, is the presence of what I have referred to as the frame of mind and freedom of thought accompanying literacy. Far more learned and lucid accounts than any I might offer here have already been written describing the psychology and epistemology of oral education and oral culture; but some account of this matter must be presented here as well. Both the recitation and the reception of unwritten poetry, preserved nowhere if not in the memories of bard and audience, require an uncritical, unhesitating mimetic surrender to the sung sounds and rhythms. "Hearing" may well be unwilling and unconscious, since the ear has no lids as do the eyes to preclude intrusion; but mere hearing is unlikely to result in the precise remembering of what was heard, particularly if the sounds inadvertently overheard comprise thousands of lines of complex poetry. School children would be a good deal more learned than they generally are if memory were effective regardless of the quality of one's hearkening. Memory requires listening; and listening involves a simple giving over of oneself, as any phenomenology of listening readily reveals. It is no linguistic accident that the Greek word *akouein* means both to listen and to obey; for soundful communication, unfolding as it does across time, must be followed as if it were a command. Indeed, poetic recitation or story-telling may be said to constitute a mode of command, a command to surrender the free movement of one's own thoughts to the poet's words so that the latter might unfold freely. Any intrusion of one's own doubts and concerns foreign to the pure flow of the sung or recited poem is as destructive to the life of the poem as is an embolism in the bloodstream of a living organism. Oral communication, in short, cannot tolerate interruption, a point made by Socrates on more than one occasion and a fact illustrated more recently, in 1830, by a man named Moerenhout, who wrote of his encounter with an old Tahitian cantor, a holy man, who recited for him the Polynesian cosmogony. The cantor could only declaim the tale spontaneously in one unbroken flow. Each time Moerenhout interrupted the cantor so as to write down that portion of the myth just sung, the cantor lost his song altogether and had to begin again from the beginning in order to regain it.

Whether in nineteenth-centry (A.D.) Tahiti or fifth-century Greece, oral cultures are obliterated by the introduction of writing. Memory is no longer necessary for the preservation of learning and the spell cast by song over the listener is broken. The text, now visible and substantially independent, lies before and between teacher and learner, at their mutual disposal and no longer beyond critique. Texts, unlike recitations, are ever open to challenge, critique and discussion. In an oral tradition, what is forgotten is lost forever; and the fact that, as Levi-Strauss points out, the tradition is transformed in the belief that it is only being repeated never fully comes to light. With the introduction of the written text, however, multiple variant versions of a single myth or poem may be preserved and critically compared, both with each other and against other sources. In the visual realm of the written text, the inquiring, discursive mind may range over the text at its own pace and selecting its own directions, just as the eye is free to focus wherever it wishes and to consider from a variety of perspectives the visual object, permanently at its disposal. In fact, the freedom of the eye provides numerous parallels with the freedom of reason consequent upon the collapse of orality.

It has been said that the Socratic question *ti estin?*—the question "what is the nature of…?"—dismantled Greek mythical thinking, a form of thinking which had prevailed in the archaic age and well into the classical period until the time of the

Sophists. Whatever truth there may be to such a claim, it must be added that Socrates exemplified his times at least as fully as he shaped them. Semonides' new art of memory, developed in the late sixth century, seems to have been predominantly visual; and Empedocles, not many years later, stressed the acquisition of knowledge through a variety of the senses. Surely the ground beneath orality is softened by both of these contributions. Similarly, the development of critical prose and its gradual replacing of poetry as the most serious vehicle of thought began with medical and philosophical treatises, chronicles and speeches, well before Socrates, who, after all, to our knowledge never wrote a page.

Not only the Socratic dialogues but the dramas of Euripides, as well, are replete with questions and speculations regarding the nature of things. Consider, for one, the following choral selections from Euripides' *Helen* [1137–1144;1148–1150]:

> What is god?
> What is not god?
> What lies in between?
> What man can say
> He has reached the edges of existence,
> No matter where he has been?
> What man has gazed upon god,
> Witnessed the wild confusion at the core of things,
> The contradictions,
> The unexpected twists of fate,
> And returned to tell the tale?
>
> There is nothing sure
> In all the turnings of men's minds.
> Only god's words are bright with truth.

If free critical inquiry, open cultural debate, and linguistic experimentation mark the collapse of oral culture and of mythical thinking, then Euripidean drama is as fertile a field as any in which to trace the movement from hearing to seeing, or from the reliving of tradition in memory to the critical examination of tradition in the often harsh light of reason. The story that Socrates attended the theatre only when he could see the works of Euripides testifies at the very least to the perceived congeniality of these two, Socrates the philosopher and Euripides the playwright. After all, in the *Frogs*, Euripides is accused of having thrown out music for the sake of hairsplitting arguments, which is not far afield from charges laid against Socrates then and ever since. Euripides played far more free with metrical codes than did his predecessors, frequently obscuring the distinction between sung and unsung lines or between what was traditionally reserved for the chorus and what was reserved for actors, and bringing the language of his dialogues into closer coincidence with ordinary colloquial discourse. He may hardly be accused with any justice, however, of abandoning music; for the music of his plays is rich and luxuriant. In his time, Euripides was associated with the "new music" exemplified by Timotheus; and in any age there are those who say of the new music that it is simply not music. Perhaps Euripides' most exotic musical innovations were the astrophic, polymetric monodies of his late plays, such as that of Ion's temple-tidying entry in the *Ion* and that of the Phrygian slave's frenzied account of mayhem in the *Orestes*.

The Socratic character, if we may call it that, of Euripides' plays, however, runs deeper than their mutual liberation from metrical conventions. The Euripides of the *Frogs* [971ff] admits without apology that he has introduced his audience to thinking, even taught them how to think [*phronein*] by presenting characters who question, reason, and debate whatever happens and whatever they do. And we see for ourselves in his plays how appropriate is this admission. It is all but unheard of, for instance, in earlier non-Euripidean tragedies for central characters to change their minds, whereas Euripides presents us with a gallery of characters who painfully reconsider and reverse their actions. On occasion the entire structure of a play is woven by the interplay of two or more characters changing their minds in tragic syncopation, most notably perhaps in the *Hippolytus* and in the *Iphigeneia at Aulis*. Socrates must have been more than once edified by the extent to which Euripidean characters, or some at least, led the examined life. Furthermore, we find Euripides' characters often talking to themselves, wondering how things have turned out as they have or why they themselves are going to do what they are indeed about to do.

If we knew of Euripides only from Aristophanes, we might imagine that Euripides squeezed his plays from books, which is far from the truth. It remains true, however, that Euripidean prologues are sometimes quite bookish and that his characters are known to break out into discourses better suited to school than to stage. The most current and pressing intellectual and political debates of his day find voice in his tragedies, for example the debate over the meaning and relative status of natural law versus convention, or the debates over the demythologization of Greek religion, the secular critique of civic religion and of folk piety, the merits of democracy and the ethics of empire. Indeed, such contemporarily charged issues as the death of god, women's liberation, radical theology, the military-industrial complex, economic imperialism, and decolonization would be foreign to Euripides only as terms, not as ideas. For someone who has been said to have composed his poetry in a cave and to have shunned the throng of the city, Euripides could not have been more in the thick of things. Associating, as he seems to have done, with Anaxagoras, Protagoras, Prodicus, and Socrates, he was both at the center and on the edge of his times; for his was a city both productive and intolerant of change, a city disposed to disown and to dispatch, in one way or another, its most legitimate progeny. "The best traditions make the best rebels," wrote Gilbert Murray in *Euripides and His Age*. [Oxford, 1946] "Euripides is the child of a strong and splendid tradition and is, together with Plato, the fiercest of all rebels against it."

In sum, Euripidean theatre constituted an open forum for a deeply divided society to display its divisions, if nothing else. The famous Protagorean dictum that there are two sides to every argument and the accompanying suggestion that a clever man ought to be able to argue either side successfully give rise and shape to one battle of words after another in Euripidean drama. In these moments of rhetorical pyrotechnics Euripides is presenting, as it were, to his audience's gaze and for their consideration the pragmatic manipulation of language to suit and dissemble one's purposes, a skill central to the Sophist curriculum and prevalent in the politics of empire. It would be an unthinking response to these moments in his plays, however, to imagine that Euripides' theatrical fascination and facility with Sophistic rhetoric indicate the location of his true sympathies. Closer, I would propose, to the sympathies of Euripides are these words of Agamemnon in the *Iphigeneia at Aulis* [333]: "The clever [*sophe*] tongue I find hateful and malignant." There are many "clever tongues" in Euripides' plays, making every effort to cover the stench of their deeds with the perfume of their words; but as a rule they do not fare well. One such smooth tongue, as we have already seen, belongs to Polymestor in the *Hecuba;* and, translated freely, Hecuba's raw response [1187ff] comes down to this: There is nothing worse than rot wrapped in finery. Behind whatever veil of words, however finely woven, a rotten life begins to smell and give itself away. The same Hecuba is no kinder to Helen in the *Trojan Women* [969ff] when Helen talks for her life, making over her deeds more thickly than, presumably, she ever had to make over her face. Without exhausting ourselves here with citations, we may say that this confrontation of words with the deeds that cower behind them is too common and central to Euripidean drama to escape anyone's notice and might be seen to present a critique of Sophistic rhetoric, or of its abuse at the very least. And, if that is the case, then we are justified in hearing the voice of Euripides himself in this fragment [N2.439]: "How I wish that facts could speak for themselves, so that they could not be misrepresented by eloquence."

Facts or actions, however, do not speak. They have no voice of their own and thus must find eventual voice in words which reveal them faithfully. Consequently, the battle for truth comes down to a contest of words, a contest between true words and false words, words which are transparent to deeds and words which are an opaque screen dissembling the deeds that lurk behind them. "The account born out of truth is simple and straightforward, standing in no need of elaborate interpretation. It makes its own case. But the word with no justice on its side is simply sick to its core and needs whatever tonics cleverness might concoct." [*Phoenician Women,* 469–472] This is essentially the claim of Medea, who, after listening to Jason painting a halo around his sins, confronts him and says to him with utter confidence "one word is all it will take to stretch you out flat." [*Medea,* 585]

The Aristophanic Euripides confessed proudly that he let everyone talk; and we might add that he let them say whatever they pleased. But to speak is not necessarily to have the final word. Refutation was often swift to follow, delivered, as we have seen, directly by another's words, more revealing of the truth. The forms of refutation in Euripidean drama are many. In the *Hecuba,* Polymestor is first contradicted, even as he speaks, by a mere stage prop, the shrouded remains of the boy whom he cut down and cast into the sea but whom he says is even now as safe as sate can be. Thinking that the corpse before him is that of Hecuba's last surviving girl, Polymestor is smug and sure that his words are working their wanted effect; but, to the ears of Hecuba and of the audience, Polymestor's words make no more sound than pennies dropped into a bottomless well. His fate is sealed. Rather more subtle is the refutation meted out to Orestes whose own words are made to mock him [*Orestes,* 646–651]:

> All right, I committed a crime. Even so, it would be criminal of you not to commit a crime now to help me out. After all, it was criminal of my father Agamemnon to muster an army and throw it against Troy. But he wasn't exactly doing anything wrong, because the wrong he was doing was done to make right the wrong that your wife did, which was criminal. Anyway, you owe me a wrong, Menelaus, for the wrong done rightly for you.

This gibberish poured from the mouth of Orestes is surely no critique of moral discourse; rather it is a parody of the sophisticated but futile disfiguration of language to conceal rather than to reveal the truth. In retrospect now, it may be more accurate to speak of Euripidean theatre's presenting not so much an open forum for the mere airing of diverse opinions as a courtroom wherein the decisive debates of his age might be adjudicated. In the Euripidean theatre, it is closer to the truth to say that Athens is on trial than to say that Athens is on display. The most obscure aspect of this trial, of course, is the identity of the judge. Here Euripides fades behind his characters, just as Plato fades behind Socrates, who, in turn, is as elusive a figure as we are likely to meet anywhere. Perhaps all we are able to say in the absence of directly imparted Socratic or Euripidean doctrine is that some opinions are better than others and that our eyes are rather more discerning after our reading of Euripides or Socrates than before. In sum, the claim I am making comes down to this: the playwright, as Euripides lives the calling, is no less committed than is the philosopher to truth: to the telling of the truth if possible, to the untelling of lies if necessary, and to the admission of ignorance if ignorance is all that seems available. Perhaps this is where scholarship rightly ends: with the exhaustion, in both senses, of ignorance.

EURIPIDES THE PLAYWRIGHT

Our discussion of Euripides as playwright is admittedly already underway and will reach to the last page written here. Consequently, the agenda of this rather slight subsection requires a modest focus, which is simply this: to come to some provisional understanding of the place of the playwright in fifth-century Athens. In what terms, we might ask, was the calling of the playwright understood? What were the expectations placed on him? By what standards was he measured?

To put first things first, we may turn to Plato, whom anyone would agree was a man with priorities. Interestingly, Plato, in the *Republic,* which along with Aristophanes' *Frogs* comprises the richest ancient source for our present discussion, makes no distinction between poets and playwrights or, more specifically, between Homeric poetry and Attic drama. In this light, Euripides stands in a direct line with Homer, and tragedy constitutes an Attic supplement to Homer. In this as in other matters, we may assume that Plato was overlooking the realm of appearances and striking what he saw to be the essential underlying unity of epic and tragic poetry.

The essence shared by epic and tragic poetry is education, which we must take to mean public or political education in the sense of the education of the polis. No one would quarrel with the altogether central place of Homeric poetry in the traditional education of the Greeks, who learned not only to speak but also to think and to act as Greeks through the mimetic absorption of Homeric verse. Homeric poetry has been described as the "tribal encyclopedia" of ancient Hellas; and it is as such that Plato confronts and challenges it. Tragic drama, on the other hand, far from encyclopedic in scope, comprises mere "slices" from the Homeric whole, served as what might be regarded as "tea" in comparison with the Homeric feast. For Plato, however, only the scale is different. Tragic poetry, no less than epic poetry, possesses as its defining function education.

It was not until Plato's founding of the academy, consequent upon his moral despair of not only Athens but any city likely ever to emerge in stone and flesh, that education ceased, in principle as it were, to be the business of the city and became the business of a precinct apart, an intellectual *temenos* known as the academy. In the fourth century, the charge of education passed, at least in theory, from civic culture to formal schooling, which Plato understood to be inevitably countercultural. Civic education, the education depicted in the parable of the cave, is, in Plato's estimation, invariably miseducation. For our purposes, however, what is essential to notice is that Plato's attempted and largely successful coup in the *Republic* takes as its incontestable point of departure the double fact that the city is the first to instruct its citizens and that the poets are the first to instruct the city. Otherwise, the massive intellectual effort of Plato to wrench education away from the city and his directing of that effort straight at the poets would have to be seen as unmitigated strategic folly.

Plato's conception of dramatic poetry as essentially instructional is not to be seen as a Platonic idiosyncrasy. After all, tragic poetry was supported by elaborate civic patronage in Athens. No less than the construction and fitting-out of a warship for the Athenian fleet, the subsidizing of a tragic production constituted a *leitourgia,* the discharging of a serious and economically onerous service to the city. We might also point to the fact that the specific word for playwright or dramatic poet in classical Greek is *didaskalos,* "teacher" or "instructor". Admittedly, this term points primarily to the playwright's task of teaching his play to the chorus and the actors assigned to him by the civic authorities. Nevertheless, it may be argued that the sphere of the playwright's teaching extended beyond the cast to the city; and such an argument would find solid support in the *Frogs,* to which we turn next.

Aristophanes, like Plato, must be cited with circumspection regarding Euripidean drama; but, in the case of both, we are on rather more solid ground when our focus falls not on the points they are arguing but rather on what they assume as common knowledge or opinion in arguing their peculiar points. In the *Frogs,* both Aeschylus and Euripides, who agree on precious little, have no cause to quarrel with the claim that tragic poets like themselves are "teachers of men." More precisely, what is affirmed in the *Frogs* is that poets, in their capacity as teachers, give counsel not to children but to youths, those who are on the brink of manhood. Poets preside, as it were, over an essential rite of passage from childhood to manhood. Elsewhere, the same would-be men receive from the city their military training and their first assignments as "ephebes," what we might call "recruits." The "basic training" provided by the theatre is directed not at muscle and nerve but at the mind and the heart. The young Athenian male, at eighteen, was to be made ready not only for the challenges of war but also for the challenges of citizenship. Not only did his chaotically passionate flesh and spirit require the tempering of rigorous discipline; but his callow, impressionable, intemperate soul, like hot wax, required the stamp of the city. In Athens, it was the poet's charge to cut that seal and to impress it upon each new generation of citizens. In short, before the inauguration of "higher education" by Plato, the poets and, in the fifth century, preeminently the tragic poets were the "teachers of men" in the sense of teachers who make men of boys.

The "rite of passage" over which the poet presides is that between the private realm and the public realm. The primary identification of the Athenian boy was with his family, tribe, and constitutional district or "deme"; but with manhood one became in the fullest sense an Athenian, whose essential loyalties and commitments were expected to transcend personal and familial considerations. At approximately the age of six, a boy was weaned a second time from his mother and removed from the women's quarters to the men's quarters where he would take his meals and associate primarily with his own sex. At the age of eighteen, however, a young man was removed from his home altogether and sent off for military training and his first tour of duty. This is the critical age, the critical point of turning, wherein a young man first enters the service of his city and discovers what may be called the public or common realm as distinct from the private realm. Thucydides likened the ancient city or polity to a common meal, a "pot-luck" we might call it, to which each citizen brings not only his hunger but also his contribution. It is to this feast that the poet invites the youth, counselling him regarding not only what he might reasonably expect of the city but also what the city might reasonably expect of him.

In the theatre of Dionysus, the stakes, as it were, could not have been higher for the city of Athens. Admittedly, the tragic curriculum was not so expansive as to challenge the Homeric encyclopedia on every front. Instead, the tragic curriculum struck at the heart and the mind and the eyes, leaving the extremities to be instructed elsewhere. The core of the tragic curriculum was political and moral, not as distinct categories but as essentially complementary dimensions of a single wisdom or skill, which Plato's *Protagoras* calls "political wisdom [*sophia politike*] or "political skill" [*politike techne*]. The three constitutive elements of this wisdom or skill, as explicated in the *Protagoras*, are: firstly, the skill of waging war [*techne polemike*]; secondly, a sense of justice or right action [*dike*]; and, thirdly, a sense of honor or shame [*aidos*]. The art of warfare, the effective employment of violence, was required in mythic or prehistoric times to secure the human realm from bestial threats, in fact to turn the tables and make man the predator instead of the prey. The art of waging war, however, which is not the subject matter of tragedy, is itself a threat to the polity which possesses it; for it may at any time turn inward. Like fire, it is civilizing; but also like fire it must be contained or it will cook more than meat and will consume the very dwelling whose construction was made possible by the tools shaped and tempered in its flames. In short, any city may wage war against other cities or even with itself; and we know from Athenian history and literature that civil war was indeed the Athenian political nightmare *par excellence*. What contains within acceptable limits the destructive potential of systematic human violence are the two other essential elements of civic wisdom or skill: a sense of justice and a sense of shame; and these are instilled, etched into the souls of Athenian youth, by the poets whose words must be hot and bright with truth.

It is further claimed in the *Protagoras* that cities cannot be formed unless political wisdom is the possession of all or nearly all citizens. Political wisdom cannot be the prerogative or the burden of a minority, if cities and thus specifically human life are to survive and flourish. Protagoras goes so far as to place in the mouth of Zeus himself the following decree, thus giving it the highest of sanctions: "If anyone proves incapable of participating in a [common] sense of justice and shame, let him be put to death as one who is a plague to his city." [*Protagoras*, 322d] Shameless immorality is not only destructive but contagious, and cannot be tolerated. With this in mind, we approach an understanding of how profoundly serious was the calling of the poet, the teacher of citizens, above all the youngest citizens. To betray that calling was to corrupt the young and to threaten the city no less than if one had laid seige to its walls.

This calling, to teach the city of Athens, is not in question when Aeschylus and Euripides square off in the *Frogs*. What is in question is the curriculum. Their quarrel is not over their responsibility to teach, but rather over what it is they ought to teach and how they ought to teach it. Since our concern here is with Euripides, we will focus on his proposals. He says that his teachings ought to be eminently practical and decent, serving to enhance life in the city, all of which may be conveyed by the word *chresta* [1057]. Furthermore, Euripides suggests that the manner of his speech should suit its message. A simple, straight-forward, humanizing lesson is best conveyed in simple, straight-forward terms. What he has to say must, in his word, be said *anthropeios* [1057], by which he must mean something like: "in simplest human terms." It would seem, then, at least as an experiment, premised on the possibility that Aristophanes is conveying with some faithfulness the acknowledged purpose of the poet in Athens, that we might approach the work of Euripides as that of a man endeavoring to counsel his fellow citizens regarding justice and honor and shame, the most fun-damental human decencies, without which common life may not survive much less flourish, and doing so in those terms most likely, in his judgement, to convey without distortion his central teaching. If we add to this his realization that he was endeavoring to counsel a city already corrupt, already plagued with civil war and fraternal slaughter, already festering with private violence, then we might approach the work of Euripides as that of a teacher with an unwelcome teaching, forced to de-ploy strategies of ironic indirection to insure that his teaching will come out straight. We might even conjecture that Euripides, aware that his words were often acid poured on open wounds, and cognizant of the time that the written word could now buy for premature proposals, wrote for the future, for any time and place in which he might be understood.

After all, we may recall the perhaps presumptuous claim of Pericles, reported for us in Thucydides' history of *The Peloponnesian War,* to the effect that Athens was the school for all of Hellas, the standard measure for all the cities of Greece. And, as if this were too modest an achievement, Pericles pre-dicted that future ages would wonder at Athens even as did his own age. Regrettably, Pericles the visionary proved strangely blind to the shamefulness and injustice of greed and self-aggrandizement on the part of a city, though he was the first to condemn them on the part of any citizen. Cities, he seemed to imagine, lay beyond the bounds of ethics. In fact, he seems to have argued quite openly that cities like Athens with imperial designs and responsibilities cannot afford to display decency, pity, or compassion. Somehow he dreamed that domestic policy and foreign policy could be sealed off hermetically from each other and that the splendor of the one could ignore and outshine the filth of the other. In this he proved himself a fool, with the result that future ages wonder at Athens not only for its culture but for its corruption, as well.

In sum, Athens was the teacher of Greece and, in some measure, of all ages; and Euripides was in the front ranks of the teachers of Athens. Singularly sighted in those darkened areas wherein Pericles and his city appear to have been all but blind, Euripides teaches us about all that shone and about all that stank in a city, which for the sheer scale of its accomplishments, good and evil, has few rivals. In the works of Euripides, we wonder indeed at Athens, its civilization and its barbarity, and perhaps even more at their coexistence; and, unless we place the dramas of Euripides under glass and gaze at them squintingly, as we would at a series of laboratory slides, we will wonder too at how little has changed. In the theatre of Euripides, the tragedy behind the tragedies is always that of Athens, in its particularity and its universality, the timeless tragedy of the path not taken, of lost potential, of what might have been. It is the tragedy we hear in the voice of Adrastus in the *Suppliant Women* [949-954], sick to death with the pointless suffering we humans cause each other:

> O wretched race of mortals,
> Why slaughter each other with your spears?
> Stop all this and lighten the load you bear.
> Settle down with each other into lives of kindness,
> And let your cities be secure in this.
> For life is a brief business.
> Better to make it as easy as you can,
> Then to go through it
> Bent over with pain.

In the *Laws*, Plato looks back at the decline of Athens and says that it was when the populace, rather than the best and wisest among them, were allowed to judge the theatrical and musical contests that the city fell apart. Presumably, what he means is that the populace wished above all to be entertained, flattered in their fantasies, confirmed in their prejudices. Regardless, what is surprising in Plato's comment is not that he attributes the decline of theatre to the arguably vulgar judgement of the people-at-large, but that he attributes the decline of the city to the decline of its theatre. It is interesting in this context that Dionysus in the *Frogs* says that he is in search of a poet because the city needs saving, as if a poet might do more than a god for a city on the skids. There was an ancient saying among the Greeks that "a city deserted by its gods is a city lost." [Aeschylus, *Seven Against Thebes*, 217–218] There may be some truth, then and now, to saying the same of a city and its poets. The theatre, after all, as we shall consider in the next chapter, was the city's "seeing place," the place of vision; and when the theatre falls upon dark times, the city goes blind.

CHAPTER TWO
⬦⬦⬦⬦⬦⬦
THEATRE

The foregoing discussion of the playwright's place and profession in Athenian public life already frames the forthcoming discussion of the place and function of theatre. The theatre was, quite simply, the locus and the medium of the tragic poet's teaching. As its name suggests, it was a "seeing-place," which is not to deny the aural, musical dimension of drama but only to give preeminence to the dimension of sight. This primacy of sight requires critical and speculative consideration, because in it lies the key to the interpretation of tragedy set forth in this volume. Consequently, we turn first to a consideration of the sight proper and peculiar to theatre.

In our earlier contrasting of seeing and hearing, we noticed the freedom of the eye in ranging over the visual object, which remains at the more or less stable disposal of the see-er. In addition to the relative independence of the eye, we may notice too the essential commonality of sight. Whether we consult formal studies of sight, ancient and modern, or whether we consult directly our own everyday experience of sight, we come eventually to the commonsense conclusion that ordinary objects of sight and our ordinary sight of them are reliably common to all sighted individuals. Despite the uneven quality of individual vision, the exceptional instances of optical illusion, and the inescapable particularity of perspective, we experience sight as the most common of the senses. Even those who have been intellectually or spiritually persuaded in theory that the visual world is illusory or radically private rely in practice from day to day on seeing their way through a shared world. Quite simply, if I were to see an object in open sight and point it out to others around me, only to find that I alone see it, I would be confounded rather than confirmed in my convictions; and I propose that I am far from being alone in this.

To say that the Athenian theatre was a seeing-place, then, assigns it to the common realm. The circular construction of the Greek theatre and the placing of the drama in the middle of that circle at the more or less equal disposal of all citizens further suggests that theatre belonged to the public realm. It was not a place where privilege or power determined the degree of one's participation. Rather, being a place of common sight, it was necessarily a place of freedom and equality. As such, it was an integral component and expression of Athenian public life. Like the pnyx where all citizens were permitted an equal voice and an equal vote, and like the agora, where all citizens had equal access by lot to service in the highest deliberative and judicial bodies, and like the acropolis, where public sacrifices for the well-being of all citizens were performed not by an ensconced priesthood but again by citizens, like all of these foci of Athenian life the theatre was defined as a public realm designed and designated for an essentially common experience, in this case the experience of a common vision. The orchestra, then, no less than the common civic hearth in the agora and the common civic altar on the acropolis, was a central symbol of the polis and a vital source of its life. In fact, I would claim that Attic tragedy, an art form nearly native to Athens, was a foundationally constitutive element of the democratic Athenian polis.

It is clearly beyond the bounds of this discussion to trace a path from Mycenaean monarchy to Athenian democracy. Nonetheless, we should be aware that the acropolis of Athens no longer vaunted a royal palace in the fifth century; rather, the place of the ancient kings belonged now to the gods. And in the common worship of their gods, Athenian citizens acknowledged not only their inequality with the gods but also their equality with each other. Ritual sacrifice, as we shall see in some detail later, was the cornerstone of Greek religion and served to delineate the divine from the human, the sacred from the profane. The absolute, authoritative word of the divine or divinely representative ruler, which formed the basis of nearly all ancient East Mediterranean regimes, found no place in Athens, nor, in principle did the rule of force. Both the sceptre and the spear, authority and force, the two rival principles of rule represented by Agamemnon and Achilles, respectively, in their bitter quarrel depicted by Homer, both were rejected by Athenian democracy. In the *Iliad*, Zeus alone possessed both absolute authority and absolute power; and it may be argued that even Homer, who is said to have given to the Greeks both their gods and their heroes, finally rejected both the sceptre and the spear as the bases of human fellowship, when he had Achilles and Priam reach across their hatred and their rage to embrace each other in compassion and to share a meal. Regardless, within the city walls, the spear represented tyranny to the Athenians; and the sceptre represented hybris.

The alternative principle of government with which the Athenians experimented was that of public debate and open vote. Not only was each vote to be counted equally but each voice was to be heard with more or less equal openness to the possibility that it might express the truth. In case any individual citizen, even without claiming special authority or threatening the use of force, might attain a personal preeminence whose practical effect would be to intimidate others and to silence dissent, there was instituted the practice of ostracism, or temporary banishment. Ostracism, until it was debased, was a leveler, serving to eliminate for a time those individuals who were too gifted or too accomplished or too influential to take their place any longer as equals with their fellow citizens in common deliberation. It was, in a sense, a barbed tribute paid to genius. Under the democracy, the good of the city was to be found out in the process of searching for its common mind. The many were to become one, not through obedience to some higher authority, nor through fear of some greater force, nor through deference to some towering figure in their midst, but rather through coming together to a common mind and to a common voice. In this process there was no place for gods or demigods or brutes. Contrary to the animal sacrifices performed on the acropolis, the deliberations on the pnyx, which was the place of civic assembly, were purely human affairs. Just as the temple temenos marked off that area reserved for commerce with the sacred, so the assembly marked off that area reserved for indulgence in the profane consortium of men, reserved, we might say, for the free play of human passions and human wits.

By now we may well wonder what light this discursus into Athenian civics and city planning could cast on the theatre. The point, however, which can be pressed home now is that, in the scheme of Athenian public life, theatre occupied a uniquely balanced position between the sacred rituals of the acropolis and the secular wrangles of the assembly. Although in saying this I do not have in mind the theatre's literal, physical location, even in this respect the ambiguity of the theatre was perhaps reflected; for the theatre of Dionysus, mounting as it does a steep slope of the acropolis, might well be seen as a bridge between the heights and the commons, between the timeless protocols of the gods and the urgencies of the all-too-human moment. The theatre of Dionysus indecisively spanned the *hiera*, the sacred, and the *hosia*, the profane. It was a place of sacrifice and cult, while at the same time it was a place wherein doubt, blasphemy, rage, and evil were hurled into open sight. It was a space reserved equally for pious and for impious words, for prayers and for curses.

The ambiguous character of the Athenian theatre ran far deeper, however, than we have yet explored here. After all, ancient theatre or, more specifically for our present purposes, tragic drama was an oral performance emergent from and controlled by a written text, and as such drew both from the oral poetic tradition and from the literary-critical tradition. Since the written text of a tragedy preceded and survived intact each rehearsal and each performance, it could be open with impunity to experimentation and criticism. Furthermore, since the written text was permanently present to prompt the actor's memory, the playwright was free to disregard the limitations of oral memory as well as any accompanying reliance on formulaic patterns and rhythms and to employ, instead, a diversity of meters and a complexity of language not possible in purely oral poetic composition and performance.

As in form so also in content, the playwright drank from two streams. By convention, tragedy drew predominantly upon the poetic tradition for its *mythoi* or plots. Even in doing so, however, it was free to alter the myths at will, perhaps as a botanist may take cuttings from the oldest and most familiar plants to create something new and boldly different or as a photographer, though working in the most literal of all art forms, may enter the dark room and work creative wonders with the manipulation of light. Thus, in the *Helen,* Euripides, taking cuttings, as it were, from Homer, Herodotus, and Stesichorus, creates a delightfully novel hybrid-Helen, more like the faithful, pining Penelope than the whore of Hellas, while in the *Electra* he casts a more intense, inwardly revealing light on the otherwise quite recognizable princess and discloses a sexually stunted and obsessed adolescent, as enraged by her inadequate wardrobe as she is by her mother's murderous treason. In short, the ancient myths roused or provoked tragedy without determining its response. What this made possible was a public debate with the past, a visible, audible *agon* or struggle between all that was conscious and all that was unconscious in the Athenian psyche.

What may not at first glance be evident here is the freedom and the power bestowed on the playwright, on the one hand, by his inheritance of the entire mythic tradition of his race and, on the other hand, by the license accorded him to work whatever transformations he may wish upon that tradition. After all, the ancient myths and legends comprised the text from which Greeks learned to speak and to think; a mostly unwritten text, to be sure, but all the more compelling and inescapable for that fact. Learning one's mother tongue from stories, a coherent cosmos of stories woven with familiar images and rhythms, is barely to be compared with learning to speak and to think from texts which systematically present the elements and rules of phonetics and grammar. Language learned as a personal tool is well-suited to self-expression but is unlikely to create deep bonds with the past or the fellowship of shared imagination. The original difference here may be likened to that between breastfeeding and the intravenous infusion of a dietetically correct formula; and the eventual difference might perhaps be witnessed by contrasting the impeccably minced discourse of the university with the unstrained effusion of the bard who tilts back his head and drinks words as if they were the sweetest syrup. Words webbed in stories are not the same as words arranged alphabetically in vocabularly lists and indentified by mostly inept synonyms. Free-running words, like free-running chickens, truly do possess a different taste. But the heart of the matter here is not words but stories and images; and the point I wish to make is that Euripides, as an Athenian playwright, received as his legacy those stories and images which he knew were precisely those in the presence of which his audience's minds and hearts had first opened to their world.

Euripides, moreover, as playwright, possessed not only the power of the traditional stories but also power over them. Through major or minor alterations in plot, discourse, or tone, the playwright was able to create a split image, as it were. With the ancient image in mind and the new image before the eye, the spectator was confronted with a conflict between the received tradition and the present reality. Often, in the crevasse created between these two conflicting images, the Athenian public were invited, even forced, to contemplate themselves and their city and the contradictions which they were living.

When, for instance, the most celebrated and beloved of all the Greek heroes—Heracles—made his appearance in Euripides' *Heracles,* he suffered a rather critical loss of stature. This was in the mind of most Greeks the ancient "superman," whose brawn and bravado spawned cycles of legends in which he seemingly tamed all that was wild in the world, save himself. In wresting power from beasts and women—achievements coveted and claimed by Athenians on behalf of Theseus, their own would-be Heracles—he made himself the titular founder and defender of Athenian patriarchy. In short, he was not a man to spend much time at home with the family or to betray the slightest weakness. The Euripidean Heracles, however, longed for nothing so much as a quiet life at home. He said farewell to his labors and confessed that he had been all wrong to have preferred them to the joys of family. He was by this time, however, a thoroughly violent man, and violence has a way of spilling over, with or without daimonic intervention. Just as, in the Euripidean account, Orestes' furies roost within him, so the Euripidean Heracles comes to realize that he is the source and the object of his greatest labor, the most savage force he will ever confront. In a matter of minutes the man who had stood taller than any other man in the ancient imagination is broken, like a match. In the theatrical hands of Euripides, even Heracles, to say nothing of the Athenian spectators, has difficulty recognizing himself as he awakens from his mad slaughter. He thinks at first that his mind is clearing from one of his heroic labors, but like Agave in the *Bacchae*, what awaits him is not myth but reality. "I'm confused…" he mutters as his wits return. "Where could I ever be helpless?" [1105] he wonders. This is certainly a question to which the tradition supplies no answer. He notices next that his father is weeping and he wonders what possible cause his father could have for tears. His father's response is simply: "even a god would weep if he knew what I know." [1115]

What, we may ask, did Amphitryon know? In a word, Amphitryon knew the truth; and so, by this time, did the Athenian theatre-goer. But these are not precisely the same truth. Amphitryon knew the truth of Heracles. He had witnessed with his own eyes his son turned, or rather revealed as, savage beast. The Athenian public, however, knew, whether they accepted it or not, the truth of Athens; for they had witnessed the city of Theseus reveal in recent years its savage, slaughterous spirit. Athens, like Heracles, whose revered, received image was one of self-forgetful boldness and courage on behalf of Greek civilization, had for all its astounding accomplishments violated the first law of humanity, the lowest common denominator of human decency: "every race of man loves the lives it brings into the world." [636] Not so Athens, however, which had sent off its sons to die and to kill for nothing. For all the difference it made, Athens might as well have killed them itself.

It is not a great distance in the Greek imagination from Heracles to Athens. From the mythical Heracles to the legendary Theseus to the historical Athens there is a worn, familiar path, just as there is a virtually paved road from the seige of Troy or the siege of Thebes to the Persian Wars to the Peloponnesian War. Thus, when Euripidies demythologizes, as it were, the glories of the mythic past, revealing the siege of Troy as a deranged misadventure, the violent orgasmic phantasy of a rabble chiefed not by noble lords but by callous non-entities, the mercilessly revealing light cast on the remote past falls on the more recent past, as well, and threatens more immediate myths with reality. Myth, legend, history, and present reality in the Greek theatre are like layers of skin. They do not peel away one at a time, painlessly, like filo dough. When Euripides offered to the Athenian public, for instance, the *Trojan Women*, he was not distracting or entertaining them any more than Medea intended to delight Jason's bride with her gifts. Words like the following [*Trojan Women*, 1158–1160], though literally provoked by the murder of Astyanax and spoken by Hecuba to Talthybius, must have been no easier to remove than Medea's gown, once Euripides had hurled them out at the same citizens who, assembled on the pnyx, had only recently called for the senseless massacre and demolition of Melos:

> Achaeans! You know how to hurl a spear; but
> not how to use your mind or your heart.
> What was it about this little child that
> made you so afraid that you had to kill him,
> and go about it so savagely?

In short, Athens's mythic icons were at the same time mirrors, and any alteration or distortion in the images of the past reflected immediately upon the present. Thus when Euripides exposed the traditional Olympian pantheon as a household wherein the most callous, petty, selfish, cowardly, vindictive, jealous, and cruel behavior was commonplace, and at the same time presented the great lords of legend as chips off the divine block, he left the Athenians with little of stature in terms of which to flatter and defend themselves.

He gave them a mythology reduced to scale, a debased mythology suited to a debased city. "Human nature," wrote T.S. Eliot, "is able to endure only a little reality." If this is true, then Euripides brought the Athenians to the edge of endurance.

It is not surprising that Euripides was accused of having denigrated the tragic tradition. Tragedy implies stature and in a great many of Euripides' plays the traditionally central figures are too small in everything but their pain to command a tragic response. Empires and the mythologies which accompany them display a penchant for grandeur; and this is precisely what Euripides denied his fellow citizens. His were dark times and he offered a vision suitable for eyes accomodated to darkness. In the search for human excellence, Euripides overlooked the seats of traditional privilege and directed the eye, instead, to the traditionally least likely places, to the margins of human existence. As we shall see later in some detail, it was to women, slaves, peasants, barbarians, the very old and the very young, all those excluded from canonical heroism, if not from humanity, that Euripides turned to display new, unconventional paradigms of nobility. Euripides overturned the traditional hierarchy premised on privilege; stood it on end, in fact.

The most privileged, of course, were the gods, whose exemption from death made them all the more unfeeling and unnaccountable in their exercise of power. Next were the kings and princes, whose relative exemption from suffering and whose disproportionate power enabled them briefly to live and to think as if they were gods. At the base of this traditional pyramid of privilege and power were those whose weakness and vulnerability left them to suffer without recourse, without respite. By revealing the corruption that accompanies power and the wisdom that comes with suffering, Euripides endeavored to redefine heroism. As a rule, it was not those who suffered last and least, but rather those who suffered first and most who stood tallest and shone forth on the Euripidean stage. Alcestis, Macaria, Iolaus, Polyxena, Theonoe and her slave, Menoeceus, Electra's peasant husband, and Iphigeneia, for example, tower over their husbands, fathers, kings, lords, and murderers, who command mostly our contempt.

By presenting its traditional ideals in moral disarray, Euripides fostered the radical critique of Athenian society; and by creating a new canon of heroism, he provided what might have been the first elements in a revisioning of that society. The Greek theatre, then, clearly made possible not only sight but insight. It was the choice of the playwright whether to question or to confirm the common vision and the common mind more or less fixed by tradition. It was indeed possible for the playwright to challenge directly the amalgam of myth, historical half-truth, prejudice, and delusion, which formed the consensus of ordinary public opinion. Although steeped in myth, theatre was uniquely vulnerable to the incursions of historical reality. Although heir to the poetic tradition, tragedy unlike epic was each time a fresh creation written with a single performance in mind. Belonging to a particular moment as epic poetry never did, tragedy resonated as fully to the immediate present as to the mythic or indefinite past. In short, everything and nothing was sacred in the theatre, reflecting as it did both myth and history, the sacred and the profane, the received tradition and the present reality.

A further light is shed on the middle ground occupied by Greek theatre when Aristotle, in the Poetics, assigns poetry, and specifically dramatic poetry, to a middle place between philosophy and history. In distinguishing dramatic poetry from philosophy and history, Aristotle makes quite clear that the most obvious difference here—the fact that poetry is written in verse and both philosophy and history are not—falls wide of the point he wishes to make. History and philosophy could be written in verse and drama in prose without altering their respective natures, as Aristotle understands them. The key to this understanding lies not in the literary form but in the essential subject matter of each. History concerns itself with actual events, with what has happened rather than with what could or should happen. Poetry, on the other hand, is free of the actual course of events, free to consider whatever is possible. In short, history addresses particulars, while poetry addresses universals. It is for this reason that Aristotle says of poetry that it is more serious and elevated, in fact more philosophical, than history. It is only fair to note here that Aristotle has in mind, as his paradigmatic historian, not Thucydides but Herodotus. It is not clear, in fact, that Aristotle knew at all the work of Thucydides, who is in Aristotle's categories as clearly a poet as he is a historian. Regardless, the distinction being made here between a concern with particulars and a concern with universals remains critically illuminating.

On the face of it, however, both tragic poets and historians are storytellers, the one admittedly less critical of his sources than the other. After all, the tragic poet's stories are mostly from the mythic past, to which no chain of human witnesses can be traced back. The historian, on the other hand, would have us believe that his stories, which relate more recent events, rest upon more reliable grounds, upon more or less trustworthy human memory and testimony. In short, it would seem that what divides the tragic poet from the historian comes down to time and its effects. And if this were truly the heart of the matter, we might say that the tragic poet is a teller of prehistoric stories, while the historian is a teller of historic stories. In saying this, we would miss Aristotle's point, however, which is that even though the stories of the theatre appear to be about particulars, namely, about individual persons and events, they truly are not. In other words, when Euripides tells a story of Theseus and when Herodotus tells a story of Themistocles, we miss the essential distinction between their accounts if we focus on our awareness that Theseus is a less historically stable individual, that is, a more fictional and less factual individual than is Themistocles, and in doing so never question their equal claim to individuality. In order to grasp what Aristotle is saying about tragic poetry, we must loosen our fixation on the distinction between fact and fiction and consider instead the distinction between fact and truth. This is made all the more difficult by the characteristically modern identification of fact and truth, an identification which cannot go unchallenged, however, if we are to approach Greek theatre with any perception.

When Aristotle says that dramatic poetry is philosophical because of its essential concern with universals, he is in effect saying that dramatic poetry is concerned with truth. We would perhaps argue that the historian is no less concerned with truth, with telling the true story, for example, of Themistocles. But Aristotle means something different by "truth" than we have in mind in arguing for the legitimacy of historical truth-telling. Of course, any full account of Aristotle's understanding of truth falls well beyond the reasonable bounds of our present discussion. Nonetheless, we cannot hope for even a provisional grasp of the ancient playwright as teacher, nor of the ancient theatre as a seeing- place, nor of ancient dramatic poetry as philosophical without some brief venture into the conception of truth inherent in Aristotle's analysis of dramatic poetry.

In appealing here to Aristotle, I am not claiming that Aristotle's teaching shaped Euripidean drama; for to claim that I would have to turn back time itself. Rather, I am claiming that Aristotle was a well-informed and intelligent commentator on Attic tragedy, sufficiently close, both in time and in sensibility, to the fifth-century tragic playwrights to reveal in their work much that is all but lost on our less knowing gaze. Further, I would argue that the few Aristotelian categories employed in my comments provide a usefully concise articulation of elements which can be shown to lie already within, indeed at the core of, Euripidean drama and, for that matter, of all Attic tragedy as we know it. Presumably, it was to his own similar perception of the convergence and congeniality of his work with that of the theatre that Aristotle was pointing when he called dramatic poetry "philosophical."

The truth whose meaning we are exploring here, the truth of theatre and of philosophy, is the truth of universals or universal truth. "Universal truth" and "universals," though the most common way of translating the relevant Greek words, are all too likely to mislead us here, however; for they have acquired too many contemporary connotations alien to our purposes. I say this because the "universal" of consummate concern in Euripidean theatre is humanity or human nature. Now, in contemporary usage, to speak of the universal truth of humanity or of human nature, is to speak of that which is true of all human beings, if indeed there is anything true of all human beings. The way we would determine whether some attribute or behavior were universally human, in the sense of universally true of human beings, would presumably be through the exhaustive observation of all individual human beings, which is, of course, not feasible. Consequently, we are left with approximations of the truth, which is to say that we are left with claims to the effect that every human being observed by us has displayed the particular attribute or behavior whose universality we would argue. Modern statistical theories and methods have provided plausible grounds for reaching and defending conclusions well beyond the scope of those individuals actually observed; but nothing can alter the essentially quantitative character of this conception of universality. The conception of universality central to, and even constitutive of, ancient theatre is not, however, essentially quantitative, but qualitative.

The truth of human nature, as it is sought out and revealed in Greek drama, is more appropriately described as that which is true *for* all human beings, rather than that which is true *of* all human beings. What this distinction permits us to acknowledge is that there are attributes and actions which are true *for* all human beings yet not true *of* all human beings. And if this is the case, mere observation is useless as a means for the discovery of universal truth. What is required, instead, is insight. And insight is the proper work and aim of the ancient theatre. Before burrowing even further into these reflections, however, a straightforward example from Euripides' *Alcestis* [779–784, 787–788, 799] may well serve to ground and to clarify the matter at hand. The voice we hear in the following lines is that of Heracles, drunken and rowdy, conducting his own private debauch in the mourning house of Admetus. He addresses the household servant who is supplying him with wine and feast.

> You there, c'mere.
> I'm gonna make you a wiser man
> Do you know what's what?
> I mean do you know what it means to be human?
> I don't think you do.
> Anyway, you listen to me.
> We all gotta die.
> There ain't one of us alive today
> That knows whether he'll be around tomorrow
> So there, that's it.
> You heard what I got to teach.
> Enjoy yourself, have a drink
> If you're mortal,
> You gotta have mortal thoughts.

The braying Heracles, of course, his tongue loosened with wine, had more than this to say; but I've preserved the core of his teaching. Essentially it comes down to this: all human beings die and they ought to live and think as if they know it. What we may notice about his teaching is that one of its tenets is true *of* all human beings. It is true of all human beings that they "gotta die." The second teaching, he would claim, is true *for* all human beings but is surely not true of all or even most. It is true for all human beings that they "gotta have mortal thoughts." Both death and the consciousness of death are prescribed. Both belong to the nature of human beings. Both are universally true. But the truth and necessity of the one must be distinquished from the truth and necessity of the other. The one we may call a literal necessity and the other a moral necessity. The one describes what it is to be mortal and the other describes what it ought to mean to be mortal. What we notice next is the relationship between these two universal truths or necessities. It is the literal truth that enjoins the moral truth. It is because we are mortal that we ought to think and to act as if we are mortal. In other words, we must, in the sense of should, live in accord with our nature.

Clearly it is the possibility of living in violation of one's nature that accounts for the fact that what is morally true for all is not actually true of them. All human beings ought to think mortal thoughts and to act accordingly; but not all do. Heracles prefaced his remarks, we remember, with the claim that what he had to say was going to make a wiser man of the servant. Presumably, Heracles' first teaching was not news to the servant, who is noticeably distressed over the death of Alcestis. That we all "gotta die" is a truism, lost only on the youngest children. But few are those, as Camus once wrote, who pursue life's truisms to their final conclusions. It is not the literal knowledge of death's inevitability that makes anyone appreciably wiser, but rather the reasonings and resolves which ought to accompany, but most often do not accompany, that knowledge.

The path of wisdom, then, requires that facts be transformed into truths, that truisms be pursued until they yield their moral conclusions. Euripides, as a teacher of his city, is engaged precisely in this endeavor. Not unlike Heracles, Euripides is concerned to make a wiser man out of whoever listens to him. No doubt such a concern rings rather pretentiously, even offensively, in many or most modern ears. After all, modern theatre is there, it would seem, to entertain, not to edify. We underestimate and trivialize ancient theatre, however, if we overlook what Aristotle called its more serious, elevated, even philosophical nature. The ancient theatre is a seeing-place, a place avowedly consecrated to communal moral insight, a place where light is shed upon universal necessities and truths, those moral necessities and truths which hold for all human beings, however widely they ignore and defy them.

The tragic theatre, in sum, is a place of disclosure, a place of truth. Even the Greek word for truth—*aletheia*—gives us privileged entry into the ideas to be explored here. *Aletheia* literally means that which has not escaped notice, that which has not gone unseen, or that which has not been forgotten. What this derivation seems to suggest is that truth, unless ferreted out and grasped tightly, is likely to slip away, once discovered, or to elude us altogether. Truth, conceived as "unconcealment," presupposes concealment as the raw condition of truth. It is as if truth, like precious metal, must be mined, extracted, as it were, from darkness. "Nature," said Heraclitus, "likes to hide," which is not far from our present point, inasmuch as the truth of central concern to Euripides is that of human nature. Perhaps it is also the case that human nature likes to hide and is likely to elude us unless it is dragged into open view and unless we, in turn, are coaxed into confronting it. One place wherein both occur, I would propose, is the ancient theatre.

In another equally enticing aphorism, Heraclitus points out how, when we dream, we inhabit a private world. When we awake, however, he says we awake to a common world. Here again we find a metaphor for truth and its disclosure. Truth is common; and to behold it each individual must be roused from private dreams to public vision. It is not only that when we dream we dwell in a private world, but also that when we dwell in a private world we are only dreaming. The city is ideally a place where humanity flourishes; and humanity is common, universal, as an obligation if not as an achievement. Therefore, when the city, guided by the playwright's counsel, is brought to a common vision, that vision is first and essentially the vision of humanity, lured out of concealment into the common light of day and into the shared light of reason to be contemplated and embraced.

How, we might ask, does this awakening occur? How is a common vision achieved? In the most preliminary and literal sense, the city is led to a common vision by being collected in the theatre and presented with a common spectacle. By vision, however, we mean more than this. We mean insight; for only through shared insight does a community form a common mind. The stories enacted in the Athenian theatre, like the fables of Aesop, are transparent to logos, to thought and idea. In the case of Aesop, the logos—usually translated as the "moral"—yielded by each fable is explicitly stated and, more often than not, represents a commonplace of folk wisdom. In the case of Euripides, however, the logos embedded in each drama is more complex and less explicit. The moral issues explored in Euripidean drama rarely admit of direct, univocal declarations. Instead, we are presented with a dilemma and a debate. There are multiple lines of force, as we shall see, in the Euripidean theatre; and, for every line of force, a voice to argue its case. The outcome, while not simplistically didactic, is far from cacophonous. The playwright's voice is discernible, even though it is fractured and filtered through his characters, like light refracted through a crystal; for there is an order, a scheme, in Euripidean theatre which rendered his drama not only visible but intelligible to its original spectators. For the most part that order is visual and thus spatial; and is prior to any words spoken. In Greek theatre, the visual order frames and provides the interpretive structure for the many voices woven together in the text. The remainder of this chapter, and in fact the remainder of this book, will address that visual order and the insight it made possible.

It has already been claimed, while discussing dramatic poetry's philosophical concern with universal truth, that the stories or *mythoi* unfolded in the tragic theatre are not truly about individuals. This fact would have been more evident to ancient Athenian spectators than to ourselves, both because they "saw" Greek theatre and because what they saw outwardly in the theatre corresponded to and confirmed, in its most essential structure, the categories of their most inward thoughts. In a word, what I am pointing to here is the fact and the significance of the fact that ancient tragedy was masked. On the face of it this is no startling revelation. Everyone knows that Greek tragedy, and all of Greek drama for that matter, was performed with masks. Whatever other ancient theatrical conventions were challenged and adapted or abandoned, all classical Greek theatre was masked. It might be argued that masks were dictated by merely practical considerations. How were men to play credibly the parts of women, for example, without wearing masks? And how could the three actors, to whom the playwright was conventionally limited, have played more than three characters without the ready changes of identity made possible by masks? There may well be answers to these questions; but we need not quarrel with the obvious utility of masks. It is not for their utility, however, that they were adopted; for the use of masks in ritual and drama, both in ancient Greece and elsewhere, precedes and oversteps the specific conventions of classical theatre, which one might otherwise imagine to have dictated that use. Besides, what I have in mind by saying that Greek theatre was masked extends well beyond the literal use of painted cloth coverings for head and face.

To say that Greek theatre was masked is to say that in Greek theatre personal identities were concealed. The closest Greek word to "personal identity" or "personality" is *prosopon*, which curiously is the word both for face and for mask. *Prosopon* means that which is looked upon, that aspect of a human being which is most visible. It is, we could say, one's visible identity. This makes evident sense, for though one may be visually identified by one's stature, or physique, by one's hands or feet or walk, it is by one's face that one is, as we say, "positively identified." To cover the face is to make one invisible, in the sense of unidentifiable. What I wish to claim in all this is that the essential function of Greek theatrical masks was not only to conceal the identity of the actor but to conceal personal identity altogether and to bestow upon the masked character a universal significance instead of an alternative personality.

Both to stress the fact that, in exploring the masked character of Greek theatre, I have something more in mind than the physical mask, as well as to illuminate what this "something more" might be, I will point to another ancient masked ritual in which no physical masks were used. This was the ritual of hospitality, which constituted one of the most sacred moral obligations in ancient Greece, under the direct patronage of Zeus himself, who was thought to take the punishment of offenders into his own hands. The aspect of this ritual which is of critical interest here is the anonymity customarily imposed upon those who make the ritual request of hospitality. The Greek word both for "guest" and for "host" is *xenos* or stranger; for host and guest are to be and to remain strangers to each other in the requesting, the giving, and the receiving of hospitality. Not until the pledge of hospitality has been made and accepted, in fact not until the stranger-host has provided the stranger-guest with a room, a bath, a fresh robe, and a first meal, which is to say not until the bond between host and guest has been sealed, is the guest to reveal his indentity. Before that moment he is a stranger.

This strange behavior has a brilliant truth at its core. If the guest's identity is known, the extending or withholding of hospitality may well be influenced by that knowledge. The host may discover that he is related to the guest or that they both come from the same town or that the guest is related to an enemy or is from a part of the world for which the host has nothing but contempt. Whatever the host finds out about the guest's individuality may influence and complicate the way he sees the man before him. And any such influences and complications are irrelevant to the obligation of hospitality, which is due to any other human being in need of a roof and a meal. The bond of hospitality is to be a bond between human beings, rooted in the recognition of a common humanity, not in the discovery of shared idiosyncrasies. What is displayed in the giving and receiving of hospitality is not the unique regard one individual has for another but the essential goodwill assumed to exist in the heart of any human being for another. The initial silence of the guest regarding his identity is a mask worn over his individuality. The function of this mask is, however, not only to conceal a reality but also to reveal one. The revealed reality is the guest's humanity, which is ordinarily masked by his individuality. Kings, slaves, employers, cousins, welfare recipients, and AIDS victims, citing several possible indentities at random, are less likely to be seen simply and straightforwardly in their humanity once their particulars are known. Personal familiarity conspires to estrange individuals from their common humanity, just as the shared ritual estrangement of host and guest serves to reconcile them to their common humanity. By now the point I wish to make is doubtlessly clear. Ancient Greek theatre was a masked ritual in precisely the same sense as was the ritual of hospitality, and with the same end in mind: to reveal the essential commonality of all its participants and to revive among them the essential goodwill and mutuality without which human community is an idle phantasy.

The anonymity imposed upon Greek theatre is, to be sure, in no way as total as that proper to the rites of hospitality. In the theatre, the human mask is admittedly particularized, and it comes in many forms. Each mask, however, as it conceals the identity of the actor and receives the identity of a specific character in the plot, remains open to and reveals the wider, more embracing, generic category to which that character belongs. In Attic drama, each character is visibly defined and positioned within two fundamental orders, which I will call the metaphysical order and the political order. Within the metaphysical order, the three essentially distinct spheres of being are those of gods, humans, and beasts. The focus of tragedy invariably falls upon the human sphere; for both gods and beasts are spared, or perhaps we should say denied, mortal poignancy. Human consciousness must define itself against the distorting irrelevancies of divine and bestial existence; and tragic consciousness is nothing if it is not human consciousness brought to brightest flame. The second order, the political order, lies wholly within the human sphere and comprises all of those distinctions between human beings which sever them one from the other and may appear to constitute essential differences between them. In the political order, men are distinguished from women, citizens from slaves, Greeks from barbarians, the rich from the poor, the young from the old, and so on. Both orders, as understood within those archaic conventions inherited by Euripides, constituted hierarchies of privilege and power. Within the immutable metaphysical order, gods were the masters of mortals, and mortals were the masters of beasts, while within the altogether mutable political order, the balance of power slides and shifts, as Hecuba reminds Odysseus [*Hecuba*, 282–284]:

> The powerful do not do well
>   To abuse their power.
> No turn of fate fails to turn some day.
> I know.
> I was once where you are now.
> You see how much remains.

Each character's place within these two orders is made visibly evident on the ancient tragic stage, not only by the mask that is worn but by other semiotic conventions, as well. The human visage is unmistakable, but in itself is possibly misleading; for gods often take human form. If we realize that the tragic stage was itself vertically divided into metaphysical spheres, then the place of each character within that most fundamental order becomes more apparent. Too removed from the human condition to feel its pain and too near to resist meddling, the gods drift over the human realm suspended from the "machine" or stand aloof atop the stage building. They speak down to mortals, while mortals speak up to the gods. The more that the gods flaunt their divinity and the more that wretched mortals acknowledge it, the greater becomes the visible gulf dividing them. Thus, in the face of manifest divinity, mortals fall to their knees or prostrate themselves flat upon the earth, not even raising their eyes. In such moments, the identity of the mortal, or that of the divinity, for that matter, is beside the point. What is seen is the otherness, the sheer immeasurable power and pre-eminence of gods and, by contrast, the abject helplessness of mortals. Thus, for example, in the *Electra,* the *Helen,* the *Iphigeneia in Tauris,* or the *Orestes,* when one or other of the gods veers in on the machine to decree what is to be, there can be no question of human resistance to the divine will. What is revealed, when gods and mortals clash, is not finally a conflict of wills or personalities but an inescapable conflict of natures. Gods and mortals are fated by the radical incompatibility of their natures to misunderstand each other and would be wrong to take their differences personally, as we too would be wrong to interpret them so.

Similarly, within the political or inter-human order, masks, costumes, stage position, posture, and gesture all conspire to make visibly evident the peculiar station of each character, as well as the relative power or weakness concomitant with that station. Youth and age, for example, are immediately visible on the ancient tragic stage. A boy has no beard, a mature man a dark beard, and an old man a white or gray beard. A modern reader or spectator of an ancient drama might be inclined to overlook or to underestimate the critical significance of these and other such categorical differentiations which serve to reveal its political design, the lines of force motive within it. In the *Alcestis,* to cite one instance, the fierce confrontation between Admetus and Pheres is less likely to be seen as the collision of two colossal egotists, if Admetus' callow youth and Pheres' cantankerous seniority are noted and given their due. Even more crucially, in the *Bacchae,* the brittle arrogance, the conflicted voyeurism, the rigid prurience of Pentheus are all made coher-ent and sympathetically intelligible by the recognition of his adolescence, a fact which would have been immediately visible to any original spectator but which we must learn in the last moments of the play from a chance reference to what we call "peach fuzz" on his severed head. In the same way, whether a woman was young or old, married, unmarried or widowed was clear for all to see from the moment of her entry. Kings are known perhaps from crowns or from their elevated stage positions or from the fact that others bow or fall to their knees before them. Barbarians too are unmistakable, as are slaves.

The entrances of characters into the Greek theatre represent at the same time the entrances of realities, natures, forces, and ideas which shadow in importance the individual character who happens to convey them there. Aristotle could not be more clear or correct on this: that Athenian tragedy is not about individual character. Rather, it is about that action into which one is propelled by forces active without and within the individual and which are beyond the individual to limit and control. It is about nature and fate, which Heraclitus aphoristically fuses together and which could not be entwined more tightly than they are on the Euripidean stage.

In Euripidean drama, individuals are prey to their metaphysical and political natures. Gods and mortals are destined either to collide or to pass indifferently in the night, but never to know commonality or friendship. And those humans whose disproportionate privileges or deprivations, power or weakness divide them from each other—as if they were radically diverse beings—must summon nearly incomprehensible will and insight to recognize their common humanity and to embrace in fellowship. More commonly, the political order mirrors and mimics the metaphysical order. Human beings lord it over each other, playing out their power and yielding to their weakness as their respective necessities demand of them. Some act as if they were gods while others, in turn, are treated as if they were beasts.

In sum, these two orders, the metaphysical and the political, describe the essential scope and structure of the Greek theatre. They are the templates for the curriculum which Euripides, as playwright and teacher, brought to vision in the Athenian theatre. They are the templates, as well, for all that follows in this particular endeavor to approach the sight and the insight still residing in Euripidean drama.

◇◇◇◇◇◇◇◇◇◇◇◇◇◇◇
THE METAPHYSICAL ORDER

The claim which has brought us to this point in our discussion is that the Athenian tragic theatre, and in particular the theatre of Euripides, had as its defining endeavor the disclosure of human nature. In this context, it has been suggested that human nature, as discerned by the ancient Greeks, is inclined towards concealment, and must be brought to light and to open view, if it is to be seen by all. This work, the proper work of the Athenian playwright—bringing to light human being—may be understood as a clarification or definition of human being; for the wonted concealment of human being is most often a matter of its confusion with other beings. Furthermore, as the aim of this work, though not necessarily its method, is philosophical, it is important to note that the classical Greek philosophers are singularly clear-sighted and articulate guides in our efforts to grasp what is meant by defining the nature of human being, which is why we turn initially to the writings of Plato and Aristotle for our preliminary orientation.

In the *Phaedo* [96a6–10], Socrates says that he too was eager to be wise, in the sense of being able to give an account of the nature of things. He goes on to say that it seemed to him a resplendent achievement to have seen the origins or causes of each thing, which is to have seen why each thing comes into being, why it passes out of being, and why it is what it is. Elsewhere, in the *Phaedrus* [230a1–6], Socrates admits that he is rather single-mindedly concerned to be able to give an account of human nature; for he confesses that, until he knows the truth of human being, i.e. the truth of his own being, he finds it rather ludicrous to pursue an understanding of other truths and other natures. In short, he says he has no time for these. It is the human question that interests him, the question of human being, which he formulates in the following manner. He wonders whether he is, as a human being, some bestial being in the savage order of a Typhon or rather a living being with some more gentle and civilized nature. He recognizes that individual human beings can aspire to either extreme possibility, that they may become in practice either the most sublime beings on earth or the most savage. Both possibilities are equally available; but they are not equally appropriate. What decides the appropriateness or inappropriateness of these possibilities is the truth of human nature, which Euripides, no less than Socrates, seeks.

Aristotle, in fact, begins his *Metaphysics* [280a22–28] with insights which have direct bearing on our present discussion. He says that all human beings by nature desire to know, which he immediately links to the special delight we take in seeing. Sight, more than any other of the senses, explains Aristotle, leads us to understanding and reveals to us the differences between things. When we see the differences between things, we see these things for what they truly are, without confusion. To have seen something in this way, clearly and distinctly, is to know it. This very confidence is embedded in the Greek language itself; for the word for "I know" [*oida*] means literally "I have seen." To know the nature or the truth of human being, then, is to have seen its coming into being and its passing out of being, and to have seen it for what it is, apart from what it is not. In short, to know human being is to have seen it "defined" or "in definition," which, as the etymology of this word suggests, is to have seen the limits of human being.

In order to remind ourselves that these questions are not foreign to Euripides, but in fact lie at the center of his concerns, we may recall the paedogogical confrontation between Dionysus and Pentheus in the *Bacchae*, "paedogogical" because Dionysus comes to Thebes essentially as a teacher, a teacher from the "old school" we might say. "Whether it wants to or not," threatens Dionysus, "this city must learn its lesson." [39] Some of the citizens, indeed, are quick to learn the lesson, as two of these, Teiresias and Cadmus, make clear when they boast that they alone have seen the light. The lesson, it seems, comes down to this: the discernment and acknowledgment of one's humanity. Cadmus sums it up when he says: "I am mortal. I don't aspire to the gods, nor do I disdain them." [199] Dionysus, speaking for himself, says from the outset that he has come and taught his dances and mysteries with one end in mind: that he might be utterly manifest [*emphanes*] to human beings as the god that he is. These two events—the theophany of Dionysus and the human insight of Cadmus—are appropriately bonded together. When a god manifests himself in his divinity, it highlights not only divinity but humanity; for the gulf between human nature and divine nature yawns open in the process. Somehow, Pentheus clings to his folly in the face of Dionysus'instructive disclosures of his divinity, a folly which Dionysus sums up and flings back at Pentheus in these words [506]:

> You don't know [literally: you have not seen]
> why you are alive,
> what you are doing,
> or who you are.

Pentheus is a fool because he fails to learn or to acknowledge his limits; not his personal limits, but the limits of his human nature. He has no sense of where he begins or where he leaves off. He would deny his roots in the bestial and imagine his equivalence to the divine. These, after all, are the borders of the human, borders on which human folly is prone to trespass. To see the human "in definition" without confusion is to see humanity as distinct both from bestiality and from divinity. This vision corresponds directly to that of the city, the polis; for the city is that place designed and reserved for human beings. As Aristotle puts it, in the *Politics* [1253a], "anyone who proves incapable of human collaboration or who is so self-sufficient as to stand in no need of others, has no share in the city, like a beast or a god." Clearly, the definition of human being and the definition of the human realm, namely the polis, coincide in the theatre where both are imaginatively envisioned for the edification and politicization of all citizens.

If we are to understand the ancient significance and urgency of defining human being and the human realm, we must realize the ambiguity with which they were once surrounded and pervaded. Human nature, as imagined in poetry, portrayed in art, and reasoned over in philosophical and scientific discussions, was seen by the ancient Greeks as poised unstably between two extreme and foreign natures, that of beasts and that of gods. The relationship between the human realm and these two inhuman realms was a matter of profound uncertainty and nearly obsessive concern. Mid-way between beasts and gods, humanity was at once the battlezone wherein radically antithetical forces confronted each other and itself an unhappy synthesis of the most fundamental cosmological categories. Humanity was at once descended and estranged from the beasts, while at the same time aspirant and hostile to the gods.

In case this idea of fundamental metaphysical ambiguity might seem to a modern reader to be a quite bizarre and benighted preoccupation, I would point to a similar preoccupation closer to home as we know it. While the modern secular critique of religion has removed from many minds any concern over the imminence of divine being, and while the modern natural and behavioral sciences have removed any conviction of an essential divide between human beings and animals, a rather new and curious metaphysical ambiguity has surfaced both in scientific discussion and in popular imagination. This recently emergent ambiguity is that between man and the manmade, between human being and artefact. In formal terms, I refer to research in artificial intelligence, bionics, and robotics; but of more immediate interest is the contemporary spillover of science into popular culture, where a genuine confusion exists between man and machine. The media are by now so infiltrated with androids that certainty no longer exists from one moment to the next whether the character who has evoked our sympathy, rage, admiration or amour is composed of sinew and soul like "us" or is, instead, composed of microchips and printed circuitry. More important, however, is the increasing sensibility which suggests that it doesn't truly matter one way or the other. Even the saving remnant who would argue that there is some essential difference between human and artificial being, most often find themselves at a loss to articulate convincingly the decisive difference between what is "natural" and what is "artificial" and are at an even greater loss to mount a compelling case for preferring the natural over against the artificial.

I have no intention of belaboring this issue here; for my only point is that pervasive cultural confusion and debate over the metaphysical status of human being have only changed their focus rather than slipped into extinction. The "human question" of Socrates remains a border dispute; but today's disputed border is a different one from those under scrutiny in ancient Greece. For the ancient Greeks, as for the entire ancient East Mediterranean world, the ambiguous boundaries requiring clarification were those we have already noted— the boundaries between humans, beasts, and gods—and to which we now turn.

Volumes could and have been written on the theme which we now set out to explore and which we can do no more than sketch. In our effort to glimpse and to grasp the ancient understanding of metaphysical ambiguity, we will turn first to visual art, then to poetry, and finally to philosophical and scientific speculation. Firstly, it is clear that no more telling evidence of ancient metaphysical ambiguity may be offered than ancient Greek, Egyptian, and Near Eastern visual art, which abounds in fantastic hybrids of all three metaphysical categories: gods in part-human, part-bestial forms, men that are part beasts or beasts that are part men, and so on. In some instances, these hybrids seem relatively stable, while in other instances they undergo frequent, unpredictable transmutations. What is manifest in all instances is the fact that ambiguity was a primary cosmological element in the ancient East Mediterranean world.

Gorgons and satyrs seem to have been among the first such hybrids to take root and to achieve prominence in the Greek imagination, and by the late Geometric period a plethora of oriental hybrid beings had entered Greek art: sphinxes, centaurs, chimaeras, and boreads, to name a few. Long before the seventh and sixth centuries, in which fantastic bestiaries flourished in Greek art, composite beings had been already common in Minoan and Mycenaean art. In interpreting this phenomenon, however, we are left with our conjectures, since neither the Greeks nor their neighbors explained their iconographic fascination with the mingling of diverse natures. If intuitions have any standing at all in these matters, however, it seems unlikely that anyone gazing with any thoughtfulness at ancient East Mediterranean gods and monsters will fail to sense the awful otherness of these beings and yet their kinship with our fears and fascinations and desires. However these peoples must have seen and thought about gods and beasts, they must have seen them as "other"— inaccessible in their beauty, wisdom, power, courage, cunning, and grace—and yet as somehow bonded to the human by virtue of human sympathy, imagination, and desire. In saying even this, we are perhaps saying both too much and too little, when the art is already eloquent on its own behalf. Surely it leaves us with a feeling that the divine, the human, and the bestial are set apart from each other by a great divide, and yet are one.

Turning now to poetry, we find that the oldest and most widely diffused tale in the ancient Near East, the epic of Gilgamesh, had as its central theme the definition and quest of human being as distinct from divine and bestial being. This tale, however difficult its influences on Greek literature may be to trace directly, doubtlessly affected Greek poetic imagination as deeply as Near Eastern sculpture and painting affected Greek visual art. Its two heroes, Gilgamesh and Enkidu, may be described as frontiersmen in the ancient endeavor to define the specifically human realm, its appropriate aspirations and necessities. At the outset of the tale, Gilgamesh is described as a man who is two-thirds divine and yet wild like a bull. Enkidu, on the other hand, begins at the other end of the metaphysical spectrum. With a gazelle for a mother and a wild ass as a father and raised by creatures with tails, Enkidu is a man who, it is written, is two-thirds beast and yet likened to the gods. In short, in these two characters we encounter metaphysical ambiguity with a vengeance. The poem describes the slow, excruciating process of their mutual humanization. It is the story of their becoming human together.

Without losing ourselves in this wondrous tale, we must note that in it the human touchstone is mortality. No matter how intimately Gilgamesh and Enkidu may have mingled with gods and beasts, no matter how hybrid their natures, they are finally defined by their mortality. It is of no ultimate consequence that they are two-thirds divine or two-thirds bestial. A one-third portion of humanity, or even less, suffices to condemn one to mortality; and from mortality all else that is human follows. "Even the sons of the gods," writes Euripides in the *Alcestis* [989–990], "go dark in death," which might as well be a line from the *Gilgamesh*. Gilgamesh, "he who knew everything," is also described as "the man who saw the abyss." With his companion Enkidu, Gilgamesh hunted the beast-favorites of the gods, rejected *hierogamy* or sacred union with a goddess, and, most decisively, watched his friend, his other self, die in his arms. In that moment, he says, sorrow came into his belly and death took up habitation in his bed, in his house, companioned him everywhere he went. In time he relinquishes his inward evasions and outward quests for any release from the truth he has come to know, and accepts the essential human truth of mortality, which brings him back to his home, to the towering, familiar walls of his city.

Greek poetry could not be more resonant with the quests and truths pioneered by Gilgamesh and Enkidu. That mortality is the defining truth of human being and the source of undeluded human consciousness is altogether central to the poetry of Homer as well as to that of Euripides. In fact, the friendship of Gilgamesh and Enkidu, which leaps like a flame from their mutual collision with mortality, may be seen as the prototype for the friendship of Achilles and Patroclus; and the idea of *ibru* or friendship manifest in the Gilgamesh text is intriguingly close to the idea of *philia* or friendship so effulgent in the *Iliad* and so pervasive in the plays of Euripides. Beyond Achilles, who like Gilgamesh is part-human and part-divine and likened to a beast, Greek literature abounds in hybrid beings. The forms and circumstances of these various beings and their metamorphoses are at once too numerous and too notorious to require any cataloguing here. Always, however, what remains decisive for humanity is the necessity of death and the consciousness which wells up from that necessity. It is this keen-edged truth and the clarity it brings with it that makes possible in drama the sorting out of essential confusions.

This same metaphysical ambiguity and confusion found frequent voice in ancient Greek scientific and philosophical speculation. Both in Greece and in the Near East there was from the earliest times a belief that in the beginning, or before the beginning, all things were fused and formless. Various theories were proposed to give a coherent account of the emergence of differentiation and order; but behind this order there lay primordial unity. More often than not, the sorting out or separation of things is neither thorough or final. Thus Anaxagoras [fr.11] suggests that "in everything there is a share of everything else, except for Mind [*nous*]." Some things, in his view, lack Mind altogether; but otherwise everything is composed of everything. What, then, could define one thing as distinct from another? Aristotle's response [*Physics,* A4,187a23] to this question is most concise. He says that "the nature of each thing is thought to be determined by that of which it has a preponderance." To resume our focus on humanity, the implications of these beliefs and theories for human being are quite clear. Humanity, like everything else, in Thales' words is "full of gods." At the same time, humanity shares animal life with the beasts and is consequently "full of beasts." Yet, despite its share of bestiality and divinity, it is the consciousness of death—"mortality" in a word—which has preponderance in humanity, and so determines its nature.

In sum, ancient Greek humanism, which is the legacy received by Euripides, assigns to humanity a reasonable place within the full expanse of nature rather than unleashing human beings upon nature as unaccountable tyrants or plunderers. In contrast with this relatively benign and self-effacing humanism, Levi-Strauss, in a recent essay on "Race and Culture," [in *The View From Afar,* NY: Basic Books, 1985] says that en route to our more arrogant modern humanism "man had forgotten that he is worthy of respect more as a living being than as the lord and master of creation." Yet it is only fair to say that this is a forgetfulness which was already well on its way in Euripides' Athens and of which Euripides, drawing upon the more ancient tradition, was an unrelenting critic.

To bring this discussion home once more to the theatre of Euripides, I wish to claim that Euripidean drama, contrary to what Nietzsche would have us believe, is profoundly Dionysian. All that I mean by this claim will be made clear in time; but for our present purposes I wish to focus on his most explicitly Dionysian work, the for there we find Euripides' most devastating assault on the arrogant humanism lamented by Levi-Strauss as well as his most radiant articulation of the ancient truths that humanity is full of gods and full of beasts and thus required to find and to inhabit humbly that middle place assigned to it.

Before we can approach the *Bacchae* with any perception we must dismiss a frequent and fundamental misconception of Dionysiac religion, namely that Dionysus is the god of the drunken debauch. Plutarch is nearer the truth when he says that Dionysus is the god of *hygra phusis,* literally "fluid nature," which encompasses all of the rippling, pulsing, erupting, sluicing forces of life: blood, water, sap, semen, milk and, admittedly, wine. Dionysus represents and presides over the unrestrained potency of animal life, in which human beings may commune. To drink from the *hygra phusis,* as we learn from the messenger's report to Pentheus, may be to drink water struck from rock or to drink milk scratched up from the soil or to drink the blood of animals torn apart in the frenzied *sparagmos,* as well as to drink wine spurting up from the face of a rock at the tap of Dionysus' wand. In whatever form, the bacchant is drinking the god and becoming one with him. This is the meaning of *baccheuein:* not so much to revel, but rather to merge with the god Dionysus, to be of life, which defy transformed by union with the boundless forces and overrun every metaphysical and conventional border.

Thus, in the *Bacchae,* Dionysus himself is transformed from god to man to beast and back again. He takes any shape he wishes; and, beyond the city walls where the animals and the mountains are wild with divinity, he draws his bacchants into corresponding metamorphoses. Even the rigid Pentheus, who stands guard personally over the boundaries which describe and maintain civic and domestic life as he knows it, even Pentheus is lured into becoming one with the god and thus suffering unforeseen transformations. First, Pentheus takes the form of a woman and then, when he is totally one with the god—a union symbolized, on the one hand, by his vision of the two suns and, on the other, by his elevation in the arms of the tree sacred to the god—he is dragged down as both god and beast to be the prey and the sacred feast of women ecstatically alive with all that is both savage and sacred. Pentheus, who would stand off from the god and not be touched, becomes the surrogate of the god and suffers in his stead. In the end, under the aegis of a smiling god, it is he who is mourned and not the god; and so he enters the destiny waiting for him in his name, "Pentheus," the "mourned one."

From even this brief glance at the *Bacchae,* we see how it is that Dionysus is the god not only of religious mania and ecstatic rites but also of the mask and of theatre. He is the god of transformations, whether they occur in the mountains or in the streets or in the theatre. This is a god whose power suffices to erase, for a time, the lines between illusion and reality and thus to allow safe, at least in the theatre, passage across boundaries whose stability and maintenance are ordinarily required for human sanity and order. Both the borders of the metaphysical order and those of the political order become permeable in his presence and in his possession. In more contemporary terms, we would add that in the theatre a fissure is opened into the unconscious, providing for the controlled release of the unconscious into the conscious. In theatre, which endeavors to do more than entertain, the control is occasionally precarious and there is released a shudder of the primal panic which engulfed both Pentheus as he hurtled from his dendritic haven and Agave when she recognized her trophy as the same head which once, similarly bloodied, had burst from her womb and brought her a similarly triumphant joy.

The bond between Dionysus and drama is, indeed, quite ancient, preceding by centuries the institution of Athenian tragedy. Dionysus was not in the fifth century a recent immigrant to Greece, as once thought, but seems instead to have been familiar to Greeks long before the year 1000. The Great Dionysia at which the tragedies were eventually performed dates only from the sixth century, while far more ancient was the Old Dionysia or the Anthesteria, also in the spring and also dedicated to the cult of Dionysus. The sequence of the Anthesteria, a three-day festival, bears certain similarities to the sequence of the Christian Passover, from the Passion to the Resurrection: the themes of sin and atonement, a communal meal in which the wine drunk is at the same time the blood of the dismembered god, and finally the restoration of the god in the midst of his devotees. More significant for our present discussion, however, is the fact that masked mummery and the veneration of the god made ritually present in his own mask were integral to this archaic festival, which means that Dionysus was affiliated with masks and with dramatic ecstasy already many centuries before the institution of the dramatic festival at the City Dionysia. In the latter festival, of course, the place of Dionysus was manifestly central. The dramatic contests were preceded by the sacrifice of a goat to Dionysus and by a procession to the theatre precinct where an effigy of the god was installed. The plays were literally performed in the presence of and to the god, with the priests of his cult near at hand. During the dramatic festival, the actors themselves were regarded as sacred officers of the Dionysian cult, one with the god as were his bacchants on the hillside of Thebes.

Although many formal elements of Athenian tragedy may well be traceable to dithyrambic choruses and explained as reasonable developments therefrom, the hot core, as it were, of ancient tragedy lies in the cult of Dionysus, god of masks, ecstatic transformation, and sacrificial immolation. The very name of tragedy [*tragoidia*], whose meaning remains a matter of dispute, may perhaps be appropriately translated as "song sung at the sacrifice of a goat"; for we know that the theatrical contests followed upon the sacrifice of a goat to Dionysus. The prize and the sacrificial victim associated with the dithyrambic contests was, on the other hand, not a goat but a bull. Tragedy, in fact, drew upon a number of pre-existing elements which it had in common with Dionysian and sacrificial ritual, such as the use of masks, song and dance at the *thumele* or sacrificial site, lamentation, and the music of the *aulos* or twin flute.

In focusing on the Dionysian and sacrificial core of tragedy, the metaphysically definitive situation of tragedy is revealed. In the tragic theatre, humanity stands face to face with death and with the divine. The inescapable outcome is the disclosure of the human. Nowhere in the corpus of Athenian tragedy is this fact more visible than in the *Bacchae,* as Pentheus—confronted by his god and by death—unwittingly provides a spectacle from which the awful truth bursts forth. Seated in the precinct of Dionysus, the theatrical spectator might well say of Pentheus "there but for the immunity of the theatre go I." But the immunity of the theatre is finally an illusion. Pentheus too imagined that he was being provided a harmless spectacle at a safe distance; but he forgot that the tree in which he sat perched was sacred to Dionysus. He was already in the grip of the god. The theatre of Dionysus was no less the place of the god; and the spectators no less in the power of the god, soon to become the spectacle, unless they were to heed the god and to confront their own mortality. The *Bacchae,* it seems evident, is Euripides' consummate statement on the theatre; and thus these words [794–795], spoken through the mask of Dionysus, were aimed at all who at that moment confronted the god:

> Instead of raging on like this,
> Thrashing futilely against a force
>   that will never weaken,
> If I were you,
>   a man face to face with god,
>   I'd offer him a sacrifice.

If we examine the extant tragedies of Euripides, we find that with very few exceptions sacrifice figures substantially in their thematic development and often defines their very structure as, for example, with the *Electra,* the *Iphigeneia in Tauris,* the *Bacchae,* and the *Iphigeneia at Aulis.* However unorthodox and innovative Euripides may have been in many aspects of his work, he recognized the centrality of sacrifice and rooted his work more profoundly than did any of his fellow playwrights in this most sacred and revealing of all rituals, thus giving his work an archaic resonance as well as a source deep within the Greek psyche, from which to launch his most savage attacks on the atrocities of his times. Consequently, if we are to reach the core of Euripides' work, we must explore the meaning of sacrifice in ancient Greek piety and thought and reveal how it was that both sacrifice and theatre served to delineate the metaphysical structure of the cosmos and, more particularly, the place of humanity within that structure.

Sacrifice [*thusia*] was the cornerstone of Greek religion, the primary and central religious activity in the fifth-century polis. Nearly all personal and civic acts of any significance—festivals, wars, athletic contests, births, deaths, marriages, oracular consultations, treaties, contracts—were marked by sacrifices. The act of sacrifice constituted the definitive experience of the sacred and, for that matter, of the human; for sacrifice clarified and acknowledged the relative status of the human and of the divine in the scheme of things. Apart from the *sphagia*—blood sacrifices performed for their own sake in extreme situations, before battle and at burials—the fundamental structure of sacrifice was that of ritual slaughter followed by a meat feast. In order to understand this structure and its significance, we will discuss each of these essential elements in turn.

Sacrifice is first and most evidently an act of slaughter. Life is violated and with it the bond between humans and beasts; for in all but the darkest and most distorted sacrifices, the victim is an animal. In cutting the throats of animals, human beings cut themselves loose from their intuitive communion with animals in life. Human beings cause and experience death and yet survive. In sacrifice, human violence is diverted to animals and sanctioned as an exception. Killing is contained by ritual and made to serve both the solidarity of humans with gods and the solidarity of humans with each other. In the violation of animal life, human beings turn their backs on the beasts; and, in sending up the sweet smoke of sacrifice, human beings turn to the gods, seeking their favor and their fellowship. By offering up the fruit of sacrifice to powers above the human, human beings consecrate and thus justify the savagery with which they have severed themselves from the beasts.

The second essential element of sacrifice is the meat feast, which may, of course, have been the primitive origin of and pretext for sacrifice. In the feast, the victim is cooked with divinely derived fire and becomes human nourishment. The death of animal life serves to sustain human life. The encounter with death is followed by the shock of human survival and consequently the affirmation of human life in a feast. Complicity in the irrevocable act of killing, the shared experience of death, the terror it evokes and the guilt it instills—all conspire to create human solidarity. The focusing of human violence on animals, it is hoped, will divert that violence from fellow humans. Homicide and homophagy are to be renounced just as the killing and eating of animals are sanctioned. The survival of the human community is thus affirmed and assured by sacrifice; for when animals become the helpless victims of human violence, the source of human nourishment, and the acceptable outlet for human aggression, then the most primal threats to human survival are removed, namely hunger and the attacks of other animate beings, bestial or human.

Even though sacrifice opens up and establishes limited communion and communication with the gods, the distinct portions assigned to each make clear the divide which separates them. Humans receive the edible, perishable portions, a meal required by their own precariously perishable existence. The gods' portion, by contrast, is consumed in flames together with spices. What they receive is the sweet smoke and scent, which rise out of human sight to delight those unimaginably remote beings who have no needs or fears.

The role that sacrifice plays, then, both in Greek religion and in Greek theatre, is to trace the most essential boundaries in the cosmos and thus to illuminate those truths which, if ever obscured, would condemn the world to darkest chaos. In the theatre, these boundaries are not only drawn but also transgressed. We learn best from contrast; and so we are made to witness both the brightest and the darkest of deeds, both crystalline clarity and impenetrable confusion. Human victims are held down under sacrificial blades, human flesh serves as human feast, mothers murder their children and children their mothers, brother slaughters brother. Every truth is denied, every nature defiled, so that they might be rediscovered and reaffirmed as the foundation of human fellowship and thus of the city.

Unless the metaphysical order remains inviolate, the moral order cannot hold. In short, when human beings forget that they are distinct from gods and beasts, they begin to act like them. With this in mind, we return to these distinct categories so that we might come to a more precise and full understanding of each as they appear in the theatre of Euripides.

Gods

The traditional Greek gods belong, together with humans and beasts, to the one cosmos. Admittedly, their elevated status within the cosmic order confers upon them certain exemptions from necessities peculiar to human or bestial beings; but, for all their immunities and privileges, the Greek gods remain integral to the same world to which humans and beasts belong. Beyond this initial disclaimer of transcendence, however, it becomes quite problematic to formulate any concise, univocal account of ancient Greek theology. No such theology ever existed among the ancient Greeks; and therefore no scholarly or creative effort on our part can call it forth from the bleached stones of their temples and altars. The ancient Greeks had no sacred texts or prophets or formal priesthood with authority to decree official doctrine or discipline. It is, in fact, finally a misnomer to speak of ancient Greek religion at all. If we are to use the word "religion" with reference to ancient Greece, we ought to speak of "religions"; for there were civic, household, chthonic, rural, local, and pan-Hellenic gods and cults, all crowded into ancient Greek piety, not to mention an array of mysteries and brotherhoods complementing or challenging the more traditional beliefs and rites. We begin, then, with this awareness of the staggering complexity of ancient Greek piety so as to place the following modest reflections in appropriate perspective.

The first Greek poets to propose orderly, systematic accounts of the divine and human realms and their mutual affairs were Hesiod and Homer; and it was their visions more than any others that shaped the images and ideas of the gods within the subsequent literary tradition. The gods and goddesses highlighted by Homer were, of course, the Olympians, whom Hesiod identifies as latecomers created by earlier cosmic powers, such as Chaos, Earth, Ocean, Sky, and Eros. In Homeric poetry, the earlier gods and goddesses of chthonic religion either lapse from sight altogether or appear in clear subordination to the Olympians. The traditional local heroes, who like the Christian saints display a proximity to the divine as well as unusual powers corresponding to that proximity, are also reduced in stature by Homer, particularly in the *Iliad*. Homer's heroes are without exception mortal and thus unambiguously removed from the divine realm. In Homer's patriarchal Pan-Hellenic vision, the primacy of the Olympians, and among them the preeminence of Zeus, is not to be challenged from any corner. What we must note even as we pass over it here is the fact that Homer's and Hesiod's conceptions of a pantheon of anthropomorphic gods and goddesses assembled on a mountain in the North, were common to virtually all of the ancient Aegean and Near Eastern world, with the exception of Egypt and Israel.

The blessed gods of Homer live altogether privileged lives. Their most singular privilege is, as we have already seen, their immortality. It is their immortality, however, which may be seen as the source of all that is petty and callous and shallow in them. Without having to pay the ultimate price for life, their lives are left without poignancy or purpose. They resemble rotten children unable to mature beyond their blindly willful assertions and quarrels. To be sure, the Olympians are capable of grandeur and graciousness and occasional loyalty; but they are ultimately unreliable and disappointing from a human perspective. In their world nothing is irrevocable. The gods' wounds, like their errors, heal even as their human counterparts molder in their graves. And apart from the fact that they "exist always" [*aien eontes*], they "live easy lives" [*rheia zoiontes*]. Unlike mortals whose already abridged lives are further reduced by necessities too numerous to count, the Olympians know only luxuriance and ease. The moral result is predictable. Without mortal tension in their fibers, they are incapable of sounding a pure note. Their courage and sorrow, laughter and love and grief are all pathetically imitative of human emotion and virtue. Apart from their power, the Homeric gods trail behind miserable mortals. Indeed, it seems not to have offended Greek piety to question the wisdom or the goodness of the gods. It was their power alone that was not to be doubted.

The Homeric pantheon, however pervasive its influence on Greek piety and imagination, was not without its critics. To many Greeks, the anthropomorphic character of the Olympians was ludicrous and offensive, all the more so because of the less than exemplary humanity mimicked by them. In the sixth century, Xenophanes, who seems to have been a deeply religious man, ridiculed Homers gods, saying that "if cattle and horses and lions possessed hands, or were able to sketch and do the things men do, horses would draw gods that looked like horses, and cattle would draw gods resembling cattle, giving them bodies like their own." [fr.15] While he confessed that "there is no man nor will there ever be one who knows the truth about the gods," [fr.34] Xenophanes spoke of "one god, supreme among gods and mortals, in no way resembling mortals, either in body or in thought." [fr.23] Others sought to demythologize the Olympians by seeing in them poetic hypostases of cosmic forces or projections of human passions and folly. Empedocles, for example, gave the names of gods to the four universal elements. According to Prodicus, however, human beings divinize those things which benefit them most. In short, theories of the gods abounded, virtually all of them skeptical, if not contemptuous, of Homeric fundamentalism.

It may be said that Euripides, in his ideas of the gods, stood in a direct line from Xenophanes to Plato, who dismissed Homer as a seditious liar, regarded the encouragement of superstition as the worst crime against religion, and yet saw in atheism the breeding ground of tyranny. It may further be said that Euripides considered and echoed in his dramas a myriad of opinions concerning the gods. The first step towards honesty, if not clarity, in these matters is the admission of complexity and unknowing. Legend has it that Protagoras first read his notorious treatise "Concerning the Gods" in the home of Euripides, the opening statement of which is well-known: "Concerning the gods, I am unable to discern whether they exist or not, or what they may be like in form. The path to such knowledge is too strewn with obstacles, the subject too obscure, and human life too brief." Euripides seems to have taken to heart this cautious admission of his friend, which may be why we hear in his plays so many conflicting voices concerning the gods and things divine. When taking aim at elusive, even invisible, quarry, a scattergun would seem a wiser and less arrogant choice of armament than an arrow.

It must be stated from the outset, then, that Euripides' personal religious beliefs remain a matter of conjecture. As we form our own conjectures, however, it is mistaken to employ useless univocal categories such as theism, agnosticism, atheism, and secularism in an attempt to designate either Euripides or Athens in the late fifth century. Both are too conflicted and too complex to be so easily categorized. It is instructive in this regard to reflect on the inability of any such category to designate the religious convictions of Americans at the end of the millennium, Americans who, we know, comprise a spectrum from snake-handlers to skeptics, from those who refuse the services of combustion engines to those who deny any essential distinction between human spirituality and artificial intelligence. In some locations one can listen in vain for sacred words from church pulpits, while elsewhere bible hymns stream from variety store loudspeakers. If we hold a mirror, so to speak, to the soul of America, do we see reflected in it a believer or an atheist? In unwarranted despair we might retort at once that America is made up of millions of individuals calling for as many individualized mirrors. The truth is, however, that America in the late twentieth century, like Athens in the late fifth century, has a character which may very tentatively and provisionally be described, though not in simplistically satisfying terms. In sum, it is misguided to expect from the fifth century and from its poets a straightforward homogeneity which we would know better than to expect from our own, and equally misguided to dismiss the possibility of ever reading one's own or others' times with any insight at all.

While Burckhardt's dichotomy of rationalism for the few and magic for the many is only once removed from sheer reductionism, it may be used to suggest the conflicted character of fifth century Athenian piety, which was both able to produce trenchant criticism of the religious tradition and barely able to tolerate that criticism. We may recall how the Athenian debacle in Sicily was partly occasioned by the paralysis of Nicias and the Athenian army in the face of a lunar eclipse. Pious observances and fears often lose their hold when they become inconvenient, much less lethal; but not so in this case, which suggests that they lay well below the skin. We may recall, as well, that the fifth century was scattered with impiety trials, as a result of which Protagoras was banished and Socrates executed. Anaxagoras was saved from prosecution only by the intervention of his friend Pericles; and we don't know what saved Euripides from the charges brought against him. The free thought for which Athens was known in the fifth century was apparently not without its price to pay. Even as we assume that Euripides might have been emboldened by the company of Athenian "free-thinkers," it is equally reasonable to assume that he may have been chastened by the quite effectual local forces hostile to any challenge raised against traditional piety. We know, for instance, from Plutarch that the line in the *Melanippe* [fr.480] which reads "Zeus, whoever that might be..." caused such an uproar in the theatre that Euripides, for a second production, altered it to read: "Zeus, as truth itself has said…" If Euripides was willing to rewrite a line, once written, we may assume that he was not above checking an impulse or reformulating an idea before it reached either the page or the stage. Just as Aristotle is thought to have masked and muted his own religious ideas so as to avoid repeating the fate of Socrates, it is surely possible that Euripides exercised a similar caution, lest he repeat the fate of Protagoras.

If there was any sanctuary of tolerance in Athens, however, it was the theatre, which enjoyed an astounding measure of "academic freedom" long before the founding of the academy. This freedom seems all the more remarkable when we remember that the theatre, apart from being a place of art and education, was also a sacred place, the *temenos* or precinct of Dionysus, whose cult image presided over the orchestra. The site for which Euripides wrote was closer to a church than a Broadway theatre, which we must keep in mind when we listen to words like these from Euripides' *Bellerophon* [fr.286], spoken face to face with Dionysus and within earshot, so to speak, of Athena Parthenos:

> Who is it, anyway, that says the gods exist
>   in starry heaven?
> They don't. They don't exist at all.
> Anyone still willing to talk in that old-fashioned way
>   is a moron.

How, we might ask, are we to hear these words? It might seem that these and similar lines are singularly well-suited to modern scorn, so familiar as to require no interpretation. The opposite, however, is nearer the truth; for it is most unlikely that a contemporary audience or reader of Euripides will hear these words as blasphemy, which I suspect is what they are. Scorn is easily achieved; and indifference requires no achievement at all. Blasphemy is a different matter altogether from these and other common forms of secular disbelief. First-rate blasphemy, as T.S. Eliot has suggested in *After Strange Gods* [NY: Harcourt, Brace, 1934], may indeed be one of the rarest achievements in literature, requiring, in his words, "both literary genius and profound faith." He proceeds to explain that "no one can possibly blaspheme in any sense except that in which a parrot may be said to curse, unless he profoundly believes in that which he profanes." Obviously, the belief from which blasphemy spews forth is not a child's faith, seamless and unsullied. Rather, it is conflicted to its very core, wounded and wandering in pain. It has already been suggested by more than one scholar that the whole matter of the gods was for Euripides a source of incurable suffering; and such suffering is indeed the matrix of blasphemy.

At the very least, I wish to suggest here that fifth-century Athens was indeed a place where blasphemy could well have been uttered and, once uttered, understood. Very few, if any, such places still exist. Neither literary genius nor profound faith, much less their convergence, are in great supply in contemporary theatre. Profanity on the other hand, like the common dandelion, is annoyingly prevalent and unimpressive. Without celebrating blasphemy, it is nonetheless easy to understand Eliot's reproach for our age, in which he thought blasphemy had become a sheer impossibility.

Not so the age of Euripides. Dionysus, when accused of overreaction, answers quite simply in his own defense: "I am a god. I was blasphemed by you." [*Bacchae*, 1347] And Dionysus was not singled out for this treatment. Zeus alone is treated with almost unexceptional deference and respect by Euripides, perhaps because Euripides may have come to regard the name of Zeus as a pseudonym of sorts for the unknowable god beyond all gods. Regardless, the lesser Olympians fare less well. To mention one, Apollo surely comes in for his share of blasphemy. In the *Ion* we are made witnesses to what may be called the birth of blasphemy. Ion, the sanctimonious temple boy, is church-perfect when he enters the sacred precinct. His faith is dewy fresh. But as the shabby misdemeanors of Apollo are unfolded before his scrupulous eyes, he erupts with scandalized rage. The evidence overwhelms him. The gods flagrantly violate their own laws and still presume to punish men for their comparatively minor infractions of the same laws. He decides to confront Apollo with his wrongs; but Apollo is not to be confronted. Apollo is neither god enough to avoid sin nor man enough to own up to his sins once committed. The final blasphemy in the *Ion* is contained in the utterly damning no-show of Apollo in the final scene. The wrong divinity rides in on the machine. This theophany is transparent to a quite pathetic reality, the reality of a god cringing within earshot of the moral outrage of mortals and coaxing his bolder sister to talk him out of his dilemma. In the end, it is Apollo who indicts himself.

Apollo, as the god of divination and prophecy, comes in for additional abuse on this second count. The frequency and the ferocity of the attacks on oracles and auguries in Euripidean drama tempts one to infer from these some thorn deep in the author's spleen; but such conjecture is secondary to the fact of the affront itself, spilled out on sacred ground in words like these from the *Iphigeneia in Tauris* [572–575]: "The one real human tragedy is when we set aside our common sense and put our faith in oracles, only to be ruined by them." This same sentiment is echoed and amplified in the *Helen* [744–748] by a servant of Menelaus, a veteran of Troy, who is sick and angry over the part played by prophecy in that war and the sufferings it inflicted:

> You know, now I see the art of prophecy
> for what it is,
> a vulgar occupation and a pack of ties.
> Nothing useful came from all the altar fires we lit,
> nor from the winged screechings overhead.
> It's daft to dote on birds,
> as if they're man's last hope.

Admittedly, in most Euripidean critiques of prophecy and divination, aim is taken not directly at the gods but at their human agents, the race of priests and prophets, whose words are assessed as useless at their best and disastrous at their worst. One is often left to wonder whether there are, in the playwright's own view, any gods at all behind the dreams and oracles and auguries through which they were supposed to reveal their wisdom and their will. In any event, the human traffickers in supernatural insight made safer and surer targets of doubt and indignation. We may recall that even Plato seems to have given limited credence and place to knowledge gained through mantic experience. Not to have done so, at least officially, would have been to take a quite radical and possibly dangerous position, a position which we might suspect but cannot prove Euripides privately held.

Myth, like prophecy, is regularly discredited in Euripidean drama, though usually with less venom. Just as native wit and common sense are proposed as superior alternatives to oracles and divination, so myths are often crossed by more plausible accounts, closer to the realities experienced by the spectators. A frequent strategy employed by Euripides is to lay down the myth central to his drama as though it were the warp on his loom, and then to weave across the myth, as weft, polychrome threads of doubt, common sense, rational critique, and contradictory experience. Nowhere is this strategy more evident than in the *Helen,* wherein the accepted myth that Helen went off with Paris to Troy is crossed by the dramatic fact that Helen never went to Troy at all, but flew off to Egypt instead, in the arms of Hermes. The two stories and the two whereabouts of Helen are explained by there being two Helens, a phantom-Helen and the real Helen. Without our unraveling here the intricacies of this most vibrant and delightful Euripidean comedy, we may note that the drama predictably calls upon its characters to sort out the discrepancies in the stories they have been living and suffering for nearly twenty years and to accept the painful truths consequent upon those discrepancies.

I have spoken of the *Helen* as a comedy, because by any modern measure that is patently what it is. Granted, it was written for the tragic stage and in the tragic form; but it is light in its touch, happy in its outcome, and frequently comic, even broadly so. The *Helen* is, nevertheless, at the same time tragedy, which is to say that it contains an essential contradiction, a contradiction revealed not altogether wittingly by the loyal, life-long servant of Menelaus as he is sorting out the two Helens and their stories and coming to the singular, startling truth, that Helen never went to Troy, that she was never once unfaithful and had pined like a perfect Penelope for her far-flung husband, in whose arms she is finally wrapped. Now, staring at the rapture of Helen and Menelaus' reunion, this shipwrecked and otherwise wrecked veteran of Troy makes a quite understandable remark and, in doing so, reveals a dark chasm beneath the bright cloud on which Helen and Menelaus are perched [700–707]:

> SERVANT
> Menelaus, help me to share your happiness.
> I can see for myself *that* you're happy,
>   yet I can't for the life of me figure out *why*.
>
> MENELAUS
> But old friend,
>   this is your story as well as ours.
>
> SERVANT
> This woman… wasn't she the one… who… I mean…
>   didn't she mete out our misery in Troy?

MENELAUS
No, not she. The gods made fools of us.
All we ever had of her was a pathetic effigy,
  modeled out of thin air.

SERVANT
Wait ... let me get this straight.
What do you mean?
That we went through all of that...
  for nothing more than a puff of air?

In this brief exchange, the head-sickening tragedy of war is laid bare, a tragedy from which Helen and Menelaus are insulated by their noble standing and their fairy-tale lives. Menelaus tries to convince the servant that the royal myth is one in which even he has a share; but the servant, unless he is a fool, knows that Helen and Menelaus' story-line splits from his own, the one into comedy and the other into tragedy. Even if this truth is lost upon the servant, it is less likely to be lost upon the drama's spectators. A similar divide is visually evident in the *Bacchae* wherein Dionysus wears a comic, or at least a smiling, mask and Pentheus wears a tragic mask. The *Bacchae,* like the *Helen,* brilliantly confuses tragedy and comedy, and in doing so discloses the cosmic divide between gods and mortals. Human tragedy is seen to constitute divine comedy. They are the warp and the weft, not only of Euripidean tragedy, but of the universe as well.

On a lesser scale, in myriad brief episodes and exchanges, myth is affronted and challenged in Euripidean drama. Again in the *Helen,* as Helen introduces herself to the audience, she relates the popular myth of her conception, according to which Zeus feathered himself as a swan and had his way with Leda. But Helen immediately follows her recounting of the myth with a dismissing quip: "if there's any truth to what they say," [211] she adds. Later, when a lost Greek named Teucer washes ashore in Egypt and provides Helen with news highlights from home the following exchange ensues [137–144]:

HELEN
What of Tyndareus' twin sons?
Are they dead or alive?

TEUCER
You hear both.

HELEN
Well, which do you hear more?
God! I have suffered so much already!

TEUCER
One story is that they've become gods,
made into stars to circuit the night sky.

HELEN
That story makes me glad.
But you say there is another version…

TEUCER
There is… that they slit their own throats
and bled out their lives…
victims to their sister's shame.
No more stories. I've wept enough already.

Once myth has become just another story, one version among many, its authority is broken irreparably. It must stand or fall now in the same terms as any other account of reality. Myth is still free to inhabit and roam the Euripidean theatre. Euripides undertakes no sweeping dismissal of myth, any more than does Plato. Instead, he merely reduces myth to human scale and permits his characters to form their own judgements in its regard, which they readily do. When, for instance, in the *Trojan Women,* Helen argues for her life that the entire Trojan mess was Aphrodite's doing, Hecuba doesn't believe a word of it and adds that neither would anyone else with any intelligence. The truth is, according to Hecuba, that Helen took one look at Paris and her wits went the way of Aphrodite. After all, explains Hecuba, "Aphrodite" is just another word for "lust." Heracles is equally incredulous of the myths of divine misbehavior, when, in the *Heracles,* he confesses that he doesn't believe any of them, never did and never will.

Heracles' disbelief in the myths of divine adultery and tyranny, however, must not be confused with disbelief in the gods. Like Hecuba, Heracles is concerned to preserve the honor of the gods from all-too-human slander. "If god is truly god," protests Heracles, "he is flawless, lacking nothing. [All those myths to the contrary] are the malicious lies of poets." [*Heracles,* 1345–1346] Iphigeneia, conscripted to the bloody service of Artemis after her miraculous rescue from the blade of Calchas, comes to a similar defense of divine flawlessness in the

Iphigeneia in Tauris. Against all appearances and against all that has been handed down regarding the goddess whom she serves, Iphigeneia raises her own solitary protest [381–391]:

> We mortals are unclean,
>> forbidden to approach the goddess,
>> if we soil our hands with bloodshed, touch a corpse,
>> or assist a woman giving birth.
> And yet she herself revels in human sacrifice,
>> finds it sweet.
> No, this cannot be.
> Zeus, and Leto his bride,
>> cannot have spawned anything so spurious.
> I don't believe the tales of Tantalus and his feast.
> I don't believe that gods ever savored the flesh of a child.
> Here in this land,
>> men not gods are murderers.
> Men make their own perversions into rituals
>> and sacralize their sins.
> No god is evil—that is what I believe.

Whether Euripides believed the same, we can never know. What we do know, however, is that this conviction— "if gods do anything shameful, they are not gods" [fr.292.7]—is expressed with frequency and passion in Euripidean drama, which allows us to say that there is in that drama an heuristic movement beyond the capricious and corrupt gods of the poets towards a more pure conception of divinity, less likely to offend human intelligence and integrity. Into the theological vacuum left by the poets and their myths, Euripides introduced a range of speculations current in his day. In fact, Euripides is commonly reckoned a disciple of Anaxagoras, whom Aristotle regarded as the first sober metaphysical thinker. Anaxagoras gave the name of Mind [*Nous*] to his First Cause, which brought order into the primordial chaos and then withdrew. It was Mind that initiated the rotary motion which drove the hot, dry, light, and rare seeds to the furthest edges of the universe to form aither. These speculations are of interest here because of the frequent occurence of Mind and of Aither as divine epithets in Euripidean drama, both the fully extant dramas and the fragments of lost dramas. "In each one of us it is the Mind that is God" [fr.1018] reads one fragment, while another refers to Aither, "which is known to mortals by the name of Zeus." [fr.877] In addition to Mind and Aither, other natural elements and forces, such as Earth and Necessity, are given the name of God or Zeus in one or other Euripidean text. There seems to be little point, however, in marshalling a fuller array of such references here; for from them we are able to conclude no more than that Euripides must have been keenly aware of and interested in the most advanced metaphysical thinking of his day.

In the midst, perhaps we may say the muddle, of theological speculation in Euripidean drama, most critics eventually indicate where they imagine Euripides' personal convictions to have been located. It may be justified, though not kind, to say of this endeavor to disclose the true mind of Euripides what was said of the notorious "search for the historical Jesus," namely that each critic, staring down into the well of history to catch a glimpse of Jesus' (read Euripides') own countenance, eventually with an elated sense of discovery glimpses his or her own face. Having said this, I foolishly take my place at the rim of the same well.

The dazzling scope of theological opinion in Euripidean drama suggests to me that Euripides neither possessed nor sought to promulgate any doctrine of the divine, even though the question of god remained a central and agonizing one for him. As we shall explore more fully in its proper time, the most urgent focus of Euripidean concern is the human realm, in particular the suffering which mortals endure from inhuman sources, as well as the suffering which mortals endure from each others' stupidity and malice. The truth of God has direct bearing, however, on both sources of suffering, inhuman and human; for justice, whether cosmic or political, is man's only hope for respite. And justice, divine or human, is a religious matter for Euripides. "Justice has great power," says the chorus of the *Electra* [958]; and, for Euripides as for Homer, whatever has great power is somehow divine. Thus, in searching for the voice of Euripides among all the myriad voices resonant in his dramas, I imagine myself to hear something of his voice in these lines from the *Hippolytus* [189–197]:

> Human life, from beginning to end,
>   is riddled with pain.
> There is no respite from its burdens.
> But something other,
>   more deserving of love than life itself,
>   lies wrapt in darkness,
>   veiled in cloudy vapors.

> We are revealed as we are,
>> hapless lovers of a brilliance
>> gleaming beyond our earthly reach.
> No one can lay it bare for us.
> Beyond this one mortal life,
>> we are inexperienced, drifting aimlessly,
>> carried along by myths.

Indeed, "there is in the human circle no clear and bright truth about divine things." [*Heracles,* 62] Human confusion and unknowing do not, however, preclude human longing and hope, which are precariously proposed in these choral lines from the *Hippolytus* [1103–1107]:

> The care of the gods for me,
> Whenever my heart welcomes such a thought,
> Is a great thing.
> It draws from me the poison of my pain.
> But the secret hope I cherish,
> That some kind Wisdom prevails,
> Slips away from me,
> When I watch what mortals do
> And what they endure.

The care of the gods for mortals is left in considerable doubt in Euripidean drama. The hearts of the gods are called "inflexible" [1268] in the *Hippolytus,* while Artemis says of herself and her Olympian colleagues that it is their custom to remain always "aloof and neutral" [1130]. Artemis, forbidden by heavenly law to weep and to look upon the dead, abandons her devotee in his moment of most profound need and wins his ironic rebuke: "it's a slight matter for you to turn your back on a long companionship." [1441] The gods, Olympian or otherwise, appear fickle. One moment they preside over human affairs, molding them in their hands like soft clay; the next moment they are gone, deaf to human appeal, blind to human agony. And so it is in the Euripidean theatre. In the *Bacchae,* the god is in total control. There is no crack in which one might hide from his power. In the *Hecuba,* however, Hecuba can no more raise a god than she can breathe her children back to life.

The power of the gods, as has already been said, is not the decisive question in Euripidean drama, any more than it is in the *Book of Job.* It is the justice of the gods that concerns mortals most; for, if the gods are not just, their existence and their power are no consolation at all. And, despite the occasional assertion of divine justice in the Euripidean theatre, justice remains therein predominantly a human concern and a human challenge. The following fragment [506] from the lost *Melanippe* may indeed express something of the mind of Euripides on this matter:

> Do you really think that injustices
>> sprout wings and fly before the gods,
>> where Zeus has them inscribed on tablets,
>> for his own records,
>> so that he can study them,
>> and administer justice to mortals below?
> The firmament itself would not suffice
>> to contain Zeus' records of human sins.
> Nor would Zeus himself be equal to the task
>> of sorting out the sins of humankind
>> and meting out to each his due.
> No, justice is already here,
>> close by us,
>> something you will see,
>> if you care to open your eyes to it.

It may well be that "human virtue accomplishes nothing without the efficacious favor of the gods." [*Suppliant Women*, 596–597] Even so, most Euripidean characters seem convinced that without human virtue, most specifically without human justice, the efficacious favor of the gods will likewise accomplish next to nothing. The gods cannot reap what they do not sow. "There is as much chaos among the gods," suggests Iphigeneia, "as there is among humans." [*Iphigeneia in Tauris*, 572–573] Finally, however, the fact that the gods have their own hands full or that they are themselves unjust or that they interfere in human affairs only at whim from a general position of indifference—all of these and other common Euripidean criticisms are contained in the undeniable metaphysical fact that the gods are inhuman. It is their inhumanity that says everything. The sheer distance of the gods accounts for all of their human shortcomings and renders inestimable and unreliable their virtues.

The ground of all human fellowship is equality, communion in a shared humanity; and the gods are simply excluded from this fellowship. Aristotle recognized this in the *Ethics* when he said that friendship or love [*philia*] cannot exist between two beings when a gulf of inequality divides them.

The example he gave was the gulf between god and human-kind, which precludes fellowship between them. "No one needs friends," says Theseus in the *Heracles* [1338], "when he is cherished by the gods." Theseus spoke these words, however, even as he held out his hand in friendship to the broken, all-too-human Heracles. There is no confidence whatsoever in Euripidean drama that human beings are cherished by the gods, which would argue that Euripidean "theology" points, at the end of the day, to humanity and to human fellowship. In this case, we are left with the last words of Heracles [1425–1426], once a would-be god who has in the meantime left behind every illusion of divinity and suffered his way to the human border only to drink the unexpected sweetness of friendship: "any man who would prefer great wealth or power to love, the love of friends, is sick to the core of his soul."

HUMANS

Second in status within the metaphysical order, suspended somewhere between the gods and the beasts, humans take up a peculiarly precarious existence. As has been pointed out already, the human condition is fraught with ambiguity, drawn as it is from two disparate, immiscible sources: the divine sphere of continuous being and the bestial sphere of continuous becoming. The radical instability of human being as imagined by the ancient Greeks may be grasped as soon as we realize that in Greek myth human being is not privileged with a clear and distinct creation. Unlike Hebrew and other Near Eastern mythologies, Greek mythology contains no account of a divine creation of human being. The Greek gods are quite capable of extinguishing human life but not of originating it. Like human beings, the Greek gods may participate in the natural process of human procreation, provided they seduce or seize a human partner; but the gods stand no nearer to the origin of that process than do their human consorts. Human being, as the ancient Greeks strove to understand it, came to be seen as the realization of a process of separation from divinity, on the one hand, and from bestiality, on the other. Humanity, in short, came to be understood as the product of a temporal process, an "original" process which must nevertheless be reflected and reaffirmed in the life of each individual human being.

Broadly speaking, there were already at the time of Euripides two quite irreconcilable anthropological theories offering divergent accounts of humanity's beginnings and of the human process into the present. The one imagined human being to have come to its current condition through a process of decline from an original state of near-divinity, while the other imagined human being to have arisen slowly from an original state of near-bestiality. In neither view had human being been uniquely fashioned, breathed into life, and assigned its proper place and purpose in the order of the cosmos. Rather, it was agreed from either side that human being had arrived at its current middle position within the metaphysical order from somewhere else. Whether that "somewhere else" was nearer to the state of the gods or nearer to that of the beasts was a matter sharply disputed. Either human being was descended from some sublime, superior being or human being was evolved from some brutish, savage being. Finally, each of these theories presented a distinct moral imperative to human being, understood to be ever-mutable and ever in process. If human being had regressed from an originally idyllic condition, it remained for it to retrace its steps, however it might, back to that first, most perfect state. If, however, everything in the human past represented darker, denser, more barbarous conditions, it fell to human being to hold the ground it had gained and to take further steps, if possible, into civilization.

Foremost among the proponents of the first theory—that humanity had regressed to its current condition—were Hesiod and Plato; and now, in order to explore this theory in somewhat fuller detail, we turn to Hesiod, whose views were surely altogether familiar to Euripides. According to Hesiod, there was once, under the reign of Cronus, a golden age of men—I say "men" advisedly, since woman had not yet been fashioned into existence—in which gods and men, though distinct beings, lived in close proximity and fellowship. They shared the same feasts, for which neither of them toiled; for life in the golden age was free of pain, relieved of the necessity for labor. There were no wars, no contention, no killing, and no sexual union. Men were uniformly of high moral character; yet, for all their near perfections, they were mortal. Death, even then, had its claim on humanity; but it came gently, like sleep. Of course, neither we nor Euripides require the informative services of Hesiod to notice that human prerogatives have undergone severe slippage in the intervening ages of man. As for the consummate curse upon man in the Hesiodic account, the creation of woman and the gods' inflicting of her upon man, we will soon consider that event in its proper place within the political order.

The second theory—that humanity had progressed to its current condition—may be found in the Homeric Hymn to Hephaestus and was proposed by a range of later writers such as Protagoras, Critias, Moschion, and Diodorus. Of more direct interest here is the fact that it is quite frequently invoked or alluded to in the dramas of Euripides. The many varied versions of this theory are complex beyond the scope of any exploration we might conduct here; but even a distilled, composite account will suit our present needs. The foundational idea here is that humanity once lived in a beastly condition, dwelling in caves and engaging in frightfully uncivilized practices, including cannibalism. A number of pre-Socratic thinkers took one further retrogressive step in the argument and claimed that humanity began its long career quite literally as an animal, quite possibly some other animal altogether. Anaximander conjectured, in this regard, that the first humans were produced within fishes and nourished until they were competent to make their own way on land, at which point they were cast up on the shore. Archelaus, on the other hand, argued that human beings had emerged originally as a hybrid, resulting from interbreeding among animals.

In the midst of these early anthropological speculations on humanity's bestially humble beginnings, various proposals were set forth to explain how and by what humanity was decisively distinguished from animals. Some pointed to fire and to the transforming arts which it made possible, while others suggested that specifically human life emerged with the cultivation of grain and the domestication of animals. The polis too, with its own distinct order, the political order, articulated in its laws, seemed to some to mark the decisive emergence of human civilization. Speech, thought, intelligence, and moral sensibility were also candidates for humankind's specific difference from the other animals. Even the gods were, on occasion, given credit for raising humankind from its primal destitution to its moderately privileged status above its former peers. "I praise that god," says Theseus in the *Suppliants* [201–204], "who lifted humanity from its primal confusion and parted humanity's path from that of beasts, first with the gift of intelligence and then with that of language... "

In fact, all of the above proposals find expression in one or other Euripidean drama, from which fact we may conclude at the very least that Euripides took an active interest in current anthropological speculations, just as he did in theological ones. Needless to say, such ranging speculations on humanity's origins and progress provided Euripides with a wealth of images and ideas which he could turn to his own dramatic purpose and profit. In the Cyclops, for example, Euripides was able to employ nearly the full array of such ideas to contrast the purportedly advanced political civilization of Odysseus, who was clearly standing in for more contemporary swashbuckling Greeks, with the primitive, near-bestial community composed of the cannibalistic Cyclops and his shepherding satyr-serfs. The tongue and wits of Odysseus prove corrupt and ineffectual; and his only contribution to the island is to promote drunkenness and provoke violence. Reduced to primal desperation by the savage slaughter and consumption of his men, Odysseus reinvents the earliest primitive weapon effective at some distance, the Paleolithic spear hardened by fire. Quite likely, beyond having a bit of fun, Euripides was, in the Cyclops, employing his characteristic irony to question just how far humanity, in the carriage of civilization, particularly Greek civilization, had truly progressed.

To return now to the core of our argument, we must note that the underlying assumption of both ancient accounts of humanity's essential process, whether understood as regress or progress, is that human being is unstable and ambiguous, requiring definition for the sake of clarity and resolve for the sake of integrity. Thus human being is seen as the fruit of human becoming, which is both a prehistoric and a personal phenomenon. Ancient anthropology addresses the "becoming" of humankind, while ancient ethics addresses the "becoming" of the human individual. What distinguishes ancient anthropological considerations, then, from ethical ones is a matter of respective scale rather than of substance. Finally, it must be stated that the scale of ancient drama coincides far more closely with that of ethics than with that of anthropology; for drama thinks and speaks and moves through stories, the stories of individual lives, however transparent those lives may be to the wide spectrum of humanity. The appropriate span of time recommended by Aristotle for each tragic drama was the circuit of one day's sun across the sky, which no plays seem to have exceeded to the extent required to trace the path of humanity from the golden age or from the bellies of fish to its present condition.

Euripidean drama, however scattered it may be with references or allusions to anthropological speculations or, for that matter, to theological speculations, finds its center in the ethical problem of human becoming. In order to press now to the heart of this problem, it is instructive to recall from the preceding discussion of the gods that it was their inhumanity which in the end proved definitive of their nature and decisive for all of their qualities; and the root of their inhumanity lay in their immortality. The final insignificance of the Greek gods and the ultimate frivolity of divine affairs may be traced to their conscious inexperience of death. Correspondingly, human significance and the consummate seriousness of human affairs may be traced in Euripidean drama to the conscious experience of death, which is what is meant by mortality.

With a few fanciful exceptions which serve only to prove the rule, all human beings portrayed or considered in Greek poetry are mortal [*thnetoi*], just as all gods are immortal [*athanatoi*]. To say this is, however, to say a good deal more than simply that all human beings die and that all gods do not. If this were the case, goats and bulls and birds would be mortals; for surely their eventual demise is as certain as ours. But they are not mortals, despite their being yoked to death. What they lack is not death but the consciousness of death. They live and then they die, while mortals live and die at once. Beasts live as if they will live forever, even though they will not; for they do not know in their minds and hearts that from their first breath they face death. It is the conscious anticipation of death and the transforming power which such anticipation exercises over a life that comprise mortality. The fact of death alone is without significance, like a geometric point without extension. As we have seen already and will see again, the fact of death is critical; for otherwise gods with all their consciousness could manage to be mortal, which they can never be. The mere fact of death, then, is critical but insufficient for mortality.

To be mortal [*thnetos*] is to be "deathful"; and life is only full of death when it is infused and heightened with the consciousness of death. Once again, we find humanity spread-eagled across the metaphysical spectrum, bound to share both the consciousness of the gods and the doom of dumb animals.

To be born of woman, however, does not bestow mortality other than as a destiny and a debt. The same is to be said precisely of human being; for human being and mortality are finally one. All that birth brings with it is human possibility, which must be realized personally in the process of human becoming, mortal becoming, which is at its core a coming to the consciousness of death and an embracing of the ethical consequences of that consciousness. We will consider first the coming to mortal consciousness and then its ethical consequences.

Whether we look to the Epic of *Gilgamesh* or to the *Iliad* or to the dramas of Euripides or to the dialogues of Plato, we find that mortal consciousness emerges through the power of human imagination, what Plato calls *eikasia. Eikasia,* as Plato understands it, is the human capacity to see an image as an image. Most, if not all, animals see images straight on as visible objects. As Leonardo daVinci explains in his notebooks, a dog may well run to a painting of its master, as if the painting were the master; but as soon as the dog licks the painting, the painting becomes mere paint. One moment the painting is the master and the next moment it is not. It is either the one or the other. At no point is it, for the dog, an image of the master. The curious thing about an image is that it both is and is not what it is. A bust of Pericles, for example, is Pericles. At the same time, however, it is not Pericles; for Pericles is no more and never was this or any other bust. Nonetheless, we humans look at a carved bust of him and say that "this is Pericles," by which we mean that we see Pericles in it. It is this same capacity to see one reality reflected in another that is refined and exercised at each critical point of turning in the ascent of Plato's divided line in the *Republic.* In short, Platonic wisdom is rooted and realized in the power and practice of human imagination.

Imagination is no less essential to Euripidean theatre than it is to Platonic metaphysics; for *eikasia* is not always mystical in its aspirations. We reach at once the heart of tragic imagination when we realize that human beings can die without dying, can confront death without passing through its portals; for human beings can see their own deaths reflected in the deaths of others. Gilgamesh, when he holds and beholds the head of his dying friend Enkidu, his other self, dies with him and then returns to life. He returns to life, however, transformed; for he now sees death as well as life in all things, including himself. He is full of death, just as he is full of life. The metaphysical truism that in humanity the immiscible streams of being and nonbeing converge becomes a volatile, enlivening, obliterating truth for Gilgamesh, as it does for Achilles in the *Iliad* and for Admetus in the *Alcestis*. Achilles, after lying with his lost friend through the long night, stripped naked of any illusion of immortality, rises and stands off from the corpse of his other self. The metaphysical dikes give way and the full ambiguity of his humanity overtakes him. He is at once a blazing god and a ravaging animal. He is, briefly, the savage, celestial event of their release and collision.

In Plato's metaphysical scheme, imagination is revelatory precisely because the cosmos is constituted as an ascending series of images. One reality reflects another, which in turn reflects another, until our minds are drawn to that reality which reflects nothing but simply *is*. Correspondingly, within the ethical and literary spheres, imagination is revelatory because all of history is constituted as a series of human lives, in each one of which we can see ourselves somehow reflected. Each life is an image of humanity, a moving, fleeting, imperfect image, with which we have a deep affinity created by the fact that we too are, each of us, images, woven of being and of nonbeing, fraught with life and with death. Finally, when we consider that the Greek theatre is peopled with masks and that those masks are images reflecting both the personages of myth and the citizens of Athens, then the theatre too becomes revelatory, a place of essential disclosure. In sum, the structure of the Euripidean theatre, like that of the Platonic cosmos, is comprised of icons or images and requires imagination at every turn to see images as images, masks as masks, and so, in them and through them, to reach insight. Platonic *peripeteia*, enacted in the ascent from sensory images to divine Being is at final odds, however, with Euripidean *peripeteia*. The end of Platonic wisdom is to think divine thoughts, whereas the end of Euripidean wisdom is to think human thoughts.

So that these seemingly incidental reflections on imagination might be brought now to a sharp and suitable focus, we turn to the earliest of Euripides' extant dramas, the *Alcestis*, in which the *peripeteia* or critical turning of Admetus to the truth of his humanity occurs through what we have described as poetic *eikasia*, or imaginative insight. What we must realize from the outset about Admetus is that the extraordinary luxuriance and privilege of his condition have made of him an *idiotes,* a man radically inexperienced in the common limits of humanity. He lives in a world of his own, a world so unique as to reflect nothing beyond itself. In addition to having inherited the ease and privileges of royalty, Admetus has the god Apollo for his slave, the hero Heracles for his friend, and has for his wife a woman willing to take his place in death. How is such a man to think human thoughts?

The first blow to Admetus' illusory insulation from the human condition is struck strangely enough by his wife Alcestis. After she whispers her last goodbye and leaves his arms holding her cooling corpse, Admetus' first words are: "In my misery I am slain" or "I am lost in misery" (*apolomen talas,* 391). The word which he uses here to describe the effect which Alcestis' death has on him means to be killed or slain or annihilated or lost. Of course he is literally none of these. Instead, he is presumably in flawless health, with a new lease on life. His words literally describe not himself but Alcestis. The truth is, nonetheless, that Admetus has endured something quite unexpected. He has, in part, died with Alcestis. His immunization from humanity has proved imperfect and let him down. He is undermined by his own inalienable human imagination; for he has seen and experienced his own death in Alcestis' death. He is not as yet fully aware, however, that this is what has happened to him. Still less has he followed that awareness to its full mortal and ethical conclusions. For the moment, he displays the stunned disorientation and depression of an animal mourning the death of its mate in uncomprehending confusion. He is coming to human consciousness, slowly and painfully. He is coming to it from a great distance.

For the lesser members of his household, whose education into the human consortium had begun at birth, the truth of Admetus' situation is obvious. He has not been singled out to endure some unique swat of fate; rather, he has reenacted a commonplace. In the words of the chorus of common citizens, which is to say in the words of common sense [416–419]:

> Admetus, your misfortune is not optional.
> You must endure it.
> After all, you are not the first man alive,
> Nor the last,
> To lose a good wife.
> Try to understand.
> Dying is something expected of us all.

For a time, Admetus keeps his rage. He clings to the conviction that he has been singularly wronged. But by whom? For lack of a more suitable or proximate culprit, Admetus unleashes his outrage on his father, Pheres, who has refused to die in Admetus' stead and so, in Admetus' distorted vision, deserves to be cursed as the most selfish of men. Pheres, however, is not prepared to accept the blind, insulting fury of Admetus and spits Admetus' words back at him with shocking savagery. This, in abridged form, is what he has to say to his son [675ff]:

> Listen, boy,
>> just who do you think you're cursing out?
> I gave you life,
>> made a man of you,
>> left you with mastery over my house.
> I'm not obliged to die for you.
> When my turn to die comes, leave it to me.
> I'll do the same for you.
> The fact is, to squeeze free of death,
>> you waged a shameless campaign.
> Well, your time came and went;
>> and you've still got your life.
> All you had to do was murder your own wife.
> You've obviously stumbled on a brilliant scheme
>> for private immortality.
> It's only a matter of convincing your "wife of the hour"
>> to do your dying for you.
> Take this much from me:
>> the rest of us are as fond of our lives
>> as you are of yours.

The fact is that Admetus finds himself less fond of his life now without Alcestis. He begins to live the life emptied of life and to nurse the never-healing wound predicted for him by the chorus and Alcestis' maid. He returns to an empty house and an empty life with a palate so embittered that the future can promise him no sweetness. Neither the radiant sun overhead nor the soft, rich soil beneath his feet have the slightest consolation to offer him in his pain. He envies the dead, particularly his wife. Relentlessly, the chorus interrupts his tiresome, self-indulgent laments and reminds him that all of this is nothing new and that, if his pain seems so without precedent, it is only because he was so inexperienced when grief struck.

The final episode of *Alcestis*, when the broken, humbled, and struggling Admetus encounters Heracles and his prize (the mysterious veiled woman so like Alcestis) is too complex and elusive to admit of easy distillation here. Nonetheless, I will venture several tentative comments. Whatever a lifting of the woman's veil might reveal is less critical than what Admetus reveals in this encounter; for, apart from poetic license, there is no return from death. Even if this Greek fairy tale is given a happy ending, life is not so blessed. Admetus has learned this much and struggles briefly with its implications. He is still a child, unequal to the demands of mature integrity. What he has outgrown is not his weakness but his blindness. He is transparent even to himself in his failures, his failed friendship to Heracles and his failed vows to the dying Alcestis. Her honor, he admits, has its claim on him; but both his weakness and the fantastic premise of this play preclude his respecting that claim. After all, this was not a tragedy but a satyr-drama, despite the absence of satyrs. It is, in the words of an ancient commentator, tragedy at play. Its playful premise, however, is, like the prize of Heracles, thinly veiled. Anyone who knows that death's word is final can lift the veil or simply peer through it, and then go on to complete the tragedy of Admetus.

What Admetus only begins to glimpse before his tragedy is ludicrously interrupted are the claims that mortal consciousness place upon him. Pheres inflicted upon him the awareness that others cherish their lives as deeply as he does his. Presumably, then, Alcestis loved her life as deeply as Admetus loves his. The damning brilliance of this truth reaches even the depths of Admetus' encaved self-absorption and reveals him for what he is, a moral troglodyte, until now snugly sheltered from the human realm. For Admetus to learn the truth that human life is each time precious and each time doomed required that Alcestis die and that Admetus go down into imaginative death with her. It is not a truth one learns on one's own. Human beings teach it to each other by living and dying and suffering. Sooner or later, in the face of the human spectacle, imagination eats away the self's protective secretions and the illusion of uniqueness is lost. We see our own death in the deaths of others. We come to despise the safe distance which we, like the ancient gods, would have kept from self-polluting communion in wretched humanity. We may recall how Theseus reprimanded his mother, Aethra, when she made her own the sufferings of the Argive women who had lost their sons in the siege of Thebes. "Their troubles are no reason for you to groan," Theseus instructs Aethra; for "you are not one of them." [*Suppliant Women*, 291,292] What he says literally is that she is not born or descendent [*ephus*] from them, that she does not have the same nature [*phusis*] as they have. Kinship, for Theseus, is a matter of blood. He sees and feels the sufferings of his family, and perhaps of his city, as his own; but his imagination is not yet so lucid and embracing as to see the sufferings of any human being as his own. I say "not yet" because we learn of Theseus, after he has been instructed in the ills of humanity, that he himself has gone down into the carnage and is washing the filth of battle from the corpses of the fallen warriors. We may presume that the herald speaks for Theseus when, in response to a shocked comment on how unspeakably shameful such work is, he answers: "What shame can there be in bearing our common human ills?" [768] Clearly, Theseus has come to see for himself what his mother saw from the beginning.

The first profound implication of mortality is fellowship, the fellowship of the doomed. Nowhere in Greek literature is this truth more strangely invoked than in the fatal encounter between Achilles and the young Lycaon, who must be counted one of the unluckiest of Priam's or anyone else's sons. Armed only with his pleading, Lycaon grips Achilles' spear with one hand and his knee with the other hand; but no number of gestures or words will save him, because Achilles is daimonically deathful on this day. He has indeed caught the chill of death from sleeping with the corpse of Patroclus through the dark, silent night. What is at first hearing so strange, however, is the manner in which Achilles welcomes Lycaon into the fellowship of the doomed with the greeting "friend" [*Iliad*, XXI.106–110]:

> Friend, you too must die.
> Why spend your tears and your cries
> On me? Patroclus, you know, is dead;
> And you will never be the man he was.
> Are your eyes blind to me?
> To my beauty, my stature, the fact
> That my father is a splendid man
> And my mother a daughter of heaven?
> Yet death stalks me as much as you.
> Nor am I an equal to my fate.

When he heard this, we are told that both Lycaon's spirit and his knees failed him; for he knew himself in that moment to be a dead man. Compelled to gaze imaginatively both upon the already dead Patroclus and upon the soon to be dead Achilles, Lycaon was emptied of hope. The *Iliad* is replete with such leaps of imagination and the unlikely fellowship which they create. Surely the greatest imaginative leap of all is when Priam and Achilles, their eyes washed pure with tears, gaze across the abyss which divides them and wonder at the sight before them. Achilles sees in the aged, mournful Priam his own old and miserable father, while Priam sees in the wondrous Achilles his own once-resplendent son. Achilles too thinks of Hector and weeps for Patroclus. The two of them draw together in their thoughts, embrace in their grief, break down, and fill the tent with their cries. Their tears and their laments mingle; for theirs is a single, immeasurable sorrow. Later, Achilles rises, takes Priam's arm, and gently lifts him to his feet. "Without a care of their own, the gods weave for us mortals lives of sorrow," he says to Priam. "For us to live is to grieve." [XXIV.525–526]

The fellowship to which Achilles invites Priam is very close to that which he extended to Lycaon, except that murderous passion has given way in the meantime to mournful compassion. Achilles stood over the helpless Lycaon both as a ravaging beast and as a glaring god. He meets Priam, however, face to face, as a human being who endures with him the caprice of the gods. This, I believe, is the consummate moment of vision in the *Iliad,* the moment of truth, in which a new model of human community emerges. The human order revealed herein rests neither upon the spear nor upon the scepter, neither upon brute force nor upon divine prerogatives. The true human order rests, it seems, upon mortal compassion; and the appropriate scope of *philia,* the bond of human love, is not familial, not civic, nor ethnic, but universal; for there are few divides between mortals, either in literature or in life, greater than that between Priam and Achilles.

This, then, is the meaning of imaginative insight: to see one reality in another, or to see one reality and to think another. What occurs in such moments is not confusion but crystalline clarity. When Achilles looks at Priam and imagines his father, and when Priam looks at Achilles and imagines his son, their vision is heightened not muddled. It is not as if properly separate realities are running together like pigments in the seething cauldron of their souls. The truth is, rather, that these two grief-chastened men are no longer sufficiently arrogant and willful to fracture and disperse into separate realities what is essentially one. When pigments mix they turn to blackness; but when colors, bands of light, converge they are luminous and pure white. This metaphor brings us closer, I believe, to what Heraclitus meant by the one light of day, the light of the waking world which we inhabit in common, the light of reason, in which each human life becomes transparent to each other human life in the hopeless, compassionate fellowship of mortals. In this light, the truth of human nature is disclosed. This same light, the light of the common human realm, is altogether luminous in Euripidean drama.

It may seem to require a similar imaginative leap to pass from Homer to Euripides, from archaic epic to classical theatre; but the truth is that, in the moments which we have been considering from the *Iliad*, we are already well within the mind of Euripides. In the *Iliad*, after all, we may trace the tragic *peripeteia* of Achilles from the folly of his quarrel with Agamemnon to the wisdom of his fellowship with Priam. He goes down into death with Patroclus and emerges deathful. He sees only death in all eyes and in all things. In time, however, this passion gives way to compassion and he embraces, in *philia*, in the loving fellowship of wretched mortals, the father of his own greatest grief and of his final ruin. This movement of consciousness and the foundational human truths which it lays bare and brings to light pervade and shape Euripidean drama. In fact, it may be said that the radically new conception of human *arete* or excellence, the radically new definition of heroism proposed by Euripides, already shone centuries earlier in the tent of Achilles. It was not, however, what Euripides' contemporaries remembered best or honored most in the *Iliad*. What Euripides did was to rediscover that seed and to plant it afresh in the fifth-century Athenian theatre. Here as elsewhere, it was Euripides' genius to discern the future in the past, to find something radically challenging in something ancient and forgotten.

The above claim that Homer, particularly in the *Iliad*, struck a well from which Euripides drank deeply must, of course, be tested against the full range of Euripidean drama; and such a test exceeds the modest limits of this book. Short of such a thorough test, however, it is to be hoped that this brief Homeric commentary finds frequent reflection and resonance in what has already been said and in what remains to be said herein about the voice and vision of Euripides, to which essential human fellowship, compassion, and love are so utterly central.

To conclude, now, this discussion of the human realm and of human becoming, we turn first to the *Heracles* and finally to the *Hippolytus;* for in both of these dramas the eponymous heroes, like Gilgamesh and Achilles before them, suffer through to the truth of their humanity and win the consoling prize of human fellowship and compassion. Theirs is an *aristeia* stripped of all divine delusions and bestial perversions, scaled to human tragedy, communal and compassionate. Only with eyes accustomed to the darkness of the times and of the human realm can they be seen to blaze forth like the heroes of old as the best and the bravest of men.

We have already traced the near obliteration of Heracles which left him prostrate in confusion and despair, surrounded by his bloody handiwork. This man was once as near as any to being a god. He had pressed the bestial border as well. His own eyes peering out out from under the head of a lion in whose skin he was wrapped, he would have been mistaken for a beast if not for a god. Nonetheless, he is now clear and unequivocal regarding his undiluted human lineage. "I own you, not Zeus, to be my father," [1265] he says to the aged Amphitryon. It is his naked humanity which he covers now in shame. Left to himself he will never rise, never uncover and accept his fragile and flawed nature. The chorus of old men, who like the chorus in the *Alcestis* were never so privileged as to imagine themselves other than as they are, anticipate the event about to occur. "When a man's dragging steps quit and he goes down," they sing as they make their own weary way, "he is to be lifted to his feet." [124–125] And that is precisely what we come now to witness.

The entry of Theseus into the human hell unveiled on stage reflects the mythical descent of Heracles into Hades, as well as the heroic entrance of Heracles into the hellishly murderous lair of the demonic usurper Lycus. Each of these represents an image of heroism. The splendors which Heracles displays, however, both in Hades and in the court of Thebes, are inhuman, one moment superhuman and the next moment subhuman. The larger than life Heracles is indomitable, but likewise untamed. With or without the ministry of Iris and stage-Madness, Heracles is out of control, metaphysically undefined, living in categorical confusion, and strewing a corresponding chaos wherever he goes. Thus, despite his intent to enter as a saving *daimon,* he proves a slaughterous demon, fulfilling rather than thwarting the threats of Lycus. In sharp contrast to Heracles, Theseus is transparently grounded in his humanity and brings to the service of Heracles powers peculiar to human beings: forgiveness, fellowship, and love. The final episode focussed on Theseus and Heracles, like book twenty-four of the *Iliad* focused on Priam and Achilles, is to be seen as still another *aristeia,* radically unconventional and yet utterly archaic, the consummate blazing-forth of human glory, such as it is in the unflattering light of truth.

What Theseus brings to Heracles is no escape nor immunity from his suffering, but rather companionship in that suffering. "I have come," he explains to Heracles' father, "to suffer with him." [1203] Theseus ignores Heracles' desperate cries and gestures, warning of pollution. "Among friends," Theseus reassures him, "there is no such thing as pollution." [1234] To Heracles' despairing protestations that he is already past the limit of endurance and will embrace death rather than reenter the human realm, Theseus answers that these are the words of an *epituchon* [1248], an ordinary man, the kind of fellow you would expect to find anywhere, without even trying. They are not the words of a hero. Thus Theseus challenges Heracles to a new heroism, a peculiarly human heroism, whose demands neither gods nor beasts can comprehend or meet. Heracles is asked to endure lucidly the shame of his unspeakable deeds, and to reenter the community of mortals, no longer as a would-be god or beast, no longer as an intimidating, unapproachable power, but as a human being, no more, no less, and no other. Surely we must keep in mind here that this challenge is being spoken out to the citizens of Athens, the savior-city turned tyrant, more slaughterous than salvific, whose atrocities are accumulating at its feet.

Each line in this stunning last episode of the *Heracles* bears commentary and contemplation, which, however, it cannot receive here. Instead, we must leave the *Heracles* with several simple images etched in our minds. The first is that of Heracles weeping. Like Gilgamesh, by his own admission, he has never wept before. His legendary labors, he says, were nothing compared to this. They were relatively easy. The second image is that of Theseus helping Heracles to his feet, which is to say helping him to assume the simple, upright posture of a human being; for this is what he finds so difficult to accept—the yoke of humanity. What makes this bearable is the giving and receiving of another yoke, the yoke of friendship, the yoke of love [*zeugos philion* 1403]. This, then, is the last image, that of Heracles with his arm on Theseus' shoulder, the two of them yoked in compassion and love, as Theseus exits with Heracles in tow, like one of the little boats, one of the little children, whom Heracles the mythical hero had swamped instead of saving.

A moment similarly bright with human truth occurs in the last episode of the *Hippolytus,* when the shredded, battered, blood-sodden Hippolytus is carried home and laid at his father's feet. Hippolytus' pain is equaled only by his father's, whose soul, tangled in the traceries of grief and remorse, has been dragged likewise mercilessly close to death, which is near enough at this moment to make the gods flee. These two once so deluded and pretentious men only now accept their humanity, because it is all they have left; and, alone with it, they draw upon its peculiar grace. They embrace; and Hippolytus, in an act so miraculously improbable that it must be the work of human freedom, forgives Theseus for cursing him so blindly and so effectively. He forgives Theseus for taking the only life he was ever given and will ever have. There is nothing more he, or any mortal, could ever do, which Theseus acknowledges when he says: "how noble a son you have proven yourself to be!" [1452] Here again we are given an Euripidean *aristeia,* a glimpse of humanity at its best.

BEASTS

The human realm must be defined and secured not only over against the gods but also over against the beasts. In fifth-century Greece, the human realm was thought to have crystallized in the polis. Thus the human realm and the political realm were understood as ideally one. In the admiring gaze of its citizens, we might add, Athens was seen to represent the consummate development of the polis. Beasts, like gods, were excluded from the human fellowship of this and of any other Greek city, though beasts, made to nod their head in assent before the blade, "willingly" spilled their blood on the city's altars, mostly set off in the *temene,* the sacred precincts, of the gods. Political fellowship is rooted in *philia,* loving friendship, the bond of the polis; and friendship requires essential equality. Friends, and thus fellow citizens, are to hold all things, at least all essential things, in common. The suffering of a friend makes one suffer; and the joy of a friend makes one joyous. The boundaries between friends, in short, are permeable; and, while retaining their own individual identities, friends become one. In theory, all fellow citizens are friends, while cities, on the other hand, may well be fierce enemies. Euripides, as has been noted already and will be explored further, would extend the consortium of the city to the consortium of humankind, lest the unity forged within disparate cities be used to divide and ravage the community of mortals.

Between humans and beasts, however, there can be no final friendship; for they lack fundamental equality and commonality. In prehistoric times, the predatory power of beasts was broken by the conspiracy of human strength and wit. Beasts became prey, the preferable object of human aggression and a staple of human nutrition. Once their power was broken, the "otherness" of beasts made possible their victimization. As quarry for the hunt, as victims for sacrifice, and as meat for the feast, beasts obliged human fellowship without any hope of sharing in it. Their inhumanity is decisive and immutable. Though the beasts share with mortals the essential limitation of death, they seem not to be haunted by death. They do not live with death as a companion but confront it only in extremity. Mortals, on the other hand, can and do on occasion lie before an open fire after a grand feast, walled in and roofed securely from any conceivable threat, and, despite youth and health and wealth, shake with terror and dread at the mere thought of their finitude. For mortals, life is not precarious only when it is at immediate risk. Rather, for mortals, life is essentially precarious. Beasts require the literal, sensorially apprehended presence of danger for their hairs to bristle, their eyes to dilate, their hearts to pound, and so on. For all of this and more to beset them, mortals require no more than imagination. And this imagination, elusive as it may be, suffices to open a chasm between mortals and their otherwise fellow animals, the beasts.

Although the literal tooth-and-claw primacy of the beasts was wrested from them in prehistoric times, they retained considerable symbolic power and eminence in the imaginations of the ancient poets and artists and, we may presume, of those ancients who have left no lasting record of their obsessions. As symbols, beasts, except when consciously anthropomorphized, always represented inhumanity and thus extremity; for the bestial, however it is imagined, lies invariably beyond some boundary of the human. From the human vantage point, the denizens of the inhuman realm tended to fuse. Otherness is otherness, or so it must have seemed; for, as depicted poetically and iconographically, beasts and gods were often strangely bonded. For that matter, within the political order, wherein the human sphere is conventionally constricted to encompass only fellow-citizens or political allies to the exclusion of women, barbarians, slaves, and enemies, outsiders were imaginatively dehumanized and likened to beasts in preparation for their being actually violated. At the present moment, however, our focus is upon the metaphysical realm, wherein the multivalent symbolic power of beasts will be made more clear by reference to several examples from Greek literature and art.

Both literary and iconographic evidence suggests that the imaginatively preeminent beast in ancient Egypt and the Middle East, as well as in Greece from the Bronze Age into the classical period, was the lion. This suggestion bears even more weight if we accept that the Gorgon is originally and essentially leonine. From Gilgamesh to Euripides, from pre-dynastic Egyptian palettes to the lions-gate of Mycenae, from Heracles to Achilles to Dionysus to Alexander the Great, the lion remains a symbol of awesome, almost divine, power, sometimes lordly and benign, sometimes utterly savage. A lesser beast and thus a lesser symbol is the dog, a symbol of snarling, vicious, small-scale ferocity, as well as of the impurity of battle. In the *Iliad*, Teucer calls Hector a *kuna lussetera*, a rabid dog, a warrior gone berserk, so beside himself that he forgets any reverence for gods or fellow mortals. Leaping to the fifth century, sooner or later, Sophocles likens every one of his heroes to one beast or another; and Euripides too employs a kaleidoscopic bestiary to imagine his characters and their deeds.

Rather than catalogue further the bestial images in Greek literature and art, we would do well to consider more closely, in a specifically Euripidean context, the two bestial symbols already noted, the lion and the dog, while adding a third, the deer; for in these three we may comprehend the spectrum of bestial symbols employed by Euripides to illuminate their corresponding human possibilities. This spectrum is primarily one of power and weakness and resembles that proposed by Thrasymachus in the *Republic*. At one extreme is near-absolute, unaccountable power, represented by the lion; and at the other extreme is near-absolute weakness, represented by the deer. Absolute power and absolute weakness are inhuman, the one being humanly unattainable and the other being humanly unnecessary. Only gods, whose sovereign otherness may be symbolized by beasts, possess and exercise unqualified power; and only beasts, particularly the hapless, harmless victims of sacrifice, display weakness unqualified by moral defiance. Mortals are always only would-be gods and would-be beasts, never capable of rising to unconditional power and yet always capable of rising above unconditional weakness.

First, we consider the dream of absolute power, the unaccountable power of the tyrant, symbolized by the lion. In Euripides' *Phoenician Women,* we witness the struggle of two brothers—Eteocles and Polyneices, the cursed sons of Oedipus—for such power. They are likened in their hideous, fratricidal struggle to "twin beasts" [1296] and to lions [1573]. The prize for which they contend and over which they soon slaughter each other is avowed with shocking candor by Eteocles in these words to his mother, Jocasta [503–506]:

> Mother, with you I will mince no words.
> I would outreach the stars,
> Run the circuit of the sun,
> Harrow the haunts of hell,
> If I could do this one thing: grasp tyranny,
> Tyranny the greatest of the gods.

It is utterly clear to Eteocles' lucidly perverted soul that only two possibilities exist for him, as for his brother: to be a tyrant or to be a slave—to be a lion, lordly and ruthlessly savage, or to be an ox, a beast of burden, yoked to another's will and ever ready for his blade. The diseased divinity in whose malignant service each individual must be mutated into either a master or a slave is noted and named by Jocasta as *philotimia* [532], the overweening desire to excel and so to win universal deference. Jocasta's decrying of *philotimia* as the most perverse of daimonic forces and as devoid of justice represents a lonely voice, not only within the poetic tradition but also within imperial Athens; for *philotimia* provided not only the foundation of traditional heroism but also the motivation of contemporary empire.

Jocasta explains how *philotimia* invariably leaves behind it a trail of devastation and death. Instead, she would have her sons honor equality [*isotes*, 536], the fair bond of friends and of cities, whose legacy is stability and peace. Like Orestes and Medea, however, Eteocles would rather drag his house to ruin than suffer the slightest diminishment. An addict to his own ambition, he is blind to the space "between everything and nothing." He must have either one or the other, which he does; but not before spilling rivers of innocent blood.

Medea too spills innocent blood en-route to near-divine power. She, of course, shines dark and triumphant at the close of her drama, appearing in the machine like a goddess. True to her threats, she manifests herself as a *daimon*, quite equal to the work of rewarding her friends and wreaking chaos on her enemies. Described in the opening episode as a lioness [187] by her children's nurse, she is in the final episode described by the undone Jason as "not a woman at all but a lioness with a nature more bestial than Tyrrhenian Scylla." [1342–1343] In this last moment of the play, perched in that place reserved in Attic tragedy for the gods, she is inhuman and thus momentarily exempt from the limits of mortality, though not from the excesses of bestiality.

Plummeting now to the nethermost point on the spectrum of human power and weakness, we come to the slave and the victim, symbolized by the beast of burden and the sacrificial victim. The fate of the slave and that of the victim would appear to be incomparably disparate, as disparate as life and death. Indeed, they are just that; but the life of the slave constitutes a living death, a daily approximation of death. The victim Polyxena, in the *Hecuba*, torn from between her mother's knees like the trembling doe in Hecuba's worst nightmare, is made to spill out her blood all at once on the tomb of Achilles. This is the fate which Polyxena prefers, in no uncertain terms, to the daily death of the slave, in which life is spilled out slowly like wasted wine dripping from a cracked cup. This much Polyxena makes quite clear to Odysseus, whom she says she will make to effort to resist [349–368].

> I was born a princess.
> I was nursed on the highest of hopes,
>   to be a bride for kings, vying for my hand,
>   to be the queen of the best among them,
>   to live to a full age in his court.

I grew to be the acknowledged mistress
    of Troy's girls and women,
    conspicuous in every respect.
Mortality aside,
    I was a goddess.
And now I am a slave.
The name alone, so alien in every way,
    is enough to enamor me of death.
Am I to be an item for sale to coarse men,
    I, the sister of Hector,
    sister to the princes of Troy?
Am I to know only harsh necessity,
    sweeping some man's floors,
    kneading his bread,
    from one weary day to the next?
Am I, the bride of kings,
    to let some crude slave from god knows where
    defile me in his filthy bed?
Never!
I will take one last look at freedom
    and consign myself to hell.

Polyxena's subsequent speech at the grave of Achilles, related to Hecuba by Talthybius, is surely one of the most stirring speeches in ancient tragedy. This young girl shames the leering mob of Troy-sacking Greeks with her bold, defiant courage. She cries out for her hands to be untied so that she might die as she has lived, a proud, free woman and no man's slave. She bares her breasts, leans back her head, and spews her one, only life across the earthen mound piled over the corpse of the greatest of the Greeks. In all this, Polyxena's literal defeat is not in question; for she is dead. Neither is her moral victory in the slightest question; for she outshines the amassed Greek army and their corrupt fame. Hers is an inextinguishable beauty; while they are for all time common butchers.

Similarly, in the *Iphigeneia at Aulis*, the decision before Iphigeneia is not whether to live or to die, but simply how to die. She cannot hope to take on and to overwhelm the entire Greek army. Instead, she can either be dragged off to her death like some squalling, netted beast or she can go to her death freely, as did Polyxena, with as much dignity as defeat permits. Bestial victims are always either unwitting or unwilling or both. Not so human victims, who, utterly emptied of hope, may lucidly accept their death with humor or bravado or grace, as did Socrates and Polyxena and Iphigeneia, respectively. Nowhere, perhaps, is the resemblance between humans and beasts more inescapable than in death; for they live and thus lose a common life. It is equally true, however, that nowhere is the difference between humans and beasts more dramatically evident than in witting, willing death, such as that of Iphigeneia.

Deceived by her own father into thinking that she awaits the hand and the bed of Achilles, Iphigeneia and her mother prepare for the wedding sacrifice. When she learns that she is the sacrifice and that Agamemnon, not Achilles, will make her bleed her virginal blood, not in a wedding bed but upon an altar, Iphigeneia's instinct is to plead for her life and to elude her fate at whatever price. So long as she imagines her fate to be alterable, she will endeavor to alter it. Soon, however, she sees that she is not merely endangered but, indeed, doomed. The perception of her unconditional weakness leads her to a peculiarly human insight and resolve. In resisting, she would slide from human grace and squander other precious lives. Instead, she wills what is willed and thus usurps the power of those who would take her life from her. She will not be alienated from her own death or in her own death. Her death belongs to her as inalienably as does her life and she will undertake it in her own way. "Hear me, mother," she says to Clytemnestra, "hear what has occurred to me and what I have in mind to do" [1374–1376]:

> I have imagined my death
>> and all is well.
> Now I want to do it right.
> I want to shine when I die.
> I want nothing to do
>> with anything craven or cheap.

And shine she does, as her father, the king of kings, never managed to do, before or since. She was led to expect a marriage; so it is a marriage she will announce and embrace. She is to be the bride of Hellas. There will be no tears, no black veils; only the wedding crown and joyous song. Then, in one shuddering moment, when the sacrificial scream replaces the love cry, she will thrill her spouse and leave him bereft, to mourn her forever. Iphigeneia enters freely now into the sordid pretense created by her shabby father to cover his own cowardice and ambition; and she expands it into myth. She turns a lie into a legend. She, not her father, and not the mob he pretends to lead, shall be the Savior of Greece. She will be the best thing about the war in this its finest moment, so far as it reflects on her. So far as it reflects on the army and the non-entities who command them, however, this is the war's darkest moment, its most damning atrocity.

However one assesses the authenticity and interprets the meaning of Artemis' final sleight of hand in substituting for Iphigeneia, as the blade descends, a young hind, the image of Iphigeneia as archetypal human victim endures. The status of no truth within the human realm is altered by the miraculous intervention of Artemis, though the reputation of Artemis may be appreciably improved thereby. From the human, ethical perspective, however, it would be no different if Agamemnon had closed his eyes and accidentally missed his mark. Like the veiled girl in the *Alcestis*, the arrival of the surrogate deer occurs too late to change anything essential; for the truth has already been glimpsed. And the audience must live with the truth, whether or not Alcestis and Iphigeneia are granted poetic reprieves.

The third and final bestial symbol we will consider here is that of the dog, which lies mid-way between the ravaging lion and the ravaged deer in the spectrum of human power and weakness. The dog, virtually indistinguishable at times from the wolf, is savage and resourceful, but hardly sovereign. It is most intimidating in its plural form, when roaming in packs, and is irresistible only briefly when it is beside itself, rabid with rage. The dog is neither invulnerable nor without recourse. It can inflict pain, even death; but not without suffering its own share of pain in turn.

Clearly there are many such "dogs" in the corpus of Euripidean drama, resigned to suffer but resolved to inflict suffering as well. Briefly—for this current discussion has already taken us across into the political order—we will consider the broken but effectual queen of Troy in the *Hecuba*. Hecuba is living proof, and knows as much, that weakness, as well as power, corrupts. Suffering brings wisdom; but excessive suffering, endured past the point of personal endurance, is disfiguring and brings not wisdom but evil genius. Hecuba longs to die before she becomes as dark as all that has been done to her; but Zeus will not let her go. Instead, with merciless largesse, he seals her every crack as if she were the last vessel in his fleet. Finally, she is consumed with a single desire, to see a bit of justice done; but neither the powers above nor the powers below will lift a finger or give a fig for justice. So she will do a bit of justice herself, poetic justice, or, in a word, revenge, which she accomplishes through a combination of wit and collective rage. She herself, however, has sustained wounds as deep as any she inflicts; and her end is not what would be described as kind. Transformed literally into a mad dog, she will climb the mast of a Greek ship and plunge to her death.

Women are, indeed, frequently likened to dogs in Greek poetry. In the Greek imagination, they are weak unless they are frenzied and united. As Hecuba points out to Agamemnon, however, the power of women evokes wonder and dread as soon as it is gathered and focused. Furthermore, she says, it proves irresistible if combined with cunning. Women, like Polyxena and Iphigeneia, are indeed Greek hunters' prey, marked victims, so long as they are alone; but, as soon as they claim their collective power, release the fury within them, and employ their considerable guile, they take up their own hunt and track their own prey.

What is as critical as it is obvious is that the lion, the deer, and the dog are all beasts; and the human possibilities glimpsed in them are likewise bestial. They find their way into Euripidean drama, presumably, because they find their way into our lives; and Euripides was committed, as we know, to presenting life as it is in fact lived. Neither their occurrence nor the frequency of their occurrence in Euripides' plays can be construed fairly as indicating Euripides' personal approval. If I may venture a Euripidean judgement in this matter, it seems that human beings do best to see themselves and their possibilities, as did Gilgamesh and Enkidu, Achilles and Priam, Heracles and Theseus: in each other.

CHAPTER FOUR

THE POLITICAL ORDER

Within the metaphysical order, or simply the cosmos, human being is distinguished from divine being and from bestial being. Human beings, defined by their mortality, stand at an essential remove both from the deathless lucidity of gods and from the deathful oblivion of beasts. Within the metaphysical order, human being is essentially one, admitting of no particular exemptions nor privileges. Even the sons of the gods, recalling a choral verse from the *Alcestis*, go dark in death. Kings, slaves, Greeks, barbarians, women, and warriors meet, on the far side of death, with the same undiscriminating obliteration. On the near side of death, however, within the political order, or more simply the polis, human being is divided into these and many other denominations. The seamless consortium of mortals is, in the city, shredded into tatters until man and woman, rich and poor, master and slave, citizen and stranger are all but unrecognizable to each other in their common humanity. Indeed, they are often left to wonder whether they have anything at all in common with each other. Screened by convention, the natural solidarity of the doomed is replaced by a spectral scheme of privilege and oppression enforced by prejudice and wilfulness.

The Greek theatre, as we have seen already, was a place of essential disclosure, wherein the truth of humanity was laid bare for common contemplation and acknowledgment. Metaphysical insight, however, is all too easily shadowed and compromised by political corruption. The essential unity of humankind, an undeniable corollary of mortality, must be argued afresh in the political realm, wherein it is the least evident of truths. In fact, the political order appears premised upon its denial. The political order, the specifically human realm, which ought to contradict the hierarchical structure of the metaphysical order, mostly mimics it instead. Characteristically, within the political order, one human being or human faction would play the god to others and, time and power permitting, would reduce the rest of humankind to bestial servitude and instrumentality. In short, the truth glimpsed briefly and brilliantly in the metaphysical realm perishes at once of its own impracticality in the political realm.

The timeless argument for the necessary and natural corruption of the political realm is nowhere stated more lucidly than in the *Republic* of Plato, wherein Thrasymachus argues that every human being strives naturally and necessarily for the absolute power and freedom of a god at the inevitable expense of every other human being's similar striving. Every good corresponding to every human desire is, so far as Thrasymachus knows and argues, fundamentally unshareable, a maddening fact made all the worse by the infinitude of human desire. Consequently, one man's happiness means everyone else's hell; and only the tyrant, whose will has its own way always, is truly happy. Thrasymachus, however, knew well that compromise is unavoidable and collusion best. Tyranny is less dangerous and more practicable when pursued collectively, which insight was foundational for Athenian imperialism, as for every form of imperialism before or since. The brazen claims of the Athenian generals at Melos, as reported by Thucydides, propound the same cynical doctrine. In fact, as noble a soul as Pericles saw less and less wrong with tyranny the more inclusive it became of the Athenian polis. Tyranny blown large to the scale of the city was no longer something despicable but was, instead, seen as simple destiny.

In the drama of Euripides, however, we glimpse a political order radically consistent with the essential human truths perceived within the metaphysical order, a political order purged of divine pretense and bestial demeanment. This is not to say that Euripides founded an actual city, any more than did Plato in the *Republic.* What may be found within the dramas of Euripides, as within the dialogues of Plato, is a city without walls, a city raised in thought and speech alone, inhabitable only for the imagination and the heart, a spiritual haunt wherein moral outrage and defiance might echo and resound. The facts, after all, are on the side of Thrasymachus; but fact is sometimes the enemy of truth. The fact is that the political realm seemingly always has been and likely will remain an arena for human competition and that conflict, rather than the site of human recognition and communion, constitutes a human scandal not a human truth. Against this scandal Euripides and others raise their voices in defiance; but, admittedly, such voices are never so many nor so powerful as to bring down the walls of the cities they despise or to raise up the walls of the cities they envision.

Nevertheless, moral protest against the corruption of the established political order may be seen to constitute a refutation of the truthfulness, if not the actuality, of that order. After all, the consummately arrogant Athenian generals at Melos and the grotesquely belligerent Thrasymachus of the *Republic* not only flexed their muscle but propounded a doctrine. In their arrogance they claimed to possess not only clout but also the truth. In short, their claim came down to this: all human distinctions, even moral distinctions between justice and injustice, decency and degeneracy, are reducible to the singular distinction between power and weakness. Naturally and necessarily, they would claim, the powerful exploit their power and the weak acquiesce in their weakness. The irony is that the Melians in their weakness did no such thing. They failed utterly to observe what the Athenian generals and Thrasymachus propounded to be a law of nature; and such exceptions to the would-be rule may be said to cast into doubt, if not into disrepute, the truth of the Athenian claim. At the very least it may be said that the moral outcome of the Melian campaign was a good deal more ambiguous than the military outcome, in which the Melian defeat was total.

Before we consider the many faces and voices of political defiance and protest in Euripidean drama, we must complicate the too simplistic image of the Athenian political order so far presented in this chapter. Without denying that Athens deserved its title as the "tyrant city," it must be pointed out that city-scale tyranny is at least two-faced and thus shows a very different side to those within the circle of its favor from that which it shows to those without. On the one hand, Athens was for most of the fifth century a democracy, a kingless city governed by the principle of *isonomia,* the equality of all citizens in making and administering the law. Political order was likened to cosmic order; and both were seen to depend upon equality. *Isonomia,* oneness before the law, and *homonoia,* oneness of mind, were seen to be the conceptual pillars of democracy; and their realization had been the slow work of centuries, in which the power of families and factions was broken and reconstituted as the common possession of all citizens. Viewed from within its walls and through the eyes of one of its own sons, Athens might well seem to be, as it was and is often seen, the guarantor of a quality of life rarely glimpsed by others and the watershed in man's trek from savagery to civilization. We sense the rightful pride Euripides himself may well have taken in the extent of *isonomia* in his mother-city, when in the *Suppliant Women* [403–408] we hear Theseus correct the Theban herald who has asked to speak with Athens' master [*tyrannos*], as if Athens, like so many other cities were a city of slaves:

> Stranger, you are already off on the wrong foot,
> > looking for a master in this place.
> This city is not under one man's rule.
> It is free.
> Here the people govern, taking their turns,
> > in yearly succession.
> Power in this place is not handed over to the rich.
> The poor have as much power as anyone else.

Athenian democracy may be said to have reached its consummate form in the vision and era of Pericles, in which the city and the cosmos became fused or, more accurately, confused. The cosmos was collapsed into the city, *phusis* into *nomos*. In this scheme of things, an Athenian was born first and foremost to Athens, which nurtured his life and thus possessed a primal claim upon it. The collective self, the civic "we," eclipsed the individual self. The collective mind and will of Athens usurped the potential tyrant within each citizen and were crystallized into an absolute political entity not unlike the Leviathan of Hobbes, who clearly did more than translate Thucydides. What was central both to Hobbes' Leviathan and to Pericles' Athens was the power and prerogative of collective human passion, will, and speech to define reality. For both Pericles and Hobbes, *nomos,* the collective assertion of will, is absolute, or rather as absolute as is the power which inflicts it upon the world. Law is nothing other than collective self-assertion; and the city is the engine behind it.

The issues raised in this present discussion are admittedly complex and seemingly obscure. They come down, however, to something quite simple and pointed. What Euripides witnessed in his own city was the creation of a radically secular state, secular to its core, no matter how girdled it might have been with pieties. The official gods of the Athenian polis in the fifth century were tame, household pets. They blessed its troops and sanctioned its edicts when and as they were told to do so. In such a regime, the metaphysical order is overturned and human beings, at least those coalesced into the collective tyranny, lord it over all of existence indiscriminately. There are only facts, no truths; and these facts are the ephemeral products of force. There is no such thing, for instance, as human being, poised precariously between, and sharing a cosmos with, bestial and divine being, except perhaps as a poetic or philosophical figure of speech. In the place of the human being there is the citizen, identified and defined by civil law; and, in the place of the rest of the cosmos—human, bestial, or divine—there is otherness, whose status is in principle at the capricious discretion of the city. In short, there is, on the one hand, the "we" and, on the other, the "they" or even the "it." If we lay bare the theoretical core of Athenian imperial policy, that is what we find.

If one were an Athenian citizen and equipped with neither imagination nor conscience, then one might see nothing amiss, much less appalling, in Athenian imperial theory and practice. However, if one were, for instance, a woman, a slave, or a barbarian, then it would require neither imagination nor conscience to notice that something outrageous was in the air. If justice is, in simplest terms, respect for the nature of anyone or anything and injustice the violation of that nature, then what was in the air was injustice. The political order—as envisioned by and embodied in imperial Athens— denied the humanity of all but its citizens, whose humanity it all the same disfigured. In Euripidean drama, we hear, as frequently as if it were a refrain, the denial of that denial and thus the affirmation of a common humanity without disfigurement.

The political order envisioned by Euripides and embodied in his plays seeks above all to be just, namely to respect the truth of human nature as discerned within the metaphysical order. The truth of human nature is violated as soon as some human beings fancy themselves as would-be gods and set out to reduce others to would-be beasts. Both cosmic justice and political justice lie in affirming the radical inequality of human being with every other being and the radical equality of every individual human being with every other individual human being. Thus the truth of the political order lies in its transparency to the truth of the metaphysical order. Jocasta sees and says precisely this to her raving son Eteocles; but he is blind to her vision and deaf to her words [*Phoenecian Women*, 528ff]:

Eteocles, my son,
The legacy of age is not all bad.
With experience can come words
    wiser than those of youth.
Child, why do you strive for a place above others?
Such striving is, of all possessing powers,
    the most perverse.
Stop this.
The divinity you worship is injustice…
Better to honor equality,
    the bond of friends, of cities, of allies.
It is the nature of equality
    to stand up steady and strong in the human circle.

Jocasta proceeds to explain to her hapless son that in the absence of equality, enmity is sown, the lesser hating the greater. The contrasting harmony we witness in the cosmos is the fruit of equality, night yielding to day and day to night, neither begrudging the other its due. Not so with her sons. "You think having more than your share is better?" Jocasta asks her son bitterly and futilely; "but what you think has nothing behind it." [553]

Within the essential equality of the human realm, however, Euripides was a keen observer of human differences. No one could with any grounds argue that the differences, for example, between youth and age, high birth and low birth, or freedom and servitude were lost on him. What he questioned was not the existence but the final significance of such distinctions. A good many of life's capricious privileges would seem to be contained in noble birth; and yet the significance of noble birth is commonly discounted in Euripidean drama, as in the following choral fragment from the lost *Alexandros* [fr.52]:

Among us mortals,
Words poured out in praise of noble birth
Are idle and excessive.
Long ago, when we were first spawned,
When the earth our mother brought us forth,
There was no telling us apart,
As the earth had made us.
Apart from what we had in common,
We had nothing.
Those born into high places
And those born well beneath them
Are still one family, one seed.
The voice of the city [*nomos*],
Has conspired with time,
To proclaim birth to the right parents
A matter of pride.

High birth is, in Euripidean drama, a matter of irrelevance. It is nobility of spirit that matters. "Of noble birth," we read in the *Dictys* [fr.336], "I have little good to say. To my eyes, the good man is the man of high birth; and the rogue, even if he comes from better stock than Zeus himself, is the one basely born." It does not take Euripides to go on to note that those nobly born have no peculiar claim or head start on decency. In fact, we find in a fragment from the *Antigone* [fr.55] the claim that "the misdeeds of the rich are many." At the very least, what we fail to find in Euripides' plays, and perhaps anywhere else for that matter, is any correspondence between privilege and decency. In Euripidean drama, the wealthy, the highborn, the powerful, the beautiful, the city's "best and brightest," for all their giftedness, seldom display a corresponding moral grandeur. Rather, they tend to lead shallow, shabby lives at best, and blind, savage lives at worst. More often than not in Euripidean drama, it is a slave, a child, a barbarian, a woman, one of the obscured or oppressed, who shines. The only inequality that finally matters to Euripides, it seems, is ethical; and, in the familiar words of Flannery O'Connor, "a good man is hard to find," which more or less sums up the following complaint of Orestes in the *Electra* [368ff]:

> There is no driven path to excellence of soul;
> for the race of mortals are an unruly lot.
> I have seen eminent fathers raise worthless sons,
> and stalwart sons come from sheer corruption.
> Within the souls of wealthy men,
> I have glimpsed gnawing hunger,
> while in bodies lacking almost everything,
> I have found a profound grasp of things.
> So how, I ask, are we to sort through our race
> and find the truly good man?
> What measure might we use?
> Wealth? ... Poverty? ... Daring in battle? ...
> Best to ignore measures such as these,
> and put them far from our thoughts.

Even without a rule of thumb for ferreting them out in advance, it remains evident on the Euripidean stage that some lives are more just than others, in that they are lived out with greater respect for the natures of all beings, while other lives trample and disfigure everything in their path. Neither the essential equality of all human beings, nor the inscrutable source of their ethical inequality, renders all human lives morally equivalent. The integrity of each life lies cupped like water in each one's hands. No one and nothing else beyond the individual is finally accountable for whether it is lost or not. Nobility or baseness of spirit emerges from deep within the life and reveals its core, its singular truth or falsity. Every other distinction is imposed from without, whether by chance or fate or human caprice, and hangs on a life like a garment. "Those who seem to all appearances to be utterly glorious," rails Andromache, "are below the surface like everyone else." [*Andromache*, 330–331] Apart from inward differences, differences of spirit, what divides one human being from another is essentially negligible. "A minute sliver of gold buys a man's daily bread," explains the peasant husband of Electra, "and on a full stomach, the poor man and the rich man are virtually equal." [*Electra*, 429–431]

In a fragment from Euripides' *Antigone* [fr.168], we read that "the only thing contemptible about a bastard is his name. In his nature he is the equal of the legitimate son." Within the Euripidean corpus we find similar comments on the names, for example, of "slave" and "barbarian." To say, however, that nothing more powerful or pernicious than names cleaves and classifies humanity into more categories than anyone can count is not to say anything remotely reassuring; for *nomos* or law is the very structure of the city and *nomos* is nothing more than words or names. In this context, to name something is to assign to it its parochial nature, to "coin" its meaning and value as if it were a piece of raw metal waiting to be stamped into currency. What is in a name? Within the city, everything. Like masks over the souls of those who bear them, the names of "woman," "slave," and "barbarian" suffice to obscure the humanity possessed in common with free, Greek, men and to justify the discounting of their lives; and so the truth of the political order, human equality, dies myriad deaths.

WOMEN

There is perhaps no more revealing an entry into the discussion of women in ancient Greece than that provided by even a brief consideration of the very words most commonly used to denote "woman," a feminine mortal. If we set aside *kore* and *graus*, which denote a woman before and after her child-bearing years, respectively, the most common word for woman was *gune*, which literally and not surprisingly means "childbearer." Clearly the central and most respectable function of woman was seen to be the bearing of legitimate children, most especially sons, for which a woman had also to be a wife. Thus *gune* may also mean "wife" or "mate," even a bestial mate. The word which in poetic diction specifically denoted a man's wife was *damar*, literally "the tamed or subdued one." *Damar* is derived from *damao*, which means to tame, to yoke, to subdue, to enslave, to rape, or to kill. The *damar* is the object of all of these activities; and, indeed, women and wives knew their share of each.

This confusion of women with beasts and slaves, embedded in the language, pervades the literature of ancient Greece as well. In the *Iliad*, for example, when warriors taunt and threaten each other, their words most often aim to turn the opponent into a woman or a beast. In the *Theogony* of Hesiod, women appear late on the human scene as a *genos* or race apart, a *kakon* or "evil thing" fashioned by Zeus, the implement of his revenge on mortal men for their possession of stolen divine fire. Adorned and garlanded by Athena, this *kakon* becomes *kalon* or lovely to behold, all but irresistible to men. Inhuman, guileful, neither to be resisted nor endured, woman—the *kalon kakon*, the "beguiling perversity"—brings an end to man's primeval well-being. Similarly, in *Works and Days*, the phantasy of an originally womanless world, uncursed with toil and evil, is shattered by the arrival of woman, this time with a name, Pandora, a bane on all men. Woman, with her insatiable appetite for food and sex, consigns men to a life of labor, that is to the ploughing of virgin soil and to the sowing of seed. Woman, in short, is a divinely set trap, a divinely fragranced beast. In the seventh century, the Aegean poet Semonides, no more a friend to women than was Hesiod, traced the perverse characters of women to the beasts where in his view they presumably belonged. Beyond Hesiod and Semonides, women were quite commonly likened to bees, sometimes favorably with a nod to their industriousness, sometimes disparagingly, with drones in mind.

Even a glancing consideration of ancient Greek art confirms the claim that women were commonly imagined in inhuman categories. Images of war, hunting, athletics, sex, and sacrifice may be said to dominate Greek pictorial art; and it may further be argued that all of these spheres of activity were tangled and entwined in the Greek imagination. The common bond between them is violence. It is surely a commonplace by now to point out that from the stone age spear to the most advanced ballistic missile, man's weapons represent him sexually, as it is to point out that athletic contests, ancient and modern, are more or less benign battles. We have already discussed the diversion of violence from human victims to bestial ones, and the consecration of such killing in sacrifice. Aristotle likens the first menstrual flow of a young maiden to the flow of blood from a slaughtered victim, though the likeness between the first blood shed by a victim on the altar and the first blood shed by a wife in bed is more commonly explored in Greek literature. Further, the ritual *sphage,* the sacrifical slaughter of animals immediately before battle, in the face of one's enemies, to be consummated not in a meal but in battle, clearly anticipates the letting of human blood to follow. In rare instances, the *sphagia,* the blood victims, may have been human; and there is perhaps no more poignant symbol or expression of the renunciation of life and of sexuality entailed in mortal combat than the sacrifice of a virgin, a theme familiar to Euripides. Even if the bed of love and the field of battle represented distinct aspirations, reflected in the distinct figures of Paris and Achilles, their corresponding activities shared a common word, *mignumi,* "to mingle with," whether in combat or in copulation.

Even these few brush strokes, as it were, convey a sense of the image and the place of woman in ancient Greece. Now, in order to bring into sharper focus the immediate context for Euripides' concerns with women, we turn pointedly to fifth-century Athens, with whose legendary founding various tales of virgin-sacrifice were connected. From the outset it is instructive to reflect upon Athena, who gave more than her name to her city. Athena, though a feminine deity, is no friend of women. In fact, she has precious nothing to do with women at all. Sprung from the axed head of her father Zeus, she is motherless, while, as declared virgin, she is likewise childless. Motherhood, the common experience and *raison d'etre* of all respectable Athenian women, is utterly foreign to her. She is a warrior, born in full armor from the skull of her father. In her most famed embodiment, the statue of Athena Parthenos crowning the Athenian acropolis, she was stripped of any semblance of womanhood and bore not only the emblems of Athenian militarism but the emblem of Athenian misogyny as well. Depicted on the outside of her shield was the Amazonomachia, the legendary defeat of the Amazons by

Theseus, marking the final fracturing of feminine power, while on the inside was depicted the prehistoric defeat of the centaurs by the Lapiths, aboriginal Athenians.

These two myths, borne triumphantly by Athena Parthenos, were utterly foundational for Athens. Together they represented the decisive wresting of power from women, on the one hand, and from beasts, on the other. The only surviving threat to Athenian supremacy were the gods; and they were for the most part either domesticated or disbelieved. The gods survived, of course, and prevailed in myth, concerning which it is telling to point out that Greek mythology is, as everyone knows, suffused with rape, the master-rapist being Zeus, the king of the gods. The conquests of Zeus can hardly be seen as the naughty fruit of celestial lust; for rape, whether Olympian or ordinary, is not about desire but about dominance. In this light, we must admit that Greek mythology, so far from condemning violence towards women, celebrates it. What has not been so commonly known or openly acknowledged is what is only fair to call the phallic obsession of fifth-century Athens. Indeed, if we consider only its phallic processions and drama, its omnipresent herms, and its plethora of bizarre phallic art, we would not be rash in ascribing to Athens a cult of the male generative principle and an adulation of the penis, all having little or nothing to do with love and everything to do with power.

An Athenian woman's claim upon citizenship and her participation in public life were indeed marginal. With certain ritual exceptions, a woman was expected to be as publically silent and unseen as possible. A certain liberation may have accompanied menopause; but this likely meant increased freedom to frequent public places rather than any enhanced part in public affairs. The simple fact that from fifth-century Athens there survives not a single word written by a woman nor, with the possible exception of some vases, a single artifact attributable to a woman's hand, is as eloquent as any chapter which may be written on the obscurity of the Athenian woman. Not only were Athenian women inconspicuous; they were officially anonymous as well. A female child's name was not listed in the records of the phratry, i.e. the clan or ward; and the citizenship of a male child was traced through his father and his maternal grandfather, without mention of his mother's name. Just as the wife was commonly seen as housing and nurturing her husband's seed, without contributing anything beyond hospitality to the procreative process, so the mother was seen as the neutral, nameless conduit through which citizenship was passed down from one male generation to the next. She was, in short, a delivery device.

The woman's or wife's sphere of influence was essentially the home, where she bore her children and managed the household's affairs. This is not to say that she was sovereign within the home. Rather, Athenian art, literature, and architecture conspire to tell a domestic story not of female sovereignty but of female solitude and subservience. From such evidence, it would seem that women, as wives, were primarily mothers, water-carriers, and weavers. They were more or less confined to the *gunaikonitis*, the women's quarters, where meals were prepared, children raised, and domestic crafts practiced; in sum, where women's lives were mostly lived out. It seems that husband and wife did not ordinarily share the same room or bed. Instead, children were conceived on the *kline*, a narrow couch designed and reserved for intercourse. It may be argued that wives often or even mostly ate their meals separately from their husbands and their grown sons, who lived a masculine life apart in the men's quarters, the *andrones*, usually more ample and adorned than the rest of the house.

Reserving their wives for legitimate offspring, Athenian men regularly entertained *hetairai* or prostitutes in the *andron*, the "man's room," a dining room equipped with couches and located with conveniently direct access to the street. Here the man of the house hosted his *symposia*, or drinking-feasts, at which his invited male companions were amply provided with food, drink, entertainment, and sex. The tales of many such *symposia* are graphically told by myriad surviving *kylikes* painted with clearly uncensored scenes familiar to symposia-goers. The *kylix* was a man's cup kept from wives' and children's eyes in the men's quarters and thus an arguably reliable witness to the events occurring therein. Admitting the exceptional moment of mutual tenderness or shared amusement, the larger story told on these cups is one of sexual abuse and humiliation, particularly if we keep in mind the never-pictured but ever-nearby wife, the presumably neither deaf nor unimaginative wife, under whose roof her husband conducted his revels.

There is a favorite phantasy among many classicists of the bright, engaging, free-spirited, fun-loving Athenian prostitute, who was the virtual equal of her male companions. The historical centerpost of this phantasy is the famed figure of Aspasia, consort of Pericles, and admittedly no mean figure in her own right. Yet even if Aspasia was as free and influential and self-possessed as she has often been described, an exception tends to prove rather than discount the rule; and the rule for women, whether wives or whores, was arguably closer to the complaint of the chorus of women in the *Thesmophoriazousai* [786–787] who claimed "men without exception attribute to the race of women a host of evils, so that we are regarded as the source and the substance of every evil afflicting men."

Apart from the female protests and partisanship to be found in Euripidean drama, to which we will soon turn, there is to be sure a counter-tradition coexistent with the prevalent misogyny ingrained and evident in Athenian society. Stated more simply, Euripides was not the only friend Athenian women had. First and foremost, they had each other. Even without the numerous surviving references to female solidarity in myth, art, literature, and ritual, we might assume the existence of a female counter-culture, rebellious and resilient. Indeed, in fifth-century Athens, in addition to the clandestine confidences which must have been shared in the women's quarters and at the communal fountain, the yearly festivals of the *Skira* and the *Thesmophoria,* for example, virtually institutionalized the political solidarity of women, while in the *Adonia* and the *Dionysia* altogether uncanonical sexual paradigms were brought to public consciousness. After all, the soft, gentle Adonis was no more a master-rapist, àl a Zeus or Heracles or Theseus, than were the maenads of Dionysus tame, harmless housewives. It is significant to note, as well, that the mysteries of Eleusis were open to all, men and women, slave and free alike.

Sharpening our focus now upon the theatre of Dionysus, it must be acknowledged that Euripides was not alone in voicing the complaints and in staging the conspiracies of women. In the years following the mutilation of the herms in the summer of 415, on the eve of the fateful Sicilian expedition, Aristophanes wrote several comedies—the *Lysistrata,* the *Thesmophoriazousae,* and the *Parliament of Women*—on the theme of women's rebellion. It has even been suggested that these plays were inspired by a one-night women's revolt in 415 responsible for the castration of herms throughout the city; and it must be admitted that this account of the infamous scandal of the herms, whether true or false, has an all but irresistible appeal. Sophocles too, despite his avowed preference for depicting people as they ought to be, presented in his lost *Tereus* [fr.524] the following quite frank assessment of the sorry lot of contemporary women. Specifically, it is the voice of Procne, a wronged wife if ever there was one, that we hear:

> So many times I have observed the status
> > of women, how we are nothing!
> While still girls in our father's house,
> > the life we enjoy is, I think,
> > the sweetest of all lives.
> Oblivion is a kind nurse,
> > the guarantor of childhood bliss.
> But when we ripen and come to our senses,
> > we are hurled from our houses.
> Far from our familiar gods and our parents,
> > we are put on the market,
> > as objects for sale to men,
> > strangers or barbarians.
> Some of us go off to decent homes,
> > while others go off to abusive ones.
> Either way, after one agreeable night,
> > spent close in our husband's embrace,
> > we are expected to sing about our situation,
> > and to consider ourselves well off.

Turning now to Euripides, we hear Procne's lament echoed in the following speech of Medea, a similarly wronged and similarly vindictive woman [*Medea*, 230–251]:

> Of all creatures endowed with life-breath and wits,
> > we women form the sorriest lot.
> To begin with, it costs us a fortune
> > to buy our husbands;
> > and so we get a master for our bodies.
> Our lot is still worse without one.
> The greatest feat is to find a decent spouse,
> > instead of some worthless sort.
> A woman has no respectable way out of a marriage;
> > neither can she say "no" to a man from the outset.
> Every fresh wife finds herself in a house
> > whose ways and rules are new to her.
> Without having learned such matters as a girl at home,
> > she would have to be psychic now
> > to know how best to make a life
> > with the man who shares a bed with her.
> Now if she manages all of this to perfection;
> > and her husband lives with her gently,
> > placing on her neck a light yoke,
> > then hers is a life to be envied.

Otherwise, it is better to be dead.
A man, when he's had enough of his wife and family,
   simply leaves the house,
   finds a friend or a companion his own age,
   and so puts an end to his boredom or disgust.
We women, however, must fix our eyes on a single soul,
forever.
What they tell us is that we women, living at home,
   are spared the perils of war,
   while they are out there nose to nose with spears.
What foolishness!
I'd three times rather take my chances
   fighting in their front ranks,
   than bear one of their children!

If there were fellow women seated in the theatre of Dionysus, which remains an open question, these words must have found deep, though perhaps inaudible, resonance among them. In any event, they would have struck home somewhere. Medea is indeed *deine,* a woman to be reckoned with and wondered at. She is a strange woman; but, as her account of the common plight of women makes plain, there is nothing strange or remarkable in her situation. In short, Medea would have been quite readily recognized. She is a woman whose mate has tired of her and has preferred to her a younger, more advantageously situated maiden, in this case no less than the king's daughter. Medea's mate is, of course, Jason, of Argonaut fame; and, like so many men who in the tradition cut a quite dashing mythic image, Jason suffers under the direct light of Euripides' critical realism. Like so many Greek icons, he is smashed on the Euripidean stage.

The truth of Jason, as it is disclosed in the *Medea,* is that he built his reputation on Medea's accomplishments. More than once he would have been a failure, even a dead man, if Medea had not bailed him out. For all of this she paid an exorbitant personal price, in return for which she seems to have expected no more than his lasting affection and loyalty. In short, she was willing to be the noteworthy woman behind the negligible man. But, in apparently timeless male, middle-aged fashion, Jason had ridden Medea like a horse for as long and far as her legs would carry him and then dismounted and looked around for a fresh mount to convey him to new heights. What else was a hero to do? As from gods, it would seem that Euripides came to expect little from heroes.

Jason's words, as it happens, are as reprehensible and recognizable as are his deeds. With altogether misdirected condescension, he claims and expects Medea to believe that this latest feat of his—his abandoning her and their two boys to marry the king's daughter—is a coup he has devised and accomplished with an unselfish eye to her, Medea's, well-being and that of their boys. His futile words, of course, fail to convince, as do most attempts in Euripidean drama to mask and remake deeds with words. Words, after all, are infinitely malleable and serve as readily to conceal as to reveal the truth. In both realms, in her words and in her deeds, Medea is more effective than her less-than-formidable male adversaries. She persuades them of her at least short-term goodwill and harmlessness; and, in the meantime, she destroys them.

Too much attention, I think, is paid by critics to the specifics of Medea's deeds and not enough to the specifics of her situation, which, unlike the extremity of her actions, link her to other women, then and since. In sketch, Medea is a woman without options, a woman against the wall. Having left a bloody trail behind her, she cannot retrace her steps in the hope of a happy homecoming. Without recourse to any bond of blood or marriage, she is, together with her sons, homeless. And, in ancient Greece, to be homeless is to possess no human niche at all. Homeless, she and her children are mere prey, as good as dead, worse than dead. Even if Jason honors his word and makes some marginal provision for her safety and support, she is a woman shamed, with nowhere to bury her rage and nothing worth waiting for but death. In sum, her situation is already atrocious before she envisions and enacts her atrocious response to it. Before Medea acts, she is cornered into a choice between two unacceptable possibilities. Either she can accept every abuse without reprisal until she is emptied of any pride or hope, or she can return abuse with abuse and regain her self-respect, if nothing else. It is clear from her encounter with Creon, that she has no access to human justice beyond that of her own revenge. Jason was prepared to leave Medea alive but with nothing to live for; and that is how she is prepared to, and does, leave him. Exiled from the house, she says that she will bring the whole house down, including her sons. Both Greek genetics and Greek politics place Jason's sons, whether he will have them or not, under his roof, as it were; and, when it comes down, it comes down on them too. The closest thing to a hapless bystander in the final carnage is Creon's daughter, who, if indeed she had any choice in the matter, betrayed the solidarity of women in accepting another woman's spouse as her own.

Medea's final solution is not true justice and is not presented or commended as such by Euripides. The fact remains, however, that poetic justice, however unacceptable it is in actuality, is imaginatively satisfying as civic justice rarely is. Revenge in kind, eye for eye, tooth for tooth, doing unto others as they had hoped to do to you, is as emotionally gratifying as it is ethically grotesque. Through the imaginative rehearsal of revenge within the marginally more safe precincts of the theatre, drama does, perhaps, as Aristotle later suggested, make possible the *catharsis* or purging of such extreme passions. At the very least, drama traces and thus explains their eruption into life, without condoning them. The clearest indication of how Euripides finally regards Medea is given by the fact that he stages her final appearance above the orchestra in the machine, the apparatus reserved for gods. She has, through her excessive, unrelenting savagery, deified herself, as it were, won a place among the gods. Her final theophany reveals her acquired inhumanity, for this is the definitive characteristic of the Euripidean gods. Unlike the final redeeming moment of the *Hippolytus,* the final moment of the *Medea* is beyond the reach of forgiveness or compassion; for it is in the grip of a convert to the gods. And converts, as everyone knows, make up for lost time.

Another Euripidean woman against the wall was Hecuba. Like Medea, she had nothing left to lose in the end but her humanity; and, if we learn anything from Euripidean drama, we learn how tenacious our grip must be if our humanity is not to be ripped away from us. When her daughter Polyxena, who is everything to her, is dragged off so that the dead Achilles might drink her virgin blood splashed on his grave, Hecuba confesses that she is losing her grip; but that grip is not finally broken until she learns that her last hope has been betrayed by the family friend, Polymestor, pledged to protect the last surviving son of Priam and Hecuba. The boy's mutilated body washes ashore and is brought to Hecuba. The unthinkable is written in his wounds. Hecuba, like Medea, rootless now, tips into the inhuman torrent coursing through her and is carried off. Like Medea, she knows better than to expect divine justice, and she soon exhausts every human appeal. Men, like the gods, are the authors of women's wretchedness; and they are not about to unwrite what they have written.

What is unique about Hecuba's revenge is that it represents the concerted revenge of a consortium of ravaged women. It is, in short, the work of collective female rage. In the *Medea*, the other women will no more join in Medea's reprisals than they will obstruct them. Their only complicity with her lies in their silence. In the *Bacchae*, the maenads are admittedly concerted in their savagery; but they do the work of the god and implement his rage, not their own. They are one with the god, possessed by him. Agave, so far from gloating in her bloody handiwork as does Hecuba, disbelieves it. In the *Hecuba*, we find the same utterly secular, psychologically explicable female rage which is at work in the *Medea*, together with the collectivity of women emergent in the *Bacchae*.

This convergence represents an unanticipated and unsettling political development, as Agamemnon acknowledges as soon as he is apprised of it by Hecuba. When Hecuba says that— even without armed assistance from Agamemnon and his men, in fact with nothing more from him than his promise to obstruct any interference—she is prepared to deal with Polymestor and to see a bit of justice done, he is at once incredulous. He wonders how she can do this work alone; and, if not alone, with whose help. She reminds him of the *ochlos* [880], the mob, of Trojan women herded into nearby tents. He scoffs at her suggestion, presumably not because he sees mobs as harmless. After all, his mob took Troy. "You mean them, the wild game we won with our spears?" [881] he taunts. Finally, when Agamemnon wonders how a mob of women is going to undo a king, Hecuba unveils a terrifying truth: "*deinon to plethos sun doloi te dusmachon.*" [884] It requires a good many more words to translate such distilled defiance. *Deine*, we recall, was Medea's epithet, a single word for what evokes at the same time dread and wonder. A familar definition of divine otherness, as that which allures and terrifies, falls close to the mark here. Strange, fascinating, and fearful is the *plethos* of women. *Plethos* conveys both the sense of multiplicity and the sense of unity. In other words, Hecuba is saying something like this: just count the women in those tents and then imagine them acting as one. As if this were not enough to bring a shudder to the leader of men, Hecuba adds: *sun doloi te dusmachon*, which is to say, "put this together with cunning (in which we women have no peers) and there is no defence against us."

To all of this Agamemnon initially responds with one word, *deinon* [885], thus acknowledging Hecuba's assessment of the force within those tents. When he goes on to express his continuing doubts, Hecuba reminds him that there are precedents for their undertaking, citing the ninety-eight-percent effectiveness of the daughters of Danaus, and the women of Lemnos who outdid them. With this said, Hecuba has made her point; and so has Euripides. In a political order wherein the balance of power and weakness is the last word, the victimization of women is no law of nature. Rather, it is a function of women's isolation and passivity. If ever they should come to see their sufferings as one suffering and together trace it to its source, coming to a consciousness of their concerted power along the way, then the outcome will be indeed *deinon,* even blinding, a truth of which Polymestor soon becomes living proof.

Arrogantly unwary, Polymestor is easy prey to the cunning throng of women. After slashing the life from his sons, they fling Polymestor on his back, wrapping his hair in their hands and slamming his head back against the rocky earth every time he tries to move. Straddling him like some netted beast, one by one the women plunge into the sockets of his eyes the pins taken from their loosened gowns until he streams with blood. The image is unmistakably sexual—that of gang-rape—an event all too familiar to these women and to their counterparts throughout the Athenian empire and points beyond.

At first glance, Hecuba may appear triumphant in all this. She destroys Polymestor utterly, with whatever satisfaction that brings. As in the *Medea,* however, the price of vengeance is ethically prohibitive. She pays with nothing less than her humanity for the pleasures of poetic justice. She and her fellow-women, as well as Polymestor, are utterly bestialized in the end, snarling and snapping at each other like dogs. In fact, lest there be any ambiguity regarding the ethical status of Hecuba, she is told that she will be literally transformed into a wild bitch with blazing eyes and will leap to her death from the mast of Agamemnon's ship before she ever reaches Greece. Thus, although the metaphysical destiny of Medea and of Hecuba stand at polar extremes from each other, they are equivalent in their inhumanity.

The truth which these reflections on the *Medea* and the *Hecuba* have laid bare is summed up by the chorus of the *Electra* [1051], when they point out that "justice can conduct itself shamefully." When we search both the *Medea* and the *Hecuba* for some ethical alternative to poetic justice, for someone who conducts herself without shame, our search inevitably comes to a rest with Polyxena and her sacrifice. Polyxena is, of course, only one of many young, unblemished sacrificial victims in Euripidean drama; but for now we will limit our considerations to her. As with Medea and with Hecuba, we must from the outset be clear regarding Polyxena's situation, her limits. She cannot choose whether to die or not. She knows that she is to have her throat slit this very day over the buried corpse of Achilles. True enough, there is a remote chance, to which her broken mother clings, of winning some reprieve or at least time from Odysseus, if she pleads pitifully with him; but she is aware that the only alternative to her announced sacrifice is a life of slavery, a living death the prospect of which is more dreadful to her than Neoptolemus' blade. Instinctively, and from watching her mother, she knows that suffering, up to a point, brings wisdom and challenges one to virtue, but that beyond a certain point suffering ravages and disfigures not only the body but often the soul as well. More specifically, she knows her own limits, knows that a girl like herself, accustomed to every comfort and unaccustomed to denial and degradation, will not bear with any grace the life of a slave. Her resolve is lucid and unflinching, as she addresses Odysseus with these words, words which we have already considered but which bear repetition here [*Hecuba,* 342–368]:

> Odysseus, I see you standing there at an angle,
>> pulling back your hand into your cloak,
>> fearful of being touched.
> Don't be afraid.
> I am not about to call upon Zeus,
>> hope of the hopeless.
> Nor am I going to beg for my life.
> I have no choice but to die.
> But as it happens, to die is my choice.
> In resisting you, I would only die a shameful death,
>> proving to be one of those who cling to life…
> I was born a princess.
> I was nursed on the highest of hopes,
>> to be a bride for kings,
>> vying for my hand.
> I grew to be the acknowledged mistress
>> of Troy's girls and women,
>> conspicuous in every respect.
> Mortality aside,
>> I was a goddess.

And now I am a slave.
The name alone, so alien in every way,
　　is enough to enamor me of death.
Am I to be an item for sale to coarse and brutal men,
　　I, the sister of Hector,
　　sister to the princes of Troy?
Am I to know only harsh necessity,
　　sweeping some man's floors,
　　kneading his bread,
　　from one weary day to the next?
Am I, the bride of kings,
　　to let some crude slave from god knows where
　　defile me in his filthy bed?
Never!
I will take one last look at freedom
　　and consign myself to hell.

Polyxena, led off to slaughter, maintains the same bravado before the voyeuristic veterans of Troy, drawn up in ranks to watch her sacrifice. As the son of Achilles approaches her with the whetted blade, he motions to his men to seize her, already bound. Polyxena, however, screams at them to stand off and for not one of them to touch her. At her bidding, they cut loose her hands. "I am the daughter of a king," she says, "I am not going down among the dead degraded as some man's slave." [551–552] Polyxena, her hands now free, takes her robe and tears it from her shoulder to below her waist, exposing her soft breasts. She leans back her neck in defiant acquiescence "to make it easy" for her executioner. Torn with pity, and perhaps with unacknowledged desire, Neoptolemus hesitates and then cuts her deep and clean below the chin, as her breath and blood burst from a single slit.

Polyxena is literally defeated; for her young life is effortlessly and irretrievably dispatched. In strength of arm, she is no match for one Greek warrior, much less for the whole Greek army. She does, however, manage to snatch from her literal undoing a human victory, an ethical victory, which, to eyes accustomed as Euripides' were to the darkness of the political realm, may be said to shine. After all, mortals are always literally defeated at the end of the day. The moral genius of mortality is to preserve one's integrity even as one is despoiled of all else, to die with grace even as one is damned.

It is clear that Hecuba and Polyxena represent two distinct, divergent possibilities for women in extremity, women at the mercy and disposal of men: the avenger and the martyr. In dramatic contrast with the avenger, the martyr remains spotless, uncontaminated by the violence she suffers. Witnessing her daughter's uncompromising purity of soul, Hecuba herself is moved. "There is beauty in your words, daughter," she says to Polyxena, "but it is a beauty wracked with pain." [382–383] Even as Hecuba wonders at the loveliness of leaving the world before it soils the soul, she finds that same loveliness lacking. She reveals complication, where Polyxena sees only simplicity; but beyond this Hecuba is not one to say more. Neither, it seems, is Euripides. In the *Hecuba,* he presents two unacceptable alternatives, which return today's reader and Euripides' own audience to the root of the dilemma, the corrupt political order in which women are often made to choose between degraded survival and innocent ruin. Hecuba, for her part, makes her choice; but, looking back at her daughter, Hecuba confesses herself to be nonetheless consoled by the exquisite nobility of the path taken by Polyxena.

At first glance, Iphigeneia, in her tragedy written by Euripides in self-imposed exile from Athens, might appear to be the mirror image of Polyxena. Both Iphigeneia and Polyxena go to their deaths the would-be consorts of Achilles, the one in life and the other in death, the one before the war and the other after. Both supposedly die for the sake of fair winds, whether to waft the Greek armada on its way to Troy or to waft it home. Both take on their deaths freely with the same piquant defiance of brute force. What separates them, however, is the fact that, while Polyxena dies in lucid despair, Iphigeneia dies in the thrall of a glorious delusion.

The truth soon disclosed in the *Iphigeneia at Aulis* is that Agamemnon's ambition has outstripped his abilities. He is no more in control of his army than was Hippolytus in control of his horses. The army has its own reasons for setting out to Troy and they have nothing to do with retrieving Helen nor with restoring Greek pride. The army's lust, its driving compulsion, is for violence and for gold. What is more, Calchas, the war-mongering cleric, has convinced the army that Iphigeneia's death is a divine demand. Hers must be the first blood spilt. Only then can the army slake its own thirst with Troy. The dark truth is that Agamemnon is so enamored of his prerogatives, so enslaved by his fears, that he is willing to kill his own beloved girl rather than compromise his career or confront the truth. And not only does he dispatch his daughter to death; but he sends her off into legend bearing a seductively glistening lie, whose perversity she is too young and too desperate to detect. In other words, he takes advantage not only of her weakness but also of her innocence. He spoils her even as he slays her.

We shed unwarranted light on this darkest of tragedies if we imagine that Agamemnon believes a word of what he tells Iphigeneia regarding why she must die. In utterly lucid bad faith, Agamemnon creates a lie the size of the atrocity he is willing and about to commit. He invents Hellas, Greece, an entity greater than the sum of all of its living daughters and sons; and so it must be if it is to demand and to justify their deaths, as many of them as are needed. He invents too the barbarians, not in their flesh but as a provocative political phantasy, barbarians whose very existence is an affront and a threat, and whose extinction or subjection thus becomes a moral imperative. In short, Agamemnon reinvents, before our eyes, politics. He subverts the simple love of life and of all that sustains it into patriotism, the sentimental love of an ideal, fictive historical entity, in this case Greece, which masks, while pretending to transcend, the shabby self-interest of moral non-entities like Agamemnon and Menelaus and the mob which flatters itself as an army, a national assault-force, marshalled to make Greek beds safe investments again.

What darkens and complicates this tragedy is that Iphigeneia is being murdered by her own father, not by some savage stranger. Neither Agamemnon nor Iphigeneia can confront this truth straight on. They share, instead, a consoling lie. Agamemnon plants its seed in Iphigeneia and she brings it to term. Greece is turning to him and to her and demanding the ultimate sacrifice. Nothing less than the freedom of Greece is at stake. With this lie, Agamemnon anaesthetizes his girl before putting her under the knife. But we should not mistake this act for one of compassion. Anaesthesia can be as much for the surgeon's convenience as for the patient's comfort; and in this instance Agamemnon's prevailing concern is to ease his own passage to Troy, not his daughter's passage to Hades. Her death is something he wants to put behind him with as little awkwardness and delay as possible. Like every sacrificial victim, Iphigeneia must show herself willing. With a handful of grain or a cup of water, cattle were made to nod their heads and goats to shiver in assent to the blade. In the case of a human victim, especially one's own daughter, the stratagem must

be more subtle and perverse. Agamemnon is, of course, prepared to admit none of this. Instead, he cries out in futile
contradiction of the obvious: "I love my children! If I did
not, I would be deranged." [1256] "Woman," Agamemnon
says to Clytemnestra, "it is a strange and dreadful thing
[*deinon*]to be daring to do what I am about to do." [1257]
Given that he regards the alternative to be equally dreadful,
however, he goes ahead and does it anyway.

Clytemnestra reminds Agamemnon that Iphigeneia will not
be the first of her children torn from her arms and slain by his
hand. She was first taken to Agamemnon's bed by force, after
he had murdered her husband Tantalus and shattered her
newborn infant's skull against the hard earth. This bit of
family history serves to put the immediate course of events in
perspective. The present atrocity is not some rare, cosmic eclipse
of an otherwise exceptionless regard for the sacredness of life.
Instead, it is the most recent incident in a recurrent pattern of
atrocities. It is the fruit of war, the first fruit of a new harvest.
Tell me, Clytemnestra taunts her husband [1185–1190]:

> After you've sacrificed your girl,
>> what are your prayers going to sound like?
> What sort of blessing does a child-slaughterer like you ask
> for?
> When you go off leaving a trail of shame,
>> will you not come home reeking?
> And how is it any more fitting for me
>> to beg the gods to bless you?
> Wouldn't we as much as call the gods idiots,
>> if we were to ask blessings,
>> for those who murder our children?

What Agamemnon receives from Clytemnestra is no blessing
but a threat. She will be waiting for him.

Meanwhile, Iphigeneia, her frenzied fear of death now
sublimated into her new-found sense of mission, explains to
her mother that "It is wrong for me to love life too much. You
bore me, not only for yourself but as the common property
of all of Greece." [1385–1386] She regards herself now no
longer pitiable but privileged. She is to be the bride of Greece;
the bright events of Troy will be her progeny. The irony lost on
her is that she, a corpse, will breed only other corpses, Polyxena
among them. The bright events of Troy will be no brighter
than the one about to occur. All the same, Iphigeneia is

committed now to playing out to its perverse consummation the charade of a marriage with which this tragedy began. She insists that there be no mourning, no funeral mound, no laments. "Shout the paean," [1467–1468] she cries out to her attendants, only highlighting the dark ambiguity of the moment; for paeans were sung not only before wedding banquets but also before battles.

The poetic and ritual parallels between sacrifice and marriage embedded in this play are too many and too rich in implication to trace fully here. In outline, however, they are unmistakable. The original lie which lured Iphigeneia to Aulis took the form of a summons to marriage; and the final lie which lures Iphigeneia to her death takes a similar form. Such a ploy is uniquely suited to possess the imagination of an adolescent princess. Between Iphigeneia and her wedding, however, there stands a ritual requirement, the *proteleia,* the preliminary sacrifice. Agamemnon and Clytemnestra and Iphigeneia share the same impatience to put the *proteleia* behind them and to get on with the main event. The main event is, however, a war not a wedding. Iphigeneia will not soon lie under her husband and spill her first blood in the act of love. Instead, in an act more hideous than incest, she will lie under her own father and spill her first blood as he plunges his blade into her virgin heart. She will die "like a spotless young animal." [1083] Instead of a love-cry, there will be only the scream of death.

For many critics, the radical conversion of Iphigeneia to her fate is too sudden and too complete to be believed. While it may be admitted that events, inward or outward, seldom take as long on a Greek stage as they do in everyday experience, we must appreciate that Iphigeneia has very little time at her disposal. As for the seamlessness of her resolve, what less would sustain her now? Besides, it only has to last another hour. If we are surprised to find no single crack in her new-found faith, we need only to recall that the truth masked by it is so hideous that, like the face of Medusa, one glimpse of it would turn Iphigeneia to stone. Like Perseus, the most that she can bear is a reflection of the monster only a blade's length away, however distorted that image may be; and there is no one who can begrudge her that. If her words sound hollow, it is because they most surely are. They are the words of speeches, sheer propaganda, designed to put down the soul like an animal that has outlived its purpose.

The *Iphigeneia at Aulis* is Euripides' last word on war, the politics which provoke it, and the victims who endure it. Surely we do not learn from this play, but are nevertheless reminded by it, that no war, not even the Trojan War, and much less the Peloponnesian War, would ever or long be fought without seducing the young to its awful momentum. Young, beautiful bodies and souls must be given some compelling reason for dying or for killing; and those whose purposes are served by war know well that the truth will not do. It is cursedly the case that the inexperience, idealism, passion, and naivete of youth conspire to make them prey to the speeches of their elders. The timeless scandal is that the latter, like Agamemnon, cynically aware of the power of their words and their effect, believe not a single word they say. "A smooth tongue," indeed, "is a mischievous and malignant thing." [333]

Set ineffectually against the practitioners and apologists of violence are those who most often endure it, women first among them. The mark of womanhood in ancient Greece was motherhood and "motherhood is a strange, powerful thing [*deinon*], a great love-charm, giving this much in common to all women: there is nothing they will not do or endure for their children." [917–918] Women's biological destiny is to give life; and it may be that they find it that much more difficult to squander it. It may be too that their traditionally assigned place of weakness in the political order gives them a peculiarly privileged vantage point on the madness of male militarism. There seems to be little question in Euripidean drama that power corrupts and that absolute power corrupts absolutely. Thus women, by dint of their very weakness, are likely to be more humanly intact. Yet, as we have seen, weakness pushed to the brink, suffering beyond the point of endurance, can be every bit as corrupting as power. No wonder, then, that Euripides often turns to women not yet dispossessed of their instincts to speak the simplest, most telling truths. "To look upon the light of day," says Iphigeneia before she succumbs to fear and to her father's spell [1250–1252],

> is for all human beings the sweetest of joys.
> In the dark world below, there is nothing.
> To pray for death is sheer madness.
> To be alive, in whatever lowly condition,
>   is better than to die a glorious death.

Of course, Iphigeneia herself soon betrays her own words; but their truth stands and reveals itself to those under less immediate duress than she.

These straight, simple words and others like them in the Euripidean corpus call into radical question the traditional heroic code rooted in *philotimia,* the questing desire to be always more than the others, to increase as they decrease. To enter the *agon,* the contest, one must step into the ring of death, willing to despoil or to be despoiled, to kill or to die. Outside that ring there is no glory, only life. Inside that ring, however, if Euripides' voice has any validity and resonance left at all, is only madness. It is a ring of fools.

> Ten thousand men dream ten thousand different dreams.
> Some of them come true and end in bliss.
> Nothing at all comes of the rest.
> What I call blessed is the life lived in simple happiness,
>   day by day. [*Bacchae,* 907–909]

The life exorcised of *philotimia,* or never first infected by it, is best. For one thing, such a life is harmless. Larger-than-life dreams are, in themselves, life-threatening. To avoid all suffering—either the inflicting of it or the enduring of it—is admittedly a dream larger or better than life, an ideal rarely if ever to be achieved; but the pursuit of it will, at worst, do no harm. "No more is to be hoped for by anyone in any life," says Hecuba, "than to elude ruin, one day at a time." [*Hecuba,* 627–628]

It is a simple doctrine, if it may be called that, which comes through in these and countless other moments in Euripidean drama. Here is a code of heroism scaled to the human, accommodated to the darkness of the political order. In succinct formulation, the Euripidean hero is the survivor. Archaic heroism, by contrast, excluded from the outset all those who clung to life. Survival was worthy of women and cowards. In the new heroism of Euripides, however, survival is the essential human virtue; and at the core of this survival is the blind and uncompromising affirmation of life, the affirmation pulsing in nature, in *hygra phusis,* the affirmation annually enacted in the resurrection of the world from the dark death of winter and celebrated in the rites of Dionysus and Demeter, the affirmation mortally imitated and shared in the act of childbirth. Nowhere in Euripidean drama is this blind, wild, and wondrous bond between mother and child, with all of its cosmic resonances, more lyrically recited than in the *Helen* [1319–1352], wherein the chorus sing of the delirium of the Great Mother when her child is abducted into the darkness below the earth:

> The sorrowing mother searched far and wide
> For any clue to her daughter's rape,
> A crime accomplished with effortless guile.
> But at last she called an end to her toil,
> Whose only fruit was frenzy and exhaustion.
> Then to the snow-white crest of Ida she climbed,
> Wherein mountain nymphs keep constant watch.
> There the mother broken with grief
> Cast herself down among the rocky thickets
>   blanketed in snow.
> So she brought blight upon the barren earth,
> Making the snow sterile, unyielding of any fruit.
> Total was the ruin she brought to the race of men.
> For the sheep and the cattle she provided nothing,
> No fresh, leafy fodder, no curling green tendrils.
> Cities lost their means of life.
> The gods went without their offerings.
> The altar flames went out.
> And with a mother's endless grief,
> Bitter for her daughter lost and gone,
> She sealed shut the earth's springs.
> The glistening streams went dry.
>
> When the raving mother brought to a halt
> Even the festivals shared by gods and men,
> It was Zeus who gave the kind command
> To calm the woman's hellish rage.
> "Go, sacred graces, Muses too, go to Deio,
> Crazed for the girl that is gone.
> With wild cries pierce her dark resolve.
> With dance and sweet song soften her heart's pain."
> First to respond was Aphrodite,
> Loveliest of all the blessed ones,
> Who took in her hand the skin-taut tambourine,
> Rimmed with brazen castanets.
> And soon her clamor reached the depths of hell,
> Where a smile broke across the goddess-mother's face,
> As she took up the blaring flute,
> And in the wildness of it all,
> Rediscovered joy.

If we forget, as we do and must, that this is a myth about gods, it tells a familiar tale of the frenzied love of mother for child, the desolation of irretrievable loss, and the miraculous rebirth of the human spirit insatiate with life. The pure, unqualified affirmation of life, emerging as it often does from beneath the heaviest burdens and within the darkest griefs, comprises the core of human courage and grandeur.

Concerning the altogether uncanonical heroism of survival exhibited in Euripidean drama, certain possible misconceptions require to be addressed. Firstly, by "survival" is meant more than the mere sustenance of life-signs. The only survival worthy of a Euripidean hero is human survival, the integral survival of soul as well as body. To save one's skin, as it were, while abandoning one's integrity, is not something admired in Euripidean drama. It would be difficult to argue, for instance, that the characters of Electra, Orestes, and Pylades, as they are drawn in the *Orestes,* are respected, much less celebrated, by the playwright. Although, or perhaps because, they will stop at nothing to preserve their lives, they are portrayed as nothing less than psychopathic terrorists. The fact that Apollo distributes rewards to these three at the close of the play is damning, not redeeming. What Apollo furnishes is an Olympian "political" solution, whose ludicrous contradiction of common sense and of common decency is nowhere more evident than in his proclamation that Orestes is to marry the same girl against whose throat he is at that very moment pressing his blade. Apollo's solution is virtually transparent to the numerous treaties already negotiated by "Olympian" Athens with an unswerving eye to its own survival and self-interest and blind to all else. It may even anticipate the inevitable terms which Athens would soon be forced to negotiate with Sparta; for the allusions to Athens in the *Orestes* are woven of the sheerest fabric. "There is not much to be done with a fallen house," [70] laments Electra, summing up her woes in the prologue. Like the house of Agamemnon, Athens in 408 was imminently threatened from without and rotting from within, leaving everyday doubts whether it would first be torn down or cave in. Orestes, Electra, Orestes, Pylades, and Athens were all indisputably "survivors"; but we find little pity or esteem displayed in the *Orestes* for their brand of survival.

Secondly, if survival is to be appropriately human, it must be not only integral but communal. The Euripidean ethic of survival is not a code of selfishness, preoccupied with personal longevity and purity. Euripidean survival is inseparable from solidarity; and nowhere do we find this solidarity more frequently and fully displayed than among women. Euripidean drama is rife with references to the actual and active fellowship of women. In the *Helen* [329], for instance, the chorus, endeavoring to convince Helen that she is not alone but companioned in her trials, explains that "it is only right for one woman to bear another's burdens." Similarly, in the *Iphigeneia in Tauris* [1061], Iphigeneia invokes the natural consortium of women, prefacing her appeal for loyalty with the following words: "We are all women and the good-will we bear each other runs in our blood."

Women's communal affirmation of life, however, is not restricted, in principle, to the *genos* or race of women but extends appropriately to the race of mortals, as well. If Euripidean women are, in practice, somewhat exclusive in their political concerns, it is because they are so often herded into tents as slaves or confined to their quarters as wives. It is they who are excluded from public affairs; and it would be one more undeserved affront to make them answer for their separateness. Indeed, it is not surprising that we possess few historical or literary accounts of women's engagement in the wider community, beyond the community of women and of their children. One such account, however, may be found in the *Phoenician Women*, wherein it is the women, young and old, Greek and barbarian, royalty and slaves, who display enlightened and unselfish concern for the common good, while their male counterparts would gladly destroy the city and each other before relinquishing their petty quarrels and private ambitions.

Once again, in the *Phoenician Women*, an ancient myth is held by Euripides at such an angle as to mirror events of his own city and of his own time. Thebes seems only a mask worn by Athens in this play. The chorus' description of Thebes—"a city wrapped in a dense cloud of spears, the air ablaze with the specter of an impending battle and its carnage" [250–252]— might as well describe Athens in any of the years from 411 to 408, when this play was likely written and performed. Athens too, like Thebes in the drama, was in tatters by this time, worn thin by war and shredded by factionalism. Both stood on the brink of doom. Within this apocalyptic context, the strong, public, challenging voice of Jocasta is particularly engaging. She is a rare Greek woman, on active duty in the front ranks of political negotiation, denouncing squarely every warring faction, and pleading with fierce will and wit the cause of equality and peace; and all this while her husband, blind and despairing, lies behind bolted doors. We may wonder whether Jocasta's royalty, her near-widow status, and perhaps her arrival at menopause suffice to account for her freedom to engage in public affairs. We might indeed speculate that in the figure of Jocasta we are permitted a glimpse of a phenomenon occuring in Athens in the late fifth century. As the Peloponnesian War dragged on, year by year thinning out the able male population of Athens, and particularly after the staggering loss of Athenian lives in Sicily, the ratio of mature women to men must have been decisively altered, leaving women not only with numerical superiority, but with correspondingly expanded freedoms and even responsibilities. Such has been the rule during other, even less protracted wars in history, such as the two global wars of this century; and such, we might surmise, was the case in Athens. Confronted with history's nearly unbroken silence on this matter, we cannot say more with any confidence.

Euripides, of course, could not rewrite the history of Athens, any more than Jocasta could turn back the torrent of events in Thebes. She was ineffectual; and her counterparts in Athens, if indeed she had any, were not only ineffectual but fell from whatever slight influence they may have held without a trace. What remains significant, however, is that in retelling a story as transparently allegorical as this one was for the citizens of Athens, Euripides raised Jocasta from traditional political irrelevance and not only assigned to her a central public role but also gave to her a voice that was lucid, articulate, and visionary. Clearly she is the only person in Thebes, as re-enacted in the *Phoenician Women,* who emerges as a possible savior of the city. As potential rulers of Thebes, Eteocles, Polyneices, and Creon—in other words, all of the viable male candidates—are blind in one way or the other to the common good and disinclined to its pursuit. If the citizens of Athens were left with a similar response to the *Phoenician Women* and it their imaginations leapt to their own city under siege, bled nearly white, and still hemorrhaging from within, did the words of contemporary women, known to them but lost to us, come to mind, words like those of Jocasta, pleading for an end to savagery and for an embracing of peace, simplicity of life, and equality? Perhaps they were as blind as the sons of Oedipus, in which case the chorus' words were likely addressed to them: "the city, if it could chance upon it senses, would weep." [1344]

The specter of *gynecocracy*, women's power or women's rule, was clearly, if we consult a wide range of traditional and fifth-century sources, an object of profound suspicion and fear. Together with rampant promiscuity and bizarre mating practices, permissiveness towards women, much less submission to them, came to be associated with barbarians, and to some lesser extent with Spartans. The prospect of power's coming into the hands of women through peaceful and proper means was all but unimaginable. In the Athenian male imagination, women, if they were ever to come to power, would do so in the same manner as would slaves, through their seizing power suddenly and violently, slaughtering their husbands or their masters indiscriminately. Even the influence of women was something pronouncedly suspect and to be avoided. Women, in sum, like barbarians and slaves, were thought to be intellectually inferior, unruly, devious, sexually uninhibited, potentially dangerous, and representative, over all, of a lower form of life. Although Euripides occasionally employed these stereotypes for reasons of his own, he also boldly contradicted them in too many instances to catalogue here, displaying at least their irrelevance to, and often their reversal of, the truth. One example might suffice.

In the *Trojan Women*, Andromache describes how she, or any captive woman, evokes the instant hate of her new master and mate, if she loyally lingers at all in memories of her slaughtered spouse. Instead, she is expected to spread wide not only her legs but even her heart to this savage stranger; and, accompanying such abuse, there is expressed the following theory about women and sex, to which Andromache makes her own seething response [665–672]:

> What they say is
> > that all any man has to do
> > to make a woman lose her aversion for his bed
> > is to show her a good time for one night.
> I would spit from my sight
> > that woman who would throw off the man
> > whose bed she used to share,
> > and resume the ways of love with another.

> Even a young filly, torn from her running-mate,
> balks at being yoked with another.
> Yet it is a dumb brute beast,
> born without wits
> and without a glimmer of our nature.

In this light, it is not women who are found to display a lower life-form, evidenced in savage sexuality.

Fear, hate, and violence go hand in hand; and women in Athens were the privileged object of all three. In the prism of Euripidean drama, however, all three are refracted back upon their source. Nowhere is this fact more manifest than in Euripides' treatment of the figure of Helen, surely the most hated of all Greek women: Helen the whore, Helen the ruin of cities. However relatively benign Homer's treatment of Helen had been, her name had made the rounds by the fifth century. Indeed, she emerged as the sum of all that is both irresistibly alluring and deservedly despised in women, the virtual embodiment of Hesiod's *kalon kakon*.

An adequate tracing of the image of Helen in fifth-century tragedy, or even in the Euripidean corpus, would require extensive citing and analysis of sources. A more brief and bold sketch, however, is called for to conclude this section on women; and I trust that the following few comments would hold up under closer, more inclusive scrutiny. Setting aside the *Helen* for a moment, essentially two possible accounts of Helen's misadventure to Troy are circulated in Euripides' plays. She may have gone to Troy quite willingly, in the thrall of a freshly excited lust; or she may have been torn violently from her home and her husband and made a captive lover in Troy. In weighing these two versions and ferreting out the more likely truth of the matter, at least as Euripides saw it, the *Trojan Women* would appear to be a privileged source; for therein the trial of Helen is effectively enacted, and the principal surviving witnesses made to take the stand. The testimony of Cassandra, given her powers, is enough to convict; but Helen damns herself by admitting that she ran away on her own feet—yet, she claims, as a slave, not to Paris but to Aphrodite, the Irresistible. Helen rests her case on what she imagines to be theological bedrock; but in the Euripidean theatre her rock softens to sand. What Hecuba says is what everyone here knows: "Aphrodite is merely a name for mortal lust." [989] And with this said, Helen has no case left. The Euripidean verdict is evident. Helen left Menelaos freely; for she loved Paris more.

Helen is accused of a good deal more, however, than adultery. At her door are laid all of the agonies of Troy, every corpse and every maimed life, Trojan or Greek, left in the wake of a ten-year war; and, strangely enough, it is Hecuba who unwittingly speaks in defense of Helen with respect to this latter, more grievous and sweeping charge. No one here hates Helen more than does Hecuba; and no one is more uncompromising in her demands that Helen must be made to suffer all that she has coming to her. Nonetheless, it is Hecuba, who, after cataloguing her disasters—those endured already and those yet to be endured—points out a curious fact. "And all this," she says, "what has been and what will be, happened because of one woman's love affair." [498–499]

What Hecuba notices is that all Helen actually did was to take a lover. She fell in love. She did not wage a war. The war was not her idea or her doing. The war was not the effect of what Helen did but rather Menelaus' and Agamemnon's response to what Helen did. Just as she chose love freely, they chose war freely; and, in doing so, they revealed their characters, characters utterly exposed in others of Euripides' plays. The simple fact is that Helen and Paris represented another path from the one worn by the Greek warlords. After all, Paris had been offered both lordship and conquest, either one of which would have pinned Agamemnon and Menelaus under his heel; but he chose beauty and love instead. Helen and Paris both preferred love to all else and thus preferred each other to anyone else. The war and all its carnage and rubble was someone else's preference, someone else's choice.

Why, then, war? Euripides' most concise answer to this comes in the *Helen*. His answer is: for nothing, always for nothing. In this same play he exonerates Helen utterly. Drawing upon a variant tradition regarding her, he explains that she never went to Troy at all. Not only is she innocent of causing the war; but she is innocent even of adultery. The Greek armies pursued and fought over a phantasy, a puff of air, nothing more. Euripides, writing this play as the first survivors staggered home from Sicily with stories of a defeat beyond belief, must have decided that it was time for the truth to come home to roost.

Helen was the consummate Greek woman; and Euripides leaves her utterly untarnished. In the last speech of the *Helen* [1686–1687], Theoclymenus, the failed Egyptian Paris, to whose unrelenting advances the faithful Helen never once succumbed, has this to say about the once most hated of women:

> In the name of Helen, the noblest of spirits,
>> and for that reason an exceptional woman,
>> I bless you all.

In the *Helen,* Euripides returns Helen to Argos to clear her own name; and, with the same play, he returns women to Athens with the same prospect in sight. Women, no matter what Hesiod wrote and Greek men believed, are not the cause of the world's woes. We need look elsewhere. These words from the *Melanippe* [fr.499.1–3] likely overstate Euripides' own estimation of women; but they are miles closer to the truth than the charge of misogyny lodged against him all these years. Anyway, if justice, while in process, is a matter of balance, the citing of them might serve its cause.

> The censure and abuse women suffer
>> from the tongues of men
>> are sheer madness.
> They are bending an empty bow.
> The truth is that women are better than men,
>> a truth I will disclose.

Finally, we must note that, in saying that women are better than men, the word chosen by Euripides for "man" is not *aner* whose opposite is *gune,* man as opposed to woman or husband as opposed to wife, but rather is *arsen* whose opposite is *thelus,* muscular, aggressive man as opposed to tender, nourishing woman. What this fact may suggest is that women are not being categorically compared and preferred to men, but rather that women's characteristic way of being in the world, of inhabiting their humanity, which is presumably available to men for imitation, is what outshines and shames the ethically homuncular machismo characteristic of men.

SLAVES AND BARBARIANS

This discussion of the political order has so far been focused on women precisely because women dominate the Euripidean corpus. If we consider only Euripides' seventeen extent dramas, we find that eight of these bear the names of women, while twelve may be said to be primarily about women; and fourteen have choruses composed of women. Apart from these statistical indications of the thematic prominence of women in Euripidean drama, it may be argued that the condition of women as explored in Euripides' plays epitomizes the corruption of the political order as he understood it. In contrast with his evident preoccupation with women and their issues, Euripides makes only occasional mention of slaves and barbarians. Consequently, the following comments will constitute little more than a series of footnotes to our discussion of women.

The issues of slavery and racism are all but inseparable from those of sexism. In all three, violence and oppression are rooted in prejudice. Women, slaves, and barbarians are defined by *nomos*—law and custom—as "other" than, and correspondingly unequal to, free, male, Athenian citizens; and, since, within the city, citizenship is functionally equivalent with humanity, otherness is functionally equivalent with inhumanity. Women, slaves, and barbarians are all three races apart and thus the object of systematic misunderstanding and institutional violence. We may speculate why Euripides chose to highlight the misunderstanding and violence endured by women. Not only by virtue of their numbers, but even more by virtue of their inevitable proximity to men—as their mothers, sisters, daughters, wives, and lovers—women were unavoidable. This proximity may have made it all the more difficult for men, including Euripides, to insulate themselves from the feelings and views of women and to exclude them from the human circle. The otherness of barbarians and slaves was likely easier, conceptually and emotionally, to maintain.

The issues of women, slaves, and barbarians are inseparable, as well, because these three categories overlap regularly on the Athenian stage, as they did in Athenian homes and streets. Most slaves were either women or barbarians or both. Even Athenian wives bore their own resemblances to slaves. Whether taken in war or taken in marriage, women were always vulnerable to a form of slavery. Curiously and tellingly, brides as well as newly acquired slaves, were welcomed into their new homes with the *katachysmata,* the ritual pouring of nuts down upon their heads. Both wives and slaves were regarded as property; and whatever marginal status they possessed under the law was derived from that fact. Wives and slaves were not only at the service of their husbands and masters but also at their disposal sexually. The lot of slaves, however, was undeniably heavier and darker than that of Athenian wives, particularly those slaves consigned to the mines and quarries, for which hell is a euphemism. Whatever reputation fifth-century Athenians may enjoy to this day for having been gentle masters, the evidence to the contrary, such as the common practice of torturing slaves publicly in the state-operated interrogation center, remains, as it always has been, damning. Slavery is not a gentle institution, however administered; and there is little to suggest that the Athenians administered it mildly.

So far from appearing an unnatural atrocity, slavery seems to have been regarded by Athenians in the fifth century as an integral element of advanced civilization, at least so long as slavery was limited to barbarians. A great many Greeks seem to have had qualms about enslaving other Greeks, which is to say that slaveholding was mostly justified in Athens as it was in America by the presumption of racial superiority. Theories to this effect were expounded, for instance, in the fifth-century Hippocratic treatise, *Air, Waters, Places,* and later, in the fourth century, by Aristotle. The above Hippocratic treatise traces the peculiar convergence of intelligence and courage characteristic of Greeks to their geographical location and its accompanying climatic influences. In the *Politics,* clearly drawing upon this and other sources, Aristotle restates the case for Greek racial superiority and points out that, provided they achieve political unity, the race of Greeks constitutes a natural master race. This claim, however, must have been a byword already in the fifth-century, as well; for we find it shamelessly proclaimed by the hapless Iphigeneia, at Aulis. "It seems like common sense, mother," she says to Clytemnestra, "that Greeks should rule over barbarians, and not barbarians over Greeks." [1400–1401] In this too, however, she is deluded by her father, a delusion we cannot imagine to have been shared by Euripides when we consider the very next line spoken by Iphigeneia in defense of the claim for the seemingly natural rule of Greeks over barbarians:

"For they are slaves and we are free." [1401] The patent ludicrousness of Iphigeneia's perception that she and her mother, and for that matter her father, are free, makes this one of Euripides' most bitterly ironic lines, an irony which surely reflects back one line upon what seems to Iphigeneia and, presumably, to "Greece" to be common sense.

In the *Politics,* Aristotle makes a general reference to those who argue that slavery is contrary to nature and is a construct of law or convention. From this reference it is clear that the case against slavery was well known by the last third of the fourth century, although the only direct statement of this case prior to Aristotle comes, compliments of a scholiast to the *Rhetoric* [1273b], from Gorgias' pupil, Alcidamas, who claimed that "God has set all men free. Nature has made no one a slave." Similarly, regarding the natural equality of all races, the fourth-century liberal, Antiphon, argued that in all things nature has constituted Greek and barbarian alike. In all the essentials of humanity, Greek and barbarian, he claimed, are identically endowed.

In the fifth century, however, Euripides comes the closest of anyone to arguing for the essential equality of all human beings, men and women, masters and slaves, Greeks and barbarians. Both because as a playwright he necessarily speaks with many voices and because he chose to speak more obliquely than later prose-writing liberals, it is not possible to point to or even to reconstruct a straightforward, Euripidean refutation of racism and slavery. Indeed, it is possible to catalogue a rather loathsome list of statements by Euripidean characters who have little good to say of slaves and nothing bad to say of slavery. One such statement comes from the *Alexandros* [fr.49]: "So worthless is the race of slaves! All belly, they never look beyond (their next meal)." In such instances, however, if we look to the immediate sources of such comments, to the characters who utter them, we find that they are mostly unsympathetic, even contemptible. Once again, as in the case of misogyny, we must note not only what is spoken, but by whom, in what context, and, most elusive of all, in what likely tone it is spoken. In short, we must confront the fact once again that Euripides wrote plays and not essays.

We have already indicated within Euripides' plays various speeches expressing the general disavowal of any natural distinctions between human beings, which implies a disavowal of the essential superiority or inferiority of any sub-category of human beings such as men, women, nobility, peasants, bastards, slaves, Greeks, and barbarians. We have also seen how, at the same time, the very structure of Euripidean drama is transparent to a spectrum of power and weakness descriptive of the oppression inflicted by some human beings on others. In other words, however untruthful it may be to the essential equality of all human beings and to the harmony which ought to proceed from that equality, it is nonetheless a truth, in the sense of a political fact, that divisions, however unnatural, are asserted and enforced by certain human individuals and groups over against other human individuals and groups. Finally, the dramatic acknowledgement of both truths—the metaphysical truth of human equality and the political fact of inequality—necessarily creates an ambiguity in the voice of Euripides, which requires interpretations whose legitimacy cannot be proven.

With respect to Euripides' own specific questions and commitments regarding slavery and racism, I would only hint here at such an interpretation. Neither the sources within Euripides' plays nor the space remaining within this chapter give warrant to anything beyond a few brief concluding remarks here. First, with respect to slavery, Euripides frequently dissolves the concept, pointing out that even the most privileged and powerful men, standing at what seem to be the furthest human remove from slavery, men such as Agamemnon in the *Hecuba* and in the *Iphigeneia at Aulis*, are best described as slaves. Thus, in the *Hecuba* [864–869], when Agamemnon explains to Hecuba the constraints upon him, she concludes:

> Then there is no such thing as a free mortal.
> All are slaves of money or of fate.
> Whether for fear of standing out against the crowd,
>> or of breaking the city's laws,
>> each one is bent into compliance,
>> against all his better instincts.
> I see your terror,
>> how you defer to the mob;
>> so allow me to set you free from your fear.

Hecuba, a woman and a slave, in an ironic reversal of roles, proposes to calm the fears of the king of kings; and, as if to confirm the truth of this reversal, the same Agamemnon, in the opening episode of the *Iphigeneia at Aulis*, is found envying his own servant-slave. Euripides further dissolves the concept of slavery by frequently giving noble natures to his slaves and base natures to his nobles. Under such a critique, slavery is denied any basis whatsoever in racial superiority or indeed in any superiority other than that of power. Repeatedly, Euripidean characters assert with their words and confirm with their actions that slavery resides solely in the name, the designation, of slave, assigned arbitrarily and kept in place by blind force. "The shame borne by slaves," we hear in the *Ion* [854–856], "resides solely in their name. In every other way, slaves, provided they lead decent lives, are the equals of the free."

The same arguments may be and are made on behalf of barbarians. Although Euripides not only presents anti-barbarian prejudice in action but may also be himself accused of presenting what may be called "stage-barbarian" characters, such as Theoclymenus in the *Helen*, Thoas in the *Iphigeneia in Tauris*, and the Phrygian slave in the *Orestes*, the overall effect of his treatment of barbarians is to dissolve the category of barbarian in much the same fashion as he did that of slave. Greeks regularly prove themselves more barbarous than non-Greeks, who in turn prove themselves on occasion quite endearing and benign. Theoclymenus and Thoas, to cite two notable barbarians, for all their fuming witlessness, are finally less savage than their Greek counterparts. Their childish superstitions and incapacity for cunning leave them at the mercy of Greeks to whom deception and calculation are second nature. In short, behind the buffoonery of these and certain other Euripidean barbarians, we may discern a disarming innocence and simplicity long lost by more cynical, sophisticated Greeks. Barbarians, like slaves and women, are quite commonly the victims of Greek violence, a violence strategically justified by their racial and moral inferiority. "That's barbarians for you," rants Hermione, who has no recognizable virtues of her own to flaunt, "they're all the same—father and daughter, mother and son, brother and sister, all doing it with each other, murdering their way out of family quarrels—law means nothing to them." [*Andromache*, 173–176] Speaking as one barbarian who suffers immeasurably from the violence unleashed and rationalized by Greek prejudice, Andromache, in the *Trojan Women* [764], minces no words: "You Greeks invented barbarian perversions."

The archetypal barbarians in Euripidean drama are, it would seem, the Trojans, just as the Trojan War is the archetypal war. It is instructive in this light to reflect upon Cassandra's assessment of Greek and Trojan losses in that war. In sum, the Greeks lost not only their lives but their souls. In her eyes, which see all, Troy, though in ashes, is blessed beside Greece; for, while the Greeks won shame, "the glory won by the Trojans shines brightest of all; for they died defending their homeland." [*Trojan Women*, 386–387] As for the cleverness of the Greeks, which accomplished for them their victory and which remains in daily use by them to defend their ongoing atrocities, it is only a satin veneer over their barbarism.

Women, slaves, barbarians—all those designated as a race apart, so as to be marked for oppression or slaughter—are disclosed in their common humanity, even as the inhumanity of their masters and executioners is revealed. The lesson learned late and hard by Admetus—that every human life is equally precious and that the seemingly superior scale of his life and his concerns is a function of his proximity to them—simply pervades Euripidean drama. It comes down to this, as the frenzied Phrygian slave in the *Orestes* [1523] so simply states it: "Everyone likes to live... slaves too!" The same slave, an unlikely seer by any usual measure, points to the foundational truth for the political order, as it ought to be, when he says that: "Everywhere, anyone who knows anything at all, knows that living is sweeter than dying." [1509] A truism to be sure; but like many truisms it contains a profound truth, neglected not because it is obvious but because its demands would change the world.

CONCLUSION
◇◇◇◇◇◇

Whether noticeably or not, I have endeavored to maintain a certain critical distance from Euripides and his work in the course of this discussion. Critical distance is not, however, the same thing as detachment, for which I have admittedly little capacity or patience. Seeing, hearing, and thinking—the most straightforward ways of approaching Euripides—are inevitably modes of engagement; and whatever insight occurs is the fruit not the foe of engagement. Doubtlessly, one human being may approach another as an object of study, as one might approach a rock in geology or a wasp in entomology or a star in astronomy; but I question the appropriateness and the fruitfulness of approaching an author in such a manner. Authors write because they have something to say; and we waste their time and ours if we are not as concerned as they that communication should occur. I am neither so uninformed nor psychic as to claim that the complexities of communication across centuries and between cultures are easily or ever fully resolved; but my instincts tell me that to forsake the heart of Euripidean drama to analyze its husk is more fittingly seen as stalling than as scholarship.

Admittedly, there is more doubt and dispute over the existence and location of a heart in a dramatic corpus than in a human corpus. Nonetheless, once the search begins, its pulse may be felt even in its extremities and the heart traced from there. First, however, we must be convinced of the fact of life. Some translations, critical studies, and theatrical productions of Euripidean drama regrettably fail to evince that fact. They display Euripides' work as if it were a fossil left long ago by something once alive rather than as something still alive and as capable as ever of leaving its mark. Digging up Euripidean drama, whether on a stage or in one's study, is not to be compared with unearthing a fossil; instead, it is more like digging inadvertently into a buried electrical cable. Once we strike it, we are convinced of its power; for, assuming we are grounded, we conduct it.

What is discovered in that moment of truth, when nothing any longer insulates us from the power of Euripidean theatre, is that Euripides—like Aeschylus and Sophocles, and perhaps like all great art—brings us back not to some remote site in times and places past but back to a center and a source always only an insight away. So much that calls itself theatre today derives whatever force it has from its own devices and resembles an internally combustible contraption able to turn a few tin wheels for our amusement and distraction. It was the genius and the courage of the Greeks, by contrast, to go out with a key and a kite, as it were, and to conduct storms.

Euripides, even more than Aeschylus and Sophocles, I believe, speaks with peculiar directness and immediacy to us today. His times were singularly darkened and confused, as ours are. The flight of the gods, the destruction of the earth, and the standardization of man—the marks of our times, in Heidegger's formulation—might as well have described Athens and the Greek world in the late fifth century. The ancient characterization of Euripides, however, as a playwright who wrote about people as they are and not as they ought to be, could not in the end be less accurate. True enough, Euripides cast a mercilessly revealing light upon human cruelty and banality; but he also left us with heroes and with a vision of how we ought to live. If his heroes seem not to be such and if his vision seems to cast no appreciable light, it may be that our eyes are not yet accommodated to the darkness of our times, as Euripides' were to the darkness of his. In fact, his heroes have little in common with the archaic daimons of an earlier age or with the Christian saints of a later age. The heroes of Greek legend and literature, like the saints of Christendom, transcend death and thus are frequently ambiguous or compromised in their commitment to life. Euripides' lowbrow heroes are more lucid and limited. The earth is their only utopia. They find themselves inspired by the vision of a future, without any ambition to envision or to construct the future. They live closer to nature than to history, history being the realm of delusion and violence. Like the Phrygian slave in the *Orestes,* they find the taste of life sweetest of all and assume that others do as well. Their heroism consists in living out the implications of that assumption. It is enough if they do nothing to add to the suffering in the world. And, if this does not suffice for heroism, then so much the worse for heroism.

It is surely a sign of their confusion and perhaps their weakness that Euripides' characters change their minds as often as they do, an activity unfitting and unfamiliar to the heroes of an age more sure of itself; but it is also a sign of their thoughtfulness. Second thoughts, after all, can be redeeming as well as damning; and certainty is as dangerous as it is re-assuring. Scruples, self- examination, and doubt may not make one singularly effectual; but at the very least they render one more or less harmless. Those who are unsure of themselves make less likely executioners or martyrs; and a world without both would be not perfect but would be an improvement.

Euripidean drama is not devoid of certainties and truths, however. There is the certainty of death and the sweetness of life. There is the beauty of human solidarity and the ugliness of its violation. There is right and there is wrong, however unclear one may be at any given moment regarding the face of each. This unclarity, after all, yields to clarity now and then. "Shameful is shameful everywhere." [*Andromache*, 144] Racism, slavery, sexism, inequality, the violence which they breed and the violence which sustains them, as well as civil wars and wars of aggression—there is little doubt that Euripides found all of these to be shameful wherever and whenever they exist, now as much as then.

Finally, there is friendship, the bond of love, the bond between all mortals of good will. This is a friendship rooted in common suffering and committed not to proliferate it, yet nonetheless resiliently capable of forgiveness when we do. Both in his plays and in the following fragment [902] ascribed to him, Euripides seeks and offers just such friendship:

> The good and decent man,
>   even if he lives in some distant place,
>   and even though I never set eyes on him,
>   I count as a friend.

H E K A B E

PREFACE
⟨⟩⟨⟩⟨⟩⟨⟩⟨⟩

The dark turbulence and elusive complexity of ancient Greek literature are often bartered at a loss for something more simple and edifying. Translucent truisms emerge and speak for all that was Greek wisdom, truisms which fail to tell the whole truth: "It is better to suffer evil than to inflict it." "Nothing in excess." "Wisdom comes with suffering." Like ancient temples and statues, stripped of their once lurid paint and bleached by Christian commentary, the texts of the past offer limited yet luminous inspiration. To anyone still able and inclined to listen to the sublime, they speak with oracular authority. To everyone else, they speak past the point.

In 1968, campaigning in Indiana, Robert Kennedy was poised to address a massive crowd in Indianapolis, when he was told that Martin Luther King had been shot and killed. It fell to Kennedy to announce this fact and to address the outrage it would ignite. He tore up his written speech and said what came to him. What came to him was this:

> What we need in the United States is not division or hatred or violence, but love and wisdom and compassion toward one another, and a feeling of justice toward those who still suffer within our country, whether they be white or whether they be black. My favorite poet was Aeschylus who wrote: "In our sleep, pain, which we cannot forget, falls drop by drop upon the heart until, in our own despair and against our will, comes wisdom through the awful grace of God." So let us dedicate ourselves to what the Greeks wrote many years ago, to tame the savageness of man and to make gentle the life of this world.

Indianapolis was calm; but Chicago, for one, soon exploded. For a time, riot was the rule. Suffering does not always bring wisdom. Grief is not always humanizing. It did not take the assassinations of 1968 or the atrocities of what was Yugoslavia to teach us this. Greek tragedy is soaked with the counter-truth: suffering and grief are disfiguring and provoke hideous reprisals. Revenge is sweet, excess gratifying. These are truths most often excluded from the canon of Greek wisdom, ignored like the plays which house them, plays like Euripides' *Hekabe*.

Hekabe is living proof that powerlessness, like power, corrupts, and absolute powerlessness corrupts absolutely. Having endured blow after blow, loss after loss, she is well on her way to becoming an icon of innocent suffering, sculpted by pain, radiant in grief. Cradling her savaged son in her arms, Hekabe is on the verge of anticipating the Pietá. She is about to confirm the simple truth that it is always better to suffer than to inflict pain, a truth whose loyalties are at best suspect. This she refuses to do. Instead, to her own great horror, she learns another law and becomes as dark as what has been done to her. What she becomes and what she does are commended to us not for imitation but for hard thought; for the truth at hand is not as simple as we have been led to believe. We cannot count on suffering—our own or others'—to be ennobling.

Hekabe tells us something we need to know: that it is better to go dark in death than to go dark in life, that it is a curse to outlive our ability to affirm. Hekabe lives too long and suffers too much. She begs to have her life taken from her. Instead, she is propped up and made to go on, as if she were testing an ancient proposition, that suffering is humanizing, that fire purifies. In doing so, she finds her only strength in others like herself, in the solidarity of the oppressed, the consortium of women, dreaded by Agamemnon and despised by Polumestor, kings accustomed to having their way.

In the end, Hekabe lives only "to see a bit of justice done." It turns out to be poetic justice, eyes for eyes, teeth for teeth, briefly and deeply satisfying. Indeed, as the Chorus in Euripides' *Elektra* put it so plainly, "Justice can conduct itself shamefully." The *Hekabe* presents a spectacle of suffering, rage, and revenge, endured and enacted by women, who, as Euripides realized, suffer first and most from war. So long as we live in a world all but defined by violence, Euripides' *Hekabe* will offer compelling witness to the courage and solidarity of those who suffer most and a fierce challenge to the simplistic assurance that suffering is somehow for the better of us all.

DRAMATIS PERSONAE

In Order of Appearance

Ghost of Poludoros
Youngest son of Hekabe

Hekabe
Queen of Troy

Handmaiden
Attendant to Hekabe

Chorus of Trojan Women
Captive slaves

Odusseus
King of Ithaka

Poluxene
Daughter of Hekabe

Talthubios
Herald to the Greek army

Agamemnon
High king of the Greeks

Polumestor
King of Thrace

Sons of Polumestor

Guards
Attendants to Odusseus, Polumestor, Agamemnon

HEKABE

*The tent camp of captive Greek women on Thrace, where the
Greek army, returning from Troy, has drifted ashore, the sails
of their ships now limp for lack of wind. The ghost of Poludoros
enters.*

POLUDOROS

I have come from the grey haunts of hell.
I have come at the leave of loner-god Hades,
    lord of the lost and the damned.
I am Poludoros, last son to Hekabe, last heir to Priamos.
I was a guest in this land,
    sent off in secret to the safety of a friend's house.
My father saw the end approaching.
Troy would soon lie beneath the bronze tips of Greek spears.
Too young to bear arms, I might yet bear the family blood.
Surviving was to be my service.
I came here as no beggar from some spoiled city.
When I came here Troy's towers scraped the sky
    and I carried with me gold enough to pay my keep
        and a good deal more.
From friend to friend I was sent.
From Priamos to Polumestor,
    from Troy-king to king of horse-loving Thrace.
And I was treated accordingly,
    so long as Troy's walls were without breach
    and Hector without equal.
Just so long as that I flourished like a well-tended sprout.
But no longer.
For as soon as the soul of my brother Hector
    went dark in death,
    as soon as our sacred hearth grew cold,
    as soon as my father Priamos was butchered
        by the son of Akhilleus at the family altar,
            hewn long ago by Apollo himself,
    when my house fell,
    in that moment the bond of hospitality
        snapped like a twig.
And our family friend took off his mask.
Polumestor cut me down in greed,
    and threw me to the surf.
My protector slit my throat to tally up my gold.

Now I am beached over there,
>   rolled up on shore by the sea's thousand hands,
>   bathed in salt and foam.
No one weeps over me.
No one sees to my rites.
For three days I have drifted in the open air,
>   watching for Greek ships from Troy,
>   watching the arrival of my ill-starred mother.
Now, bereft of my body, I hover here,
>   close over my sweet mother's head.
I have seen the Greeks sit idle by their ships
>   sulking at the empty sails.
I have watched the ghost of Akhilleus appear
>   astride his own tomb,
>   and check the entire Greek army
>   in their eager journey home.
I have listened to the son of Peleus lay claim
>   to my sister Poluxene,
>   as victim and trophy to mark his remains
>   and to sweeten the bitterness of his death.
And he will have her, a gift from his old fellows.
Today is assigned by Fate to my sister's doom.

But today, mother,
>   you will see two of your children as corpses,
>   me and my ill-fated sister.
In quest of a grave,
>   I will wash up at the feet of your servant.
I have prevailed upon the powers below
>   to let this happen,
>   so that you, Hekabe, might lay me to rest
>   with your own aged hands.
I have longed for this and it shall be.

Now, I must vanish.
She comes from the tent of Agamemnon,
>   unsettled by a dream she has had of me.

>   *Hekabe enters. She is supported by two attendants.*

Oh mother, first a queen, now a slave,
>   you are bent every bit as low as ever high you stood.
Some god jealous of exceptions makes you pay with grief
>   for every joy you ever knew.

HEKABE

Walk beside me, women of Troy.
Stave up an old woman, once your queen,
    now another slave among you.
Here, take hold, lead my steps, bear me up or I fall.
I put my arm like a gnarled branch in your grip
    and push my useless feet to keep up with yours.
O light flashed from god! O heavy cloak of night!
Why do I shudder at what I have just seen in sleep?
Why am I in dread over a mere dream?
O mother goddess earth,
    you who spawn the dark winged forms
        caved within our souls,
    I would scratch from my eyes
        this clinging vision come in night.
Call off these fiendish hounding images
    of my daughter and my son!
You gods who watch over this land, watch over my son.
He is my anchor, the last hope of our house.
He is in good hands.

But I am almost foreseeing something else,
    something unforeseen.
Never before have I known such clawing at my heart.
I shake all over without knowing why.
I need Helena the seer
    or my own prophetess-daughter Kassandra
    to read for me these runes
        burning themselves into my mind,
    and to tell me what it is I have seen.
There was a dappled fawn.
It clung to my knees in despair and I held it there.
But to no avail. There was a fox too.
It drove its razor claws into the fawn
    and tore its flesh from between my fingers.
Whatever I still held was left behind.
Soaking in its own blood,
    the quivering fawn was dragged off.
There was no hint of pity shown.

And then a second vision came to me.
I saw the ghost of Akhilleus mounting his own tomb.
He wailed for a token of honor.
One of the war-sick Trojan slaves was his idea of a prize.
Gods, call off these omens. I am begging you.
Exempt my daughter from what by now is Fate.

The Chorus of Trojan women enters.

CHORUS

Hekabe,
We come to you in all haste,
Quitting the tents of our would-be lords.
A throw of the dice made us theirs,
Once our city fell to their spears.

Hekabe,
Our haste is not to lighten your grief,
But to tell what must be told.
What we bring is beyond all bearing.
You, it seems, are the last to know.

Hekabe,
The Greeks have met
And formed one mind on this:
Akhilleus is to have his way.
Your daughter is to be his prize.
A victim very to his liking.

Hekabe,
You know already how he mounted his tomb,
A ghost in golden armor,
And reined in the ready ships,
Bellowing like a maddened bull.

"Greeks, where do you think you are off to,
Leaving my tomb without its prize?"
These words swept over the crested host,
Like a storm at sea.

Hekabe,
Greek was set at odds with Greek.
Some would sate the lust of Akhilleus at any cost.
Others at the same expense
Would deny him his desires.

Hekabe,
There was sheer deadlock among them
Until one man sped to speak on your behalf.
No slight spokesman this,
Agamemnon,
Lord of lords among them all.

Hekabe,
To save his bacchant bride for his own bed,
Agamemnon made his case as best he could.
But then there rose against him
No less than the two sons of Theseus.

"Greeks,"
Spoke the two as if they were one,
"Do we owe more tribute to a slave's prowess in bed
Than to a fallen warrior's pride?"
These words brought the deadlock back.

Hekabe,
This battle of words swung from side to side
As evenly as a pendulum,
Until one wily man spoke up, Odusseus,
Sweet-tongued, slit-eyed liar.

"Greeks,"
He cried and brought silence
Like a shroud upon them all.
"Shall we slight the best of the Greeks
To spare our hands
Some slavewoman's blood?"

"Greeks,"
He went on catching every eye in his web,
"Shall we let tales be told to the gods below,
Tales of how we forget those who die for us,
Let them go below without their due?"

Hekabe,
Whatever needed to be said to sway the throng,
It came to his lips as if on call,
And now he comes to pry loose your brittle grip
From a daughter you cannot hope to save.

Hekabe,
Go to the temples, go to the shrines,
More to the point, go to Agamemnon.
Play the suppliant at his knees
Invoke every god in sight.

Hekabe,
Your entreaties are all that stands now
Between your hapless child
And a long sharp blade.
If you fail,
Your sweet girl will lie in a swelling pool
of her own dark rippling blood.

HEKABE

I am undone. Undone.
What kind of groans, how many screams do you prescribe?
It is over with me. Who is left of my house?
Who is left of my city to come to my side?
My husband gone. My sons gone.
What does that leave?
Where does someone with no one turn?
Is there a god or some other power likely to help?
Women of Troy, you bring the worst of all news.
Your words bring me to my brink.
What now could make me want to live?
There, a little further,
　　　help this ruin of a woman take a few more steps.

Child! Daughter! Your cursed mother calls you.
Come out and hear me.
Talk with me about these rumors bearing on your life.

Poluxene enters from the tent.

POLUXENE

Yes, mother? Mother, why do you cry out like this?
The panic in your voice has startled me like a skittish bird.
What is it?

HEKABE

Oh my baby.

POLUXENE

What? I already know it is something dreadful.
What is it?

HEKABE

I fear for your life.

POLUXENE

Mother, don't try to spare me.
Just tell me… no… no… I am afraid.
I'm shaking with fear, mother.
Why are you wailing?

HEKABE

My poor child, my poor, poor child.

POLUXENE

Mother, you'd best tell me what news you bring.

HEKABE

The Greeks have met in full assembly.
They voted.
They are going to sacrifice you on Akhilleus's tomb.

POLUXENE

Mother, how can your lips form such words?
Tell me what you are saying, mother.
My fear did not let me hear you.

HEKABE

What I am saying is the blackest of rumors…
    the Greek decree of what is to become of you.
They…

Hekabe breaks down, and Poluxene goes to her.

POLUXENE

My poor sweet mother.
You have endured so much.
Your life has become a wound that never heals.
What new outrage have they conjured up for you now?
I would have been a child to you,
    bringing whatever consolation
    a child might bring to her mother.
I would have been miserable with your misery,
        a companionship worth something.
But it seems even this will not be.
I hear you now.
I know what is to be.
You will see me dragged away,
    squalling like some young fawn blind with fear.

They will open my throat with one swift slice
    and I will bleed my way to hell.
But you, mother of sorrows,
    I cry your laments not mine.
I am the lucky one now.
Death turns out to be a blessing set against your woes.

Odusseus enters.

ODUSSEUS

Woman, by now you surely know
    the resolve of the Greek army.
But I will tell you all the same.
This is what shall be.
Your daughter will die spread across Akhilleus's tomb.
He has asked for her from death,
    and we have seen fit to give him what he wants.
We Greeks do nothing arbitrarily.
We came to this by vote.
I have been duly appointed to bring you this word
    and to take the girl away.
The son of Akhilleus will have the honor of presiding
    as priest of the sacrifice.

Have I told you all you wish to hear?
Then you know where you stand.
Don't indulge yourself with gestures of force,
        only forcing my hand.
Recognize your weakness and embrace your ills.
There is wisdom to be had in giving ground
    to what will happen anyway.

HEKABE

O gods!
Still another world of mine must fall apart.
Where will the wonted groans and tears come from this time?
I needed to die in Troy, but I could not.
Zeus would not take me.
Instead, in his largesse,
    he gave me more and more cursed strength.
God seals my cracks
    as if I were the last vessel in his fleet.
And yet I serve only to suffer always more and always worse
    than what I suffered last.

If slaves have any place at all to ask their masters "why?"—
 why you crack our hears beneath your heels
  like the dry shells of locusts –
 then I ask you: why must this be?

ODUSSEUS

Ask whatever you care to ask.
I have a few minutes.

HEKABE

I want to ask if you remember the time you came to Troy,
 a spy in a beggar's disguise, all rags and filth.
You played your part well.
Real tears filled your pleading eyes.

ODUSSEUS

O course I remember.
It's not the sort of thing you forget.

HEKABE

I should think not; for you were found out.
Helena recognized you.
She told me who you really were.
I was the only one she told.

ODUSSEUS

I remember well enough.
I was as good as dead.

HEKABE

At any rate you lost your pride.
You fell to your knees before me.

ODUSSEUS

Yes, and the hand I reached out to you
 was already growing cold at death's approach.

HEKABE

And what did you have to say then,
 when you were in my position... a slave?

ODUSSEUS

I found what words I could
 to talk my way out of death.

HEKABE
You talked your way out of nothing!
I spared you and sent you on your way.

ODUSSEUS
In any case, I'm very much alive today.

HEKABE
And you can stand there without despising your own words,
    you who owe your breath to me?
I gave you your life when it was gone,
    and you give me the greatest grief I can imagine.
You are the worst of a bad breed—
       you politicians, panderers—
    you pretend to focus the energies of a people
       and do no more than unleash your own greed.
I loathe you all.
I don't want to know you.
You forsake your friends
    to fawn over faceless crowds.
But tell me, politician, since you have a few minutes...
What neat case did you make for this blood-vote?
Just how did you propose a human sacrifice,
    when custom calls for cattle?
Or is it a matter of revenge—life for life?
If that is it, tell me.
How did you Greeks, who do nothing arbitrarily,
    indict my little girl?
How many of Akhilleus's wounds is she accused of inflicting?
How in god's sight did you pass over Helena?
That bitch's blood screams for spilling!
Akhilleus sailed to Troy on her account.
On her account he died.

But maybe all you want is looks. Is that it?
Did my daughter win a beauty contest?
You took your pick among slaves to give your horny ghost
    the kind of lay to silence his complaints?
But if it is loveliness you are after, don't shop in Trojan tents.
You Greeks already have Helena,
    uncontested queen of beauty.
And, as a bonus,
    Akhilleus ought to want to see her dead
       for all the grief she heaped on him.

So much for the logic of your case.
Now I make my own. Hear me.
I am asking only what I gave,
    when you asked the same of me.
I go to my knees. I reach out my hand.
I play the other part
    in a scene you say you remember well.
Don't take my child from me. Don't kill her!
Surely there has been enough killing.

She is the only joy I have left.
With her at my side, I have moments
    when I almost forget what I have been through.
She is my world...
    filling in for everything I have lost.
She is my solace, my nurse, my staff.
She guides my on my way.
Take her and you take everything!
The powerful do not do well to abuse their power.
No turn of fate fails to turn some day.
I know. I was once where you are now.
You see how much remains.

Akhilleus, look at me. Have pity.
Return to the Greek army
    and bend back their wills from this new resolve.
Show them what they are doing and its shamefulness.
When they tore us from our homes in Troy,
    they could easily have cut us down then and there.
But they took pity, spared us our lives and made us slaves.
That is where matters stand.
Your law is clear on this. Point that out.
To kill a slave or to kill a freewoman come to the same thing.
Murder!
Your word carries a lot of weight, for good or for ill.
They will heed you.

CHORUS
Human nature admits of many forms;
    but none so callous and remote
        as not to be touched by this woman.
Hekabe, your laments would bring tears from a stone,
    much less from a man.

ODUSSEUS

Hekabe, now it is for me to instruct you.
I have spoken with good will and good sense.
If I seem the villain, your wrath has made me so,
    twisting my words out of form.
You spared my life, granted.
I stand no less ready to spare yours.
That propriety is not in question.
Some things, after all, are sacred.

Your daughter... is another matter. She is called for.
I pledged her long ago to our most shining champion
        as soon as Troy would fall.
Troy, you know, has fallen, and my pledge stands.
Akhilleus, first among us, wants her with him dead.
She is the least we can do for him.
Among some other race this might not happen, granted.
Some people pay no more honor to the best and the bravest
        than they do to the least among them.
This is why their strength and spirit wane.
We Greeks possess the vision to measure worth
        and the heart to reward it.
And there was no man of greater worth than Akhilleus.
It is just that simple.
He was the fairest of all who gave their lives for Greece.
Woman, you tell me this: would there not be shame
        in revoking friendship from a corpse,
            even as it stiffens?
What would be left to say
        the next time we draw up our ranks for battle?
"Fight with all your hearts"?
Or "Best cling to life,
        seeing that in death you will be overlooked"?

Speaking for myself, in life I expect little enough;
        but in death I want my share of honor.
Honor done the dead never dies.
A good investment.

Woman, you say you have it bad.
Well, hear me.
We Greeks have our old women too who mourn their sons.
Too many Greek brides lie alone in cold beds,
        while their men lie in Trojan fields, colder still.
There is grief enough to go around.

So bear up.
And let us honor the best of our dead.
It is our right and our duty.
If we thought otherwise, we would know nothing,
    like you, barbarians, who forsake your friends
    and forget your dead.
And still you wonder why we are the ones to prosper!

CHORUS

This is what it means to be a slave:
    to accept the unacceptable,
    to endure whatever comes along,
        always without a word;
    to be too weak to think of doing otherwise.

HEKABE

Daughter, whatever arguments I assemble,
    they are blown away like chaff.
I speak to no avail.
What little time remains is yours
    to prevail if you can where I have failed.
Surpass the nightingale. Sing for your life.
Crawl if you must. Break his heart.
Even this man may have a crack in his wall.
After all, he has children of his own.
In you he may see them,
    and find pity he didn't know was there.

POLUXENE

Odusseus, I see you standing there at an angle,
    diverting your eyes.
You are a man in flight,
    afraid of being touched or of meeting eyes,
    afraid of a young girl.
Permit me to put you at ease.
In me your fear has no cause.
Don't worry, I am not about to call upon Zeus,
    hope of the hopeless.
I am going with you.
I have no choice but to die.
Yet, as it happens, to die *is* my choice.
It would be the mark of a base soul to resist you.
In doing so I would prove myself a coward.

What sense does it make for me to live now?
I was born a princess.
I was nursed on the highest of hopes,
　　to be a bride for kings vying for my hand,
　　to be the queen of the best among them,
　　to live to a full age in his court.
I grew to be the acknowledged mistress
　　of Troy's girls and women, conspicuous in every respect.
Mortality aside, I was a goddess.

And now I am a slave.
The name alone, so alien in every way,
　　is enough to enamor me of death.
Am I to be an item for sale to coarse and brutal men,
　　I, the sister of Hektor, sister to the princes of Troy?
Am I to know only harsh necessity,
　　　　sweeping some man's floors,
　　　　kneading his bread,
　　　　making his bed
　　　　　　from one weary day to the next?
Am I, the bride of kings,
　　　　to let some crude slave from god knows where
　　　　defile me in his filthy bed
　　　　　　and call it love?
Never! I will take one last look at freedom
　　and consign myself to hell.

Odusseus, lead me to my death.
I see no reason to trust or to hope
　　that life will ever again be kind to me.

Mother, I am asking you not to say or to do anything
　　aimed at breaking my resolve.
Join me, instead, in my will to die
　　before I know a shame I do not deserve.
One who is unaccustomed to misfortune
　　is bound to bear it badly.
Death for such a one is preferable to life.
Life without some grace is an effort not worth making.

CHORUS
Nobility of birth leaves its mark, conspicuous and singular.
But when the life that follows proves as noble as its birth,
　　we have a wonder past all telling.

HEKABE
There is sheer beauty in your words, my child.
But it is a beauty bordering on despair.

Odusseus, hear me.
If Akhilleus must have his victim and you your repute,
    do not slay this girl.
Lead me instead to the site of this sacrifice.
Let me be its victim.
It would make more sense.
My son's arrows felled your chief.
I am the assassin's mother.
I ought not, it would seem, to be spared.

ODUSSEUS
Perhaps, old woman, there is sense in what you say.
But Akhilleus has his own mind in this matter.
He doesn't ask for you. He wants her.

HEKABE
Then at least take the two of us. Slaughter us together.
The earth and that demanding corpse of yours
    can drink my blood as well.
Surely Akhilleus will not complain
    if his cup is filled a second time.

ODUSSEUS
Her death will do just fine without any help from you.

HEKABE
I must die with my daughter! It can be no other way.

ODUSSEUS
You seem to think you are in a position to say what is to be.
Take another look!

HEKABE
I will cling to her like ivy to oak.

ODUSSEUS
Not if you have any sense.

HEKABE
I will not let you leave with her.

ODUSSEUS

And I have no intention of leaving without her.

POLUXENE

Mother, listen to me.
And you , Odusseus, try to understand a mother's feelings,
    natural enough under the circumstances.

O my poor, poor mother,
    please don't take on the whole Greek army.
You will only be torn away from me by arms
    twenty times your strength.
Then they will throw you to the ground
    and kick you around in the dust.
You are old. You will be hurt,
        and you will be dishonored.
Is this truly what you want? It is not what you deserve.
O mother, dear mother, give me your hand,
    and lean your head against mine.

Never again will I see the light of day.
Now for the last time I watch the sun
    trace its brilliant path across the sky.
I must form my last words.
Mother, you gave me life.
Now I go below to darkness.

HEKABE

And I remain behind, in the light, a slave.

POLUXENE

I go to death unwed.
The time for bridal songs never came
    and now must wait forever.

HEKABE

Piteous and wretched, the two of us.

POLUXENE

I fall so far from you,
    to lie in some dark corner of hell.

HEKABE

O gods, what will I do? When can *I* die?

POLUXENE
I was born free, but I die a slave.

HEKABE
Fifty children, and I am alone. Not one is left to me.

POLUXENE
Do you have a message for Hektor or for father?

HEKABE
Tell them I am wretched, more than they imagine.

POLUXENE
Embracing Hekabe.
O gentle arms that held me, sweet breasts that nourished me.

HEKABE
O my baby, this fate of yours is all wrong.

POLUXENE
Good-bye, mother. Say good-bye to Kassandra for me.

HEKABE
"Good-bye." It has the wrong ring.
There is no word for this.

POLUXENE
Softly, to Hekabe alone.
Good-bye, dear Poludoros.

HEKABE
Also softly.
If he lives.
I am so shadowed I fear even for him.

POLUXENE
He lives.
He will be the one to close your eyes in death.

HEKABE
I am in death. I have not died,
    but my grief has already brought to me a kind of death.

POLUXENE

Shroud my head, Odusseus, and lead me away.
Even before I die the death you have designed for me,
    I have broken my mother's heart, and she mine.

O light of day, I am still able to turn to you,
        but only so long as it will take
        to reach the tomb of Akhilleus
            and the blade made sharp for me.

*Odusseus covers Poluxene's head with her robe and leads her
out. Hekabe collapses.*

HEKABE

I am faint. My legs give way.
O child, take hold of your mother.
Reach out to me. Give me your hand.
Don't leave me childless!
Women, it is over with me.
O gods what I wouldn't give to see Helena in her stead.
That one Spartan bitch, with her large, luring eyes,
    dragged thriving Troy to ruin.

CHORUS

Listen, listen, listen, listen, listen.
Winds of the sea,
The wine-dark waters shimmer at your approach.
Even to the tips of shore-side cliffs,
You waft the scent and tang of the salt-soaked sea.
You fill the long-limp sails with hope
And send the scudding ships to shores unseen
Save in the pining dreams
Of war-sick, homesick Greeks.

Listen, listen, listen, listen, listen.
Winds of the sea,
You fill your lungs to send us swiftly on our way.
But where will you lift these lost lives of ours
And set us down to stand for sale?
Where will this blind journey end,
So we might begin to spill out our lives in slavery
Like wasted wine
From cracked cups?

Listen, listen, listen, listen, listen.
Winds of the sea,
You carry in your breath a thousand cries.
You moan with a grief
We know well.

O children charred in ashen Troy,
O men sent to hell in your sleep,
At least you know a kind of rest
While our end lingers like a dying lamp.

> *Talthubios enters from the Greek camp. Hekabe is lying*
> *prostrate on the ground.*

TALTHUBIOS
Women of Troy, where might I find Hekabe,
    once your queen?

CHORUS
She is only right there, Talthubios, lying in the dust,
    shrouding her head in her cloak.

TALTHUBIOS
O god, what am I to say?
That you watch over our lives, solicitous and caring?
Or that we are fools to believe in a breed of provident gods
    when blind chance alone walks, or drags,
        us through our days?

This woman, was she not queen of gold-laden Troy?
Was she not wife of long-blessed Priamos?
Now, what is left of Troy grovels under Greek spears.
And the queen... she is a broken slavewoman,
    older even than her long years,
      without strength or child of her own
        to lift her to her feet;
      without pride or purpose
        to raise her head from the dust.
It is almost too much to believe or to bear.
I too am old, and I hope to god I die
    before I fall prey to such a shameful state.

Rise, lady, lift your face, so wan and weary,
    and stand on your feet.

HEKABE

Who is it who will not leave me be?
Whoever you are, why do you disrupt my grief?

TALTHUBIOS

I am Talthubios. I run errands for the Greeks.
Poor lady, Agamemnon has sent me to tell you…

HEKABE

Interrupting.

…that the Greeks want my life too?
That I am to die with my daughter?
O sweet man,
    I welcome you and your words.
Here, give me your hand. I am in a hurry,
Take me there.

TALTHUBIOS

You do not want my hand. I can lead you nowhere.
I have come to see if you will bury your daughter.
She is dead.
The army and the generals want you to see to her rites.

HEKABE

What am I to say?
Is that what you've come here to tell me?
That I cannot die with my daughter;
    and even worse that… ?
    O my child, torn from these arms… you…
You are dead. Dead!
With you… all of my children… dead!
I am cursed!

Confronting Talthubios.

How did you do it?
Was there any respect given her?
Or did you go about your work savagely.
Tell me, old man.
Say what there is to say, whatever the pain involved.

TALTHUBIOS

Lady, I am a compassionate man.
I raise no walls against my feelings.

You are asking me to pay a second time in tears
    for your sweet daughter's death.
And so it must be.
I wept not long ago, watching her die.
And I shall weep again now,
    in the telling of that dark event.

The entire Greek army was gathered there
    at the tomb of Akhilleus,
      waiting to see your daughter die.
The son of Akhilleus took Poluxene by the hand,
    led her through the ranks of men
    and stood her on the burial mound itself.
I was there, very near to her.
When she was in her place, a cordon of handpicked guards
    closed in around your girl,
    in case she might decide to run for her life.
Then, taking in his hand a pure-gold cup,
    brimming with wine,
    the son of Akhilleus held it high,
      to pour a libation to his dead father.
Next he looked to me
    to summon the Greek throng to silence.
I took a step or two nearer and then,
    circled by that vast assembly, I cried out:
    "Greeks, silence! Silence in the ranks! Be still."
At once a hush swept over the Greeks, and he began to pray.

"Akhilleus, son of Peleos, Father,
    receive these libations, poured in propitiation,
      to raise up your spirit.
Crawl near and drink this gift
    from your son and your fellows,
    the gift of a virgin's blood, dark and pure.
Akhilleus, Father, be gracious to us.
Throw loose the ties that bind our ships to port
    and favor us all with fair journeys home."

These were his prayers, and he was joined in them
    by the whole army of the Greeks.
Then, his hand fitted itself to the hilt of his sword,
    and he slid it, gleaming gold, from its sheath.
With barely a nod from him,
    the guards circling the young girl
      closed in to seize her.

Yet before they could lay a hand on her, she cried out.
"Wait! Troy-sacking Greeks, not one of you touch me!
I am a free woman, and I will die that way!
Freely I offer my throat to your blade.
Untie my hands. I have no need of your constraints.
I said untie my hands!
I shall die a free death.
All of you, stand off!
I go down among the dead the daughter of a king.
I am no man's slave, and I will not die like one."

With one voice the army roared its support.
And lord Agamemnon, mightiest among them,
    stepped forth and spoke to the guards.
"Untie her hands and let her be."
These were his words.
They were done at once.

Then Poluxene, her hands now free, took her robe
    and tore it from her shoulders to below her waist,
    leaving bare her soft unblemished breasts.
She was to the eye the loveliest of statues, and more.
Then she lowered herself to her knees
    and knelt before the throng of Greek men.
These were her words, strong and boldly spoken.

"See here, man, if it is in my breast
    you wish to plant your blade, the way is ready.
Or if it is across my throat
    you think to slash your steel, here,
    I lean back my head to make it easy for you."

Torn with pity, the son of Akhilleus
    cut her deep and clean below the chin
    as her breath and blood burst from a single slit
    and spewed her life over the earthen mound.
Even as she swooned in death, she fell in modest form
    and covered from the eyes of men
        what was not theirs to see.
Lady, I have honored your request
    and told you what there is to tell.
This is what I heard and saw.
And now I see in you, of all women, a mother
    at once profoundly blessed and cursed unspeakably.

CHORUS

Some deep well of suffering
     is sunk within the house of Priamos.
Its dread dark waters seep within the soil of Troy.
Such is our lot to which the gods have yoked us.

HEKABE

O my child,
I need to confront the evils hounding me on every side.
But they are too many and too insistent for me
     to cope with them.
If I would turn to one, another cries out for my care.
I seem set upon some pitiless course of blow after blow,
     without respite.
How am I to cauterize my mind of you and your savage end,
     to forget and spare myself these groans and grief,
     which for all I know may never end?
All this I could not bear
     were it not for the tale this man has told of how
     you shone even beneath the shadow of your doom.

Strange the force of chance and fate over the fruits of the earth.
Even barren soil will harvest well when blessed from above.
And the richest soil throws up unwanted fruit,
     if starved of its own needs.
Not so with us. We hatch our deeds within,
     good from good, evil from evil.
We are without excuse for what we do.

Talthubios, go to the Greeks and tell them
     no one is to touch my daughter.
Curiosity will bring crowds,
     and I want them far from her.

Talthubios leaves, and Hekabe turns to her handmaiden.

HEKABE

Old companion, do this for me.
Take a pitcher and go to the sea.
Dip the vessel into the brine and bring it brimming here,
     so that I might pour it over my daughter's corpse
     and give my girl her last bath.
Then, when I have washed away the filth of death,
     I shall lay her out as befits an unwed bride of Hades,
          a virgin spoiled in hell.

But how am I to do this? I have nothing that I need.
I must make do with what I can collect
    from other women in the tents.
Some of them may have secret spoils,
    which they managed to thieve
        from their own homes in Troy.

The Handmaiden leaves.

Troy! Home once so blessed.
You used to overflow with beautiful things
    and beautiful children.
Priamos... you and I...
    a worn old woman, mother of your children,
    how have we come to this?
How has everything come to nothing?
Even our spirit is broken in two.

All our vanity is vanity.
Our private wealth, our public honors,
    all come to nothing.
All that we turn over in our hearts
    and toss about upon our tongues
    comes down to this:
There is no more to be hoped for
    by anyone
    in any life
        than to elude ruin
        one day at a time.

Hekabe enters the tent.

CHORUS
The roots of whatever happiness I knew
Were hacked and cut to death
The day Troy's comeliest prince
Took axe to towering pine
And shaped himself a ship.
Sown was the seed of my undoing
When pointed Trojan prows
Rammed the soft white surf
And set themselves to sea.
All this to fetch one woman from her bed,
Helena, sight of all sights
Beneath the seething sun.

Our avalanche of ruin began
With one small slip of soul.
One young man's unknowing,
The folly of a single fool,
Sufficed to doom us all.
In a never-ending storm of pain,
We watched iron-wielding rage
Hack apart our lovely sons
And redden the River Simois.
To survive all this is now to sit within those tents
And to keep open with our thoughts
Wounds that never close.

The Handmaiden enters, followed shortly afterward by two
of the Chorus carrying a bier and a covered corpse.

HANDMAIDEN
Women, our queen wears a crown of sorrow.
In this she is without rival or peer.
Her misery is beyond all measure.
Where is our lady now?

CHORUS
Why do you ask… and in that manner?
Already I dread your news. What is it now?

HANDMAIDEN
Hekabe must find room for still another grief.
O gods, how can I lighten the weight of these words?
I fear to crush her.

CHORUS
Look. She is coming now from her tent.
It seems she is in time for whatever it is you bring.

HANDMAIDEN
Lady, what can I say?
You are accursed beyond description.
You are a perished queen,
    no matter how your life lingers on.
Like an egg sucked dry,
    your existence is a shell about to crack.
Nothing is left to you.
Not your city, not your spouse, not your children.

Nothing is left but life's empty gestures.
Give any animal a violent enough end,
    and it will go on moving all the same for a while.
I fear we are no different.

HEKABE

I find your words offensive, but true enough.
In any case, you tell me nothing new.
But why have you brought my daughter's body here?
I was told the Greeks were making ready a pyre for her.

HANDMAIDEN

My lady, there is more to come.
After all this, you still do not know the worst.

HEKABE

No! Gods, no... no!
Tell me you don't cover there the sweet face
    of my god-struck child, Kassandra.

HANDMAIDEN

Kassandra lives. But your grief has cause.
O lady, come. You must see a sight beyond belief.

    The handmaiden draws back the shroud to reveal to Hekabe
    the corpse of her last son, Poludoros. At the sight of her dead
    son, Hekabe begins to groan from a black and bottomless depth
    which she inhabits now for the first time.

HEKABE

Aoaoaoaoaoaoaoao... aiaiaiaiaiaiaiai...
My son... my son... my darling son!
Safe... in a friend's house... I lose even you.
I am no more.

Child... my child... aiaiaiaiaiaiai...
I have outlived the world I knew.
I think strange thoughts.
My blood learns another law.
Why should I not give way to powers as dark
    as what I have become?
Child, my child... how? How can this be?
What power, what fate, what fiend
    did this to you?

HANDMAIDEN
My lady, I know no more than you.
I found him in the surf.

HEKABE
In the surf? Drowned at sea and washed ashore?
Murdered?

HANDMAIDEN
All I know… I found him sliding with the tide
        overlaid with kelp and scum.
It was like an awful dream.

HEKABE
A dream… my dream!
I see it now… those dark, winged forms…
        over you, my son, dead, even as I dreamed them.

HANDMAIDEN
What are you saying? Murdered?
Do you see in your dream who killed him?

HEKABE
Our friend, his protector, for gold and nothing more.

HANDMAIDEN
I can't believe my ears.
Poludoros slain to feed one man's greed?

HEKABE
My mind falls blank on such a deed.
He tossed away friendship like a used match.
He is the worst of men.
See what a hellish mess he made of my darling boy.
How many thudding blows does it take
        to hack out the life of a child?
I see each one of them now in his mangled flesh,
        and feel them as my own.

CHORUS
You are singled out, my queen, for suffering.
Some demon god must hold a heavy grudge
        against you and all you love.

Look, it is lord Agamemnon.
He is coming our way.

Agamemnon enters.

AGAMEMNON

Hekabe,
    why do you wait to bury your daughter?
I was told that all was ready for her rites.
Your delay seems strange to me. What keeps you?
There, behind you, what corpse is that,
    wrapped in a Trojan cloak?
Did one of the aged women die in this heat?
Tell me, who is it?

Hekabe says nothing.

Your silence disturbs me. You are hiding something.
Unlike your daughter, I have no psychic skills.
I cannot hear what you fail to say.
But why should I care who this is, if you do not.
One more Trojan dead alters very little.

Agamemnon turns to leave.

HEKABE

Lord Agamemnon, wait. Please!
I beg you, wait and hear me.

> *Hekabe lowers herself to her knees and grabs hold of Agamemnon's cloak.*

I must ask you something.

AGAMEMNON

What is it, woman?
If you want your freedom,
    I give it to you without the asking.
It is a slight matter.

HEKABE

Yes, it is a slight matter. Not so with what I ask.
I want your help.

AGAMEMNON

My help? With what?

HEKABE

I seek revenge on one who well deserves it.

AGAMEMNON
On whom? For what?

HEKABE
You will know all you need to know, my lord,
    if you look under that shroud.

Agamemnon walks to the corpse and bends over it. He hesitates.

HEKABE
Please!

Agamemnon uncovers the corpse and studies it briefly.

AGAMEMNON
A young man who came to no good end.
But this tells me nothing.

HEKABE
He is my son.

AGAMEMNON
How? Which of your sons is he?

HEKABE
No one of those that died for Troy.

AGAMEMNON
You bore others besides those?

HEKABE
Only one, my youngest… born for nothing.
You see what remains of him.

AGAMEMNON
I am grasping none of this.
Where was this boy when Troy fell?

HEKABE
Fearing for our last son's life,
    my husband sent him away.

AGAMEMNON
Where to?

HEKABE
Here to Thrace, where he was found dead.

AGAMEMNON
You sent him to Polumestor, king of Thrace?

HEKABE
Yes, with gold enough to keep him well.

AGAMEMNON
Then who did this, and why?

HEKABE
Our family friend, for gold. Now you know it all.

AGAMEMNON
Poor woman, there seems to be no end to your woes.
You think Polumestor slew your son in greed
    for one more chest of gold?

HEKABE
I know as much.
When Troy fell, he had nothing to lose,
    and a sum of gold to gain.
One thing is clear. It caused him no great pain.
His mind was made at once,
    and as quick the deed was done.

AGAMEMNON
Who found the corpse and brought it here?

HEKABE
This woman, my companion, saw him in the surf,
    washed ashore as flotsam.

AGAMEMNON
Then you are right.
Polumestor, his protector, cut your son down
    and flung him in the sea.

HEKABE
To float as bloody bait, luring demons from the deep.

AGAMEMNON

Woman, I pity you
and how your grief must dredge your soul.

HEKABE

I died of grief some time ago.
What you see now is something else.
Agamemnon, hear me out, please!
Then, if you dismiss the charge I bring,
I will have no more to say.
But if you judge me sorely wronged,
I will call on you to help in my revenge
on the most impious of men.

AGAMEMNON

You may go on, Hekabe. I will listen.

HEKABE

That man, defying gods above and gods below,
betrayed every sacred bond between fellows and friends.
He ate at our table, called himself our friend,
gave every warrant for our trust.
And then, given one ripe moment for his greed,
he thought new thoughts,
as if all the rest had been a dream.
He saw his chance and sent my son to hell,
without the bother of a burial.
The sea would serve as well as any tomb
for what to him was mere debris.

I know my place. I am a slave,
as are these other women of Troy.
And slaves are weak.
But even the gods, in all their awful strength,
are accountable to law.
There is right and there is wrong. No god can alter this.
And it is wrong to slay a guest.
This much, slave though I be, I know for sure.
Deny this and there is nothing left
but an endless night of blind desires.

Agamemnon, you are not a god, but you are strong.
And, like a god, you too are ruled by law.
Do not turn away from me.
There is no escape from what I say.

Pity me and punish him.
It is his due; and it is mine to ask.
Look at me.
I have nothing left but this:
    to see a bit of justice done.

    Agamemnon appears unmoved by Hekabe's words.

I sense I have failed as yet to find the mark
    and strike your heart.
Think then of your long nights of love in bed
    beside my girl, Kassandra, sister of the slain.
Is there not some debt or bond incurred in love's embrace?
There is no grace shown to mortals
    sweet beyond the charms of love.
I am the mother of your love.
He was the brother of your gladness.
Do right by him, and you do right by Kassandra.

    Agamemnon remains unmoved.

All that now remains for me to do is to plead.
I beg you, peerless lord,
    you who are a light to your fellow Greeks,
        give way to my request.
Help an old woman, wronged beyond belief,
    to get her revenge.
It may be I am nothing to you.
Even so, justice is the work of noble men.
Prove yourself the man you are,
    and do not shirk your calling.
Bring evil home to roost.
Consign the wicked to their own harvest.
Destroy the fiend who killed my son!

CHORUS
Strange how things turn out.
Our lives are many-sided dice,
    picked up and thrown again
        by powers we never grasp.
Today's friends are tomorrow's foes.
Love and hate are back to back.
Only law will hold us to our course,
    when all else shifts and turns
        and shows to us a strange face.

AGAMEMNON
Hekabe, how can I do otherwise
    than pity you, your son, and your misfortune?
The gods, sheer justice, and my every inclination
    argue on your behalf.
The case is clear.
Polumestor is a villain,
    and you should have your way with him.
No revenge would be too dark for such a man.

You must see by now I am a compassionate man,
    not unfeeling toward your pain.
I have placed myself in your position
    and understood your plight.
Now I ask the same of you.
I have no doubt I would ally myself with you,
    if I were only free to do just that.
But I am not.

Can you look at things another way
    and see with Greek eyes for a change?
Whatever I might do on your behalf,
    to see your vengeance through,
    will seem to my own men
        a private favor done to please my mate.
Here is where the trouble lies.
All that Polumestor did to earn your hate
    would bring applause where I come from.
To the Greeks he is a friend.
And, when he kills a prince of Troy,
    he is all the more a friend.
Here we have no common ground
    for the law of which you speak.

In short, it comes to this.
In me you have a man
    who wants to take your cause and treat it as his own.
But I must be slow to rouse my fellow Greeks,
    very slow indeed,
        no matter what the rush in your regard.

HEKABE
Agamemnon, if you are as constrained as you describe
    I wonder if there is such a thing as freedom,
        save among the gods.

We mortals all are slaves, you as much as I.
We are blind in our desires
    and fail to see beyond our fears.
Our masters may well vary,
    but their yoke is the same.
You, a lord, allow a common crowd to lord it over you.
You say you fear what they might think,
    if you make common cause with me.
But this is one fear you may set aside,
    one constraint you need not heed.
If you will be a partner in my plot,
    you need not be a party to the deed.
What I ask is very small.
When the Thracian fiend falls prey to my designs,
    there may be Greeks inclined to give him aid.
You are a clever man and you will surely find a way
    to keep such meddlers far from me and what I do,
        without disclosing any common pact we've made.
Obstruct your fellow Greeks,
    give me the few free moments that I need,
        and I shall see that all is done to suit
        this man-turned-savage-beast.

AGAMEMNON

These are big words coming from a woman, Hekabe.
Just how do you propose to do what you describe?
I doubt your aged arm could lift a sword like this
    much less wield it with the speed you'll need
        to slice apart a man of half your years.
Poison serves a woman's anger best,
    unless she has a man to do her killing for her.
And you have no one at your side,
    no manly arm to raise against your foe.
You are alone in what you plan to do
    and thus seem doomed to fail.

HEKABE

Agamemnon, your lordly eyes are not as keen
    as one might think.
You see clear past the point in this affair,
    and overlook the power that is mine.
You may be right in claiming that a woman's arm
    is no likely match for manly force.
But I am not *a* woman. I am many. *We* are many.

You say I am alone in what I do,
    and in saying this you prove yourself the fool.
There are many women in those tents,
    who are not fond of men who slay their sons.
I am not alone.

AGAMEMNON
You mean our slaves… Greek hunters' prey?

HEKABE
Can you look at things another way,
    and see with women's eyes for a change?
What you see may be a mask worn at our discretion.
You know us not at all.

AGAMEMNON
I know that women are weak.

HEKABE
In force of arm, I will not quarrel,
    one to one you men prevail.
But when we count our common strength
    we soon add up to one of you.
The rest is craft,
    and there we women have no peers.

AGAMEMNON
I mistrust the power you describe.

HEKABE
You may trust to find us equal to our task.
We have our precedents for what we do.
Did not women slay the sons of Aiguptos
    without the help of men?
And how did Lemnos come to have no men?
Murdered one by one with weakness you dismiss!
I will say again what I have said.
Leave this to us.
All I ask of you is safe passage for this woman
    through your ranks.

*Agamemnon nods his assent, and Hekabe turns to her
handmaiden.*

HEKABE

Go to Polumestor.
Tell him that Hekabe, once queen of Troy,
 summons him, and his sons as well,
 to come here, to me, for covert reasons,
  cogent none the less for everyone concerned.
If he wonders how his children figure in my scheme,
 say no more than this:
 They too must know the secret that I bear.

 The Handmaiden leaves, and Hekabe turns to Agamemnon.

Agamemnon, I ask one thing more.
Delay the burial of my girl,
 so that brother and sister may share a common flame
 and know each other's touch
  when they lie side by side beneath a single mound
   of this foul Thracian soil.

AGAMEMNON

It shall be as you have said.
With sails as limp as ours are now,
 we Greeks are going nowhere,
 and can delay as suits your wish.
As for what you undertake, I wish it well.
You are not alone to gain,
 when justice finds its way on earth.
It is a common not a private thirst,
 which you set out to quench.

 Agamemnon departs and Hekabe returns to her tent.

CHORUS

Women of Troy,
We belong to a city sacked
And brought to ruin.

Like a deafening, darkening locust-cloud,
Invading Greeks swarmed across our plains
And camped outside our gates.
From that day on we spent our lives
In the tightening coils of a viperous foe.
Our ten years of bitter siege
Were an unabating storm
Of pain and sorrow.

Women of Troy,
We shall never forget the fateful night
The coiled serpent struck.
Deceived into thinking the Greeks were gone,
A delirious city danced and feasted and drank its fill
Deep into the night.
Spears were hung again high upon the walls
And warriors went to bed without their swords.
Even in the tallest towers mounted on the city's walls
Thoughts of Greeks at last were gone,
And weary watchmen slept.

Women of Troy,
We were the last to bed that night
In our city glad with peace.
We stood naked before gold-glistening mirrors,
Combing from our hair and from our hearts
The snarls of bygone strife.
But then the night was rent in two
And all its demons flooded in.
We heard the shouts of hateful Greeks
Pouring through our streets
Like a poisonous plague.

Women of Troy,
We covered ourselves and fell to our knees,
While our husbands leapt for their spears.
In seconds we moved from peace to war
But even those seconds were too slow.
We watched our husbands die without a fight,
Swallowing Greek spears and crying to us
With mouths of blood.
With our eyes turned back to Troy in flames
We were herded into ships
And blown across the sea.

Women of Troy,
We have nothing now but our memories
And our anger.
Our souls are the embers of a smouldering Troy
And we must preserve its flame.
With every exiled breath we breathe,
In a land and a life no longer ours,
We summon rage.

A curse upon Helena and her love.
A curse upon all Greeks
And their friends.

> *During the last lines of the Chorus, Hekabe emerges from her*
> *tent, as Polumestor enters with his two small sons and several*
> *guards. Hekabe does not acknowledge him.*

POLUMESTOR

Dearest Hekabe,
    wife of my beloved friend Priamos,
    may-he-rest-in-peace,
    at the very sight of you tears well up in my eyes...
        for Troy...
    and now for your lovely daughter's tragic end.
We live in dark times.
Where can you put your trust these days?
It's all we can do to keep our honor intact, much less...
Anyone of us can be on top of things today,
    and ruined tomorrow.
The gods can make a mess of any life... and will!
The best laid plans...
I suppose it's all to bring us to our knees,
    as if life makes some deeper sense down there.
But it doesn't do any good to go around moaning
    about what's over and done with.

My good lady, I sense your anger.
Forgive me, and try to understand.
As king of Thrace, I have many responsibilities,
    and some of them take me far afield.
I could not have come to you any sooner than I have.

HEKABE

Old and dear friend, you misread my anger...
    not anger at all.
It is shame that bows my head,
    shame that I a queen should fall so low.
When you last saw me, I stood wrapped
    in all the splendor this poor life may briefly offer.
And now you see for yourself what has become of me.
It is you who must forgive me;
    for I cannot raise my eyes to look you in the face.
Take this as no sign of my ill-will, my friend,
    but only of my shame.

POLUMESTOR
I understand, Hekabe, give it no more thought.
But now, tell me, what more can I do for you?
Your servant spoke of some new urgency.

HEKABE
Yes, there is something I would share with you…
        and your sons… in privacy…

Staring toward Polumestor's guards who stand nearby.

        if that is to be had.
Do you think we can be alone?

POLUMESTOR
To his guards.
You may leave. I am alone… with a friend.
I will be safe here.

His guards leave, and Polumestor turns to Hekabe.

Now, you must tell me how I can use my good fortune
        to be of some help to you in your affliction.
Think of what I have as yours.

HEKABE
You are very gracious, just as I remembered you.
But first, my thoughts are of my son, entrusted to your care.
Tell me, Polumestor, is he well?

POLUMESTOR
He could not be better. He is your one cause for joy.

HEKABE
Dearest friend,
        you have told me what I so sorely needed to know.
Knowing this much, I can go on.

POLUMESTOR
But now there must be more that you would have of me.

HEKABE
Yes, of course there is.
Yet I want to know more of my son.
Does he speak of me?

POLUMESTOR
He speaks of little else.
If it were not for my firm hand,
    he would be here now.
He wanted to come to you in some disguise.
I thought it best to keep him out of sight.

HEKABE
And the gold… is it in your hands?

POLUMESTOR
Safe within my vaults.

HEKABE
Best keep it there.
That much gold can bring forth greed.
I trust it would not tempt a friend.

POLUMESTOR
My life is full with what I have.

HEKABE
Yes, how could it be otherwise?
Now, do you know why I needed to see you and your sons?

POLUMESTOR
Not at all. We are waiting to find out.

HEKABE
Dearest Polumestor, I intend to be as good a friend to you
    as you have been to me…
        to return favor with favor.

POLUMESTOR
You needn't think in such terms.

HEKABE
O, but there are no others for a woman in my place.
There were secret stores of ancient gold
    belonging to the house of Priamos…

POLUMESTOR
And this concerns me and my sons?

HEKABE
Indeed, for you are a man of honor…
    one of the last, it seems.

POLUMESTOR
But why did you want me to bring my sons?

HEKABE
I have more to say of this gold of mine.
And it is best that they too should hear it all,
    in case anything untimely should befall you.

POLUMESTOR
I see your point.
This war has taught us all a cunning
    we never knew we'd need.

HEKABE
Speaking for myself, I know this to be true.
But tell me, do you recall where Athena's temple
    once stood in Troy?

POLUMESTOR
The gold lies there?

Hekabe nods assent.

POLUMESTOR
Will I find a marker of some sort?

HEKABE
A black slab of rock jutting up from the earth.

POLUMESTOR
Is that it?
Is the entire family treasure hidden there?
Or is there more besides?

HEKABE
It is all there… save a bag of priceless jewels,
    which I carried in my cloak from flaming Troy.
I cannot keep them hidden long.
Will you take them now and keep them safe?

POLUMESTOR

You have them here, now?
Are they concealed beneath your cloak?

HEKABE

They are well hidden in my tent.

POLUMESTOR

You keep them here, with Greeks on every side?

HEKABE

Our tents belong to us.
In that small sphere, they leave us captive women
    to our own devices.

POLUMESTOR

You think it safe within your tent?
There are no men inside?

HEKABE

No men. Only women.
Come, be my guest, as my son is yours.
I have a debt to pay.
You cannot begrudge me this.
Come quickly. We may not have much time.
The Greeks are keen to launch their ships
    at the first breath of homeward winds.
Then, after we are done,
    you will want to go at once and join my son.

*Polumestor enters with his sons into Hekabe's tent. The
Handmaiden and the Chorus follow Hekabe into the tent.*

CHORUS

King of Thrace, all debts come due,
Even for a man who wears a crown.
Once you thought the gods too slow
To catch you in your evil deeds.
But now you know
How swift the gods can be.
Always in the end, evil and ruin
Lie side by side.
You may think to steer a private course
Free of every rock and shoal.

But then you strike the unforeseen
And your once sound ship
Drinks the sea beneath your feet.
What man is equal to the ocean's rage,
Clinging to the wreckage of a splintered life?
What good are hopes of unseen shores,
When swirling waters drag you flailing
Down to hell?
King of Thrace, all debts come due,
Even at the hands of women slaves.

*The chorus enters the tent. Silence. Then uproar and screams
from the tent.*

POLUMESTOR
Oh my god... help! Help!
No! You're blinding me!
Children! Where are you ?
Run! Run for your lives!
I am blind. I see nothing.
Children! Oh god no... No!
You filthy demon bitches! You've murdered my sons!

Hekabe emerges from the tent, followed by the other women.

POLUMESTOR
Never... I will never let you escape!

HEKABE
Cry out all you like, Polumestor.
No power on heaven or on earth can bring light to your eyes
or life to your sons.
As for your revenge on me,
already you have done all there is to do.

To the women.

You see, the Thracian monster
finds his way from the tent.
Stay clear of him. He is not yet tame.

*Polumestor emerges from the tent, lunging and scrambling on
all fours like a wounded animal, grabbing blindly after Hekabe
and the women with his hands. His eyes are streaming blood.*

POLUMESTOR

Where are you? Murderous hags, I'll find you
    if I have to crawl over every rock in Thrace.
Where are you? You'll pay for this.
I'll hound you to your graves.
Cursed Trojan bitches! Where are you hiding?
I know you're here. Oh if I could only see!
I hear you. I hear your steps. I hear you breathe.
One right lunge and I would drag you to the ground,
    tearing your flesh apart with my hands and teeth,
        glad in the spattering rain of your blood.
I will be sated with each of you. You will make my feast.

Where am I to go?
I cannot leave my children
    to be clawed apart by hellish Bakkhai,
        a meal for savage mountain bitches,
    their carcasses picked clean and left
        to whiten in the sun.
Where? Where am I to go?
Like a ship tacking into port,
    I must go back to that death-sodden lair.
I must shroud and guard my young.

*Polumestor finds his way back into the tent. He drags the bloody
corpses of his sons from the tent, covering them with a cloth he
has found inside. He crouches over the bodies of his sons as if
to ward off any further evil.*

CHORUS

Wretched man, you are poisoned from the well
    of your own deeds,
Some god has seen to your undoing with pitiless dispatch.

POLUMESTOR

Help! Help!
Men of Thrace, warriors, bring your sharpened spears.
Come to me!
Greeks! Help! Rescue me, in god's name!
Doesn't anyone hear me? Won't anyone come to me?
Is no one there?

I am the victim of women, utterly ruined by women.
What has happened to me is strange and dreadful
    beyond belief.

Where do I turn? Where do I go?
If I had wings to leap into the sky,
    I would quit this darkened earth
      and soar like a giant moth to the fiery vault of heaven
        until, like a torch, I burst to flame.
Otherwise, I wait even now for the hooded ferryman
    to journey me to blackest hell.

CHORUS

No one can be blamed for wishing to be rid of life,
    when life becomes a burden too heavy to bear.

Agamemnon enters with his guards.

AGAMEMNON

What is all this uproar?
The mountains are alive
    with echoing screams and cries of anguish.
Troy fell with less tumult than this.

POLUMESTOR

Dearest Agamemnon, is that you?
Yes, I know your voice, my friend.
Look at me. Do you see what I have suffered?

AGAMEMNON

What an ungodly sight.
You poor wretch, who has done this to you?
Who has bloodied your eyes
    and left them dense as stones?
Who has butchered your two boys?
This is the work of a hatred I dread to imagine.

POLUMESTOR

Hekabe! It was Hekabe and her hags!
They have destroyed me.
They have worse than destroyed me.

AGAMEMNON

What are you saying?

To Hekabe.

You did this, Hekabe?
This unspeakable atrocity is *your* doing?

POLUMESTOR
You mean that bitch is here, now?

Lunging aimlessly, in hope of grabbing hold of Hekabe.

Where? Tell me where she is.
All I need is one hand on her
    and I'll rip her open like rotten fruit.

AGAMEMNON
Restraining him.
Hold on. What's come over you?

POLUMESTOR
For god's sake, let me go!
Let me have my way with her.
I'm telling you to unhand me.

AGAMEMNON
And I say "no"! Cage this savagery of yours
    and give me your account of what's gone on.
If I'm to judge with any justice in this case,
    I must hear your side of things.

POLUMESTOR
All right, I will tell you what there is to know.
I took in the youngest son of Priamos,
    a boy named Poludoros, sent to me in fear
        of Troy's imminent collapse.
I was to protect and nurture him; but I took his life instead.
This much I admit. It was the only prudent thing to do.

I was afraid, and my reasoning ran as follows.
How could I afford to house the last surviving heir to Troy?
When this child would come of age
    would he not be driven by one dream:
        to resuscitate his race and seek revenge?
And if you Greeks found out about my secret guest,
    would you stand by and let this boy become a man?
No. It was clear to me
    this boy would bring a second Trojan war to Thrace.
And I would rule a land of ravaged fields and smoking ruins.
You see I was hostage to this boy,
    and I freed myself the only way I could.

All was well again…
    until Hekabe found out what I had done.
She lured me here with tales of hidden Trojan gold.
And to avoid unwanted ears and eyes,
    she led me to her tent with my two boys.

Once inside, I sat upon the ground,
    closed in on every side by Trojan slaves.
What then took place was strange but smoothly done,
        too quick to question at the time.
It seemed that everything I brought into the tent
    was made the sudden object of some fuss.
My cloak was held up to the light
    to display its Thracian weave.
My sword and spears were handed around the tent.
Their craftsmanship was held in awe.
The atmosphere was close and warm,
    and I thought it not amiss that I had been relieved
        of my only means of self-defense
    and separated from my sons.
Suddenly, at some unseen signal from their queen,
    the women threw their doting ways aside,
    drew glinting daggers from their robes,
    and slashed the life from both my boys.
I barely saw what happened to my sons
    as I was tackled by a wall of frenzied women
    and hurled upon my back into the dust.
My hands and feet were pinned in place
    by a concerted strength I could not hope to match.
Even when I tried to lift my head,
    they grabbed my hair and wrapped it in their fists,
        slamming my head against the rocky ground.
I was now a victim made ready for their lurid plans,
    spread apart and bawling like a netted beast.
One by one they took their turns with me,
    in acts hideous beyond the reach of words.
Straddling me whose struggles were in vain,
    they plunged into the sockets of my eyes
        the brooch-pins taken from their loosened gowns.
My eyes went dark with a pain I've never known
    and my face became a river running deep with blood.
Their ritual complete, my women captors,
    leaping to their feet, fled the tent
        and ran from my exploding wrath.

Set free from their snares at last,
 I leave a bleeding trail in their pursuit,
  groping and lunging at empty air,
  without a trace of sight or scent
   to guide me to my prey.

Agamemnon, you see the awful price I've paid
 for my simple zeal on your behalf,
  clearing from your path a likely future foe.
Finally it comes down to this.
I am not the first man to take abuse from women,
 nor shall I be the last.
I call upon that consortium of men
 who have suffered much from women at their worst
  to confirm what I have learned today
   to be the simple truth.
No sea nor soil nor womb of any sort yields creatures
 so vile and worthy of our hate as women.

     HEKABE
Agamemnon, we would do wrong
 to let a desperate man's loud words
  deafen our ears to the message of his deeds.
Worthy deeds make for worthy speeches,
 but odious deeds plead their case in the basest of terms.
There is nothing worse than rot wrapped in finery.
Behind whatever veil of words, however finely woven,
 a rotten life begins to smell and give itself away.
Cover your ears to the craft of this man's words
 and you will smell the kind of man he is.

    Turning to Polumestor.

You say you slew my son for friendship's sake,
 to spare the Greeks a second toilsome war.
But how many favors would it take
 to enamor Greeks of savage Thrace?
More favors than your barbarous mind could conjure up.
And when did you start courting Greeks… and why?
What ties of your blood or common cause
 obtain between you two?
Or *was* it fear that pushed you to the path you took?
This fear is sheer contrivance on your part.
You are transparent in what you've done and why.

You slew my son for gold. He was the victim of your greed.
We would have to be as blind as you've become
    not to see you standing naked in your guilt.
Polumestor, surely you know this:
    if you had proved yourself worthy of our trust,
    rearing our child in safety while he came of age,
        your honor as a man would be intact.
True friendship shines forth most,
    when put to such a test as this.
And in my son you would have had a friend for life,
    sharing his own wealth with you
        should you ever fall in need.
But you took a very different path;
    and, even in your blindness,
        you can see where it has led.
You have your gold and nothing else.
May it bring you happiness and length of days.

HEKABE

To Agamemnon.

To you, Agamemnon, I say this:
    If you take this man's side,
        you prove yourself as base as he.
This godless man has betrayed his friends,
    murdered his helpless guest,
    lied and stolen and proved himself
        in every way a villain.
You treat him well, and you are the same as he.
With this, I've said enough.

AGAMEMNON

I have no liking for the place I'm in.
If I judge another's wrongs, it is because I must.
Hearing what I've heard from both of you
    and seeing what I've seen,
    I would live in shame throughout my days,
        if I were now to turn my back and simply walk away.
Polumestor, it seems amply clear to me you killed your guest,
    not as any favor to us Greeks,
        but for the gold you wanted as your own.
All the rest you've said is sheer pretence,
    fast thinking under courtroom pressure,
        nothing more.
To you it seems a slight matter to slay a guest.
We Greeks have very different thoughts in this regard.

What you have done we find contemptible...
    not the sort of fault we overlook.
I would condemn myself in acquitting you.
And this I shall not do.
Since you have unleashed evil,
    you must let it drag you where it will.

POLUMESTOR
Bested by a woman. What a bitter judgement.

HEKABE
You think you suffer too much for what you have done?

POLUMESTOR
My sons... my eyes... you bitch!

HEKABE
You complain to me? You think I suffer less?

POLUMESTOR
Hag, you exult in ruining me!

HEKABE
Would you begrudge me that?

POLUMESTOR
Your triumph will be brief.

HEKABE
It will suffice.

POLUMESTOR
I know more than you suspect.
Dionusos, our Thracian seer,
    has read for me the future like a book.

HEKABE
There must be pages missing in his tome.
Pity he told you nothing of today.

POLUMESTOR
Wretch, mocking me like some superior being!
You shall drown at sea,
    hurling yourself from the masthead of a Greek ship.

HEKABE
I spit your prophecies back into your face.
You see a lot for someone with no eyes.

POLUMESTOR
I see your daughter slain…

HEKABE
Kassandra?

POLUMESTOR
By this king's wife. She keeps a grim house.

HEKABE
Never so mad as that would she be driven.

POLUMESTOR
Mad enough to hack her own husband down
    with an axe, while he…

AGAMEMNON
Enough! You've raved on long enough!
Do you want to suffer still another blow?

POLUMESTOR
Play bold now; but a bath of blood
    is being drawn for you at home.

AGAMEMNON
Seize him… and drag him off!

POLUMESTOR
My words strike home?

AGAMEMNON
To his guards.
Gag him!

POLUMESTOR
Fair enough. I've said it all.

AGAMEMNON
Waste no time with this man.
Let his own insolence of tongue
    entertain him on some desert isle.

Polumestor is dragged off my Agamemnon's guards.

And you, Hekabe,
  bury your dead as best you may.

Hekabe leaves with her Handmaiden.

Women of Troy, be ready for our sailing.
I feel a breeze across my face, and it will take us home.
A blessing on our journey now.
May we leave our long miseries behind
  and find our homes at peace.

Agamemnon exits.

CHORUS

To the tents,
  to the ships,
    to the lives no longer ours.
This is the way of slaves: to echo others' lives.
When fate stands in our path, it is we who must give way.

The Chorus exits.

H E L E N

INTRODUCTION
○◇○◇○◇○◇○

What follows is intended not only for classical scholars, but also for those who have stumbled across or been assigned this text and wonder why Euripides and the *Helen* should lay claim to their time and energies, much less to their imagination and heart. I shall begin with Euripides.

EURIPIDES

The names of Aischylos, Sophokles, and Euripides are so often said in sequence that they might for all practical purposes be hyphenated as a single designation for ancient Greek tragedy. An uncritical reading of Aristotle's *Poetics* might be added to confirm one's sense that Greek tragedians wrote to a formula as fixed and tedious as today's pulp romances or Broadway musicals. The truth is, however, that classical tragedy was a tempestuously diverse art form tolerating works at moral, political, and aesthetic extremes from each other. Euripides, admittedly, was barely tolerated by his contemporary critics, who judged his drama to be the demise of tragedy, discontinuous with the tradition and indeed destructive of it. In short, he was seen then and is best seen now as a rebel. Let us consider the roots and the nature of his rebelliousness.

Euripides was only one generation removed from his most distinguished dramatic mentors, but he might as well have lived in another age from them. To imagine the extent and character of the gulf separating Euripides from Aischylos and Sophokles, one might contrast the American generation who grew up in the afterglow of World War I and fought in World War II with that generation who came to adulthood in the 1960s and either fought in or resisted the Vietnam War. Indeed, the parallels between Athens in the fifth century BCE and the United States in the twentieth century are quite striking and are altogether illuminating of Euripidean drama.

Twice in the first two decades of the fifth century, Athens had played the crucial hand in the allied Greek victories over the Persian "barbarians." Twice the Persians had invaded Greece with epic force and arrogance, and each time Athens, together with its allies, had repelled the Persians and made the world safe again for democracy. The battles of Marathon and Salamis became the touchstones of Athenian moral and military preeminence. In passing, we should note that Aischylos fought both at Marathon in 490 BCE and at Salamis in 480 BCE, and that Sophokles led a chorus of boys in the festivities marking the victory at Salamis, events that neither playwright would ever or could ever forget. Euripides, on the other hand, born four years before the glorious Athenian victory at Salamis, came to maturity during the inglorious period of Athenian imperialism, and he wrote all but two of his extant plays during the Peloponnesian War.

In the years after Salamis, Athens abused its moral and military leadership to acquire an empire, in which its allies were cajoled and coerced into accepting the status of subjects. In time, Athens came to treat the Greek world as if it were the family business. Athens's own national security and national interest became sovereign concerns, fictions sufficient to encompass and lay claim to the world it had once fought to save from the similarly bold and ambitious designs of the Persians. Athens gambled for absolute power and soon became an addict of its own aspirations. The more immoral its policies, the more self-righteous its rhetoric. The more it departed from its own past, the more it appealed to that past.

Apart from the ever-conspiring but daunted Persians, Athens had only one rival in its ascendancy, Sparta, its erstwhile ally in the Persian Wars. For those with any vision, a total war between these two superpowers and their satellites came to be seen as an inevitability for which it was only prudent to summon one's energies in avid preparation. And, since there was no averting this conflict, one might as well provoke it at one's convenience and to one's initial advantage. Such was the logic that prevailed, although both Athens and Sparta were internally divided in sentiment over the coming war and remained divided over the war itself, once it came in 431 BCE, nearly fifty years after the Persian defeat at Salamis. What ensued were twenty-seven years of savagery, a gathering spiral of destruction and degeneration, chronicled by Thukydides in his history of the Peloponnesian War and dramatized by Euripides in so many of his plays.

Although Euripides never wrote plays as martial and patriotic as Aischylos's *Persians,* one can find strewn in what he did write the shattered but recognizable remnants of a lost Athenian idealism. He knew that Athens had once stood for decency and self-determination. He knew that Athens had once shone like burnished gold, victorious in virtue, virtuous in victory. He also knew what Athens had become and what it now stood for, *realpolitik* and imperialism. Such was the discrepancy between its myths and realities. In play after play, Euripides struck two notes: one sounding the legacy and a second sounding the present state of affairs. The resulting dissonance enraged Euripides' contemporaries, for it had the tormenting ring of truth to it. Relentlessly, Euripides sounded out the clash between Athens's professed commitments and its operative commitments, employing various strategies—notably irony, allegory, and parody—to orchestrate his brutal melodies.

According to Sophokles' rather tame characterization of the difference between himself and Euripides, Sophokles presented people as they ought to be, whereas Euripides presented people as they are. However, this is not precisely accurate, for Euripides reminded his audience of how people ought to be, even as he revealed them as they actually are. Otherwise, Euripides would have written straight Attic comedy, whose employment it was to speak directly and mercilessly to the present situation. As a tragedian, Euripides mostly confined himself to the legends and mythic material of which tragedies were made, but he brought that legacy into disarray just as Athens had debased its own inheritance. Thus, on the stage of Euripides, the Olympian divinities are often callous and cruel beyond our grasp, while the great lords of legend appear as petty, amoral, deceptive, cowardly, selfish, and often bungling nonentities unworthy of their epic place. Tragedy implies stature, and Euripides refused to allow his contemporaries to flatter themselves and their travails with delusions of tragedy. Instead, he gave an adulterous generation a suitably adulterated mythic structure in terms of which to see itself.

At the same time, Euripides fashioned a new conception of heroism, coined for all those long excluded from the traditional Olympian and baronial heroism. His was a heroism devoid of privilege, the all-too-divine privilege of immortality and the all-too-human privilege of wealth and unaccountable power. Euripides' heroes were those whose effulgence is eclipsed in all but the darkest times, those who are the first to suffer most, but whose sufferings elapse without official notice: slaves, children, women, peasants, foreigners, and old people. We might say that Euripides unmasked tragedy. It is indeed difficult to imagine his characters wearing theatrical masks, which visually defined each character in terms of certain fixed categories like age, sex, social standing, and race. Euripides develops the individuality of his characters in a manner and to a degree not found among other classical tragedians. But his characters assert more than their individuality. Euripides' characters openly defy their masks. Men act like women and women like men. Kings behave like slaves and slaves like kings. Children outstrip warriors in bravery and Greeks outdo the barbarians in barbarism. Peasants display their nobility of spirit, while nobles display their innate depravity. Euripides' is a theater without secrets, but surely not without its point. And the point seems to be that nobility of spirit, the nobility traditionally ascribed to the Greek gentleman, the *kalos k'agathos,* is the only true heroism, and that no one is born into it. Further, the climb to decency is shown to be more steep for those born into privilege.

"I made the drama democratic," says the Euripides of Aristophanes' *Frogs,* "I staged everyday life, the way we live it." In keeping with his commitment to the least of men and women, Euripides admits without apology in the *Frogs* that he presented in his plays the dialogue of ordinary conversation; "for," he argues against the heightened language of Aischylos, "you ought to make people talk like people." (I would interject here that if Euripides did not sound like Aischylos or like Sophokles to his contemporaries, he should not sound like them in translation.) It is not surprising to learn that this poet of the people was adored by his audiences even as he was scorned by the judges. Only four of Euripides' twenty-three tetralogies were awarded first prizes, while Sophokles may have won as many as twenty-four victories. Nonetheless, when the surviving remnants of the Athenian army were herded into Sicilian quarries to desiccate in the sun, it was those who could recite the poetry of Euripides who were set free. Fitting tribute to a man who hated war as much as he esteemed compassion.

The Peloponnesian War cast a long shadow over Euripides' work. In fact, one perceives in his writing an obsession with imperialism, however global or domestic its arena, with war, and with the oppression of women—thematic concerns that in Euripidean drama reveal themselves as convergent. Euripides understands war to be the inevitable engine of imperial greed, while he sees the oppression of women not only as the most pedestrian form of imperialism but also as the most brutal legacy of war. In short, men make war and men oppress women, who are, together with their children, the most innocent victims of war, and all for the assertion of a privilege which is no more than a vile fiction. The only true privilege in Euripidean drama is integrity, and neither men nor women, by virtue of their sex, possess any special claim on it. It is power not androgen that corrupts, and if men are more corrupt than women, it is because they are more powerful. With Euripides in their midst, the Athenians did not need Lord Acton to tell them that "power corrupts and absolute power corrupts absolutely"; nor did they need I.F. Stone to point out that "governments lie." When, in the theater of Euripides, women acquire power, they employ it as savagely as do their male counterparts, though with more swift efficiency.

If power corrupts, so does suffering. A recurrent theme in Euripidean drama is the brutalization of women through suffering. In moderation, pain tests the spirit and purifies the heart; in excess, pain brings out the savage. Everywhere on the stage of Euripides there are limits, and no one crosses them with impunity. Jason, Eurystheus, and Polymestor, to mention a few, overstep the limit and pay for it, their power snapped as easily as a match; but those women whom they brutalized, their victims Medea, Alkmene, and Hekabe, prove every bit as bestial as their oppressors when they find themselves finally with the advantage of power. All that can be said in the latter's favor is that they were driven against their grain to what they did and that their deeds do accomplish a certain poetic justice. Poetic justice is, however, not justice, not ennobling, only satisfying.

It was most likely Euripides' long, outspoken opposition to the war party and its war that caused him to be hounded from Athens in 408 BCE, four years before Athens's unconditional surrender to Sparta. But even while he retained his citizenship and wrote for the theater, he lived the life of an outsider. Legend has it that he wrote his plays in a cave overlooking the Bay of Salamis. His once great city was now without its former might and morals. In the words he wrote for Iolaos in the *Herakleidai*: "very few men these days live up to what their fathers were." Even the cosmos was no consolation to him, for to him, as a disciple of Anaxagoras, the planets and stars were no more than oversized rocks, some hot and some cold. The traditional gods are dead in Euripidean drama, though the sacred is very much alive. Euripides' one consolation and what he held most sacred, if we are to believe his own plays, was love, *philia,* the bond of fellowship and compassion, the peculiar solidarity of those condemned to mortality. In one play after another, Euripides pointed to the natural solidarity of women. Their common oppression had taught them *koinonia,* commonality, according to Aristotle the root and foundation of love. Men are less privileged in this respect. They must cross a great divide in order to embrace each other in love. But cross over they do in the *Herakles,* Euripides' perhaps most poignant tribute to love. In the *Herakles* we learn that Herakles has descended into hell to retrieve his friend Theseus, and we watch Theseus, in his turn, enter the inner hell of Herakles' soul, scarred by his own atrocities, to lift him to his feet again and so restore his friend to human stature. The last words of that play surely reveal the heart of Euripides: "Any man who would prefer great wealth or power to love, the love of friends, is sick to the core of his soul."

Before turning to the *Helen,* there are two notable slanders against Euripides that I wish to challenge and, as if it were in my power, to dispatch to the oblivion they deserve. The first of these is Euripides' unwarranted reputation as a misogynist. It is perhaps an occupational hazard of writers to become identified with precisely those views or actions they most abhor. Such is the case with Euripides and misogyny. Women simply dominate the corpus of Euripidean drama. Some of those women, like Medea, Phaedra, Hekabe, and Klytemnestra, are demonstrably corrupt, while others of them, like Makaria, Polyxene, and Iphigeneia, are singularly pure; but all of them are victims and all of them, in spite of their oppression, are strong nd decisive, which is more than can be said of their male counterparts. It was an unlikely misogynist who wrote this line for Medea to hurl out at her predominantly male audience: "I would rather fight in the front ranks three times [which is nearly to say "die three deaths"] than bear one child!" In part, Euripides must have won himself the title of misogynist by openly attributing sexual passion to women and by confronting his audience with women who met affront with affront, brutality with brutality. There is no question that his plays evoked and thus laid bare the misogyny of his audiences, and that, on occasion, he gave voice, through one of his characters, to an unmitigated hatred of women. But it is false to impute that voice and its hatred to Euripides. Consider, for example, the following speech of Polymestor in the *Hekabe:*

> I am not the first man to take abuse from women,
>   nor shall I be the last.
> I call upon that consortium of men
>   who have suffered much
>   from women at their worst.
> To confirm what I have learned today
>   to be the simple truth:
> That no sea nor soil nor womb of any sort
>   yields creatures so vile and worthy of our hate
>   as women.

Admittedly, these words would suffice to convict Polymestor of a certain antipathy toward women, but there are simply no grounds for assigning that same antipathy to Euripides. No one reading the *Hekabe* could argue in good faith that Polymestor is portrayed as anything but the most despicable of humans. Hekabe's and the chorus's contempt for Polymestor maybe taken for granted, but it is Agamemnon who silences him and condemns him without reprieve to a certain but unmercifully slow death, blind and marooned on a deserted island.

The second slander from which Euripides deserves to be exonerated may be found in as ancient a critic as Aristophanes or in as modern a one as Nietzsche. What I have in mind is the charge that Euripides was a Sophist, addicted to the excessive rationalization of action, motive, and character. Nietzsche's reading of Euripides in *The Birth of Tragedy* surely represents one of the most brilliantly wrong achievements in the history of criticism. The central difficulty with Nietzsche's proposal is that on Nietzsche's own terms Euripides is a Dionysian, not an Apollonian, poet; for no more Dionysian drama has ever been written than the *Bakkhai*. Granted, Euripides was a student of the eminent Sophists Protagoras and Prodikos, but all that can be legitimately inferred from his association with the Sophists is his thorough familiarity with their ideas and methods, not his concession to them. Sophistry in simplest terms is the discipline of argumentation, which enables one to argue any case persuasively regardless of its merits or of one's own commitment to it. Sophistry espouses morally neutral reason, reason abstracted from any straining after or commitment to truth. If one wished to pursue sophistic training today, one might join a debating society or enrol in law school, where the art of advocacy is taught.

There is no denying that Euripides' plays are rife with sophistry. Euripides paraded before his audiences a long line of fast talkers who were desperately endeavoring to put their shabby lives in a better light. We may recall Jason's efforts to convince Medea that, in abandoning her and their sons, he had only their best interests in mind. His royal, nymphian bride-to-be did not figure in his decision. Equally absurd was Polymestor's complaint that he had been in fact a hostage to the helpless, hapless Polydoros, and that his murdering the boy in cold blood had been an act of self-defense. Euripides' plays abounded with vain speeches such as these, precisely because Athens abounded with the same. After all, Athens had a reputation to maintain as well as an empire to acquire; only a verbal blizzard could conceal its atrocities. Year after year it defended its policies and promoted its war effort in the most sterling terms. What else but Athens could Euripides have had in mind when he wrote the *Iphigeneia at Aulis* and created the devastating scene in which Agamemnon convinces his beloved Iphigeneia that she is dying nobly for Greece? No one in that play, no one but Iphigeneia, believed those words, least of all Agamemnon. He knew he was lying, knew that his daughter was dying to buy him time, to conceal for another day his depravity, and to slake the army's greed. And as Agamemnon's filthy words were being written, only the youth of Athens, the myriad Iphigeneias who comprise each new generation of warriors, were sufficiently naive and idealistic to believe that Athens's wars were worth the killing and the dying they entailed.

Euripides knew only too well the cosmetic influence of slick speech, whether from listening to Protagoras in the agora or from listening to his fellow citizens in assembly at the Pnyx. I suppose we cannot know with any certainty what Euripides thought of the desperately clever speeches he heard in his life and imitated in his art, speeches donated to the common cause of civilizing savagery with rational discourse and of sanctioning barbarity with the rule of law. We cannot know but we can guess. And I would guess that Euripides shared the disgust of Hekabe for what she heard and that he would have responded much as she did:

> Worthy deeds make for worthy speeches,
>   but odious deeds plead their case in the basest of terms.

There is nothing worse than rot wrapped in finery.
Behind whatever veil of words, however finely woven,
A rotten life begins to smell,
    and give itself away.
Cover your ears to the craft of this man's words,
    and you will smell the kind of man he is.

The same would seem to be true of cities, and of nations, then and now.

HELEN

Among the myths and legends of ancient Greece, there is no story more lovely and luring than that of Helen. From kings, warriors, and bards alike she summoned the ultimate effort. Her surpassing beauty not only launched the Greek fleet of a thousand ships to Troy but also bemused legions of ancient poets to sing her praise and her shame: praise for her loveliness and shame for her adultery. In all Greece, and in all ancient poetry, there was no woman so adored and so hated as Helen. She was at once goddess and whore, prize and scapegoat, fantasy and flesh. In short, she was the consummate woman, compelling, complex, fracturing any light shed on her into a spray of defiant color. She is at once the promise of bliss and the assurance of doom. She is fantasy incarnate, and her story must be one of magical ambiguity, a fairy tale for all time.

The origins of the story of Helen are too complex and elusive to trace in a sketch as brief as this one. The poetic glimpses of her provided in ancient Greek literature are mere images of images of images, as far removed from the original as are the shadows cast upon the wall of Plato's cave. They are like shells heaved up from the sea, resonant with lost legends and myths. Before considering, then, the figure of Helen as presented in Homeric epic and Attic tragedy prior to her appearance in the *Helen*, some mention of her former lives, without any expectation of comprehensive clarity, would seem appropriate.

The story of Helen is almost certainly of Indo-European origin. The core of the Helen story—the mustering of an army and the waging of a war to regain an abducted bride, the destined mother of one's children, the utterly irreplaceable woman prized above all other women—is without precedent in the older literatures of the ancient Near East, such as the *Epic of Gilgamesh* and the Middle Egyptian romances. The theme of romantic love and rivalry, however, is central to the

Indo-European epic and represents its own peculiar literary innovation. Indeed, this theme came to permeate the east Mediterranean texts of the Amarna/Mycenaean Age, shaping not only Greek epic but the patriarchal narratives of Genesis. Helen and Menelaos may constitute the exemplary embodiment of this theme, but we can discern its outlines, as well in a range of other Greek and Hebrew (i.e., Homeric and biblical) couples such as Achilleus and Briseis, Odysseus and Penelope, Hektor and Andromache, Abraham and Sarah, Jacob and Rachel. A bridge between Homer and the Bible may perhaps be found in the Ugaritic *Epic of Kret,* which tells of Kret's march on the city of Udum with a reputed force of three million men to reclaim his beloved Hurrai. Whether or not Kret is the eponym for Krete, the influence of this epic on the Minoan and Mycenean sources of Homeric epic would be difficult to dispute.

Helen's Indo-European roots are especially clear from her association with the Dioskoroi, the divine twins Kastor and Polydeukes, whose genetic counterparts may be found in the Asvins, or "horsemen," of Vedic mythology. The Asvins, whose frequent occupation it is to rescue the distressed, have a particular concern with the rising and setting of the Sun, Sūrya in the form of Sūryā the Sun Princess, whom they rescue or retrieve each day from the darkness. Thus they are called "the Retrievers." Often identified naturalistically with the Morning Star and the Evening Star, one twin follows the Sun Princess Sūryā into night and the other twin precedes her into the day. Together they are her escorts, and are variously seen to be her husbands or her groomsmen. The correspondences between Helen and the Indic Sūryā as well as those between the Dioskoroi and the Asvins are numerous and complex, but even a brief mention of some of them may prove illuminating and suggestive.

Like the Asvins, the Dioskoroi are portrayed in Greek literature as both horsemen and luminaries or celestial horsemen. When Helen is raped by Theseus, long before she is carried off by Paris, it is the twins Kastor and Polydeukes, who retrieve her from Athens, the city of her captivity. Later, when Paris abducts Helen to Troy, she is again retrieved by two brothers, Menelaos and Agamemnon, husband and groomsman, respectively. Further, in Homeric epic the destined land of her *nostos,* her homecoming, is Argos, which is curious because Argos is not Helen's home, unless by Argos is understood the Argolid or the entire Peloponnesus. At the very least we may hear a pun in Helen's Argive epithet, for *argos* means "bright" or "shining." Thus *Argos* could conceivably designate on some underlying stratum of meaning the day, the land of brightness, or even the land of the living. On this stratum, Helen, "the bright and shining one," would be retrieved by Argive brothers, twin horsemen (recalling that Homeric Argos is the land of horsemen) and brought back from night to day, from the land of darkness to the land of light.

Helen's stature in Homeric epic is remarkable; though a mortal, she is given the epithet of *koure Dios*, daughter of Zeus, an epithet reserved for the three great daughters of Zeus: Athene, Artemis, and Aphrodite. It is widely held that these three preeminent goddesses hail from a time and place antecedent to the reign of Zeus, perhaps representing the three functions of an earlier pantheon. Too powerful to be absorbed into Zeus's regime as his consorts, they were conceded a share in his blood rather than his bed, and granted a certain subordinate autonomy. The fact that Helen is included in this privileged circle suggests that she too was once a goddess of the first order, long before she became not only the daughter of Zeus but also the whore of Greece. Another clue to the existence and character of Helen's former radiance is her special affiliation with Aphrodite, who both favors and tyrannizes her in Homeric epic. Helen's association with Aphrodite suggests a link with sexuality and fecundity, and there is indeed ample evidence that Helen was worshipped as a fertility goddess, with her own shrines at Therapne, Dendra, and Rhodes, and with a Spartan festival, the Helenephoria, named after her. Her birth from an egg, her irresistible beauty, her multiple husbands, and her association with rape, being born both of rape and for rape, leave her identity as a fertility goddess in little doubt.

When we put together these two elements—Helen's legacy as the Sun Princess and her association with Aphrodite—we are able to grasp the broadest outlines of her complex character. In fact these two elements are not as disparate as they might at first appear. After all, the sun is the source of life and is intimately linked to fertility; thus Helen's identity as a sun goddess and her identity as a fertility goddess are to be seen as cognate identities. Further, it must be noted that the circuit of the sun, both as it marks the passage of day and night and as it marks the cycle of the seasons, involves a descent into death, the death that is night and the death that is winter. Once a year the earth dies and must be reborn, just as once a day the light dies and must be retrieved. Helen, intimate with both these cycles, cannot escape an association with night and death. As Sun Princess, she would spend half of her time in the land of darkness, and, like Persephone, as a fertility goddess, she would spend half of her time in Hades, the kingdom of death, whence the fearsome aspect of Helen and her mythic association with Nemesis and night. It is not surprising, then, that *Helene* has been associated with Selene, the moon goddess, and that Helen under her own name became the Spartan goddess of the moon. Helen's association with death is clear in the *Iliad*, wherein she is frequently referred to and frequently refers to herself as the *kuon*, the dog or bitch, and this in a poem where the word *kuon* is employed almost invariably to summon the horrific image of the dreaded scavenger dogs who roam the battlefield of Troy and rip the fetid flesh from the carcasses of unburied warriors. *Kuon* is also used in the *Iliad* to refer to Kerberos, the three-headed guardian dog of Hades. Such is the company Helen keeps in the Homeric imagination. She is at once Helen, bright and shining, and Helen, death of men and cities. Like Aphrodite, she is both irresistible and awful in aspect, indescribably lovely and terrible to behold.

It is clear that the face of Helen, as it emerges from a complex and elusive past, expresses more than we are able to grasp. The fact is that there were many Helens as there were many Troys. Just as ancient cities lie beneath each other, so disparate mythic strata lie one atop the other in literary traditions. Always, the past is both buried and preserved as the future is built, the rubble of one tradition providing the cornerstone for the next. This is simply to suggest that ancient writers like ancient architects did not create ex nihilo; rather, they re-created the new from the old, leaving their mark mostly in the form of alterations. Helen is no more the creation of Homer than she is the creation of Euripides, or of any other Greek poet. Her bards, one by one, recall and rework her story within their own lights and for their own purposes; and, like *matrioshkas*, the many, many Helens from Euripides clear back into faded prehistory lie nested one within the other, defying us to tell them finally apart.

It would be pointless and futile to attempt a composite sketch of Helen drawn from the myriad accounts of her in ancient Greek poetry. There is simply no consensus regarding her most essential features. Is she human or is she divine? Was she raped by Paris and dragged off against her will, or did she run off with him all too willingly, after having lured him into lust? Was she the preeminent cause of the Trojan War or its most pitiful victim; was she perhaps both? Did she employ every device to escape from her Trojan captivity, or did she use her considerable magical powers to try to foil a Greek victory? There are no vibrant answers, only cacophonous claims and counterclaims, to be found in Greek epic, lyric, and dramatic poetry.

Without the slightest pretense to an exhaustive or even balanced assemblage of the many images of Helen, I would nonetheless risk one or two questionable generalities regarding her tradition, from Homer to Euripides. The Homeric Helen has a certain aura of divinity about her that is increasingly shadowed in later Greek poetry. The Helen of the *Iliad* and the *Odyssey* displays a more or less consistently sublime calm. Her bearing and her beauty mostly evoke wonder. She possesses powers of divination and prophecy. She has an uncanny ability to recognize faces she hasn't seen before and to imitate voices she hasn't heard before. She administers potions powerful enough to banish all cares. By virtue of his mere association with her, Menelaos becomes immortal. For the most part there is a diminishing of Helen's divinity after Homer. No longer a goddess, nor even a divinely gifted woman, Helen descends to the condition of woman and, by most accounts, woman at her worst.

The Homeric Helen may have conferred immortality on her mate, but for later poets Helen's affiliation is with death, not life. The chorus in Aischylos's *Agamemnon* describes her as a blood flower never to be washed out, and as a demon of death stalking the house and bringing only agony with her. Euripides' Hekabe cries out with nothing but hate for her memory: "That one Spartan bitch with her large luring eyes dragged thriving Troy to ruin." And Andromache taunts Menelaos with his epic efforts to regain a worthless wife, arguing that he should not have lifted one single spear for such a slut as Helen. What he should have done instead, in the words of Andromache, is "just sat there and spat once in her direction." Understandably, Helen receives the most venomous abuse from those who suffered most on her account. Yet neither Priam nor Hektor, in the *Iliad*, blamed her for the plague that had followed her from Greece. But with these gracious exceptions, even in the *Iliad* Helen is crushed between two great hatreds, to borrow Aphrodite's phrase, the hatred of the Trojans and that of the Greeks.

Ancient Greek poetry is strewn with brief efforts to lift the blame for the Trojan War from Helen's memory. I will mention a few. Hesiod blames Aphrodite and Zeus. Homer suggests in the *Odyssey* that the war was fought for the honor of Agamemnon, and, in the *Iliad*, he reveals with celestial clarity the conflicting divine stakes in the war, all of which might suggest that Helen was a pretext and a pawn. Stesichoros traces the fatal flaw to Tyndareos, the father of Klytemnestra and Helen, who slighted Aphrodite and so brought down on his daughters the curse of notorious unfaithfulness. Then, of course, there is the curse laid upon Paris before his birth, and the fateful beauty contest from which Paris could not have emerged without two divinely vindictive enemies. And it is clear from many sources that Aphrodite promised to one man the wife of another, which leaves her surely with a share of the blame for what ensued. None of these extenuating circumstances, however, alters the fact that Helen went to Troy, and Kassandra, who ought to know this because she knows everything else, reveals in Euripides' *Trojan Women* that Helen's was a "willing love."

There is, however, another tradition which claims precisely this—that Helen never went to Troy. Before considering this claim, there is an important commentary on Helen's "willing love," in Euripides' *Trojan Women*, which ought to be considered. First, before Helen appears, there is the disbelieving remark of Hekabe, who has no kind words for Helen, to the effect that all this carnage and grief came about "because of the way one woman chose a man." At the very least she accuses the Greeks of overkill. She holds Helen to be guilty but acknowledges at the same time a disproportion between her sin and the Greeks' retribution. In simplest terms, Helen made love and the Greeks made war. Scarcely equivalent occupations. Helen chose love. Menelaos, her warlord husband, and Agamemnon, his ambitious brother, chose empire and bloodshed. Paris too chose love, the fact and implications of which Helen points out to Menelaos when she finally confronts him. Paris was given three options: empire, conquest, or love. The first option would have given him sovereignty over Menelaos, Agamemnon, and the rest of the Greeks. The second option would have given him victory over their armies. Instead, he opted for love, leaving empires and wars to them. Helen, it might be surmised, made the same choice. "Think about the meaning of this," says Helen. And if we do just that, we might conclude that the Greek army and its captains have certain debts to pay. To Paris they owe immeasurable gratitude for his indifference to power and to his preference for love. To Helen they owe the admission that she is hated not for causing the war but for despising them and their warring ways. Contemptuous of empire and of male prerogatives, Helen chose her own man and her own life. This was her unpardonable sin. However, Euripides' pointing this out was either too oblique or too unwelcome to exonerate Helen or her heirs.

Only the literal, if absurd, claim that Helen never went to Troy would suffice to clear her name. Euripides, it should be noted, was not the first poet to file this claim on Helen's behalf. Stesichoros, in his "Palinode to Helen," had stated: "There is no truth to the story that you sailed away in the benched ships. You never went to Troy." Homer, while he left no doubt that Helen went to Troy, had also placed her in Egypt, along with Menelaos, detoured in the homecoming. Herodotos, on the other hand, related in close detail how it was Paris and Helen who were blown ashore in Egypt, to Paris's great misfortune, for he escaped without Helen and barely with his life. Finally, it was Helen's divine siblings, the Dioskoroi, who announced at the close of Euripides' *Elektra* the theme of Helen's forthcoming vindication in the *Helen*, produced the following year: "Helen never went to Troy. Instead, Zeus fashioned and dispatched to Troy a phantom Helen, so that men might perish in hatred and blood."

In writing the *Helen*, Euripides was at his ironic and bitter best. In presenting a faithful Helen, chaste and secure in Egypt, Euripides not only left the Trojan War without its traditional excuse, but also left Athens's most recent folly without excuse as well. In 415 BCE, Athens, obsessed with the dream of extending its empire to the westernmost boundaries of civilization, had launched the most extraordinary armada in its history against the island of Sicily. And, when the first fleet met with disaster, it sent another. In doing so Athens played its last card. When the few survivors of this second expedition straggled back to Athens with the news of total Athenian defeat, they were greeted with hostility and disbelief. It was in that same winter of Athens's despair that Euripides wrote the *Helen*, a delightful, playful fantasy at whose center lay the darkest of truths. The Athenians had pursued a phantom in Sicily, and their disaster was the fruit of sheer folly. The homecoming veterans of Sicily and the homecoming veterans of Troy had at least this in common: whatever they braved and endured was for nothing. What they failed to have in common was victory. The lightness and brightness of the *Helen* only served to highlight ironically the unremitting darkness of what lay behind it, for the spotlight is on Helen and Menelaos and their happy ending. In the Sicilian misadventure there was no Helen and no Menelaos, and no happy ending. Inevitably, the Athenians would have identified not with Menelaos but with his battered servant, who wonders why the fact that they fought over a phantasm constitutes good news. "Menelaos," he asks, "help me to share your happiness. I can see for myself that you're happy, yet I can't for the life of me figure out why."

In brief, the *Helen* provided escape for those sufficiently dense or determined to overlook the truth it contained, but to the rest it told that truth with savage directness. "Empire" like "woman" is a fantasy, a fact that does not diminish the mad intensity with which men pursue it. The *Helen*, like Aristophanes' *Birds*, produced several years earlier, shortly after the departure of the first armada for Sicily, explores the psychology and the politics of erotic fantasy and reveals the deep complicity of sexual lust and the lust for power. This link between sexuality and violence was not a new theme in Euripides' dramas and it was to lie at the center of his two last plays, the *Iphigeneia at Aulis* and the *Bakkhai*. Nowhere, however, are the fantasy of woman and the folly of war revealed with more poignancy and bitter delight than in the *Helen*.

In many of his plays Euripides experimented at the border of tragedy and comedy, in recognition of the psychological fact that tragedy pushed to the extreme yields a dark, absurd humor. The border between laughter and tears in Euripidean tragedy is as thin as it is in life. Euripides frequently forces his audience to cross that border and so to revel when they know they ought to weep. In the *Helen*, I believe, Euripides would have us dance on the border itself, as if on the edge of a blade; we are meant to bleed even as we laugh.

TRANSLATION

Any translation of a play should, it seems, be itself a play. When someone changes a play into a novel or a novel into a play, we call it an adaptation, and so we should. So too, when an ancient play is changed into a text intended for propping upon one's desk and reading to oneself with incessant reference to glossary and endnotes, I think we must call that text an adaptation. Any translation of a play must be playable, first and foremost. In saying this I am not favoring arbitrarily the claims of the producer and actor and theatergoer over the claims of the student and scholar; the plays of Euripides belong inalienably to the theater and the concerns of the theater must rightfully prevail in any translation. Furthermore, Euripides wrote for his contemporary theater, for the ordinary citizen, for the people. And so it is the task of a translation to aim toward the contemporary public theater, not the university theater, which may or may not have absorbed the uncommon patience and privileged understandings of the academy.

What this means, to cite one example, is that Euripides' humor must be made to play humorously today. A pun, for instance, must be translated with a pun, not merely explained with a footnote indicating the existence of a pun in the original Greek. So too, savagery must remain savage, irony ironical, vulgarity vulgar, and so on. A literal translation, then, is not one that renders the Greek word for word, but one that creates a play that will play to its audience as closely as possible to the way in which Euripides' original played to its audience. This may be an unattainable ideal, but it is the ideal nonetheless. We may call this point "north," and every other endeavor of mine in this translation may be plotted from it.

If we are to believe Aristophanes and others, Euripides' plays did not sound and look like those of Aischylos or Sophokles. Thus translations of the former should not be made to play to a contemporary audience like those of the latter. In the *Frogs* we learn that Euripides' verse was freer than that of his peers and spoke to everyone, and that there was in his works a peculiar mix of homeliness and magnificence. Finally, regarding not the form but the substance of his dramas, the fact that Euripides was driven from Athens is the clearest indication we could have that he was understood. In this translation, though I have no desire to revive his agony nor to share in it, I hope for nothing more than that he be understood again.

DRAMATIS PERSONAE

◇◇◇◇◇◇◇◇◇◇◇

IN ORDER OF APPEARANCE

HELEN
Wife of Menelaos

TEUKROS
Surviving Greek Veteran of Troy

CHORUS OF CAPTIVE GREEK WOMEN

KORUPHAIOS
Leader of the Chorus

MENELAOS
King of Sparta

PORTRESS
Of the Palace of Theoklymenos

MESSENGER
And Member of Menelaos's Crew

THEONOE
Seeress Sister of Theoklymenos

ATTENDANTS TO THEONOE

THEOKLYMENOS
King of Egypt

SERVANTS OF THEOKLYMENOS

MESSENGER
And Servant of Theoklymenos

DIOSKOROI
Divine Twin Brothers of Helen

◇◇◇◇◇◇◇◇

HELEN

The scene is Egypt, seven years after the fall of Troy. The stage is set against the outer wall of the palace of Theoklymenos, son of the dead king Proteus, whose tomb is to one side. Helen has spread out a pallet of straw at the base of the tomb, where day and night she claims sanctuary. Helen is found propped against the wall of Proteus's tomb. She rises and walks to the center of the stage, where she addresses the audience.

HELEN

Here is where the Nile, unblessed with rain,
    swells with winter's pale snows
    flowing in the summer sun.
Glistening and pure,
    its streams flood the thirsting soil of Egypt,
    where Proteus ruled supreme so long as he drew breath.
Proteus, king of Egypt,
    made his dwelling here, on the island of Pharos,
    and took to his bed Psamathe, daughter of the seas,
    once married to Aiakos, until she quit his side.
Psamathe gave to the house of Proteus two children:
    first a son, Theoklymenos;
    and then a splendid daughter,
    whom at first they called Eido,
    her mother's pride and joy.
Later, when Eido came of age,
    a woman fit for some man's bed,
    her name became Theonoe, "seeress,"
    divinely sighted with a vision of all that is
    and of all that is yet to be.
This power was a legacy from her mother's line,
    from Nereus of the Seas.

As for me, my home is well known… Sparta.
My father… Tyndareos.
Oh yes, people tell a story about Zeus…
    how he once feathered himself into the likeness of a swan,
    feigned flight from a pursuing eagle,
    lit upon my mother Leda,
    and won his way with her.
It may have happened that way,
    or it may not have.
Either way, my name is Helen,
    and my story a long list of woes.

It all began when three goddesses,
    snarling among themselves over who was most beauteous,
    sought out Paris, tucked away on Mount Ida.
These three:
    Hera, Aphrodite, and Athene,
    the virgin sprung from Zeus himself,
    presented themselves to Paris,
    and set their quarrel in his lap.
Aphrodite bribed her way to victory.
I know… I was the bribe.
Paris was pledged my hand in marriage,
    and the rest of my charms as well,
    if a woman as cursed as I may boast of charms at all.
With thoughts now for nothing but my bed,
    Paris left Ida and his herds behind
    and made his way to Sparta.
Hera, for her part, displayed no grace in her defeat.
Her rage turned me and my promised bed
    to so much steam… vapor lost to the open air.
And Paris, none the wiser, brought home instead of me
    a stand-in fantasy made to my likeness,
    conjured from thin air and puffed into life.

Meanwhile Zeus had plans of his own
    to add misery to my misery.
He fanned the flames of war between Greece and hapless Troy.
This fire would purge the wearied world,
    overgrown with ordinary men,
    and would reveal once for all the greatest of the Greeks.
Spear to spear,
Greeks and Trojans faced-off over me.
I was the prize for which they fought.
Or so they imagined.
My name was on their lips,
    but my name was all they had of me.
It was Zeus who kept careful track of me
    and missioned Hermes to spirit me away.
Overcast with clouds,
    I trailed through the sky like a wisp
    until I was set down here in the house of Proteus,
    a man chosen for his singular integrity.
He would help me keep my bed unstained,
    ready for Menelaos's return.
So here I am.

Meanwhile, my hapless husband has marshaled an army
    sworn to my recapture
    and miscarried them to the towered walls of Troy.
Too many bodies bob in the River Skamander
    because of me.
And I, a victim in all of this, am slandered as a slut,
    as if I cheated on my husband,
    and engineered the war myself.

Then why do I go on living?
Hermes himself told me that one day
    I will go home to lustrous Sparta, on my husband's arm,
    after he has learned the truth,
    that I never went to Troy,
    nor ever made room in his bed for anyone else.
No man so much as made a move for my hand
    so long as Proteus walked the earth.
But now his eyes have gone dark in death,
    and things are different.
The dead king's son hunts daily for a wife,
    and I am his chosen quarry.
For my husband's sake,
    I bend my knees and play the suppliant here,
    at the tomb of Proteus, my honor's last resort.
No matter how sullied my name may be
    among the Greeks by now,
    here, in this place, I would keep the rest of me free of stain.

Enter Teukros, who does not at first see Helen.

TEUKROS
I wonder who's in charge of this place?
Stout walls... nicely crafted.
Top to bottom this is a king's house, nothing less.
I wouldn't be surprised to find Pluto himself in a place like this.

Catching sight of Helen.

Wait a minute!
My god, what am I seeing?
You look to me like the spitting image of the woman I loathe.
There's a lot of blood on that bitch's hands.
And because of her there's not much left of Greece...
    or of me, forth at matter.
Damn you for looking so much like Helen!

If I weren't a stranger here on strange soil,
    I would show you with one of my arrows
    how dearly you should pay for looking like her.

HELEN

Wait, poor devil, whoever you are.
Why do you turn away from me?
Tell me why I deserve your hate for what she did to you.

TEUKROS

You're right. I'm wrong.
I had no business loosing my anger on you.
I'll tell you something.
I'm not the only Greek who hates that woman.
I don't know anyone who doesn't.
But to you I owe an apology. Forgive me, Lady.

HELEN

Who are you and where did you come from?

TEUKROS

I am a worn and weary Greek… one of thousands.

HELEN

Then it's no wonder why you hate Helen so.
But I still want to know who you are.
You must have a name.

TEUKROS

My name is Teukros. Telamon was my father.
He planted my seed in Salamis,
    the land that reared me.

HELEN

What brings you here to the valley of the Nile?

TEUKROS

I am an exile, banished from my homeland.

HELEN

Poor man, who banished you?

TEUKROS

My father, the one who ought to love me most.

HELEN
Why? What grounds does he have
    for bringing such ruin down on you?

TEUKROS
My brother Aias's death.
When he died at Troy, it spelled the end of me.

HELEN
How so? He didn't die at *your* hand, did he?

TEUKROS
No… at his own hand, when he leapt on his own sword.

HELEN
Then he was crazed?
Sane men don't slaughter themselves.

TEUKROS
Do you know anything about Achilleus, son of Peleus?

HELEN
I know that he once courted Helen, or at least I heard as much.

TEUKROS
Well, when he croaked,
    the armor he left behind nearly started a whole new war,
    this time among his comrades.

HELEN
And that had something to do with your brother's death?

TEUKROS
Everything to do with it.
When the armor went to someone else,
    Aias bowed out.

HELEN
Then your brother died of nothing contagious.
How did his ruin spread to you?

TEUKROS
I failed to die with him.
That's where I went wrong.

HELEN
So you marched into legendary Troy instead?

TEUKROS
Yes… and while I was wasting Troy,
    my own life was coming apart.

HELEN
Tell me, did you put the torch to Troy and set her ablaze?

TEUKROS
Yes…
    so that if you'd look today for a trace of her walls,
    you'd find nothing.

HELEN
Helen, miserable Helen,
    how many wretched Trojans were plunged into hell,
    because of you!

TEUKROS
Don't forget the Greeks.
There was grief enough in Troy to go around.

HELEN
How long has Troy lain in ruins?

TEUKROS
Almost long enough for seven harvests.

HELEN
And how long a time in all were you camped at Troy?

TEUKROS
Moon after moon grew and slivered itself away over us…
    for ten years.

HELEN
Tell me about the woman of Sparta.
Did you take her captive?

TEUKROS
Menelaos wrapped her hair in his fist and dragged her off.

HELEN
Was this something you saw with your own eyes,
    or are you telling me what you heard from others?

TEUKROS
I see you, don't I?
Well, I saw her the same way.

HELEN
You don't suppose that what you saw then could have been
    a fantasy... wrought by some strange god?

TEUKROS
Can't we talk about something else?
Helen isn't exactly my favorite subject.

HELEN
I still wonder how you can be so sure of what you saw.

TEUKROS
I already told you.
I saw *her.* I see *you.*
It comes to the same thing.
I see what I see.

HELEN
Then Menelaos is home now... with her?

TEUKROS
He hasn't seen Argos yet... nor the Eurotas,
    much less his home.

HELEN
This dark news of yours shadows whoever hears it.

TEUKROS
The story is that Menelaos vanished with his wife.

HELEN
Didn't all the Argives sail home together?

TEUKROS
They did... until a storm rose up
    and scattered them like dice.

HELEN
Where were they in the sea's expanse
when the storm struck?

TEUKROS
Half-way across the Aegean.

HELEN
Since then… no one has seen Menelaos?

TEUKROS
No one.
In Greece he is spoken of as dead.

HELEN
Then I am lost.
The daughter of Thestia does she live?

TEUKROS
Leda? No, she's dead and gone.

HELEN
Don't tell me she died of shame…
from stories of her girl Helen!

TEUKROS
That *is* what they say.
No one else slipped the noose around her aristocratic neck.

HELEN
What of Tyndareos's twin sons?
Are they dead or alive?

TEUKROS
You hear both.

HELEN
Well, which do you hear more?
God! I have suffered so much already!

TEUKROS
One story is that they've become gods,
made into stars to circuit the night sky.

HELEN

That story makes me glad.
But you say there is another version...

TEUKROS

There is... that they slit their own throats
        and bled out their lives...
        victims to their sister's shame.
No more stories. I've wept enough already.

Now for what brings me here,
        to this royal house.
I must see Theonoe, the seeress.
Go to her for me and arrange a consultation.
I must learn how best to set my winged ship on course
        to sea-encircled Cyprus.
From Apollo's own mouth I have it
        that I will found a city there and name it Salamis,
        in happy memory of my island home.

HELEN

Friend, believe me, once you set sail,
        the way to Cyprus will be self-evident.
Your only concern should be to quit this place at once.
Get out of here before you're seen by Proteus's son,
        the local king.
Right now he is off in the woods with his hounds.
They share with him the same keen scent for slaughter.
He greets any Greek guest to this island
        with a sharpened blade.
Don't ask why. I have nothing to say.
If I did, what good would it be to you?

TEUKROS

Lady, you've said enough already.
May the gods reward your kindness with kindness.
You may look like Helen,
        but your heart is another story.
You two are as different as night and day.
Wrack and ruin to her, I say!
Let her drink the sea... to the last drop!
And thirst for Eurotas at the same time!
But to you, Lady, every blessing... always.

Exit Teukros.

HELEN

From wounds deep within me my agony wells up.
What voice can I give to such grief?
What muse could I approach with these tears,
    with these pitiful groans?

Come, maidens, virginal daughters of earth.
Winged Sirens, come to me.
How I wish for your accompaniment.
Let my tears fill your eyes.
Bend low beneath the weight I bear.
Learn the melody of my grief.
Then lift your flutes and lyres
    and turn my sufferings into song,
    a song to reach Persephone,
    encaved in unending night.
 There, in her awful haunt,
    may she find those who would echo the chant
    in notes deeper and darker still.
Queen of the dead,
    my laments are my libation,
    poured down into darkest hell,
    a canticle of despair to the lost and the damned.

Enter Chorus.

CHORUS

We were at the water's edge,
Where the river's dark currents
Curl 'round pale green reeds.
There, over the tall restless grass,
We spread the royal crimson robes
To dry and brighten in the sun.
Then a cry broke through the stillness,
A cry shrill with panic and grief.
It was no sound nor song we knew.
It could have been some sea nymph,
A Naiad delirious with terror.
Imagine her, fleeing Pan's advances,
Lost among the jagged sea-side cliffs,
Wailing with every step.
Exhausted and despairing,
She quails in the hollows of the rocks
And fills the air and the sea
With sounds to make your heart stop.

HELEN

Women, you who were once herded into barbarian ships
    and brought here as human booty,
    now, as fellow Greeks, listen to me.
Only a moment ago, a Greek sailor stood there,
    where you stand now.
His eyes and his words made me weep.
Troy has gone down in flames.
She is no more.
I murdered her... brought her every grief,
    with my name alone.
My mother has died of shame...
    and of the noose she slipped around her neck.
My husband... flung across the sea, and lost.
Gone too are Kastor and his twin.
Together they were the pride of my father's house.
Now they are nowhere,
    not on the open plains where they galloped their steeds,
    not in the meadows beside the Eurotas
    where they ran and wrestled and strove as young men do.
Wherever they once were, they are no more.

CHORUS

Lady, yours is a fate that would make a stone weep.
When Zeus came down from heaven,
Winged and white in the semblance of a swan,
And seeded your mother's womb with you,
Your lot was cast.
Yours would be a life not worth living.
For what misfortune would you be spared?
Which of life's blows would you not endure?
Your mother is lost and gone.
Your brothers, once the darlings of Zeus,
Have watched their luck turn.
And you, Lady, who have lived in exile,
Slandered from one city to the next,
As a woman pleasured in barbarian beds,
Now learn of your husband's death among the waves.
Lost with him is any hope you ever had of a homecoming,
When you would bless again the walls that saw your birth,
And kneel again at the altar
Where you prayed your first prayers.

HELEN

Who in the world, Trojan or Greek, felled the pine
    fated to bring down all of Troy?
Stripped and hewn to size, its timber gave first shape
    to Paris's cursed ship.
Soon enough, barbarian brawn was fitted to its oars,
    and Paris skimmed across the sea…
        to my front door.
My beauty drew him like a moth to all-consuming fire.
He wanted to be one with me.
In all of this, Aphrodite, the most murderous of mistresses,
    was weaving a tapestry of undiscriminating doom
    for Greek and Trojan alike.
Meanwhile, Hera of the golden throne,
    lofty consort of Zeus,
        sent down to me the son of Maia, Hermes,
        whose feet have wings.
When Hera's messenger came to me, I was plucking roses
    and gathering them gently in my gown
    to bring to Athene in her brazen shrine.
Up into the bright air Hermes snatched me
    and put me down here in this hapless place,
    while back there I became a point of contention,
    a prize glittering enough to die and kill for.
There, where the Simois runs pure,
    my name was polluted with fantasies and lies.

KORUPHAIOS

We know well how aggrieved you are, Lady.
Your only recourse, it seems,
    is to bear as lightly as you can
    what you are helpless to change.

HELEN

Women… friends, I know I am yoked to some fate.
But what is it?
Was I born to be some kind of freak,
    carrion for men's scavenging eyes?
I am a freak… a monster,
    and I lead a monstrous life.
I blame Hera for this.
And I blame my own beauty.

If only like a painting on a canvas
    I could be wiped away and painted over,
    this time an ordinary woman,
    somewhere between an idol and a dog.
Then the Greeks would forget
    what a wreck fate has made of me.
And I could be remembered
    for something better than my worst.

To fix your every hope on one thing,
    and then in that to be disappointed by the gods,
    is admittedly a heavy blow.
But it is bearable.
Not so with me.
My misfortunes are many.
Blow after blow, they beat me down.
First of all, I am blameless,
    and yet I am blamed.
It is easier to bear what belongs to you
    than what does not.
Next, the gods took me from my home
    and brought me here to live among barbarians,
    without family or friends.
I was born free... but no matter.
I am no less a slave now.
For among barbarians there is never room
    for more than one free soul.

In my sea of grief, I've had one single anchor,
    and nourished one last hope:
    that one day my husband would come for me here
    and rescue me from all my ills.
But my husband is dead...
    and so is any hope he kept alive in me.
My mother too is dead.
I killed her.
It may be wrong to say that,
    but what is one more wrong on my list?
My daughter,
    who once brought light to my home and my heart,
    watches her hair turn gray... alone.
And the twins,
    once called the sons of Zeus,
    are gone.

As for me, I go through the motions of life,
    though everything I love is lost.
The worst of it is that,
    even if I were to reach my home somehow,
    I would be clamped in irons at once.
After all, I am the Helen who launched the ships to Troy.
Or so everyone else imagines.
If my husband were alive, he would recognize me.
We have our secret signs,
    a language between the two of us.
But he is not alive.
He is beyond wishful thinking,
    and so am I.

So why go on living?
What can I look forward to?
I could trade in my misfortunes
    for marriage to a barbarian.
It could mean a lavish life.
But it would also mean eating my meals beside him,
    and sharing his bed.
A woman cannot despise the man beside her,
    without despising herself.
Not for long.
Death is best.
But how does one go about dying…
    with a little grace?

My misery, in short, comes down to this.
Every other woman in the world prays to be beautiful…
because to be beautiful is to be happy.
But look at me.
My beauty is my hell.

KORUPHAIOS
Helen, don't be so sure that that stranger, whoever he is,
    told you the whole truth.

HELEN
It was clear enough when he said my husband is dead.

KORUPHAIOS
To be said clearly is one thing.
To be true is another.

HELEN

Yes, which applies to your words as well as to his.

KORUPHAIOS

You are more inclined to misery than to joy.

HELEN

Not "inclined" but dragged... by my dread,
    toward what I dread most.
It is everywhere I look.

KORUPHAIOS

In the house of the king... is no one on your side?

HELEN

They are all on my side,
    except for the man who hunts me for his bed.

KORUPHAIOS

Then you know, don't you, what you must do?
Sitting here by this tomb... I mean... day after day... it...
    there just isn't... what you *should* do...

HELEN

If you have advice to give, give it all at once.

KORUPHAIOS

We think you should go to the palace and seek out Theonoe,
    the daughter of the sea-born Nereid.
The girl knows everything.
Ask her about your husband
    whether he still sees the light of day... or not.
Then, depending on what you learn,
    you can mourn or leap with joy.
But now, what do you gain from all your tears,
    shed before you really know anything?
Lady, do as we suggest.
Leave this place of death.
Confer with the girl from whose eyes nothing is hidden.
Why look any further than the palace and the girl, when they
hold the answers to your questions?
Lady, we will go with you into the palace,
    and together we will ask the girl for her divinings.
We are all women;
    and it is right for us to shoulder one another's burdens.

HELEN
Friends, I welcome what you have said.
Come, come with me now into the palace
    to learn what lies in wait for me.
I beg you, come with me.

KORUPHAIOS
You don't need to beg. We want to go with you.

HELEN
Already I hate this day for the grief it will bring.
I am miserable as it is.
And just imagine what heart-breaking news
    I am about to find out.

KORUPHAIOS
Helen dear, your gifts are not in the order of prophecy.
Don't imagine your prophecies before they arrive...
    much less moan over them.

HELEN
But my poor husband... what has become of him?
Even now does he live to see the light?
Does he watch the fiery chariot of the sun
    careen across the sky?
Does he trace the glittering voyages of the stars overhead?
Or has he gone down among the dead,
    where there is neither day nor night...
    only the long duration of doom.

KORUPHAIOS
Greet the future with a bold embrace, Helen,
    whatever face it turns to you.

HELEN
Eurotas, whose pure streams wash the pale green reeds,
    I call upon you to witness
    the oath I swear to your name.
If the sailor's tale is true,
    —and why would it not be?—
    `and my husband is dead,
    I will tighten the deadly noose around my own soft neck,
    or I will draw the whetted blade across my throat,
    until the cold steel cuts deep and releases my blood
    in a warm spattering spray.

I will tender my life as a sacrifice
    to the three rival goddesses
    and to Paris, who long ago watched over his herds
    and graced the air with the music of his flute.

KORUPHAIOS
Lady, I pray that you have seen the last of misfortune
    and that something good is coming your way.

HELEN
Troy, poor doomed Troy,
    you perished to no purpose,
    condemned for doing what you never did.
Aphrodite's largesse on my behalf
    cost you dearly in tears and blood.
Without respite, pain was added to pain,
    wound to wound, lament to lament,
    as mothers lost their sons,
    and young girls sliced away their long flowing hair
    in grief over brothers butchered
    on the banks of the billowing Skamander.
Greece too cries out in grief and pain.
Her groans glide across the sea.
She beats her head with grief
    and scores her soft cheeks with her nails
    until they stream with blood.

Kallisto, once a young Arkadian bride of Zeus,
    loping on four legs you left his bed.
But still I call you lucky.
Measured by my mother's fate, you fared well.
After all, you shed the burden of your grief
    when you took on the lioness's tawny coat
    and savage eyes.
Lucky too was the Titanian child of Merops.
Banished from the company of Artemis,
    she became a deer, with antlers of gleaming gold.
It was a small price she paid for her beauty.
Not so with me.
My beauty's price was the towered city of Troy
    and many of my own people.
For this one woman's beauty, they lost everything.

Exeunt Helen and the Chorus. Enter Menelaos.

MENELAOS

O Pelops,
> mounted on your chariot behind your legendary steeds,
> one day long ago on a Pisan field
> you vanquished Oinomaos utterly
> and won yourself a wife.
If only you had never lived as long as that.
If only you had left this life behind
> and gone to live above, with the gods,
> on the day they nearly feasted on your flesh,
> long before you sired my father Atreus,
> long before Atreus took Aerope to his bed,
> long before they had their famous pair of sons,
> Agamemnon… and me, Menelaos.
Yes, famous!
I don't want to boast, but in my opinion
> we launched against Troy
> the mightiest armada in history.
We were leaders, not tyrants,
> and we led not an army of conscripts,
> but a generation of young Greeks
> whose hearts we had won to our cause.
Many of those same men are numbered now among the dead.
Their comrades who gladly survived the sea
> must bear home the names of the fallen and the drowned.
As for me, I languish, lost on the gray, heaving sea.
Years have passed… as many as it took to bring down Troy.
I ache to go home,
> but of that the gods still find me undeserving.

Meanwhile I have sailed along every inhospitable inch
> of Libya's barren coastline.
Every time I've reached out for my homeland,
> sudden headwinds have hurled me back.
The winds I needed to fill my sails and send me home…
> never came.
Now I am nothing but a shipwreck.
I have watched my ship founder
> and my comrades slide beneath the waves.
Splintered on the rocks,
> my ship mingles with the flotsam.
It was a miracle I was saved… with Helen,
> whom I had snatched from flaming Troy.
Ours was a narrow escape, as we clung to the ship's keel,
> shattered loose from its intricate fastenings.

As for where I am or who lives here, I know nothing.
I was too ashamed to walk boldly into public sight and ask.
I have fallen too low for that.
In my embarrassment, I keep my present state
    as hidden as I can.
When a man long accustomed to good fortune
    falls on hard times,
      he falls all the harder for his inexperience.
Those long familiar with misfortune have skills I lack.
My need consumes me.
I have no food… nor clothes, as anyone can see
    from these tatters I've wrapped around myself…
    rags washed ashore from the wreck.
My splendid robes and raiment—every last luxury I owned—
    were swallowed by the sea.
As for the woman who originated all my woes,
    I've hidden her deep in the recesses of a nearby cave,
    enjoining those of my comrades who survived
    to watch over her for me while I come here alone.

So here I am…
    hoping to scare up some provisions for my friends,
    if anything we need is to be had here.
As soon as I caught sight of this walled palace,
    whose stately portals promise the residence
    of a man of means,
    I drew closer.
From such a house and its wealth, I
    might well expect some largesse for my men.
After all, no help is to be had from have-nots,
    however generous their hearts.

Pounding on the palace door.

Yo, gatekeeper! Anyone in there?
Anyone I can tell my troubles to?

The palace door opens. Enter Portress.

PORTRESS

Who are you? Go away!
If I were you, I wouldn't stand around at the king's front door,
    presenting a public nuisance.
I can see you are a Greek,
    which could cost you your life around here.
We have laws against Greeks.

MENELAOS

I hear you, Granny. You've made your point.
It's all right... calm down... I'm leaving.

PORTRESS
Pushing him away from the doorway.
Go away, I tell you!
I've got my orders, stranger...no Greeks inside!

MENELAOS

All right... but keep your hands off me!
Stop pushing me!

PORTRESS

Blame yourself for this, not me.
You're not doing as I say!

MENELAOS

Then take my appeal inside, to your master.

PORTRESS

What? I carry *anything* in there from *you*...
    and I'll be the one to pay.

MENELAOS

Say I'm a shipwrecked sailor...of spotless... descent.

PORTRESS

Take your story somewhere else.

MENELAOS

No. I'm going inside.
So do as I say and move aside.

PORTRESS

You certainly are becoming quite the pest.
I think the time has come to have you thrown out.

MENELAOS

God! Where are my glorious armies now when I need them?

PORTRESS

Obviously not around here. Who knows,
    you may have been quite dashing and formidable once.
But not any more.

MENELAOS
God, I don't deserve such abuse!

PORTRESS
Well, crying about it won't help!
What are you moaning over, anyway?

MENELAOS
Over the happiness I once enjoyed.

PORTRESS
Why won't you go away and cry on the shoulder
    of someone who cares one way or the other about you?

MENELAOS
Just tell me this much. Where am I?
What is the name of this place and its king?

PORTRESS
You're in Egypt… and this is the palace of Proteus.

MENELAOS
Egypt! My luck really has run out!
What a place to wind up!

PORTRESS
What do you have against Egypt? It's a lovely place to live.

MENELAOS
I don't actually have anything against Egypt.
It's what's become of me that I can't bear.

PORTRESS
Hard times come to lots of people.
You're not the first.

MENELAOS
The king you mentioned… what's his name… is he in there?

PORTRESS
Proteus? No, he lies over there…

Pointing to the tomb.

in his tomb. His son rules now.

MENELAOS
Then where is he, the son… inside or not?

PORTRESS
Not inside.
But listen…he hates Greeks…more than you can imagine.

MENELAOS
And how did we Greeks manage to win his hate?

PORTRESS
It was Helen's doing…Zeus's Helen. She's inside.

MENELAOS
What? What kind of a story is this? Well, go on!

PORTRESS
I'm talking about the daughter of Tyndareos.
She once lived in Sparta…many years ago.

MENELAOS
But from where did she come here? Explain that to me!

PORTRESS
She came here from Lakedaemon.

MENELAOS
When?

Aside.

I left her hidden safely in the cave.
How could she be gone again?

PORTRESS
Stranger, she came here long before you Greeks ever went to Troy.
Now, get out of here… quietly.
Something's going on in there,
    and it's throwing the whole palace into a panic.
Let's just say you've come at a bad time.
And if my master finds you here,
    his hospitality will be the end of you.
Look, I like Greeks.
When I snapped at you before… I was afraid.
It's my master. I fear him.

Exit Portress into the palace, closing the door behind her.

MENELAOS

What am I to think?
What sense does any of this make?
I find out now that my troubles are... breeding!
I snatch my wife from Troy... get this far with her...
        seal her safe in a cave...
        and meanwhile some *other* woman
        —with the same name—
        is living here in this palace!
And the Helen here is supposed to be the child of Zeus.
Maybe there's someone around here named "Zeus,"
        with a little place of his own on the Nile.
God knows there's only one Zeus up there!
But where on earth is there another Sparta,
        apart from the only one I know,
        along the banks of the Eurotas,
        where the pale, slender reeds glisten in the sun?
As for Tyndareos... it's a celebrated name, given only once.
And are there two Lakedaemons... and two Troys?
All this leaves me without words.

But admittedly the world's a big place.
And everyone knows that many different men
        have the same names.
The same is true of cities... and of women.
So I guess there's nothing so surprising in all of this after all.

And I'm certainly not going to run scared
        because someone's *maid* threatened me.
There is no man so barbarous to his core
        that he'd refuse a free meal to Menelaos.
It's just a matter of mentioning my name.
The flames of Troy are a legend by now,
        and I lit them!
There isn't a country on earth where the name of Menelaos
        doesn't ring bells.
So I'll just wait around here for the king to return,
        and, meanwhile, I'll weigh my options cautiously.
If he does turn out to be a common savage,
        I'll make my way back to the wreck
        without letting myself be seen.
On the other hand, should he prove a gentleman,
        I shall ask for what I need in my present plight.

This, of all the hardships I endure, weighs heaviest on my soul:
    that I, a king, must bend my knee to some other king,
    and beg my daily bread.
But this *is* what things have come to.
He spoke wisely—it wasn't I —who said:
    there is no arm strong enough to bend back dread necessity.

Enter the Chorus and Helen from the palace.

CHORUS
The royal halls resound with prophecy.
The seeress sings what she has seen.
Not yet is Menelaos lost to life,
Not yet dispatched to Erebos,
Land of twilight doom.
He languishes instead on the open sea,
Without a homecoming,
Without the embrace of familiar harbors.
Friendless, scavenging for his sustenance,
He is wasted of everything but his will,
As he wanders from one unknown shore to the next,
Ever since the day the long, sea-soaked oars
Put Troy into the past.

HELEN
I return now to the refuge of the tomb,
    heartened by Theonoe's words.
They could not be more welcome, nor more true,
    for her eyes see all things as they are.
She says my husband lives in and looks upon
    the same light as do I,
    even though he crisscrosses the seas,
    tossed about like a piece of cork.
She says too that he will come... *here*... seasoned by the sea,
    as soon as he reaches the appointed end of his trials.
But of his fate once here,
    whether he will escape with his life... or not,
    she said nothing.
This oversight was mine.
When the girl told me that my husband had survived so far
    I was too thrilled to think of asking more.
According to her, he is already very near,
    shipwrecked and washed ashore with a few companions.
But when? When will you come to me?
How I long for you!

Catching sight of Menelaos.

And who is this?
Am I to consider myself snared in some trap
    set by Proteus's impious excuse for a son?
Should I lift my robes and run like a filly for the finish post?
Should I lunge like a crazed bacchant
    to touch the edge of the tomb?
This man has a wild look about him, like a hunter on my scent,
    about to spring his trap.

*Helen runs in a panic for the wall of the tomb. Menelaos blocks
her way.*

MENELAOS

Woman, you who are straining so desperately to reach asylum
    at the base of the tomb,
    near its pillars scorched in sacrifice—wait!
Why do you run from me?
One glimpse of you has clogged my mind and left me speechless.

HELEN

Women, this is unfair.
See… he blocks my way to the tomb.
He wants to seize me and hand me over to the tyrant
    whose bed I've been avoiding.

MENELAOS

I seize nothing that isn't mine,
    and I do no one's evil bidding.

HELEN

Well, your clothes are wild enough!

MENELAOS

Woman, don't be afraid… and stop running away from me!

In one final dash, Helen has reached the tomb.

HELEN

I *have* stopped… now that I've reached the safety of the tomb.

MENELAOS

Who are you?
I'm looking straight at *you*… but whose face am I really seeing?

HELEN

And who are *you*?
We are wondering the same thing… you and I.

MENELAOS

I've never in my life seen such a resemblance!

HELEN

O gods…
A god *is* at work…when we recognize someone dear to us.

MENELAOS

Are you Greek… or from around here?

HELEN

I am Greek. And you?

MENELAOS

Woman, to these eyes you are so like Helen!

HELEN

And to these eyes, you… so like Menelaos.
I don't know what more to say.

MENELAOS

No matter. You have already said the truth.
I am that most cursed of men.

HELEN

At last you come back to your wife's arms!

MENELAOS

Wife? Don't you touch me! What wife?

HELEN

The wife Tyndareos, my father, gave to you.

MENELAOS

Torch-bearing Hekate,
be more kind in the specters you send to me!

HELEN

In me you see no specter,
no moon light accomplice of the mistress of crossroads.

MENELAOS
I am only one man, so I cannot have two wives.

HELEN
Well... what *other* wife do you have?

MENELAOS
The one I rescued from Troy and concealed in a cave.

HELEN
I am your only wife. There is no other.

MENELAOS
What? Are my wits intact and my eyes... gone?

HELEN
Just look at me!
Don't your wits and eyes agree that I am your wife?

MENELAOS
You *look* like her.
Beyond that I can't say.

HELEN
Open your eyes!
What more do you want?
Who knows me better than you do?

MENELAOS
You look exactly like her. I won't deny that.

HELEN
Well, who will you listen to... if not to your own eyes?

MENELAOS
The problem is... I have another wife.

HELEN
It was a phantom that went off to Troy.
I've never been there.

MENELAOS
And how do you make a phantom with a body like that...
that breathes...and blinks its eyes...and... ?

HELEN

From thin air… the stuff of which your "other" wife is made…
the personal handiwork of the gods.

MENELAOS

Specifically, which of the gods wrought her?

Before she can answer.

By the way, this whole desperate story of yours is wasted effort.

HELEN

It was Hera's doing…
so that Paris would run off with a look-alike, instead of me.

MENELAOS

But how could you be here and in Troy at the same time?

HELEN
Approaching Menelaos and grasping him.
My name could be in many places where I was not.

MENELAOS

Let go of me.
I already had all the grief I could manage
before I ever came to this place.

Menelaos turns from Helen and walks away.

HELEN

So you're going to leave me for your vacant nuptials
with that phantom of yours?

MENELAOS

Exactly. Just be glad you at least look like Helen.

HELEN

Turn away now and you destroy me.
My husband, I have found you…
and now I am losing you all over again!

MENELAOS

All I know is what I went through at Troy.
It persuades me.
You do not.

HELEN

O, what woman was ever more wretched than this?
The man I love as I love no one else
    turns his back on me.
And never again will I see the land or the people of my birth.

Enter Messenger, who does not at first notice Helen.

MESSENGER

Menelaos, at last I've found you!
I've wandered over every foot of this barbaric land
    looking for you.
The shipmates you left behind sent me to...

MENELAOS

What is it?
What happened?
Were you raided by barbarians?

MESSENGER

Nothing I say can describe what happened...
    it was so strange.

MENELAOS

One look at your panic
    tells me the sort of news you bring.
So speak!

MESSENGER

This much I can say:
    that you have endured immeasurable hardships...
    all for nothing.

MENELAOS

I know that, but those agonies are ancient history by now.
Tell me what's new.

MESSENGER

Lifted into thin air... your wife...blown away...
    she's gone... vanished!
She's up there somewhere now... hidden from our eyes.
Anyway, as she slipped free of the deep cave,
    where we were keeping her sealed away,
    she had this to say:

"Pitiful Trojans… and all you Greeks,
    who day after day and year after year
    spilled out your lives for me
    on the banks of the Skamander…
    taken in by Hera's tricks
    you imagined all along that Paris had Helen in his bed.
But he never did.
As for me, I have put in the time assigned to me,
    and kept my date with destiny.
So now I'm off… back to the sky that sired me.
All for nothing has the unfortunate daughter of Tyndareos
    heard her name become a household word for shame;
    for she is truly guiltless."

Noticing Helen.

Oh… daughter of Leda… hello!
Have you been here all along?
I was just telling how you had found your wings,
    quit your cave, and leapt up among the stars.
In other words,
    I was just making a fool of myself.
But not again.
I've heard enough of your taunts…
    of how you made your husband suffer,
    made all who fought at his side suffer,
    and all for nothing!

MENELAOS

Wait… now it all fits!
Everything she said turns out to be true!
O how I've longed for this day,
    when my arms would hold you again!

HELEN

O Menelaos, dearest man, we have waited a long time,
    but now our joy is full.

Embracing Menelaos.

Women… friends, how many days I have watched the sun
    run its fiery circuit overhead…
    and now, at last I wrap my sweet spouse
    in my glad arms again.

MENELAOS

Me too.
There is so much to tell about so many years,
    I don't know where to begin.

HELEN

I feel my excitement even in the strands of my hair,
    and there is no holding back my tears.
I am so happy!
O my husband, my sweet, I cling to you.

MENELAOS

Sweetest of all sights to my eyes,
    I throw aside every complaint I've ever spoken.
Daughter of Zeus, child of Leda—my wife,
    once more you are mine.
Long ago, mounted on gleaming white steeds,
    and bearing torches that set the night ablaze,
    your twin brothers brought you to me,
    with blessing upon blessing for us both.
How blind we all were then to what lay ahead.
Then it was a god who tore you from my house...

HELEN

And now it is a god again who drives us both
    toward some brighter, more compelling destiny.
A wrong made right makes us one again,
    however long it took.
And from the gods I pray a blessing.

MENELAOS

A blessing on us both.
I make your prayer my own.
We two are one, and it is ours to share a common fate.

HELEN

Women... friends, no more will I bemoan the past.
My time of travail is over.
I have my husband back.
The one I have awaited is in my arms.
How many years I waited to get him back from Troy.

MENELAOS

You have me and I have you.

It was a long trek through more days than I remember,
    until this day came,
        when the divine schemes fell open before my eyes…
    like a book.
These tears of mine come from joy.
What bitterness there is in them is nothing now
    against my gratitude.

HELEN
I have no words for this.
Beyond any human hope has this come to pass.
I hold you close where I thought you'd never be again.

MENELAOS
And I hold you,
    who all the world thought went off to Idaean Troy,
        to grace her grim towers.
By the gods, how were you spirited from my house that day?

HELEN
O… you go back to the bitter beginning!
The story you are dredging for lies deep and dark.

MENELAOS
Tell me… it's something I must hear.
Everything that happens in our lives is given… from above.

HELEN
I would spit from my mouth… this story you want told.

MENELAOS
Tell me anyway. Old troubles make sweet stories.

HELEN
Never did I elope to any barbarian dandy's bed,
    not on the deck of any ship, not in the thrall of any lust.

MENELAOS
Then what holy hand or fatal force
    tore you from your fatherland?

HELEN
Husband, it was Zeus's child, his son Hermes,
    who wafted me hereto the Nile.

MENELAOS
Incredible... and strange, what you say!
But who sent him?

HELEN
I wept and wept... see, my eyes are still moist with the tears.
Zeus's mate ruined me.

MENELAOS
Hera? What inclined her to make trouble for us?

HELEN
The trouble began in the baths,
    in the glistening spring waters,
        where the goddesses cleansed and purified themselves
        for their beauty contest.

MENELAOS
But how did the contest spell ruin for you in Hera's mind?

HELEN
Her scheme was to rob Aphrodite...

MENELAOS
Rob her of what? Go on.

HELEN
Of me. I was Aphrodite's promise to Paris.

MENELAOS
What a curse.

HELEN
Curse and all, I was conveyed to Egypt.

MENELAOS
And Paris got your double, as you said before.

HELEN
But worst of all was your lot, Mother.
Within your walls what torment you knew!

MENELAOS
What do you mean?

HELEN
I mean my mother is dead.
In the shadow of shame cast by my infamous affair,
    she braided a deadly noose.

MENELAOS
O... no. But our child... Hermione... she lives?

HELEN
With neither child nor mate, yes... she goes on in life, my dear,
    moaning over a marriage that never was.

MENELAOS
Paris, you brought my house down... stone by stone.
But it cost your life...
    and the lives of countless Greek warriors,
    whose burnished armor once glinted in the sun.

HELEN
The hand of a god flung me far from my fatherland,
    far from my city and from you.
I was made a curse and a menace.
But when it seemed I left your bed and house
    for some scurrilous affair, I did no such thing.

KORUPHAIOS
If only now you are blessed with good fortune
    for whatever days remain to you,
    they will be enough to heal your legacy of grief.

MESSENGER
Menelaos, help me to share your happiness.
I can see for myself *that* you're happy,
    yet I can't for the life of me figure out *why*.

MENELAOS
But old friend, this is *your* story as well as ours.

MESSENGER
This woman... wasn't she the one... who...
I mean didn't she mete out our misery in Troy?

MENELAOS
No, not she. The gods made fools of us.
All we ever had of her was a pathetic effigy,
    modeled out of thin air.

MESSENGER
Wait… let me get this straight. What do you mean?
That we went through all of that…
    for nothing more than a puff of air?

MENELAOS
Three goddesses started it all with their quarreling.
From there on it was Hera's doing.

MESSENGER
Then she… this woman here… really is your wife?

MENELAOS
Yes, take my word on it.

MESSENGER
My child, the path of god takes many turns.
There is no mapping it out.
We are drawn this way and that,
    and somehow it all makes sense.
One life is constant struggle, while another,
    seemingly exempt from pain,
    is suddenly destroyed.
There is nothing certain or forever when it comes to human fate.

You and your husband have certainly had your share of strife.
Yours was a battle with words; his with spears.
And the more he tried to win through to something,
    the more empty were his hands.
But now, effortlessly,
    he comes into the most precious blessings.
You were never a disgrace to your aged father,
    nor to your divine twin brothers.
For you did none of the shameful things ascribed to you.
It all comes back to me now… your wedding long ago.
I remember how I ran next to your four-horsed chariot,
    waving a torch in the air.
And, leaving your home behind,
    you rode off in gladness beside your husband.

It is the mark of a mean servant
    not to honor what happens to his master,
    by being glad when he is glad,
    and grieved when he is grieved.

For myself, I may have a bondsman's blood,
> but I hope to be counted among those servants
> whose souls soar high above their blood…
> free-spirited, though still in name… slaves.
Better this than to bear a double burden on my one back,
> the name of slave and a soul to match.

MENELAOS

Old friend, you have labored at my side in every struggle,
> fought at my side in every fray.
Now, take your share in my good fortune,
Go, tell the men my news, how fate has come to smile on me.
Tell them to stay by the sea where I left them.
There they are to await the outcome of my next trial,
> which I suspect is imminent.
And in case we find some way of escaping from this place,
> tell the men to stand in readiness,
> so that we might embrace each others' fate,
> and all together elude the barbarians,
> if such a feat is feasible.

MESSENGER

It shall be done, my lord.

You know, now I see the art of prophecy for what it is—
> a vulgar occupation and a pack of lies.
Nothing useful came from all the altar fires we lit,
> nor from all the winged screechings overhead.
It's daft to dote on birds, as if they're man's last hope.
Kalchas only watched as his fellows spent their lives
> for a puff of air.
He never let on; never said a word to the army.
Helenos on their side was no different.
And so a city was brought to ruin… for no reason at all.
Some would excuse the silence of priests
> as deference to the gods.
Then, I ask, why have truck with them at all,
> these prophesying priests?
We would do better to beg our own blessings
> in sacrifice to the gods.
Best just to leave priests alone.
Their art was a scheme from the start… a way to an easy living.
But no one gets rich on magic without a *little* work.
Anyway, the best magic is a balanced mind,
> and a little common sense.

Exit Messenger.

KORUPHAIOS

My own feelings about prophets
  follow the same course as that old man's.
Make friends with the gods
  and you will have the best magic of all
  abiding in your own house.

HELEN

Well. Things here have been rather uneventful until now.
But tell me, my poor dear, how you came from Troy unscathed.
Admittedly my knowing will alter nothing,
  but when you love someone,
  you long to know what hardships he's been through.

MENELAOS

With a single question about a single voyage,
  you've asked much of me.
Must I tell stories of men drowned in the Aegean?
Why talk about the false beacons Nauplios
  lit on the cliffs of Euboea to lure our ships to disaster,
  or about Krete and the Libyan cities we put into?
Why mention Perseus perched on his craggy overlook?
My stories would never bring you any satisfaction,
  and I would only go through it all again in the telling,
  when already I am worn thin with suffering.
All you and I would do is multiply our pain.

HELEN

Your response is wiser than my request.
Leave it all behind then… except for one thing.
Just tell me how long you languished on the open waters,
  wandering to no avail on the sea's bleak expanse.

MENELAOS

I made the rounds of seven years
  after the ten years spent in Troy.

HELEN

My poor man, such a long time you tell of!
And now you've made it safely to this place
  only to rendezvous with death.

MENELAOS
What do you mean? What do you have to tell me?
Your words are enough to put an end to me.

HELEN
Just go! You must leave here at once, or else
    the lord of this house will *really* put an end to you.

MENELAOS
Why? What have I done to merit such treatment?

HELEN
Your unexpected arrival
    complicates certain nuptial designs on me.

MENELAOS
You're saying that someone plans to wed my wife?

HELEN
Yes, as the final outrage, after everything else I've endured.

MENELAOS
Is this something this fellow's emboldened to do on his own,
    or is he exercising the rights of some office he holds?

HELEN
He is the lord of this land, the son of Proteus.

MENELAOS
Now the riddling words of the portress come clear to me.

HELEN
At which of the outer gates were you standing
    when she spoke to you?

MENELAOS
There. I was chased off as an ordinary beggar.

HELEN

You weren't really "begging"! I feel so ashamed.

MENELAOS
I *acted* like a beggar, which doesn't mean I *was* one.

HELEN
Anyway, it seems you already know all about
    my impending marriage.

MENELAOS
More or less. What I don't know is how successful you've been
    in eluding the king's bed.

HELEN
Rest assured... I've kept your place safe and unsullied.

MENELAOS
Welcome news... if true. How can I be sure?

HELEN
Don't you see my misery here at the side of the tomb?

MENELAOS
Poor woman, what I see is a straw pallet.
What I don't see is what this has to do with you.

HELEN
Fleeing from the king's bed, this is where I lie, a suppliant.

MENELAOS
For lack of an altar... or in keeping with barbarian custom?

HELEN
This tomb has afforded me sanctuary
    as safe as any temple of the gods.

MENELAOS
Then can't I just carry you home from here across the seas?

HELEN
You would end up on a sword... not in my bed.

MENELAOS
Then I would be the sorriest of men.

HELEN
Don't be ashamed. Just run for your life... now!

MENELAOS
And leave you? I sacked Troy for you!

HELEN
Better to flee than to find death in my arms.

MENELAOS
You are proposing cowardice to a veteran of Troy!
It does not suit me.

HELEN
I suppose you're keen to kill the king. But you can't.

MENELAOS
Why not? Is his flesh impervious to steel?

HELEN
Time will tell.
But it is no mark of wisdom to rush into hopeless ventures.

MENELAOS
Then shall I silently stretch out my hands to be bound?

HELEN
The point is that the dilemma you're in
    begs a stratagem of some sort.

MENELAOS
Death is more palatable when you're doing something.

HELEN
I see only one hope for our escape.

MENELAOS
A bribe… a bold stroke… or fast words?

HELEN
Our one hope lies in keeping the king ignorant of your arrival.

MENELAOS
But who is about to betray me?
On his own, the king will never recognize me.

HELEN
Pointing to the palace.
Inside those walls the king has a force on his side
    which might as well be divine.

MENELAOS
Do you mean an oracle of some sort,
　　seated in some secret corner of the house?

HELEN
No. I mean the king's own sister. Her name is Theonoe.

MENELAOS
"Theonoe"… she even *sounds* like an oracle!
Tell me what she can do.

HELEN
She knows everything.
And she will inform her brother of your presence here.

MENELAOS
Then I'm as good as dead, because I have no hope of hiding.

HELEN
Unless we were to go to her on our knees
　　and win her to our side.

MENELAOS
Do *what?*
You see something we might hope to win from her.
What is it?

HELEN
Her silence… not a word to her brother
　　about your presence in his land.

MENELAOS
And with her silence we could walk freely from this place.

HELEN
Yes, with her on our side it will be easy;
　　without her it will be impossible.

MENELAOS
This is for you to accomplish.
Women have a way with other women.

HELEN
No way will her knees break my suppliant grip!

MENELAOS
But what if our words have no effect on her?

HELEN
Then you are a dead man, and I am an unwilling bride,
    wed to misery.

MENELAOS
You would be more willing than you admit.
The truth is you would betray me.

HELEN
Never. I swear by all that is holy…

MENELAOS
What? That you will die rather than switch beds?

HELEN
Yes. You and I will die by the same sword;
    and in death I will lie with you.

MENELAOS
As a pledge of these words, take my hand.

HELEN
I take it… pledging to forsake the light
    when you go down in darkness.

MENELAOS
And I pledge to end my life,
    the instant I am bereft of you.

HELEN
Then how shall we conduct this death of ours,
    so that we might shine in it?

MENELAOS
Here, against the wall of this tomb,
I will first spill your blood…then mine.
But before that I will put up no small fight for your love.
Let him who dares take me on!
I will do nothing to tarnish the glory won in Troy.
Never will I run home to Greece and reap only ridicule.
I made Thetis mourn her son Achilleus.

I saw Telamonian Aias mounted on his own sword.
I watched Neleus become childless.
After all this, will I not prove man enough now
  to die for my own wife?
You bet I will!
For if there are knowing gods above,
  they themselves shroud with dust the tomb of a man
  who dies valiantly at the hands of his foes.
But cowards the gods fling out from the land
  onto some barren reef.

CHORUS

O gods, be kind this once to the race of Tantalos,
  and call an end at last to their afflictions.

HELEN
  Hearing the approach of Theonoe and her Attendants.
My luck hasn't turned after all; I'm wretched as ever.
It's all over for us, Menelaos.
She's coming from the palace… Theonoe,
  the girl who sings the unseen.
Inside… I can hear the door bolts being thrown back.
Run! Hide! But how… and for what?
No matter where she comes or where you go,
  she knows of your arrival all the same.
I'm so unhappy… so beyond any hope.
And here you are… all the way from Troy,
  preserved from death in one barbarian land
  only to stumble onto someone's sword in another.

*Enter Theonoe, preceded by her Attendants, to whom she speaks
before she turns to Helen.*

THEONOE
Lead the way.
Let your torches burn a brilliant path before me.
Let the holy ritual fumes rise and purge the air,
  so that we might breathe the purity of heaven.
Lest anyone's unhallowed feet
  have crossed my path with pollution,
  sweep the way before me with your purifying fire,
  that I might pass.
And when you have rendered to the gods
  the rites they exact of me,
  carry the hearth flames back into the house.

To Helen.

Helen, what do you think now of my prophecies?
Your husband has come to you and stands here before our eyes,
    without his boats, and without the would-be Helen.

To Menelaos.

Poor man, you have made your way here
    through a long list of narrow escapes.
And for what? Your homecoming... or a long exile in Egypt?
You cannot know which.

To Helen.

For this very day the divine tempers will flare,
    as the gods convene around the throne of Zeus
    and debate your destiny.
Hera, your sworn foe in days now gone,
    finds herself well disposed toward you now.
She would bring you safely home, as witness to all of Greece
    that Aphrodite is a cheat
    and only pretended to wed your wife to Paris.
Aphrodite, of course, would wreck your homecoming,
    to avoid having the truth dragged out:
    that she bought her beauty title with a counterfeit coin,
    a Helen that was no Helen at all.

To Menelaos.

As it happens, I hold the balance.
Either I bring about your ruin, as Aphrodite would have me do,
    by informing my brother of your presence here,
    or I take Hera's side and save your life,
    keeping my brother in the dark,
    even after he has enjoined me to tell him at once,
    the moment you happen upon our shore.

To the Chorus.

Which one of you will secure my safety now,
    by going to my brother with the news of this man's arrival?

HELEN
Flinging herself at Theonoe.
Maiden, I throw myself at your knees in supplication.

Bent and broken in my misery,
    I plead for myself and for this man.
One moment I welcome him in my arms after years of waiting,
    and the next moment it seems I must watch him die.
Say nothing to your brother of how my husband,
    my most beloved, has returned to my embrace.
Only keep him safe, I beg you.
Never forsake your own integrity
    to do your brother some kind of favor.
Any thanks you'd win from him would reek with foul play.

It was a blessing mixed with misery,
    when Hermes entrusted me to your father,
    in safe keeping for my husband.
Well... my husband is here to claim what is his.
But how can I be claimed by a dead man?
How can one who is living be given back to one who is dead?
Put yourself in Hermes' shoes... and your father's.
What would Hermes want;
    what would your father, rest his soul, want?
Would they not want borrowed goods
    restored to their rightful owner?
I think they would.
You would do wrong to defer to your wanton brother
    and ignore your worthy father.
If you, a seeress, a women of the cloth,
    defile your father's righteousness,
    and accommodate your no-good brother,
    then you are a disgrace.
What a shame... to see the secrets of the gods,
    to see everything, even the future,
    and not to see the difference between right and wrong.

I am a woman mired in wrongs done to me.
Set me free from my misery.
As it happens, this is a grace within your giving.

It has become a habit among men to hate Helen.
My reputation has made the rounds in Greece.
I am the woman who cuckolded her husband
    and set up house in gold-laden Troy.
But if only I get back to Greece and reach Sparta again,
    then they will see and hear the truth:
    that the gods played deadly tricks on them,
    but that I never played false those I love.

Then my name and my honor will be restored.
I will give my daughter in marriage, the girl nobody wants.
And I will leave behind this squalid vagrancy I've known,
    and enjoy again the comforts of my own home.

If my husband had died,
    and his ravaged remains were strewn across the flames,
    from afar I would weep for love of him.
Now, when he is safe and sound, is he to be torn from my arms?
No, maiden, I beg you... no!
Imitate the honorable ways of your honorable father,
    and be kind to me.
For the child of a kindly father can strive no higher than this:
    to follow in the footsteps of the one who gave her life.

KORUPHAIOS

Pitiable words from a pitiable woman.
Now I long to hear what Menelaos will add on his own behalf.

MENELAOS

I'm afraid I can't bring myself to fall at your knees
    and let loose floods of tears.
One such display of faintheartedness would suffice
    to tarnish every bit of glory won in Troy.
I know they say it suits a hero to weep
    when the situation warrants.
But that is one heroic prerogative I waive,
    if "prerogative" is even the right word.
I prefer to show some courage.

Now... if coming to the rescue of a stranger like me,
    who wants his rightful wife returned,
    seems to you a thing worth doing,
    then simply give her back and save the two of us.
But if you think other thoughts and decline,
    you will not initiate me into grief.
Grief is something I already know well.
What you *will* do is come out in the open as an evil woman.
Standing here close by your father's tomb,
    and wishing he were alive to listen,
    I will say what I feel is fitting and just,
    and perhaps most likely to touch your heart.

Addressing the tomb of Proteus.

Aged Sir, denizen of this deathly rock,
    give me back my wife.
I claim this woman, your ward,
    whom Zeus sent to you to keep safe and sound,
    for me and for this moment.
I know you cannot be the one to hand her over,
    not from where you stand, in death.
But surely your daughter here will not see fit
    to let her once-revered father be wakened in his grave
    and made to hear his honor spoiled.
The decision is hers.

Hades, lord of the netherworld, I would enlist you too
    as an ally in this struggle.
Your halls are filled with slain warriors
    dispatched to you by my sword in this woman's name.
You have been paid your full price.
Now, either breathe those bodies back into life again,
    or compel the maiden here to match her father's piety
    and restore my bride to me.

To Theonoe.

Now I will say what my spouse has left unspoken.
I will tell you what to expect,
    if you despoil me of my wife.
Make no mistake, maiden, I am under oath;
    first, to do battle with your brother.
It's he or I. One of us must die.
It's that simple.
But if he shrinks back from meeting me in combat
    and tries instead to trap and starve us suppliants
    at your father's tomb, this is my resolve.
First I will slay my wife,
    and then, here, at the base of the tomb,
    I will plunge my two-edged sword deep into my own heart.
Our blood will spatter your father's grave,
    and my wife and I will lie, two corpses, side by side,
    against the hewn stone,
    an everlasting reproach to your father,
    and to you a wound that never heals.
Never will your brother wed this woman.
Nor will any other man take her to his bed.
I will be the one to carry her away...
    to her home, if possible.

Otherwise, to death.
Why have I said all this?
If I were to turn woman and weep,
     I would prove more pitiful than effective.
Put an end to me, if that is your pleasure.
But you will never put an end to your shame.
Far better to let my words sink in and move you.
Then you will have your righteousness;
     and I will have my wife.

KORUPHAIOS
To Theonoe.
Maiden, it is for you now to weigh all that has been said.
Judge these matters, and let your judgment be one
     to please all concerned.

THEONOE
Reverence for all that is right runs in my blood.
It is also my choice here today.
I would no more betray myself than I would a close friend.
And I would do nothing to stain my father's honor.
Neither will I gratify my brother
     at the cost of my own good name.
My heart and my soul are a sanctuary
     wherein justice is held sacred.
Such is my legacy from Nereus,
     and I will do all I can, Menelaos, to preserve it intact.
Seeing that Hera means you well,
     I will cast my vote with her.
I would rather not offend Aphrodite,
     but she's beside the point.
I intend to do my best to remain a virgin... forever.
As for your harsh words spewn over my father's tomb,
     I take them to heart.
I would do wrong not to return your wife to you.
For my father, if he were alive today,
     would see to your reunion.
And there is a reckoning, I know, for such deeds,
     among the dead as well as among the living.
When the mind of the dead mingles and becomes one
     with the immortal air, the mind, though dead,
     possesses an immortal knowledge.
But I have no wish to go on at length.
I will keep your pleading words to me in perfect confidence.
And I will be no accomplice to my brother in his folly.

I do him true service, although it may seem otherwise,
  when I deflect him from impiety,
  and try to make a decent man of him.
But it is up to the two of you to devise your own escape.
I will not stand in your way, and I promise you my silence.
You would do well to begin on your knees,
  praying to the gods.
Beg of Aphrodite safe passage to your fatherland.
And implore Hera not to change her mind now,
  but to stand fast in her resolve
  to see you and your husband safely home.

Turning to the tomb.

And to you, my dearly departed father, I promise this:
  to spare nothing to preserve your name.
Never will you, who revered all that is right and holy,
  be called a rogue.

Exeunt Theonoe and her Attendants.

KORUPHAIOS
The wicked never truly flourish.
What hope there is of well-being resides in righteousness.

HELEN
Well, we no longer have anything to fear from the girl.
Now it's up to you to do some quick thinking
  and come up with a scheme to save the two of us.

MENELAOS
Listen. This has been your home for some time now.
And all along you've lived side by side,
  mingled freely, with the king's servants.

HELEN
What do you have in mind?
There's hope in your voice,
  as if you were about to work something wonderful
  for the two of us.

MENELAOS
Do you think you could persuade one of the men
  in charge of the chariots... to give us one...
  with four horses attached?

HELEN

Yes… I could.
But in what direction would we take flight?
Neither of us knows our way in this barbarous land.

MENELAOS

You're right. That won't work.
So what if I hide in the palace
    and cut down the king with my sword?

HELEN

No. The girl wouldn't let that happen.
If you were about to kill her brother,
    she'd break her silence for sure.

MENELAOS

And I don't have a ship in which we could make good our escape.
I had one. The sea has it now.

HELEN

Wait! Listen!
Maybe a woman can be the one to hatch something clever.
Would you object to my announcing your death…
    before you're dead?

MENELAOS

Well, it's a lousy omen.
But if you think I saying I'm dead will do any good,
    I guess I'm game to die a death of words…
    assuming I live through it.

HELEN

Then I will go before the impious king
    and play the "woman in mourning" to the hilt…
    shorn hair, desperate wailing and groans… all for you.

MENELAOS

But what… I mean, how will that lead to our safe release?
Besides, the "pretended death routine" is nothing new.

HELEN

It will be as if you died at sea.
I will beg the king to allow me to bury you in effigy.

MENELAOS

All right, assuming he goes along with your request,
    and you give me a full funeral in absentia…
    we still don't have a ship.
So how are we going to escape?

HELEN

I will insist that he give me a boat of some kind,
    from which to throw your funeral tokens
    into the sea's open arms.

MENELAOS

It's a good plan… except for one thing.
Suppose the king insists that you conduct my funeral
    on dry ground.
Then your scheme turns to dust.

HELEN

Not so. I will simply inform the man
    that Greek law does not tolerate the scattering of dirt
    over a man who died at sea.

MENELAOS

I see you have it all figured.
So I will set off with you in the same boat,
    helping you with the funeral tokens…

HELEN

Of course… you *must* be there, you and your entire crew,
    everyone who survived the wreck.

MENELAOS

Once we're on the anchored ship,
    my men will assume battle positions.

HELEN

That's your business. You see to it.
Let's just hope that homeward winds fill our sails
    and move our ship along.

MENELAOS

They will, for the time has come.
The powers above are calling an end to my trials.
One last question.
From whom will you say your learned of my death?

HELEN

From you.
Just say you sailed with the son of Atreus… saw him die…
    and alone swam faster than fate.

MENELAOS

Of course… and these rags I'm wrapped in make it obvious
    I'm fresh from a shipwreck!

HELEN

Well, your untimely wreck meant your timely arrival.
And now your misfortune may well work in our favor.

MENELAOS

Tell me. Should I go with you into the palace,
    or sit here quietly by the tomb and wait for you?

HELEN

Stay here.
If he's inclined to be rough with you,
    the tomb, along with your sword, will keep you safe.
I will go into the palace, shear off my hair,
    trade my white robes for something black,
    and claw rivers of blood into my face.
I see a bitter struggle ahead for me,
    with two possible outcomes.
Either I will be found out in my treachery,
    and be made to die for it.
Or I will salvage your life and accompany you home.

O queen and goddess Hera, reclining in the bed of Zeus,
    we lift high our arms to you in the sky above,
    where you dwell amidst the sequined splendor of the stars.
We two pitiable mortals implore you,
    bring us respite from our woes.
And you, daughter of Dione, Aphrodite,
    who bought your prize with me and my bed,
    do not ruin me now.
It was outrage enough when you made free with my name,
    though not with my body,
    leasing me out to barbarians.
If you have a craving to kill me,
    let me do my dying at home.
Why this addiction of yours to evil?

Why do you traffic in lusts and deceits,
    plotting and scheming and cheating,
    concocting love potions thickened with family blood?
If only you could learn moderation, I confess it,
    of all the gods you would be to men the sweetest.

*Exit Helen into the palace. Menelaos sits off to one side, against
the tomb.*

CHORUS

Sweet nightingale, nested deep in your shadowed grove,
Perched in your place of song,
Of all birds queen of melody and sorrow,
I cry out to you… come to me.
Spread wide your brown quivering mouth
And sing with me.
Accompany my laments.
I sing of Helen, her burdens and her misery.
I sing of Troy's mournful destiny,
Delivered on the tips of Greek spears,
When barbarian oars ploughed the sea,
And Paris rode the rolling waves,
A man wed to doom,
Carrying from Lakedaemon, from *you* Helen,
To the people of Priam, a cargo of death,
Compliments of Aphrodite.

I sing of warriors at rest now in Hades' gloom,
Legions of Greeks dispatched by spear and crushing rock,
Martyrs to a myth, mourned by desperate women,
Chopping at their hair in grief,
The beds they lie in growing cold.
I sing of how one man, a loner on the seas,
Lit the flame of his deception,
And set the Euboean headland ablaze with light,
Luring ships of Greeks to ruin in the swirling Aegean surf,
The wood under their feet splintered on the rocks of Kaphereus.
I sing of the harborless mountains of Malea,
Without welcome for the Greek fleet,
Driven far from home by winter gales,
Boasting the prize of its long war… no prize at all,
A phantom cloud of death and hate,
The handiwork of Hera.

What is god? What is not god? What lies in between?
What man can say he has reached the edges of existence,
No matter where he may have been?
What man has gazed upon god,
Witnessed the wild confusion at the core of things,
The contradictions, the unexpected twists of fate,
And returned to tell the tale?
You, Helen, were born the daughter of Zeus.
Your father, in feathered form, planted you
Deep in Leda's loins.
Yet all of Greece decried your "godlessness."
"Impious," "traitorous," "faithless" became your epithets.
There is nothing sure in all the turnings of men's minds.
Only god's words are bright with truth.

You men are crazed who run off to war,
To prove yourselves in the clash of steel,
Dreaming the fool's dream,
That with sharpened spears,
You will drive off human tribulation.
For if we depend on bloodlettings to resolve our differences,
There will be no end to hate in the cities of men.
It was hate that stormed the bedrooms of Priam's city,
When with a few clear thoughts and straight words
They might have disarmed their quarrel over you, Helen.
Now they line the gray halls of hell;
And ravenous fire, as sudden as a bolt from Zeus,
Leapt the walls of Troy and brought them down.
Meanwhile, you, Helen, reel with blow after blow
In a life fit only for pity.

Enter Theoklymenos and Servants.

THEOKLYMENOS
To the tomb of Proteus.
Monument to my dead father, I salute you.
It was for this I buried you here, Father,
    so near the palace gate.
That I, your son Theoklymenos, might greet you…
    might pay my respects,
      every time I come and go from my house.
Boys, take my hounds and the hunting nets inside the palace.

How many times I've complained of my own leniency,
    sparing riffraff who deserved to die.

And now I'm told another Greek's been seen,
 a new arrival to my land,
 who so far has eluded my guards…
 some kind of spy, no doubt,
 or someone scheming to steal Helen away from me.
This one *will* die.
All I have to do is catch him.

   Noticing Helen's empty pallet but not Menelaos.

Wait! What's this?
It seems I've come home only to find the mischief already done.
Look! No daughter of Tyndareos.
The empty mat beside the tomb is all she left behind
 as she was carried off from here.

   Theoklymenos pounds on the palace door, which opens, and,
   as it does, he catches a glimpse of Helen inside.

Ho in there! Open up!
Men, untie the horses from their stalls!
Wheel out the chariots!
This woman who's been whisked away
 is the woman of my dreams.
And I'm not going to lose her sitting down.
Wait! Hold on!
I see the ones we're after… still in the palace.
They haven't yet made good their escape.

   To Helen, as she enters.

Woman, why are you in black?
Why cast off your white robes?
And your long, lovely hair!
What possessed you to go at your noble head with a knife
 and… and… cut it all off?
You're crying. Your cheeks are all wet with tears.
Why are you doing this?
Did some dream in the night unsettle you so,
 that you begin wailing like this?
Or have you had some awful news from home
 that's torn your heart with grief?

HELEN
Lord and master—the time has come to call you this—
 I am lost! I have nothing left. I am no more.

THEOKLYMENOS
What's happened to you? What fate has struck?

HELEN
It's Menelaos—how do I form the words?—he is dead.

THEOKLYMENOS
I am not glad to hear these words,
    even though I profit from them.
How do you know? Did Theonoe tell you?

HELEN
Yes... she did.
I also heard it from a man who was there
    when my husband died.

THEOKLYMENOS
Someone has come *here* with a report we can trust?

HELEN
Yes... someone has come.
And soon he will go where I wish I too could go.

THEOKLYMENOS
Who is he? Where can I find him?
I would like to be certain about this.

Pointing to Menelaos.

HELEN
He's sitting over there, slumped against the tomb.

THEOKLYMENOS
Apollo! What a sight! Disaster is written in his rags.

HELEN
O! My husband must have looked the same way.

THEOKLYMENOS
What nationality is he?
And where was he before he came here?

HELEN
He is Greek, an Achaean.
He was aboard my husband's ship.

THEOKLYMENOS
And what kind of death does he say your Menelaos died?

HELEN
The most piteous of deaths... on the open sea.

THEOKLYMENOS
On which foreign waters was he sailing?

HELEN
His ship foundered on the rocks,
    somewhere along Libya's havenless coast.

THEOKLYMENOS
How was it that that fellow survived the same wreck?

HELEN
Sometimes luck favors the least deserving.

THEOKLYMENOS
Well, now that he's here,
    where did he leave the remains of the ship?

HELEN
Where I wish he had perished, instead of Menelaos.

THEOKLYMENOS
But it was Menelaos who perished.
Tell me. In what boat did he come here?

HELEN
He said something about sailors who happened on him
    and took him aboard their boat.

THEOKLYMENOS
And where is the malignancy sent off to Troy in your stead?

HELEN
You mean my vaporous double? Gone... into thin air.

THEOKLYMENOS
Priam... Troy... how you were dragged to your ruin...
    by mistake!

HELEN

And I am shadowed by the same dark destiny
  as the people of Priam

THEOKLYMENOS

That fellow... did he cover your husband with dirt,
  or leave him unburied?

HELEN

He left him unburied... another grief for me to bear.
I am so miserable!

THEOKLYMENOS

And so that is why you've cut off your billowing golden hair?

HELEN

I love him.
Wherever he is now, he is here... with me.

THEOKLYMENOS

Your story and your tears... how real are they?

HELEN

How easy is it to deceive your sister?

THEOKLYMENOS

It can't be done.
So now what? Will you go on "keeping house" at the tomb?

HELEN

Why taunt me?
Won't you permit the dead a moment's peace?

THEOKLYMENOS

So loyal you've been to your spouse,
  shunning my every advance.

HELEN

But no more. You may begin the preparations for my wedding.

THEOKLYMENOS

I've waited a long time, but all the same... I approve...
  with gladness.

HELEN
Do you know what we should do? Let bygones be bygones.

THEOKLYMENOS
Be more specific. Graciousness should be mutual.

HELEN
Let us make a truce. Be my friend.

THEOKLYMENOS
I dismiss my quarrel with you.
May it sprout wings and fly away.

HELEN
Well, then, now that we are friends,
    I go down on my knees and beg....

THEOKLYMENOS
What do you want from me,
    stretching out your arms and playing the suppliant?

HELEN
I want to bury my dead husband.

THEOKLYMENOS
How? How do you construct a tomb
    around someone who's missing?
Or do you plan to bury a ghost?

HELEN
In the case of someone who died at sea, the Greek custom is...

THEOKLYMENOS
To do what? Tell me.
I trust the wisdom of the royal house of Pelops in these matters.

HELEN
It is our custom to bury an empty shroud.

THEOKLYMENOS
Then do it. Bury him with all due honors.
Select whatever site you wish and raise his funeral mound.

HELEN
But that is not the way we bury sailors lost at sea.

THEOKLYMENOS
How, then? I am at a loss with Greek customs.

HELEN
We take out into the sea all that belongs to the dead.

THEOKLYMENOS
Then what can I give you for your dead?

HELEN
He knows. Until now my luck's been good
     and left me inexperienced with death.

THEOKLYMENOS
To Menelaos.
Stranger, you've brought welcome news.

MENELAOS
Not so welcome to me, nor to the dead.

THEOKLYMENOS
Tell me, how is it that you bury the dead that drowned at sea?

MENELAOS
It depends on how rich or poor the dead man was.

THEOKLYMENOS
Assume great wealth.
Then tell me what you want from me on her behalf.

MENELAOS
There must be a spilling of first blood to the gods below.

THEOKLYMENOS
The blood of what victims? I will abide by your prescriptions.

MENELAOS
You decide that. Whatever you provide will suffice.

THEOKLYMENOS
Among us barbarians, custom would call for a horse or a bull.

MENELAOS
Whatever you give, give the best.

THEOKLYMENOS
My herds are full of the finest.

MENELAOS
Next, a shrouded bier is to be borne in procession,
    minus the corpse, of course.

THEOKLYMENOS
It shall be as you say.
What else would it be customary to carry in procession?

MENELAOS
Brazen armor, for Menelaos was a warrior at heart.

THEOKLYMENOS
Then I shall provide armor worthy of a warrior-king
    of the house of Pelops.

MENELAOS
We will also need fair fruits of the earth,
    whatever flourish on your soil.

THEOKLYMENOS
Why? How do you intend to sink all of that into the surf?

MENELAOS
There will have to be a ship standing by,
    with a crew assigned to man the oars.

THEOKLYMENOS
How far out from shore does the ship have to go?

MENELAOS
Out where the breakers are barely visible from the land.

THEOKLYMENOS
Why this? What lies behind this Greek observance?

MENELAOS
A precaution… lest the waves wash foul pollution
    back up on shore.

THEOKLYMENOS
In that case, a swift Phoenician vessel will be at your disposal.

MENELAOS
Excellent. Imagine how pleased Menelaos would be!

THEOKLYMENOS
Now, surely you can manage this affair on your own...
    without her.

MENELAOS
No. it must be performed by the mother, the wife,
    or a child of the deceased.

THEOKLYMENOS
You're telling me that this grim burial of her husband
    is something *she* must do?

MENELAOS
Piety requires that the dead not be cheated of their due.

THEOKLYMENOS
Then so be it. She may go.
It is to my advantage to foster piety in my wife.
Go into my house and take what is fitting for the dead.
And once you have done this woman's wishes,
    I will send you off from my land with your arms full.
You have brought bright news to me,
    and since I see the sorry state you're in,
    you shall have the clothes and food you lack
    to make your journey home.
And you, poor dear, try not to be consumed
    with a grief that goes nowhere.
Menelaos, your husband, has met his fate.
For him there can be no crossing back from death to life.

MENELAOS
Young lady, your work is cut out for you.
You must content yourself with your husband at hand
    and let the other would-be husband go.
Under the circumstances, that is the best you can do.
As for myself, if I set sail for Greece and reach home safely,
    I will put an end to your shame... on one condition.
You must be... for your husband here...
    the sort of wife you were meant to be.

HELEN

It shall be exactly as you prescribe.
Never will my husband find fault with me.
And you yourself will be near enough
    to see the truth of what I say.
Now, poor man, go inside,
    where a bath and fresh robes await you.
I will be prompt in seeing to your wishes.
For the sooner I give you what you deserve,
    the better disposed you will be
    to perform the rites of my dearest Menelaos.

Exeunt Helen, Menelaos, and Theoklymenos into the palace.

CHORUS

Once long ago,
Darting in and out the trees of shaded mountain glens,
Leaping the banks of rivers in flood,
Racing through the thunderous surf,
Wild with worry and longing,
Her shrill cries of anguish
Piercing the merry thrumming of maenad drums,
The mountain mother of the gods,
Searched for her lost girl,
Whose name may not be spoken.

Then the goddess harnessed to her chariot
The lunging speed of savage lions,
To hunt her daughter torn from the soft grip of other girls,
As they danced the circling choruses.
And at the mother's side stood Artemis,
Swift and sudden as a storm,
A quiver of arrows slung across her back.
Athene too was there, armor clad, spear in hand,
Her eyes bright and fierce.
But Zeus, from his luminous seat in the sky above,
Set a different course for fate.

The sorrowing mother searched far and wide
For any clue to her daughter's rape,
A crime accomplished with effortless guile.
But at last she called an end to her toil,
Whose only fruit was frenzy and exhaustion.

Then to the snow-white crest of Ida she climbed,
Where mountain nymphs keep constant watch.
There the mother broken with grief
Cast herself down among the rocky thickets blanketed in snow.
So she brought blight upon the barren earth,
Making the soil sterile, unyielding of any fruit.
Total was the ruin she brought to the race of men.
For the sheep and the cattle she provided nothing,
No fresh, leafy fodder, no curling green tendrils.
Cities lost their means of life.
The gods went without their offerings.
The altar flames went out.
And with a mother's endless grief,
Bitter for her daughter lost and gone,
She sealed shut the earth's springs.
The glistening streams ran dry.

When the raving mother brought to a halt
Even the festivals shared by gods and men,
It was Zeus who gave the kind command
To calm the woman's hellish rage.
"Go, sacred Graces, Muses too, go to Deio,
Crazed for the girl who is gone.
With wild cries pierce her dark resolve.
With dance and sweet song soften her heart's pain"
First to respond was Aphrodite,
Loveliest of all the blessed ones,
Who took in her hand the skin-taut tambourine,
Rimmed with brazen castanets.
And soon her clamor reached the depths of hell,
Where a smile broke across the goddess-mother's face
As she took up the blaring flute,
And in the wildness of it all,
Rediscovered joy.

Within your private chambers, child,
You lit an unholy fire,
Whose flames burned without sanction.
And when you showed no reverence for her sacrifice,
You won the great goddess-mother's wrath.
Profound is the power of the dappled fawn-skin.
There is magic too in the sacred fennel-wand,
Wound bright and green with ivy,

And in the whirling clamor of the tambourines,
Spinning high overhead.
Hallowed is the feral hair,
Blown with the frenzy of Bromios.
Hallowed too are the moonlit rites of the goddess,
Whom the moon graciously reveals to sight.
But your one boast, child, was your beauty.

Enter Helen.

HELEN

Friends, everything is going our way in the palace.
The daughter of Proteus has proved herself
   our accomplice in stealth.
Even when pressed by her brother's questioning,
   she has said nothing to betray my husband's presence.
Instead, for my sake, she confirms his death,
   and says he lies buried deep in the earth's inner darkness.
Meanwhile, my husband has seized a splendid set of arms,
   the ones he's supposed to toss into the sea.
He has lifted the massive shield onto his powerful arm
   and with his right hand taken up the spear,
   ostensibly to play his role in the dead man's rites.
But in fact he is practicing for battle fully armed,
   alive with anticipation.
You would think that he plans to raise up trophies
   over a mountain of dead barbarians,
   slain singlehandedly by him,
   the moment we step on board their boat
In waters drawn from the purest streams,
   I have given him a bath he badly needed,
   and clothed him in fresh robes,
   exchanged for his shipwreck rags.
But enough of that;
   for I see coming from his house a man who thinks
   his marriage to me is imminent, as good as in his grasp.
For my sake, say nothing.
We would have you on our side,
   so be kind and hold your tongue.
And if we succeed in reaching safety,
   some day we shall save you too.

Enter Theoklymenos, Menelaos, and a procession of Servants.

THEOKLYMENOS

Move along, men; bring the funeral gifts to the sea.
And stay in the order the stranger assigned to you.
Helen, if what I say seems right to you, listen to me.
Stay here.
You will fulfill your duty to your husband all the same,
    whether you go or stay
I am afraid.
Some sudden madness might possess you.
All the joys you knew once with him, your husband,
    could rush back and unsettle you.
And you might, I fear, hurl yourself into the tossing sea.
For this grief of yours for a man who is, after all, gone,
    seems to me excessive.

HELEN

Sweet spouse to be.
I must honor my first love, the man I loved as a young bride.
Yes, I could die with my husband... for all my grief over him.
But what kind of a favor would it be to him,
    to accompany him in death?
Just let me go and see him to his grave.
And may the gods bestow on you all that I wish you to have.
I pray the same prayer for this stranger,
    who is no stranger to our efforts.
For your kindness to me... and to Menelaos...
    you will get your reward.
For you shall have me in your house as your wife
    as long as you deserve.
All that we now undertake shall work for what is best.
Now, give the command to whoever shall provide the ship
    in which we may convey our gifts.
Then my heart will be full with your kindness.

THEOKLYMENOS
To one of his Servants.

You, go and put at their disposal
    a fully manned, fifty-oar Sidonian galley.

HELEN
Pointing to Menelaos.

And this man will both officiate at the funeral
    and captain the ship?

THEOKLYMENOS
Of course. My sailors must obey him.

HELEN
Could you give that command again
    to remove any uncertainty in your men?

THEOKLYMENOS
I command it twice… or three times, if it matters to you.

HELEN
A blessing on you… and on our undertaking.

THEOKLYMENOS
Don't cry more than you have to. It's bad for your skin.

HELEN
Today is the day I will pay you back… for everything!

THEOKLYMENOS
Just remember, you owe nothing to the dead.
What you do for them is wasted effort.

HELEN
For the moment, my thoughts encompass both.

THEOKLYMENOS
You will find in me a husband no worse than Menelaos.

HELEN
My questions are not about you.
All I really need now is some luck.

THEOKLYMENOS
But that depends on you.
If only you give yourself to me graciously…

HELEN
Now is not the time to lecture me on how to love my loved ones.

THEOKLYMENOS
Would you like me to accompany you
    and to see you on your way?

HELEN

That is the last thing I would like.
You are the *king*.
Don't try to play the servant
    to those whose part it is to serve you.

THEOKLYMENOS

Then go.
The laws of the house of Pelops are your affair, not mine.
My house is without stain.
For it was not within my walls that Menelaos died.
One of you, go tell my vassals it is time
    to bring wedding gifts to my house.
I want my entire kingdom to burst into song.
I want to hear hymns of joy and bliss.
I want to hear the wedding song sung for Helen and for me,
    and for our lasting happiness.

To Menelaos.

Now, you, stranger, go and cast into the sea's open arms
    these offerings in honor of Helen's onetime husband.
Then waste no time in bringing back to me my wife,
    so that you might share with me our wedding feast.
After that, the choice is yours… set out for home,
    or stay here, where I will see to your happiness.

Exit Theoklymenos into the palace.

MENELAOS

O Zeus, of all the gods it is you we call wise,
    you we call father.
Look upon us and deliver us from evil.
Now, as we shoulder our fortunes to the brink,
    be quick to reach out to us your helping hand.
One touch of the tips of your fingers is all the grace we need
    to reach our wanted goal.
Already we have endured our life's share of suffering.
O gods, how often I have raised my voice to you,
    asking to be heard, in time of blessing
    and in time of pain.
I do not deserve to cower under some curse forever,
    but to walk tall and straight again.
Be on my side this one time,
    and because of you I will live out my days in happiness.

Exeunt Helen and Menelaos.

CHORUS

Sea-swift Phoenician galley,
Fresh from Sidonian waters,
You stir the sea to life with the labor of your oars,
And lead the chorus of dolphins,
As they leap and plunge in the still waters
Of the unruffled sea.
May Galaneia, serene daughter of the open sea,
Her brine-blue eyes bright and gleaming,
Speak to you with words like these:
"Unfurl your sails,
Leave them open to the whimsical swelling
Of the ocean winds.
But you men of the sea,
Ply your fir-wood oars
And lift the Lady Helen home
To the welcoming shores
Of the land of Perseus."

Helen,
I wish your long-awaited homecoming,
To the company of the daughters of Leukippos,
On the banks of the swirling Eurotas,
Or before Athene's brazen shrine.
It will be time to join again the festal dances,
To revel and make merry the night of Hyakinthos,
The boy slain by Phoibos in the games,
With a whirling disc thrown too far,
And honored by a day of solemn sacrifice,
Ordained by the child of Zeus
To be observed on Spartan soil.
And may you come home at last
To the girl you left behind,
Whose wedding torches are yet to be lit.

If only with sudden-sprouting wings
We might leap into the open air
And join the wide-winged ranks of migrant birds,
Fleeing Libya and its harsh winter storms,
Veering this way and that way,
On cue from the eldest of the birds,
As he scans and plains and fruitful fields far below,
Piping his commands.

You cranes who course the skies
In consort with the clouds,
Soar beneath the Pleiades in their zenith,
Glide through the night aglow with Orion,
Fly to Eurotas and perch among the reeds,
Crying out the glad tidings,
That Menelaos has taken Troy,
That Menelaos is homeward bound.

Twin sons of Tyndareos, wherever you are,
High in the luminous upper air,
Careening on your heavenly course,
Mounted in your celestial car,
Come down to us now,
Threading your way through the whirling web
Of stars ablaze with light.
Come, saviors of Helen,
Who make your home in the heavens above,
Come over the blue-billowing sea,
Over the dark menacing waves crested with froth,
And into the sails of your sister's ship
Send god-given gusts of homeward winds.

Fling far from your sister
Shaming tales of barbarian beds,
The stigma stamped on her in rage,
After the jealous quarrel on Ida,
Though Helen never went to Troy,
Never saw Phoibos's towering handiwork.

Enter Theoklymenos from the palace as a Messenger enters, out of breath.

MESSENGER

King, I've found you!
I bring the worst of news to your house.
What I have to say is nothing you expect to hear.
And it's going to upset you.

THEOKLYMENOS

What is it?

MESSENGER

You should work on wooing another wife.
Helen is gone… left the country.

THEOKLYMENOS
What? Lifted away on wings of some sort, or did she walk?

MESSENGER
Menelaos has made off with her.
He was the same one who brought the word of his own death.

THEOKLYMENOS
This is awful! I can barely believe what I'm hearing.
What kind of vessel carried her from my land?

MESSENGER
The same one you gave to the stranger.
The short of it is that he made off with your ship and your men.

THEOKLYMENOS
But how? I must know!
It never entered my mind
        that one man could overpower so many sailors…
        under your command!

MESSENGER
As soon as she left the royal palace,
        the daughter of Zeus walked, under escort, to the sea,
        where she displayed her wiles.
Treading the sand with her delicate feet,
        she began to wail for the husband who was far from dead;
        in fact, was standing close beside her.
Now, when we came to your shipyards and docks,
        we launched a Sidonian galley on its maiden voyage,
        with a full complement of fifty oarsmen at its benches.

One by one the needed tasks were done.
The mast was set in place;
        the oars were secured in their locks;
        the white sails were gathered;
        and the double rudders were lowered and lashed together.
Now, while we were at work, it seems we were being watched,
        for along came a band of Greeks,
        the shipmates of Menelaos, no doubt,
        trekking down the beach, clad in shipwreck rags.
They looked the worse for wear but were still striking to behold.
When the son of Atreus saw these men nearby,
        he called out to them.
There was, for our benefit, the pretense of pity in his voice.

"You men… down on your luck, I see.
How is it that you came here?
Clearly, you've cracked up your ship.
It must have been a Greek ship… but which one?
Would you join in the funeral of the perished son of Atreus?
The daughter of Tyndareos here is going to bury him in effigy,
    since he is missing."
Of course they cried their made-up tears.
Then they boarded the ship,
    carrying the offerings to be consigned to the sea.
Meanwhile, we were growing suspicious,
    and began to murmur among ourselves
    about how many these passengers were.
But we did not speak up, in deference to your instructions.
You tied our hands… and ruined everything,
    when you gave the stranger command of the ship.

Now the rest of the cargo was light, and we had an easy time
    stowing it aboard the ship.
Except for the bull, that is, who stood his ground,
    and refused to mount the gangplank.
Instead, bellowing loudly
    and rolling his eyes 'round in their sockets, the bull
    arched his back and leered over his lowered horns,
    defying anyone to lay a hand on him.
It was then that Helen's husband spoke up.
"Come on, you Troy-sackers,
    why don't you lift the bull up onto your young shoulders,
    Greek-style, and heave it onto the prow?"
At this point he drew his sword in readiness and added:
    "Something to slaughter and offer to the dead!"
Well, the Greeks sprung to his command,
    hoisted up the bull, hauled it aboard,
    and set it down among the rowing benches.
Then Menelaos, stroking the bull's neck and nose,
    managed to coax it further into the ship,
    though it was without tether or yoke.

Finally, when everything had been secured aboard the ship,
    Helen's shapely feet threaded the ladder's rungs,
    and she went to sit in the stern, on the quarter deck,
    beside the very Menelaos, who was supposed to be dead.
Meanwhile, the rest of the Greeks split into two equal ranks,
    and lined both sides of the ship.

They sat close, shoulder to shoulder,
     clutching swords concealed beneath their cloaks.
But we rowers, as soon as we heard the bosun's chant,
     made the pounding sea resound with our refrain.
And when we were at a point neither close to land
     nor far off shore, our helmsman called out like this:
"Tell us, stranger, shall we put out further or will this do?
For it's up to you to give the orders on this ship."
"This is far enough for me," he said,
     and, sword in hand, he made his way to the prow.
There he positioned himself next to the bull
     marked for sacrifice.
He made no memorial mention of any of the dead,
     as he slit the bull's throat and said his prayers:
"Poseidon, lord of seas, denizen of the depths,
          and you, chaste daughters of Nereus,
          from this land to the shores of Nauplia,
          grant safe conduct for me and for my wife,
          inviolate after all."
And as he prayed, the bull's blood sprayed into the sea…
     a bright omen for the stranger.
Then someone cried out:
"This whole voyage is a trick. We must go back!
Helmsman, give the command… turnabout!"
But the son of Atreus put his back to the slain bull and
summoned his comrades:
"Pride of Greece, what are you waiting for?
Slice… slash… slaughter the barbarians,
     and jettison them into the sea."
Then the bosun raised the countercry to your seamen :
"Come on, men, grab the spare spars, rip up the benches,
     pull loose your oars from their pins,
     and bloody the heads of these war-mongering foreigners."
Both sides were on their feet.
We swung the ship's spare lumber, and they swung their swords.
This time it was Helen who cried out, rallying the Greeks
     from her spot in the stern:
"Where's all the glory you won in Troy?
Show it to them… let the barbarians have a taste of it!"

The fighting was fast and hard, and many fell.
Some got up again; some didn't.
You could see the dead just lying there.

Menelaos, outfitted in heavy armor, surveyed the scene, and,
    when he saw one of his fellows getting the worst of it,
    he came, sword swinging, to his side,
    driving one after another of us to jump ship.
Eventually, he emptied the benches of your seamen.
Then he went to the helm and told your helmsman
    to steer a course straight to Greece.
Next they hoisted sail, and fair winds came to favor them.
So… they're gone.

I escaped being slaughtered by lowering myself
    down into the water by the anchor rope.
I was as good as dead when someone fished me from the sea
    with a line, and brought me ashore,
    so that I could bring this word to you.
You know, a little healthy skepticism goes a long way
    in this life of ours.
Knowing when *not* to believe someone…
    now that's the kind of wisdom we could use!

KORUPHAIOS

King, I never would have dreamt it possible
    that Menelaos could be right here,
    and not be found out by you or by us.
But that's what happened.

THEOKLYMENOS

What a miserable fool I am,
    taken in so totally by a woman's wiles.
So! My wife and my wedding have eluded me!
If there were any way to pursue that ship and overtake it,
    I would make short work of capturing those foreigners,
    whatever the cost.
But now it is my sister who will satisfy my vengeance,
    my sister who betrayed me, my sister
    who saw Menelaos in our house with her own eyes
    and said nothing.
I am the last man she and her prophecies are going to deceive!

Theoklymenos rushes toward the palace; but the Chorus blocks
his way, with the Koruphaios in front.

KORUPHAIOS

Lord! Lord! Where are you running off to?
There's murder in your eyes… but whose?

THEOKLYMENOS
I am following the course of justice. Get out of my way!

KORUPHAIOS
Grasping Theoklymenos's cloak.
No! I'm not going to let go of your cloak,
    for you are on the verge of doing something very wrong

THEOKLYMENOS
So *you,* a *slave,* are going to dictate to your master?

KORUPHAIOS
I have your own good in mind.

THEOKLYMENOS
Not my good… not unless you let me…

KORUPHAIOS
No… I'm not going to let you…

THEOKLYMENOS
Kill the most hateful of sisters!

KORUPHAIOS
The most holy, you mean.

THEOKLYMENOS
Who turned on me!

KORUPHAIOS
A fair turn… in the direction of doing right.

THEOKLYMENOS
And gave away my wife to someone else!

KORUPHAIOS
To someone whose claims outweigh yours.

THEOKLYMENOS
Who has claims over *my* possession?

KORUPHAIOS
The one who received her from her father's hand.

THEOKLYMENOS
But Luck gave her to me!

KORUPHAIOS
Yes. And Necessity took her away.

THEOKLYMENOS
Anyway, you're not the one to judge me.

KORUPHAIOS
Not unless I speak the truth.

THEOKLYMENOS
So I'm not king anymore? I'm told what to do?

KORUPHAIOS
To do right and not wrong.

THEOKLYMENOS
You seem to be in a hurry to die.

KORUPHAIOS
Go ahead. Kill me!
You have my permission to kill me,
    but never to kill your sister.
There is no greater glory for a well-bred slave,
    than to lay down her life for her mistress.

Enter the Dioskouroi, theophanously.

DIOSKOROI
Theoklymenos, lord and master of this land, bridle your rage,
    or it will drag you where you have no right to be.
We are the Dioskoroi, the divine twins.
Leda bore us long ago, Leda the mother of Helen,
    who has fled your house.
Theoklymenos, we call upon you...
Your rage is over a marriage that never was to be.
Your sister, Theonoe, daughter of divine Nereus,
    did you no wrong.
What she did was to honor the wishes of the gods
    and the upright legacy of your own father.
For it was always written as destiny that Helen would live
    here in your home until this moment came.

But now that Troy is torn up from her very foundations;
    now that Helen's name is no longer on loan to the gods,
    she shall dwell here no more.
Her own marriage makes its claims on her.
She must return to her home
    and to her life there with her husband.
So do not raise against your sister
    your sword with all its grim, dark stains.
Be assured, instead, of the wisdom of her deeds.
Long before this we would have come to Helen's rescue.
After all, Zeus made us into gods.
But even so, we are weaker than destiny,
    weaker too than the gods who willed all this to be.
This much we say to you.

What we say now is for our sister.
Sail on with your husband; fair winds will fill your sails.
And we, your twin brothers, will watch over you.
Astride the rolling sea, we will accompany you
    to the land of your fathers.
And when you approach your life's close and breathe your last,
    you will be hailed as a goddess.
With us, the Dioskoroi, you will share
    in the libations men pour out,
    and together we will enjoy the gifts of mortal hospitality.
For this is the way Zeus would have it be.
And where Maia's son first assigned you,
    when he swooped down from heaven
    and snatched you from your home in Sparta,
    stealing you away lest Paris make you his wife—
    we mean the sentinel island
    lying just off the coast of Attika—
    shall henceforth be known as *Helene,*
    for its hospitality to you, freshly stolen from your home.
And to wandering Menelaos, the gods have allotted a home,
    on the island of the blest.
For heaven never hates the high born.
It is for those without number or name
    that life is one long labor.

THEOKLYMENOS
Sons of Leda and Zeus, concerning your sister,
    I will set aside my differences with you.
And no longer would I think of taking my sister's life.

If the gods wish it so, then so be it.
Godspeed to Helen on her journey home!
Just know that you are born of the same blood
    as the purest and most perfect sister that ever was.

In the name of Helen, the noblest of spirits,
    and for that reason an exceptional woman,
      I bless you all!

CHORUS

Heaven has many faces.
The gods bring to pass many things we never hoped for,
While what we wait to see happen… never does.
And for what we never even dreamed could be,
God finds a way.
And so it happened here today.

⬦⬦⬦⬦⬦⬦⬦

I P H I G E N I A

INTRODUCTION
◇◇◇◇◇◇◇◇

The two distinct plays which I have grouped under the single title IPHIGENIA were not written by Euripides to be performed together, much less in the order presented here. Perhaps as many as ten years separate the two; and the *Iphigenia at Aulis* was, in fact, written after the *Iphigenia in Tauris*. As with the Theban Plays of Sophocles, however, narrative logic arguably begins to count for something after two dozen centuries. There is, after all, a certain appeal and logic to placing them in sequence so that the whole drama of Iphigenia might unfold before our eyes. A similar attachment to the "whole story" may be what once prompted an ancient interpolator to contribute his own miraculously happy conclusion to the *Iphigenia at Aulis* in the form of a chorus, which I like many other translators have chosen to omit. As it happens, that likely spurious chorus announced the unlikely deliverance of Iphigenia found in the *Iphigenia in Tauris*, which to a modern audience—well vaccinated against ancient myth—appears as nothing more than poetic escape, both entertaining and unconvincing, which is how I suspect Euripides intended it to be enjoyed and understood.

THE LEGEND

It is not possible to place a date on the story of Iphigenia. Most stories worth telling over and over defy postmarks. Hers is no exception. The defining historical event at the center of her story —the Trojan War—may be placed, however, roughly where Herodotus put it long ago, in the thirteenth century before the common era. Although she may well have been sung in some lost Mycenaean epic, Iphigenia is never mentioned in Homer. Hesiod, on the other hand, is said to have told how Iphigenia, through the intervention of Artemis, managed to escape death forever and become herself the object of cult. A similar account is found in the post-Homeric epic, *The Kypria*, wherein Artemis, substituting a stag for the ill-fated girl, is said to have lifted her away to the land of the Taurians and transformed her into a goddess. Centuries later, in the fifth century, most notably in the theater, Iphigenia made frequent appearances as sacrificial victim, sometimes rescued, sometimes not.

Regardless of its source, Iphigenia's story—the story of her sacrifice at the hands of her own father and of her last-minute rescue at the hands of Artemis—provides one of the most captivating stories in all of ancient literature, a story for our time as much as for any other. In its spell, cast all the more powerfully in the theater, we come to see that the past is not past and that the darkest and brightest truths never change.

THE DRAMA

As already pointed out, the *Iphigenia at Aulis* and the *Iphigenia in Tauris* were written and first produced, in all likelihood, nearly ten years apart. The *Iphigenia at Aulis*, though first in this volume, was one of the last plays written by Euripides and was produced for him, together with the *Bakkhai* and the *Alkmaion*, posthumously, only months after his death. From his grave, Euripides won first prize with these last plays, something he had rarely accomplished while both he and his plays lived.

The arrangement of these two plays in this volume is, as explained above, for the sake of narrative integrity. Together, in two dramatic episodes, they tell the whole story of Iphigenia, providing for a modern audience the fullness of context required to appreciate either play on its own. Additionally, when we consider that the traditional ending of the *Iphigenia in Aulis*, beginning with lines 1532 in the Greek text, is dismissed by most scholars as a contribution from some later anonymous donor, we may be justified in regarding the *Iphigenia in Tauris* in its entirety as the closest we can come to an authentically Euripidean conclusion to the unfortunately corrupted and compromised *Iphigenia at Aulis*. Judging from an Euripidean fragment, apparently from an *ex machina* promise by Artemis to send a doe as sacrificial substitute for Iphigenia, and knowing Euripides' penchant for wheeling out eleventh-hour divinities willing to suspend in the theater fates that take their certain course everywhere else, it is perhaps safe to say that the original lost ending of the *Iphigenia at Aulis* called for the saving appearance of Artemis, doe in hand, much as Iphigenia herself described the event in the *Iphigenia in Tauris*: "… goddess Artemis stole me from the knife and fire, leaving a deer to bleed and burn in my stead, while I was blown through luminous aether here, to Taurica, a barbarous land with a barbarous king."

In moving from legend to drama, however, we must keep in mind the conventional license enjoyed by Greek playwrights to draw selectively from and to improvise freely upon traditional stories in sketching the plots of their plays. Although, with few exceptions, the tragic playwrights retold old stories, their retellings told as much about the present as about the past. In the hands of Euripides, the stories of the past were given precisely that light and slant and shape required for them to mirror the present with candor. For Euripides, a playwright in dark times, this meant disabusing his contemporaries of any illusions of stature and tragedy. In his dramas, Euripides gave a corrupt generation a suitably corrupted mythic structure in which to see itself as it was.

THE SACRIFICE

It is not possible to explore here every challenge hurled by Euripides at his own generation and, for that matter, at ours. There is one such challenge, however, from which his two Iphigenia plays permit no escape.

Central to both plays is the act of sacrifice, finally human sacrifice, an act unspeakable, an act on which our minds fall blank. Yet, if we fail to confront the idea and reality of sacrifice, in its many faces and forms, then we must fail to grasp these plays. And again the loss is ours. Euripides wrote, after all, not to entertain but to illumine. The ancient theater was, as its name—*theatron*—suggests, a "seeing place," a place of insight, not distraction. The experience of these plays is thus to be an experience of heightened vision. Undoubtedly, the spectacle of human sacrifice, as well as the sight of a goddess miraculously interrupting the affair, would serve to dilate the eyes and imaginations of any witnesses. But Euripides has something more in mind than sheer spectacle and the voyeurism it provokes. If Euripides confronts his audience with the unthinkable, the unspeakable, it is to provoke thought and speech; not to suppress them. It has been said many times that the theater of Euripides is a theater of ideas. Perhaps that is why Socrates is said to have made a point of attending his plays. Regardless, if we inquire into the idea of sacrifice, we find ourselves at the heart of the plays at hand.

To anyone other than a practitioner, the act of sacrifice is bound to seem barbaric. Surely its name is euphemistic. How, anyone might ask, does making someone dead also make them sacred? Sacrifice, it would seem, is a fancy word for slaughter. Anyone or any people who practice it have slipped back into savagery, crossed the line into bestiality. Or so it would seem to civilized common sense, as we know it today or as Euripides' fellow Athenians knew it then.

Common sense, however, is often neither. After all, it is humans, not beasts who practice sacrifice. Furthermore, many of the earliest traces and recollections of humanity's passage from nature to culture, from savagery to civilization, suggest that sacrifice served to distinguish human beings from the animals. Sacrifice, including human sacrifice, was and perhaps is a mark of the human, a foundation stone of civilization. Indeed, ample evidence of the practice of human sacrifice from the paleolithic period to the bronze age is depicted in the legend of Iphigenia, representing a continuity of tens of thousands of years. We, anyone who would eschew the practice of human sacrifice, may be the aberrant, inhuman ones. It is a possibility to be considered.

The act of ritual sacrifice was, quite simply, the central cultic act of ancient Greek religion, the sacred experience *par excellence.* In it the essential order of the universe was acknowledged and reinforced. The proper performance of sacrifice was seen as a stay against chaos rather than as a collapse into it.

The fundamental structure of the sacrificial act was twofold: ritual slaughter of the victim followed by a communal feasting on its flesh. Human victims were admittedly the exception. Human sacrifice and ritual cannibalism were reserved for moments of extreme peril or crisis. On Minoan Crete, for example, there is evidence of child sacrifice and homophagy to avert the imminent threat of earthquake. Another form of sacrifice, attested in legend, involved the ritual banishing or killing of *pharmakoi,* human or bestial "scapegoats," made to carry with them the burdensome evils of a community polluted by disease or crime, a ritual whose intended outcome was *katharsis,* purification. Another pretext for human sacrifice was the need for "weather magic" to avert famine or flooding or whatever. Finally, when armies met and found themselves on the brink of battle, the sacrifice of a virgin was sometimes indicated. Her blood, the first blood of the ensuing conflict, whether as provocation or charm, somehow seemed a fitting prelude to murderous frenzy.

Before dismissing the act of sacrifice out of hand as an act born and bred in darkness, however, we must consider this: that the destruction of the victim is, in theory, for the sake of many others' survival. The slaughter is followed by a feast. The denial of life leads to a celebration of life. What begins as and appears to be boldly life-destroying becomes manifestly life-affirming. In surrendering or taking life, its sacred worth is re-discovered. Such is the theory of sacrifice.

It may be instructive to consider, as well, that there is nothing uniquely Greek about either the theory or the practice of human sacrifice. Abraham, the father of Jewish faith, was no less willing to slay his own child than was Agamemnon. The fact that he did not complete the act altered very little, except for Isaac. Later, when on the brink of battle Jephthah promised to Yahweh, in return for victory, a burnt offering, which turned out to be his own beloved daughter, his offering was accepted. No substitution was made. Neither, we know, was any substitution acceptable when Jesus prayed to his father for release. In the words of Caiphas, "It is better for one man to die for the people."

Death for the sake of life. One for the sake of the many. Herein lies the core conviction of ritual sacrifice. Such was the conviction of Paul and of the early Christian Church who saw Jesus as the perfect victim, the sacrificial lamb of God, slain for the many, his flesh and blood a feast for all of lost humanity. To the eyes of faith, the crucifix presents a glorious sight, while non-Christians stare at the same crucifix and see something altogether hideous, something unspeakable. A similar void opens up in the final scene of the *Bakkhai*, when the god abandons Agave to her own devices and to simple human sight. In that moment the brilliant trophy in her hand becomes the head of her own boy, fresh from his shoulders, ripped loose in what seemed at the time a joyous frenzy. Nowhere are the sacred and the profane so far apart as in the act and experience of sacrifice.

Whose vision, we must wonder, penetrates to the truth? When the god Dionysos releases Agave from his possession and her eyes see the hideous head in her hands, in that moment does she return to reality or does she depart from it? Which is the truth of the crucifix: atrocity or triumph? These questions bring us back to Iphigenia. Is she a martyr or a murder victim? A heroine or a "road-kill" on the way to Troy? And is there any difference?

Klytemnestra, the mother of Iphigenia, is clear on this much. Her daughter is being murdered by her own father. Everything else—every appeal to a cause, a will or a compulsion higher and greater than a mother's love or a daughter's life—is a pitiful screen thrown up between common decency and a vile crime. In the court of Klytemnestra, Agamemnon is without excuse. She is deaf to his invocations of Greece, necessity and the divine will. If there are gods, she says, we insult them when we murder in their name. In the *Iphigenia in Tauris,* Iphigenia has come around to her mother's assessment of sacrifice and of the goddess who supposedly craves and commands it. "Here in this land," she declares, "men, not gods, are murderers. Men make their own perversions into rituals and sacralize their sins. No god is evil. That is what I believe." It is also, I am convinced, what Euripides himself believed. This belief found simple and profound expression in the *Bakkhai* when the Chorus of women sang: "Those who scoff at the happiness of simple days and sweet nights, our god hates. It is ordinary wisdom to keep the mind away from extraordinary men and their excesses. Common sense and common decency. I aspire to nothing more." As for oracles claiming to speak for the gods and as for priests claiming to do the gods' will, in the *Helen* the Messenger, an ordinary, decent man, reiterates what I suspect to be the opinion of Euripides: "You know, now I see the art of prophecy for what it is, a vulgar occupation and a pack of lies... Best just to leave the priests alone... Anyway, the best magic is a balanced mind, and a little common sense."

What, then, are we to make of the appeals of Agamemnon to his daughter, for her to see his act—his taking of her life—in a different, higher light? His words to her are nothing less than a sermon, an outpouring not of reason but of faith. In this case, bad faith. Euripides leaves no room for doubt on this. By the time Agamemnon mounts his pulpit, it is too late for him to touch us with his words. We know too much. Iphigenia, on the other hand, knows too little.

After failing to convince his wife that he is in the grip of grander designs or, at the least, extenuating circumstances, Agamemnon turns to his daughter. He offers her a "higher" truth, an altered, heightened vision of what he is about to inflict and of what she is about to suffer. Beneath this aria, however, Euripides has also provided the base line, for all but Iphigenia to hear, the reality, as it were, beneath the hymn.

THE LIE

The truth revealed early on in the *Iphigenia at Aulis* is that Agamemnon's ambition has outstripped both his abilities and his luck. He is no more in control of his army than he is of the weather. The army has reasons of its own for sailing to Troy, and they have nothing to do with retrieving Helen or restoring Greek pride. The army is hellbent on violence and plunder. Meanwhile, Agamemnon is so enamored of his prerogatives and so enslaved by his fears, that he is willing to murder his own beloved girl rather than compromise his career or confront the truth. And not only does he dispatch his daughter to death, but he sends her off embracing a seductive lie, whose perversity she is both too callow and too desperate to detect. In other words, he takes advantage not only of her weakness but also of her innocence.

There is no reason for imagining that Agamemnon believes a word of what he tells Iphigenia regarding why she must die. In utterly lucid bad faith, Agamemnon creates a lie the size of the atrocity he is willing and about to commit. He invents Hellas, Greece, an entity greater than the sum of all of its living daughters and sons; and so it must be if it is to demand and to justify their deaths, as many as may be needed. He invents too the barbarians as a people whose very existence is an affront and a threat, and whose extinction or subjection constitutes a moral imperative. In short, Agamemnon invents, before our eyes, politics.

What so darkens and complicates this tragedy is that Iphigenia is being murdered by her own father, a truth which neither Agamemnon nor Iphigenia is able to look straight in the face. Instead, they agree to share a consoling lie. He plants it, and she carries it to term. Greece, he says, is turning to him and to her and demanding of them the ultimate sacrifice. Nothing less than the freedom of Greece is at stake. With this lie, Agamemnon anaesthetizes his girl before putting her under the knife. Never should we mistake this act, however, for one of compassion. Anaesthesia, after all, is administered as much for the surgeon's convenience as for the patient's comfort. In this instance, Agamemnon's prevailing concern is to ease his own passage to Troy, not his daughter's passage to Hades. Her death is something he wants to put behind him with as little awkwardness and delay as possible.

The *Iphigenia at Aulis* is Euripides' last word on war, the politics which provoke it, and the victims who endure it. No war would ever be fought without seducing the young to its awful momentum. Young, beautiful bodies and souls must be given some compelling reason for dying or killing; and those whose purposes are served by war know that the truth will not do. It is cursedly the case that the inexperience, idealism, passion and naiveté of youth conspire to make them prey to the speeches of their elders. The timeless scandal is that the latter, like Agamemnon, know both the power of their words and their emptiness.

THE CONVERSION

For many critics, ancient and modern, the radical conversion of Iphigenia to her fate is too sudden and too complete to be believed or accepted. One moment, Iphigenia begs on her knees for her life. She longs for the persuasive powers of Orpheus and uses her younger brother instead to try to break down her father's murderous resolve. Running out of words, she reminds her father that "to look upon the light of day is for all of us the sweetest of joys. In the dark world below there is nothing. To pray for death is sheer madness. To be alive, in whatever lowly condition, is better than to die a glorious death." It is not long, however, before Iphigenia, resolving not to clutch her life too tightly or, for that matter, at all, offers herself freely to just such a "glorious" death. "I give my life to Greece," she announces. "Sacrifice me and lay waste to Troy." Her last speech has clearly been scripted by her father. She has swallowed his words as if they were the sweetest milk.

There is much that could be said to anyone, including Aristotle, disappointed by Iphigenia's change of heart; but it all comes down to this. She knows she is lost. Worse, she knows her own father is going to kill her. She has only one last choice to make and only moments in which to make it: whether to die a hideous death at the hands of a father turned maniac or to die a martyr to a cause so bright as to cast out forever the darkness of this moment. Of course, this choice exists in her mind and nowhere else. Its only effect is that, for her few remaining breaths, she may be able not to hate her own father, to believe in his love and to imagine that he knows more than she does. Who, I wonder, can begrudge her this? Besides, it is all sadly true.

THE MIRACLE

As for the miraculous and salvific appearance of Artemis and all that follows upon it, we do well to enjoy it while we can. It was meant for our delight, the delight available in the theater where life is only watched and not lived and where any of life's necessities may be reversed or altered at will. Euripides wrote a number of plays whose darkness is lifted in the last instant by a visitor from on high, a divine aunt or uncle, as it were, carrying the one gift we most desire. He went even further, in fact, and wrote what are best described as romantic melodramas or comedies, plays seasoned throughout with levity and humor and ending with a promise of happiness forever after. Such are the lost endings of the *Iphigenia at Aulis* and the entirety of the *Iphigenia in Tauris,* ironic escapes from what admits of no escape, playful exceptions which serve only to prove the rule. In realizing how close laughter is to tears and in exploring their border, Euripides extended the meaning of *katharsis,* the purifying release from inner pain and pollution which was to be the climax of the tragic experience.

THE TRANSLATION

These two translations, like the originals which they imitate, are written for the theater, to be staged first and studied next. A play printed on a page is like a butterfly pinned to a wall. We cannot say we have seen a butterfly until we have seen it on the wing; nor can we say we have seen Euripides until we have seen him on the stage. Most translations of ancient plays are written for the desk or for the lap, to be examined as cultural fossils or to be read as poetry. Very few translations of Greek tragedy are written for the stage. Actors and directors, in reading through a script, know at once whether it is actable, whether it will play. The lyrics of the chorus must be able to be set to music and danced. The dialogue must ring true. The characters must be convincing as they reveal themselves in their words. Insults must be insulting. Rage must be resonant in the language used to convey it. Humor must be funny on the face of it. If we are required to learn from program notes that what one character just said to another would have been an insult or would have been a joke in the theater of Dionysos, then we are not watching a play. We are reading about one. A book allows for cross-referencing and for back-scanning. If we don't get something,

we can look it up or read it again. Not so in a play, which, like music, either carries us with it or leaves us behind. In short, the first commandment to be observed in translating a play is that thou shalt not make a good play into a bad play, much less into a poem or a study guide. This, to my mind, is the appropriate meaning of "literal" translation. It is also the goal I set for myself in the two translations which follow.

DRAMATIS PERSONAE

IN ORDER OF APPEARANCE

AGAMEMNON
High King of the Greek Forces

OLD SERVANT
Slave in the House of Agamemnon

CHORUS
Young Women from Khalkis and
Attendants to Klytemnestra and Iphigenia

CHORAL LEADER
Leader of the Chorus

MENELAOS
Brother of Agamemnon and Husband of Helen

KLYTEMNESTRA
Wife of Agamemnon

IPHIGENIA
Daughter of Agamemnon and Klytemnestra

MESSENGER
In the Entourage of Klytemnestra

ORESTES
Son of Agamemnon and Klytemnestra

AKHILLEUS
Greatest of the Greek Warriors

IPHIGENIA AT AULIS

*The scene is Agamemnon's camp at Aulis. It is night.
Agamemnon enters from his tent and looks around in the
darkness for his Old Servant, who is lying awake and unseen
off to one side.*

AGAMEMNON
Calling out to his Old Servant.
Old one, come here…to the front of my tent.

OLD SERVANT
From offstage.
I'm coming.
What is it, lord Agamemnon?

AGAMEMNON
I want you to hurry!

OLD SERVANT
Entering.
I *am* hurrying! I'm certainly not sleeping.
At my age, I lie down… that's it.

AGAMEMNON
Tell me. What star is that directly over us?

OLD SERVANT
Near the Pleiades… it's Sirius,
    square in the middle of the sky.

AGAMEMNON
Listen. Nothing. Not a sound.
Not from a single bird. Even the sea is still.
The river too is mute…without the winds.

OLD SERVANT
My lord, what are you doing out here
    in the middle of the night?
There's nothing but peace and quiet in Aulis.
Not even our own sentries are stirring.
Why don't we go inside?

*Agamemnon nods and turns to re-enter his tent, gesturing to
the Old Servant to follow him inside.*

AGAMEMNON

O how I envy you, old one.
I envy anyone who can live a life without risk,
 unnoticed, free of fame.
In fact, the more significant a man is,
 the more I pity him.

OLD SERVANT

Just what do you pity in a man who has everything?

AGAMEMNON

The fact that everything he has can, and probably will,
 slip away.
Privilege is sweet one day and bitter the next.
When the gods slip, it's we who fall.
And when we land on our feet,
 our fellow mortals wait for us,
  sleeplessly scheming our ruin.

OLD SERVANT

I have trouble hearing such laments
 coming from a king.
Lord Agamemnon, Atreus fathered you into the world,
 not paradise.
Down here, in addition to enjoying yourself,
 you must suffer.
Even you were born mortal.
So, with or without your consent, the will of the gods
 is what's going to happen.
But tell me...
Your lamp burning bright at this hour...
 and these tablets...
I can see you've been writing something...
 and that you still hold it in your hand,
  sealed and broken open many times...
   written and unwritten,
  hurled to the ground and written again.
I heard you weeping.
Now I see that you soaked the ground with your tears.
Whatever it is you're struggling with,
 you seem to be losing...
  at least your wits.

*Agamemnon slumps into a chair, lowering his head into
his hands and weeping.*

What is it, my king? What new shadow pursues you?
Tell me everything. Let me into your pain.
You don't need walls against a simple, decent man,
    someone you know you can trust.
 Remember, I've been with you a long time,
    from the day Tyndareos sent me
    with your bride, a worthy item in her dowry.

AGAMEMNON

Phoibe, my wife Klytemnestra, and Helen.
Those were the three sisters born to Leda,
    daughter of Thestios.
Now when Helen's time arrived, her suitors came
    from every corner of Greece, young men who already
had everything… except Helen.
They whiled away their time together boasting
    and making dark threats, in case they failed,
        promising to slay the one among them
            whose dream would have come true.
All the while Tyndareos was torn two ways.

He could either go on with the marriage or call it off;
    and it was difficult to predict
        which would be the more disastrous.
Then it came to him.
He would unite all the suitors in a common oath,
    sealed with a burnt offering to make it last.
And so the famous pact came to be.
The suitors one and all swore to stand behind, not against,
    the fortunate groom, whoever it might be.
If anyone, barbarian or Greek,
    should ever drive Helen's husband from his bed
        and carry her away,
        together they would march against that fool's city
        and raze it to the ground.
So, duped by an old and clever man,
    the suitors made their oath.
And to his daughter Tyndareos gave the final word.
Hers would be a love-choice.
Helen would lift her heart's sail,
    and watch the winds of desire do the rest.
Somehow that meant Menelaos.
Looking back, I wish it had been anyone else.
Then, fresh from his famous beauty contest,
    a Phrygian dandy made his way to Sparta.

It was Paris, in the bloom of youthful beauty and allure,
    swathed in silks, appointed in gold,
        Paris at his barbarian best.
There was love at once between them... Helen and Paris.
As soon as Menelaos went away, the herdsman from Troy
snatched up his prize and brought her back
        to graze on the slopes of Ida.
Next came the fury of her lawful spouse,
    who made the rounds of Helen's one-time suitors,
        unearthing an old promise,
    invoking a consortium of revenge.

As it happened, all of Greece ran for its arms,
    launched itself and got just this far,
        to the straits of Aulis,
           where every sail went limp.
Ships, armor, horses, chariots...
        all beached now on the strand.
And I am in command, by acclamation.
I suppose because I am the brother of the cuckold.
It is an honor I would be relieved to wish on anyone else.
So, here we are, an army in full muster,
    a fleet trimmed to sail.
All we lack is wind.

And for that, Khalkis the seer found the solution.
To Artemis, who prevails in this place,
    I am to sacrifice my own daughter Iphigenia.
If I do this, our sails will fill with wind,
    and Troy will fall.
Neither will happen if I don't.

When I first heard this "solution,"
    I told Talthybios our herald
        to proclaim in his loudest voice
    that the army was dismissed.
Never would I be willing to kill my own child.
It was my own brother who laid siege to me then
    with every argument he could conjure,
        until he had my hands willing to do
    what my heart could not even imagine.
I inscribed a tablet and dispatched it to my wife,
    telling her to send our daughter here to Aulis
        to be wed to Akhilleus.

I shared with her my excitement
    over the stature of this man
        our daughter would marry,
    adding that Akhilleus was refusing to sail to Troy
    unless his house and ours were bound in marriage.

All this—the whole story of our daughter's marriage—
    I made up, a ruse
        to get my wife to play into our hands.
Kalkhas, Odysseus, Menelaos: they were there with me.

No one else knew anything.
Then I came to my senses.
In the benign obscurity of night, on a fresh tablet,
    I untold my own lie, sealing it, unsealing it...
But that you already know.

    Picking up a tablet and handing it to the Old Servant.

Old one, go. Take this tablet to Argos.
It holds a deep secret.
And, knowing your loyalty, I will tell you what it is.
This is what I have written:
"Daughter of Leda, contrary to what I wrote earlier... "

    Agamemnon pauses and does not go on.

OLD SERVANT
Go on. Tell me the heart of the message,
    so that, if need be, I can deliver it verbally,
        exactly as you've written it.

AGAMEMNON
"Do not send your daughter to the calm shores of Aulis,
    braced by Euboea against the sea's wild moods.
We will celebrate the marriage of our girl
    another place, another time."

OLD SERVANT
What about Akhilleus?
Suddenly single again, won't he explode...
    in the direction of you and your wife?
The wrath of Akhilleus is a dreadful thing.
Give me some idea what you will say
    when confronted with it.

AGAMEMNON

His wedding was not fact but a fiction,
   in which he was our unwitting accomplice.
Akhilleus knew nothing of the proposed marriage,
   much less of our real plans.
So far as he knows,
   I've never promised my daughter to his bed.

OLD SERVANT

I see.
A blood victim for your army and a bride for Akhilleus.
A war and a wedding…
   your own daughter would provide both.
All you had to do was lie a little.
Lord Agamemnon, the flames you were lighting…
   did you think you would be able to put them out?

AGAMEMNON

I didn't think at all.
I leapt into the flames instead, in the hope of going mad.
But now, go… go, old one. Don't listen to your feet.
Stop for nothing.

OLD SERVANT

I'm not going to waste any time.

AGAMEMNON

Then, when you reach the shade of the forest
   and the cool springs, don't stop.
Fight off sleep.

OLD SERVANT

God forbid!

AGAMEMNON

Whatever you do, when you reach the fork in the road,
   keep your eyes open
      and watch for a chariot carrying Iphigenia
   along the shore road toward the ships.
It may be moving very fast; so don't let it slip by you.

OLD SERVANT

As you say my, lord.

AGAMEMNON

Assuming she is already on her way,
    when you come upon her and her escorts,
        block their way.
Grab the bridles of their horses, giving them no choice
    but to turn around and go back
        to the walls the Cyclops built.

OLD SERVANT

So I tell your wife and daughter to turn around
    and go back where they came from.
But why should they listen to me?

AGAMEMNON

Here. Take this ring. It bears my seal.
The same seal is on the tablet you carry.

Now go.
Already the four-horsed flames of Helios and his chariot
    advance upon the night.
It will be light soon. Go!
Do your best for me.

The Old Servant exits.

AGAMEMNON

For us mortals, life is a brief moment.
Even so it is outlasts our longest joys.
Pain waits somewhere for each of us.

Agamemnon returns to his tent. The Chorus enters.

CHORUS

From nearby Khalkis my homeland, where
With the sea on every side
The famed waters of Arethusa
Find their radiant source,
We have crossed the swirling straits of Euripos,
Steering a course to Aulis,
Beaching our boat on these sandy shores.
We come here for one thing:
To see with our own eyes
The Akhaean host, the fleet sailed by men
Who might as well be gods.

We came to see the thousand ships.
Sent—our own men say—
By fair-haired Menelaos
And high-born Agamemnon
To bring back Helen.
Paris, the herdsman-prince
Collected her from the reed-lined banks of the Eurotas
As a token from Aphrodite,
For that day when she stepped from her bath
To do battle with Hera
And Pallas Athena,
Drawing her beauty
Like a glistening sword.

Too excited to walk,
We ran just now
Through the grove of Artemis,
Over ground soaked with sacrifice,
To reach the camp.
We blush to admit
How much we wanted to see
Their tents, hung with war-gear,
Their burnished shields stacked into a wall around them,
Men on the verge of war,
Armed and mounted,
The swelling might of Greece.

First I caught sight of the two Aiases,
One the son of Oileos,
The other the son of Telamon
And held to be the crowning pride of Salamis.
With these two was Palamedes,
Whose grandfather is Poseidon himself.
The three of them sat bent over a game board,
Addicted to its demands,
Each one enthralled with his own cleverness.
Meanwhile, Diomedes threw the discus,
With visible solitary pleasure.
Nearby stood Meriones, an astonishing sight.
The blood of Ares runs in his veins.
I saw too the son of Laertes, from craggy Ithaka;
And then Nireus who, in beauty, stands all alone.

Next my eyes fell on the child of Thetis,
Tutored into perfection by the centaur Kheiron,
Akhilleus, whose feet, as if wings,
Carry him aloft.
Like a sudden burst of wind,
He ran the expanse of the beach.
It was a race:
Akhilleus in full armor and bare feet
Against a four-horsed war-chariot
Driven by a son of the house of Pheres, Eumelos,
Who was trying to shout and goad his team
Out of their imminent defeat.
What a lovely sight they were:
Four perfect foals bridled in gold,
The middle two—the yoke pair—dappled gray
With flecks of white in their manes;
And the other two—the trace pair—bays
With spotted fetlocks.
I gazed at them as they drove hard and close
Around the turning-post,
With the son of Peleus so near
That his armor clanged against the chariot's railing
And made the wheels sing.
Not even the gods have words for what I saw next:
The spectacle of the ships.
My woman's eyes drank in that sight
With the pleasure I can still taste.
On the far right lay the fleet of the Myrmidons from Phthia,
Fifty sleek, sea-skimming vessels,
Their up-curved sterns crowned with the figures of Nereids,
Divine daughters of the sea, wrought in gleaming gold,
Emblems of Nereid-born Akhilleus.

Next and comparable to these were the Argive ships
Under the command of Mekistes,
The son and product of Talaos.
Beside him Sthenelos, Kampaneos' child.
Further to the left lay the Attic fleet,
Fifty ships bearing the image of goddess Athena
Mounted in a sky-borne chariot
Drawn by a team of winged horses,
A bright omen for the sailors who man those decks
And for the son of Theseus who leads them.

My gaze then fell on the Boetian contingent,
Fifty more emblazoned ships fitted out for war.
This time it was Kadmos and a golden dragon
Perched on the ships' sterns;
And it was Leitos the earth-born who led them.
There too was the son of Oileos, who sailed
To Aulis from the famed city of Thronion in Phokis,
With a fleet of fifty Lokrian vessels.

Next from Mykene whose walls the Kyklops set in place,
The son of Atreus filled a hundred ships with men
And brought them here.
He and his brother, sharing the high-command,
Share a common purpose too.
In the name of all Greece,
They will make Helen pay for what she did,
Turning her back on where she belonged
In heat for some barbarian's bed.
Then, from its blazonry,
I recognized the fleet of Geranian Nestor…
Atop each ship the Pylian River Alpheos,
In the image of a bull.

I counted twelve Ainian vessels next,
Under the command of their king Gouneos.
And, immediately beside these, the ships of Elis,
Commanded by Eurytos.
Right there at hand I saw the lords of Elis,
Whom everyone calls the Epeians.

Next there were the white-oared Taphian galleys
Under Meges, son of Phyleos.
These had sailed from the islands of Echinai
Whose rocky shores other sailors shudder to approach.

Now, on the extreme left flank of the armada,
My eyes fell on Aias of Salamis,
With the twelve most trim, agile craft of all,
Charged with keeping the entire fleet
Drawn up in order,
Moving as one,
Like a great net sweeping the seas.

This is what I have seen…
A vast host under sail.

God help any barbarians in boats
Who cross its path.
They will never see their homes again.

Later, years from now,
When the stories come back
And fill the halls of my house,
I will listen to them and remember
That here, today,
With my own eyes,
I saw it all begin.

*The Chorus exits. Menelaos and the Old Servant enter, engaged
in a bitter quarrel. Menelaos carries in his hand the tablet.*

OLD SERVANT

Menelaos, you can't do this.
You're going too far!

MENELAOS

Get lost, old man!
You're the one who went too far.
You're too loyal to your master.

OLD SERVANT

Thank you. I take that as a compliment.

MENELAOS

You're going to regret not learning your place.

OLD SERVANT

And is it your place to read a message I was carrying
    for someone else?

MENELAOS

What you were carrying was mischief…for all of us.
You haven't that right.

OLD SERVANT

Argue that point somewhere else.
Just give me back the tablet.

MENELAOS

No way.

OLD SERVANT
Seizing the tablet.

Then neither will I.

MENELAOS

All right.

Brandishing his sceptre.

In that case I'll club your head to a bloody pulp.

OLD SERVANT
It would be an honor to die for my master.

MENELAOS
Raising his sceptre to strike the Old Servant.
You have a big mouth for a slave.

Re-enter Agamemnon. The Old Servant drops at once to one knee and reaches out his hands toward Agamemnon. As he does so, Menelaos snatches back the tablet.

OLD SERVANT
My king, we have been wronged.
This man tore your tablet from my hands.
He doesn't care about right and wrong.

AGAMEMNON
Enough of this racket!
So. You choose the front of my tent to hold your quarrel.
Why?

Agamemnon turns his back on them both.

MENELAOS
I think it is my place to speak first…before him.

AGAMEMNON
Then explain your private war with him…
and your use of force.

MENELAOS
Turn around and look me in the eye.
Then I'll say what I have to say

Agamemnon turns around to face Menelaos. As the argument between them heats up and catches fire, the Old Servant exits.

AGAMEMNON
Son of Atreus, if I prefer not to look at you,
    do you really think it's out of fear ?

MENELAOS
Then look at this tablet and the foul treason it contains.

AGAMEMNON
I'm looking.
Now give it back to me.

MENELAOS
Opening the tablet.
No, not until I read it…
    loud enough for every Greek to hear.

AGAMEMNON
So, you've broken my seal…
    and learned what is none of your business.

MENELAOS
Learned all about your treachery, you mean.
It's something you will pay for.

AGAMEMNON
How was it you intercepted him?
God, you have your nerve!

MENELAOS
I was actually looking for your daughter,
    to see if she had arrived yet from Argos.

AGAMEMNON
You really are shameless.
What persuaded you to pry into my affairs?

MENELAOS
I persuaded myself.
I was born your brother, not your slave.

AGAMEMNON
So what?
Is someone else going to keep my house?
I don't like the sound of that.

MENELAOS

I'll tell you what I don't like. Forget your house.
You can't keep your own head straight.
A few days ago you felt one way;
    now you feel another way.
I'm sure if we wait around a while longer…

AGAMEMNON

You certainly have a way with vicious words.
Your kind of eloquence is a disease, you know.

MENELAOS

And what about a mind that changes like the weather,
    or a heart that betrays today yesterday's friends?
Signs of health?

Now it is my turn, Agamemnon, to indict you.
Try not to let your anger blind you
    to the truth in what I say.
And I, for my part, will try not to go too far.

Surely you remember how keen you were at first to lead
    the Greeks to Troy, although you did your best
        not to let it show.
You put on your humblest airs,
    and you shook nearly every hand in Greece.
At your palace it was all "open doors" and "first names."
You made constant conversation,
    whether anyone wanted it or not.
With mere tokens, you tried to buy your way into power.
And it worked.

So, sceptre in hand, you quickly changed your ways.
You dropped your friends like leaves off a tree.
You lived behind bolted doors.
You had time for no one.
When a decent man succeeds and rises in the world,
    he holds his ground, an anchor of trust,
        especially for his friends.
His good fortune becomes theirs.
Somehow the opposite was true with you.
I have mentioned this first,
because it was my first quarrel with you.

King of kings, commander-in-chief of the Greek forces…
    that was you when you first came to Aulis.
Soon you were a non-entity.
Limp sails—one token of divine displeasure—and you fell apart.
Your army had enough of futility and shouted to go home.
Meanwhile, your wretchedness was etched across your face.
The vision of a thousand ships and of a vast host of men
    thronging the plains of Troy, all under your command…
    the vision was fading and you were desperate.
You called for me.
"What do I do? What way is there out of this?"
"I can't just give up my command,
    let fame run out between my fingers like water.
There must be something I can do. What is it?"
This was your question to me…
    to which Kalkhas found the answer…
        somewhere in the bowels of his birds.
He told you to sacrifice your daughter to Artemis.
Then your ships would sail.
You breathed easy and seemed almost light-hearted as
    you promised to bring your daughter to the blade.
When you sent for her, telling your wife
    to bundle off the girl at once,
        as would-be bride for Akhilleus,
    you did so on your own… don't deny it.
No one twisted your arm. No one had to.

Then you changed your mind and sent a second message,
    revoking the first.
Now you say, "Never will I murder my own child."
Indeed. I call upon the sky above, where the gods dwell,
    to witness what you've said.
In fact, you couldn't be more trite.
The arduous climb to power only to plummet to ruin…
    it's an old story… with a couple of variations:
Sometimes it is the fault of the followers.
They forget how to follow.
Sometimes it is the fault of the leaders.
They forget how to lead… or, as in your case,
    they discover that they never knew how.
Still, I save my pity for Greece, hapless Greece,
    poised for the bold and brilliant stroke,
        yet doomed to be a joke for barbarians,
    laughing from their walls at the army that never came.
All because of your daughter.

No one should sit on a throne or lead an army because he
    shook a few hands or collected a few old debts.
Kings and generals need minds that work,
    producing an idea every now and then.

CHORAL LEADER

It is a dark, disturbing sight,
    when brothers are locked in hate,
        and savage each other with their words.

AGAMEMNON

It is my turn now.
Unlike you, I will be brief, careful, and moderate.
You can see already the difference in my eyes.
I speak to you as a brother,
    and as one who knows the meaning of shame.
There's blood in your eyes and hate on your tongue.
Can you tell me why? Who has wronged you?
What is it that you want... a faithful wife?
Is that what your whining is about?
If so, I can't help you. Remember, you had a wife once.
You just did a bad job of keeping her.
And who should pay the price for that? *Me?*
For what went on, or didn't, in *your* bed?
Or is it the honors I've received: my stature, my power...
    have they gotten under your skin?
No. You're worked up over a woman.
I can tell from the way you've stopped thinking,
    and lost all sense of shame.
You just want a woman, don't you?
For a man like you, with no pride,
    desire can be a pretty shabby thing.

Now back to me.
If I, having made a mistake,
    recognize my error and correct it,
        does that make me a madman?
No, you're the one who's mad.
The gods did you a favor, ridding you of a worthless wife;
    and all you can think about is getting her back.
Long ago, Helen's love-sick suitors took Tyndareos' oath
    for all the wrong reasons.
Something or someone drove them to it,
    and it surely wasn't you.
Let's say a god called Hope did it.

So go ahead, take them on a war.
They're game for any lunacy you have in mind.
But don't assume the same of god.
The air up there is clearer than down here.
Mindless oaths taken in heat are seen as such.
I'm not going to kill any child of mine.
Besides, what kind of luck or blessing do you expect
    on this misadventure of yours?
You get perverse revenge on the worst wife that ever was,
    and I spend the rest of my days and nights in tears,
    wasting away, as I should, for what I did,
        against all law and sense,
            against my own flesh and blood.
That is all I have to say,
    words as brief and wise and congenial
        as I could make them.
You can prefer madness if you like;
    but I'm going to keep my house in order.

CHORAL LEADER

Agamemnon, this is not what you said before,
    but it is welcome;
        for it means life, not death, for your child.

MENELAOS

I see I have no one left on my side.

AGAMEMNON

Why should you,
    when you're willing to kill those closest to you?

MENELAOS

How can you call yourself my brother?

AGAMEMNON

You leave your senses and I leave you... why not?
Get your mind back and you get me back.

MENELAOS

What about friends... don't they share each other's pain?

AGAMEMNON

I'll gladly share your pain... when you stop causing mine.

MENELAOS

Forget me. Think of Greece!
Should you stand off from her struggles?

AGAMEMNON

Yes. It's all the same.
You and Greece share the same disease.
Whatever you've got is bigger than both of you.

MENELAOS

Big words... from the man with the sceptre.
To your own brother you're a traitor.
Fortunately I have other friends and other ways of...

The Messenger enters.

MESSENGER

Agamemnon, High King of the Greeks,
    I come to you bringing your daughter, Iphigenia.
She is accompanied by her mother, your wife, Klytemnestra.
And, as a special treat for your eyes,
    your little boy, Orestes, too is here.
Already it has been too long since you saw him last.
They've endured a long, tiring journey.
They are refreshing themselves now, dipping their feet
    in the coolness of a nearby spring. Meanwhile,
    we've put their horses out into the meadow to graze.
I've run ahead to give you word of their arrival,
    so that you might be prepared for them.
The men already know your daughter's here.
Word travels fast through the ranks.
The whole army lined up along the road,
    just to get a look at her.
That's about as close as ordinary people get
    to magnificence... staring at it for a moment.
Anyway, the army is asking questions.
They want to know what's happening.
A marriage, or what?
They wonder whether you missed your daughter so much
    that you had her brought to you.
I also heard them saying that it was all well and good to bring
    the child to the altar of Artemis, Mistress of Aulis,
        in preparation for her wedding.
But who's the bridegroom?
That's what they really want to know.

So… where's the basket of barley for the sacrifice?
Come on, both of you… yes, you too, lord Menelaos,
     it's time to crown your heads with garlands.
The moment is coming for the wedding song.
Let the flute's piercing cry leap into the air
     and call everyone from the tents.
Let's dance and beat the earth with our feet like a giant drum.
For this is the day your daughter learns the meaning of bliss.

AGAMEMNON
Yes…thank you. You may go now.
As for the rest, it will go as well as it can in the hands of fate.

The Messenger exits.

AGAMEMNON
What a wreck of a man I am.
How do I begin over from here?
I'm so tangled in my own fate I can't move.
I counted on my cleverness…
     on staying two steps ahead of doom.
One leap took care of that.
I see now that the common people have their privileges.
They can share their pain
     and cry their hearts out, if they need to.
Not like us. We sit apart on our thrones,
     slaves to the people we purportedly rule.
I'm ashamed to cry… so alone, so ruined.
Yet, I hurt so much I'd be ashamed not to cry.
What do I say to my wife?
What kind of greeting do I give,
     when I can't even look her in the eyes?
On top of everything else, for her to come here now,
     in the middle of this… I can't…
I sent for my daughter not my wife!
Well… it's understandable…
     a mother wanting to accompany her daughter,
wanting to be there
     to give her precious girl away.
But it means she will find out what I've done.
And the unlucky bride? Bride indeed.
Hades will see to that.
She will consummate her marriage in hell.
O my god. I can already hear what she will say to me.

"Father, are you really going to kill me? If so
    I hope that you and whoever is dear to you
    someday know a wedding night as long and cold
    as mine shall be."
Orestes too will barely stand nearby, sobbing.
In time he will understand why.
Priam's son has created a masterpiece of chaos
    from what used to be my life, a life that ended
        the day Helen climbed into his bed.

CHORAL LEADER

I am a woman from a land far from yours;
    yet I feel close to your pain.
A sorry king is a pitiable sight.

MENELAOS

Brother, give me your hand. I want to hold you.

AGAMEMNON

Here. You win. I lose.

MENELAOS

Agamemnon, I swear by Pelops our grandfather
    and Atreus our own father, that I speak to you now
        straight from my heart.
What I say is what I truly think and feel,
    nothing more, nothing less.
The sight of you in tears
    has pried open my soul to your pain.
Like you, I have had a change of heart
    and now take back my own words.
You have nothing any longer to fear from me.
We are at one. Don't take your child's life.
Not for my sake.
There is nothing fair about your grieving on and on,
    so that I might know a moment's satisfaction.
Nor is it right for your child to go dark in death,
    while mine revels in the light.

And what about me?
If I develop a craving to be married again,
    I can always take another bride.
But the last thing I can afford is to lose my brother.
I can think of no worse trade than you for Helen...
    treasure for trash.

I've been a child lately, without sense,
    watching this whole affair from too safe a distance.
Now that I'm closer, I see what it means
    for you to murder your daughter.
Besides, when I remember that the poor piteous girl,
    soon to be a victim to my marriage,
        is my family, too,
    my own feelings for her well up within me.
"Why Iphigenia?" I ask myself.
"What does she have to do with Helen?"
So I say, disband the army and send it home from Aulis.
For my sake if not for yours, brother,
    stop crying… so that I can.
Whether the words of Artemis regarding your daughter
    still speak to you or not,
    they say nothing to me.
I leave the matter with you.

In short, I've changed my mind.
No more bitter words, not from me.
The fact is I've stumbled onto where I belong…
    with you, dear brother.
It's been a struggle to find my way here.
I guess I can't be all bad if I kept trying.

CHORAL LEADER

Menelaos, you have spoken like a true son of Tantalos,
    child of Zeus.
Your ancestors would be proud of you.

AGAMEMNON

Menelaos, I honor you and your words.
What you have said,
    with such becoming candor and integrity,
        has put the two of us in perfect accord.
We both know how easy and common it is for brothers,
    confused by lust or greed,
        to quarrel over a woman or an estate.
Enmity between brothers is a poison.
I spit it out once and for all.
But the truth is that our shoulders are against a fate
    that will not give way.
I have no choice anymore.
I am compelled to kill my daughter.

MENELAOS
Compelled? By whom?

AGAMEMNON
By the army we gathered.

MENELAOS
No. Not if you send your daughter back to Argos first.

AGAMEMNON
Yes, *she* could sneak away. But afterwards, *we* couldn't.

MENELAOS
What are you saying? Your fear of that mob is excessive.

AGAMEMNON
Khalkas will tell them his prophecy.

MENELAOS
A dead man can't tell them anything. I can see to that.

AGAMEMNON
Prophets, ha!
The only thing they see clearly is their own self-interest.

MENELAOS
They're a waste of flesh and blood, that's all.

AGAMEMNON
But there's someone else we've been forgetting.
Aren't you afraid of him?

MENELAOS
I might be if you said his name. I can't read your thoughts.

AGAMEMNON
The son of Sisyphos. He knows everything that's gone on.

MENELAOS
Odysseus? He's neither inclined nor in a position
   to make trouble for us.

AGAMEMNON
He's shifty… and he rides that mob as if it were his horse.

MENELAOS

I grant you he's ambitious.
It's an addiction with him… a deadly one.

AGAMEMNON

So can't you see him, pedestaled on a rock,
    with the army pressing on all sides?
Can't you already hear him, revealing the oracles of Kalkhas
    and telling the army how I promised the sacrifice
        demanded by Artemis
    and then went back on my word to her?
Won't he simply wrap the mob's reins in his fist
    and turn its rage on you and me,
        calling on the army to murder us
            and to see to the girl's sacrifice?
Or suppose we do escape and reach home safely…
    then the army will march on Argos instead of Troy,
    and it will be our city that will be all ashes and blood.
So now you see why I despair.
My only choice is to endure what happens.
The gods are in control now.
But there is one thing you can do for me, Menelaos.
Go to camp and make sure no one tells Klytemnestra any-
thing until my daughter is safe in Hades' arms.
If I am to do this, the last thing I need is an hysterical wife.

Menelaos exits. Agamemnon turns to the Chorus.

And you, women, wherever you're from, be careful.
Say nothing.

Agamemnon goes into his tent.

CHORUS

Blessed are those who sip the pleasures of Aphrodite
Slowly, from a shallow cup.
In her bed, peace of mind is a rare prize.
Blessed is anyone who finds calm there,
Where most are driven mad.
Eros, the golden-haired boy with the bow,
Has but two arrows in his quiver.
The one brings bliss.
The other casts a net of confusion
And chaotic pain.

Keep that boy and his arrows,
I beg you, radiant lady,
Far from me and from my bed.
I pray for the middle path,
For a tame love that knows its place.
I want my share of Aphrodite.
But no more.

The race of mortals is a diverse lot.
They go their different ways.
Yet wisdom walks only the road of integrity.
Children, like trees, grow toward the light
If held straight, early on, by a firm hand.
Wisdom begins with reverence
And knows the meaning of shame.
It cleanses the mind,
Enamoring it of truth.
The result is an honorable life,
Which lives on forever
In the stories men tell.
Virtue is quarry worthy of a great hunt.
For women it means keeping their lives
And their love secret from the world.
For men it means in myriad ways
The service of their city,
Making it flourish,
Leaving it always greater
With the passing of time.

Paris,
Long ago you were taken to the slopes of Ida
To live among the flocks you kept.
Soon you filled the mountains with your songs,
Barbarian melodies from a Phrygian flute.
From the sound of it, to a wistful ear,
It could have been Olympos.
One day, as your herds grazed,
You gazed upon inhuman beauty
And made a fateful choice,
Propelling you to Greece
To a luxuriant palace and a luxuriant queen.
Your eyes met and made love at once,
In the exchange of a glance.

So, one quarrel has spawned another,
And, with ships and sharpened spears,
Greece makes its way to towering Troy.

Klytemnestra and Iphigenia approach in their chariot,
escorted by Attendants from Argos.

CHORAL LEADER

Look, see how generous fortune is to the fortunate.
It runs in their blood.
Here is Iphigenia, daughter of the great king, my mistress.
And Klytemnestra, daughter of Tyndareos, with her son.
They have the blood of kings in them.
When they empty their cup of happiness,
    someone refills it.
The gods themselves, the source of all blessings,
    are barely more blessed than these,
        the cream of mortals.

Daughters of Khalkis,
    let us stand here where we are,
    and help the great queen down from the chariot,
        lest she lose her balance and fall.
Here, we offer you our hands,
As strong as they are soft.

To Iphigenia and Orestes.

Famed daughter and son of Agamemnon,
    so new to this place, relax. Have no fear.
We too are strangers here.
Calmly, quietly, strangers to strangers, we welcome you.

KLYTEMNESTRA

I regard these words of yours,
    so kind and gracious toward us,
        to be a bright omen for this day on which
    I bring my daughter to what I have every hope
        will be a splendid marriage.

To her Argive attendants.

Now if you would first lift down my daughter's dowry
    from the chariot and—carefully now!—
        bring it into the tent.

To Iphigenia.

Next, my sweet girl,
    lower your delicate feet over the side of the chariot.
Young ladies, take her in your arms and lift her down.

The Chorus assist Iphigenia down from the chariot.

I too will need someone's arm for support,
    if I'm going to get down from here with any dignity.
And someone stand in front of the yoke horses.
They're looking wild and ready to bolt.
Finally, little Orestes, son of Agamemnon.
Lift him down, will you?
He has legs of his own; but they don't do much yet.
O… are you still sleeping, little one?
Does the chariot rock you to sleep?
Wake up now, smiling.
This is your sister's wedding day!
It's a special day for you, too. You will get a brother-in-law,
    a fine man, in fact nearly a god,
        the grandson of Nereus.
But for now, sit down here by my feet.
Come here, Iphigenia, stand close to me.
Show these young women
    how sweetly blessed I am in you.
Look, look who's coming… the father you love so much.

The sound of Agamemnon's footsteps precedes him.

IPHIGENIA

O mother, don't be upset
    if I run ahead of you to hug him.

Agamemnon emerges from the tent.

KLYTEMNESTRA

August lord Agamemnon,
    you summoned us and we have come.

IPHIGENIA

Father! I long to run to you
    and throw my arms around you.
I've missed you so much!

To Klytemnestra.

Don't be angry with me.

KLYTEMNESTRA
It's all right, child.
Of all the children I've borne to your father,
    you've always loved him most.

*Iphigenia runs to her father and clings to him. Then, still
holding his hand, she steps back and looks at him.*

IPHIGENIA
O father, it has felt like such a long time.
Seeing you makes me so happy!

AGAMEMNON
You speak for us both. You make your father happy.

IPHIGENIA
O yes, be as happy as I am… please!
Father you've done such a wonderful thing
    in bringing me here to you.

AGAMEMNON
You find words where I don't, child.

IPHIGENIA
Father, I know you're happy to see me;
    but it doesn't show.

AGAMEMNON
As king and general, I have a lot on my mind.

IPHIGENIA
Well put it all away somewhere for now.
I want to be your only concern.

AGAMEMNON
All right. I'm here with you… nowhere else.

IPHIGENIA
Then stop frowning. Make those furrows go away.

AGAMEMNON
There. Now you can see how happy you make me, child.

IPHIGENIA
But now you're crying, father. Why?

AGAMEMNON
Because there's a long separation ahead for us.

IPHIGENIA
I don't understand.
O dearest father, I don't know what you mean.

AGAMEMNON
If you did, I would cry even more.

IPHIGENIA
Then let's pretend that neither of us knows anything.
Maybe that will help you smile.

AGAMEMNON
Sighing deeply and speaking to himself.
How much longer can I say nothing?

To Iphigenia.

All right, whatever you say.

IPHIGENIA
Father, just stay home with us.

AGAMEMNON
O I wish… but I cannot… and how painful that is!

IPHIGENIA
Why can't all the spears in the world be broken in half
    and Menelaos' troubles just go away?

AGAMEMNON
I will be long gone and so will many others
    before that happens.

IPHIGENIA
But you've been away so long already here in Aulis.

AGAMEMNON
Yes, something prevents us from setting sail.

IPHIGENIA
Father… these "Trojans" everyone is talking about…
    where do they live?

AGAMEMNON
In the city of Priam, the father of Paris.
I wish they didn't exist.

IPHIGENIA
So you're leaving me, Father, and going far away?

AGAMEMNON
Just as you are, my child.

IPHIGENIA
But I want to go with you. Couldn't you take me along?

AGAMEMNON
You have a journey of your own to make,
    across a different sea.
Don't forget your father there.

IPHIGENIA
Will I set sail with my mother, or alone?

AGAMEMNON
Alone, without father or mother.

IPHIGENIA
So you are making a home for me somewhere else? Where?

AGAMEMNON
That's enough. You're still only a child.
You don't need to know.

IPHIGENIA
Then finish whatever you need to do in Troy,
    and hurry back to me.

AGAMEMNON
Before that I must sacrifice a victim, here in Aulis.

IPHIGENIA

Of course.
The offering of victims to the gods is a sacred duty.
You must see to it.

AGAMEMNON

We will see to it together.
Your place will be beside the bowl of purifying waters.

IPHIGENIA

Then, around the altar and its victim… will we dance?

AGAMEMNON

O sweet thing, I would give anything for your innocence.
Now go inside the tent.
Young girls don't belong out in public view.
First, hold my hand and give me a kiss.
Soon you are going away from your father
    for all too long a time.
Your breast and cheeks and golden hair… all so soft…
Why, on this sweet head, must Helen
    and the walls of Troy come crashing down?
I touch you and the dam within me breaks.

Agamemnon begins weeping uncontrollably.

Run… run inside.

To Klytemnestra.

Daughter of Leda, I'm sorry. Excuse this bath of self-pity.
Who would believe that all I'm doing
    is marrying off my daughter to Akhilleus?
It's supposed to be an occasion of joy.
But when a father who has watched over his daughter
    as closely as I have gives her away,
        his joy comes mixed with grief.

KLYTEMNESTRA

Do you imagine I don't know that?
How could I find fault with your tears,
    knowing well how I will weep
        when I hear the wedding song
            and lead our little girl away?
But it is what happens, over and over;
    and time will dry our tears.

Now, this man
 to whom you have betrothed our daughter…
To be sure, I've heard of him;
 but I'm anxious to hear more.
Tell me where he comes from and about his family.

AGAMEMNON
I'll begin with Asopos. He had a daughter named Aigina.

KLYTEMNESTRA
And who married her? A god or a mortal?

AGAMEMNON
Zeus did; and she bore him a son Aikos,
 who eventually took Oinone for his wife.

KLYTEMNESTRA
And which of the sons of Aiakos became his heir?

AGAMEMNON
Peleus, who then married Thetis,
 the daughter of divine Nereus.

KLYTEMNESTRA
Did he do so with the gods' blessing,
 or did he take her by force?

AGAMEMNON
Zeus himself betrothed her to Peleus.
Then, on the appointed day, briny Nereus gave her away.

KLYTEMNESTRA
And where did they wed… in the depths of the sea?

AGAMEMNON
No, no. They were married at the foot of Mt. Pelion,
 in a sacred place, where Kheiron makes his home.

KLYTEMNESTRA
Was it the same place where they say the centaurs live?

AGAMEMNON
The same.
It was there the gods made a splendid feast
 for Peleus and his bride.

KLYTEMNESTRA
So who reared Akhilleus? His father or his mother?

AGAMEMNON
Neither did.
Kheiron brought him up to know nothing
    of the weakness and corruption of mortals.

KLYTEMNESTRA
So he had a wise teacher in Kheiron,
    and an even wiser father in Peleus,
        who made it all happen.

AGAMEMNON
And now you know the kind of man
    your daughter is marrying.

KLYTEMNESTRA
He will do. Where in Greece is his city located?

AGAMEMNON
It lies within the borders of Phthia,
    on the banks of the River Apidanos.

KLYTEMNESTRA
Then he will take our daughter there?

AGAMEMNON
Once she is his, that will be for him to decide.

KLYTEMNESTRA
May they flourish together!
What day has been set for their wedding?

AGAMEMNON
They will marry at the next full moon,
    a bright omen for their life together.

KLYTEMNESTRA
Our daughter's pre-nuptial sacrifice to the goddess…
    have you seen to that yet?

AGAMEMNON
I am about to. That's exactly where we are at.

KLYTEMNESTRA
And after that, of course, you will hold the wedding feast?

AGAMEMNON
Yes, after I have made the requisite sacrifice.

KLYTEMNESTRA
And where shall I set out the women's meal?

AGAMEMNON
On the beach, beside the ships.

KLYTEMNESTRA
Well, it seems we make do. It should be all right.

AGAMEMNON
Now, as my wife, do you know what you should do?
Listen to me now, and do as I say.

KLYTEMNESTRA
Just say it.
Deferring to you is a habit by now.

AGAMEMNON
Right.
I shall stand at the wedding
     between the bridegroom and my daugh...

KLYTEMNESTRA
Interrupting.
You'll do what? You... in my place... taking my part?

AGAMEMNON
Along with the army, yes.
We men shall give your daughter away.

KLYTEMNESTRA
And where are we women to be while this is going on?

AGAMEMNON
Where you belong, home in Argos
     minding your other daughters.

KLYTEMNESTRA
You expect me to abandon my little girl
    on her wedding day?
Who is going to raise the wedding torch?

AGAMEMNON
I will provide whatever light suits the bridal pair.

KLYTEMNESTRA
You're trampling our customs as if they don't matter.
But they do!

AGAMEMNON
How customary is it for you, a married woman,
    to stay here among an army of men?

KLYTEMNESTRA
I'm the one who brought that girl into the world;
    and I'm going to give her away.
It's only fair.

AGAMEMNON
How fair is it for our daughters at home
    to be all alone?

KLYTEMNESTRA
They aren't alone.
They're safe in their quarters, well looked after.

AGAMEMNON
Obey me, woman!

KLYTEMNESTRA
No! By the goddess who rules over Argos, I refuse!
You see to your affairs,
    and I will see to mine.
I have a wedding to get ready for.

Klytemnestra enters the tent.

AGAMEMNON
    Sighing audibly in evident confusion and despair.
It's no use.
Wanting her out of the way
    isn't enough to make her leave.

Whatever I try to do, the opposite happens.
But I must go on, sharpening my wits
    against those I love most,
        scheming their ruin.
It is time to meet with Khalkas,
    who has a taste for sacrifice.
In league with him, I must carry out
    something sweet to Artemis and ruinous to me,
    something for which Greece shall pay a heavy price.

This much I know.
A man is better off living alone
    than with a woman who defies him.
Keep a faithful wife or none at all.
That's the rule to be followed.

      Agamemnon exits; and the Chorus enters.

CHORUS

They will come.
Aboard their thousand ships
Bristling with arms,
The Greeks will swarm to Troy.
To the swirling waters of Simois,
Silver in the sun, to the plains of Ilion,
Cherished by Apollo,
They will come.
Already I hear the cries of Kassandra.
Even now she flings her head,
Crowned with the crisp green leaves of her god,
From side to side, lashing the air
With her wild, knotted golden hair,
As divine lips whisper into her ears
The story of all that must be.

Perched on their walls and towers,
Soon the sons and daughters of Troy
Will stand and stare and wait,
As bronze-clad Ares,
His wooden sea-steeds churning the sea beneath him,
Nears the mouth of Simois.
With all the whetted bronze stacked aboard the ships
Like one giant blade in his hands,
Ares will labor savagely
To return from the city of Priam,

To Greece where she belongs,
Helen, whose twin brothers
Sparkle in the night sky.
Around the towered walls of Troy,
Ares will draw a circle of blood,
Marking out the city for slaughter.
With the king's head hanging from his belt,
He will dismantle Troy stone by stone,
As the women and their sorry queen
Hemorrhage their souls in wails that no one hears.
Helen too will cry out on that day.
Helen, child of Zeus or not,
Will learn to regret the day
She flew her husband's bed.
Never this for me or for my children
Or for theirs!
Never to sit and wait at our looms,
Like the women at Troy,
For the gates of hell to open.

"Who," they whisper to each other,
"Who will wrap my long hair around his fist
And drag me from the ashes
Of everything I know?"
All this, Helen, is your doing!
Who cares now whether the tale is true
That Leda bore you to a swan,
Surrendering to a wild flutter of wings,
The barely hidden frenzy of god,
Or whether Leda and her swan
Are a figment of the Muses,
A story for some other time?
Either way, you bring the same doom.

Chorus exits, and Akhilleus enters.

AKHILLEUS
Calling into the tent.
Where is the commander of Akhaians?
Will one of his attendants inform him that Akhilleus,
    son of Peleus, stands outside his tent
        and wishes to have a word with him?
He should know that this sojourn of ours
    beside the Euripos
        weighs on each of us differently.

Those of us who are unmarried
    have left behind empty houses,
      while others have virtually deserted their wives,
        leaving them childless besides.
All for us to sit on the beach
    and count the weeks go by like clouds.

Yet Greece aches with longing for this war.
The army is feverish with desire.
This is a fire some god has set.

Like anyone else who would present his own case,
    I have a right to speak my mind.
I have forsaken Peleus and our city of Pharsalia,
    only to languish here beside the Euripos,
abandoned by the winds.
Meanwhile, day by day, I must placate my Myrmidons.
Their complaints are incessant :
    "Akhilleus," they cry out,
      "what are we waiting for?"
"How much more of our lives must we waste
    on this so-called invasion of Troy?"
"To hell with the sons of Atreus and their delays.
If there's going to be action, we want to see it now.
Otherwise, lead the army home."

Klytemnestra enters.

KLYTEMNESTRA
Child of divine Thetis, I heard your voice,
    and I come to greet you.

AKHILLEUS
Staring at Klytemnestra and muttering to himself.
O goddess, guardian of modesty,
    who is this exquisite woman before my eyes?

KLYTEMNESTRA
You have no idea who I am?

Akhilleus shakes his head in response.

Well, that's not surprising.
You've never been in my presence before.
I do appreciate your modesty and respect.

AKHILLEUS

Who are you?
What is a woman like you doing here in the Greek camp?

KLYTEMNESTRA

I am Klytemnestra, the daughter of Leda.
My husband is lord Agamemnon.

AKHILLEUS

You have said with admirable succinctness...
    that I don't belong here.
I am ashamed to have been conversing
    with another man's wife.

KLYTEMNESTRA

Wait! Why are you running off?
Give me your hand, a blessed beginning
    to the marriage that will soon be ours.

AKHILLEUS

What are you saying?
I should touch your hand?
It is forbidden!
Doing that would shame me before Agamemnon.

KLYTEMNESTRA

Forbidden?
Child of Nereid Thetis, goddess of the seas, since when
    is it forbidden for a mother to hold the hand
        of her daughter's future spouse?

AKHILLEUS

Spouse?
What are you talking about?
My lady, you leave me speechless.
You're delirious!
This whole thing is in your head... nowhere else.

KLYTEMNESTRA

This happens to everyone, you know.
Men always get embarrassed
    when they meet their in-laws for the first time.
It reminds them they're getting married.

AKHILLEUS
My lady, I'm not, never have been, espoused to your daughter.
If I am to marry into the house of Atreus,
     I have not been told.

KLYTEMNESTRA
What's happening?
Now I am as confused by your words
     as you have been by mine.

AKHILLEUS
Between the two of us we'll figure this out.
One of us must be close to the truth.

KLYTEMNESTRA
Something quite vicious has been done to me.
I see now that the marriage I've come here to celebrate
     doesn't exist, except as a figment in someone's mind.
Now I am the one who is embarrassed.

AKHILLEUS
Someone has made a mockery of both of us.
Pay no further attention to it. Try to let it pass.

KLYTEMNESTRA
I've been drawn into someone else's lie… shown contempt.
I'm too ashamed to look you in the eye.
Good-bye.

AKHILLEUS
I know exactly how you feel.
Good-bye. I'm leaving… to look for your husband.

*As they turn away from each other, Akhilleus to exit and
Klytemnestra to return to the tent, the Old Servant calls to
them from a distance and enters as he speaks.*

OLD SERVANT
Wait! You, child of a goddess and grandson of Aiakos,
     wait for me.
I would speak with you.

To Klytemnestra, watching him from the door of the tent.

With you too, daughter of Leda.

AKHILLEUS
Who are you to shout at me like this?
You look and sound distressed.

OLD SERVANT
I am a slave… not something I'm proud of…
    not something I can change, either.

AKHILLEUS
Whose slave are you?
Not one of mine… not in Agamemnon's camp.

OLD SERVANT
I belong to this lady.
Tyndareos made me part of her dowry.

AKHILLEUS
Well… I'm here, waiting to learn why you've detained me.
So speak up.

OLD SERVANT
Are you certain there's no one else close enough to hear?

AKHILLEUS
We are alone. So come here and speak.

OLD SERVANT
I can only hope that what I know,
    combined with a little luck,
        may yet save those I want to help.

AKHILLEUS
It sounds as if you know more than we do
    about what is happening.

To Klytemnestra.

This may be important to us.

*The Old Servant, reaching for Klytemnestra's hand, begins to
lower himself to his knees. Klytemnestra impatiently stops him.*

KLYTEMNESTRA
Don't waste time kissing my hand, old one.
Just tell us what you have to say.

OLD SERVANT
You know me, lady. You know how far back
    my loyalty goes to you and your children.

KLYTEMNESTRA
I remember that,
    when I was still only a child in my father's house,
        you were already one of his servants.

OLD SERVANT
Then I came to the house of lord Agamemnon
    as part of your dowry.

KLYTEMNESTRA
Yes, you came to Argos with me
    and have belonged to me ever since.

OLD SERVANT
Exactly.
I am loyal to your husband, but more loyal to you.

KLYTEMNESTRA
Then tell me about this secret you're keeping.

OLD SERVANT
Your daughter... her own father is about to kill her...
    himself, with his own hand.

KLYTEMNESTRA
What? I spit out your words, old man!
You're out of your mind.

OLD SERVANT
He will slit the wretched girl's soft pale neck with a knife.

KLYTEMNESTRA
*Gasping and struggling to breathe as if every bit of air has
    been sucked from her lungs by the Old Servant's words.*
No... not this.
You're telling me my husband's gone mad?

OLD SERVANT
Only when it comes to you and your girl.
Otherwise he has his wits.

KLYTEMNESTRA
Why this?
What demon from hell whispered this in his ear?

OLD SERVANT
If you believe Kalkhas, it is a demon from the gods,
    a condition for the army's arrival.

KLYTEMNESTRA
So my husband is after my little girl with a knife.
Iphigenia… you and I…
Arrival? Arrival where?

OLD SERVANT
Troy. Menelaos wants Helen back.

KLYTEMNESTRA
And my girl is the price of her homecoming.
Iphigenia for Helen. Is this what they're calling "destiny"?

OLD SERVANT
You've said it, word for word. She will soon be a gift,
    to Artemis from your husband.

KLYTEMNESTRA
My daughter's marriage…
    that was his way of getting me to send her here…
        far from her home… and from me?

OLD SERVANT
He knew that you would be only too glad
    to give up your daughter to Akhilleus' bed.

KLYTEMNESTRA
Iphigenia… you and I were in such a hurry…
    running toward the void!

OLD SERVANT
What you two must suffer breaks my heart;
    but what Agamemnon does terrifies my soul.

KLYTEMNESTRA
Then it's done.
I…I…I can't even stop my own tears!

OLD SERVANT
It's time for tears, when you lose a child.

KLYTEMNESTRA
All this you've been telling me, old one...
    where did you say you learned it from?

OLD SERVANT
From a tablet I was taking to you,
    a second tablet from your husband.

KLYTEMNESTRA
Reaffirming his demand
    that I lead my daughter to her deathbed,
        or was he having second thoughts?

OLD SERVANT
He was telling you not to send Iphigenia.
He was at the time thinking as a husband... and a father.

KLYTEMNESTRA
So you were carrying that word to me...
Why didn't I ever receive it?

OLD SERVANT
Menelaos is to blame.
He stopped me and took away the tablet.

KLYTEMNESTRA
To Akhilleus.
Grandson of Nereus, child of Peleus,
    have you heard all this?

AKHILLEUS
Every word of your misery and of the part I've played in it.
I take none of it lightly.

KLYTEMNESTRA
With you and your bed as bait,
    they would lead my girl to slaughter.

AKHILLEUS
Your husband will answer to me...
    not just for his abuse of my name.

Klytemnestra falls to her knees in supplication before Akhilleus.

KLYTEMNESTRA

As I am simply mortal,
    and you spring from a divine womb,
    I feel no shame in falling before you
        and clasping your knees in supplication.
What good are the airs to me now?
My daughter matters more than my pride.
Child of divine Thetis,
    champion me and the girl they call your wife.
Save us... as if their story were true.
I did, after all, bring her for your wedding.
Now I see I must give her over to slaughter.
If you do nothing to stop this,
    your name will go dark forever.
You may not have a bond with that poor girl,
    but all the same, on the world's lips,
        you are her dear, devoted spouse.
By your beard... by your right hand...
    by your divine mother, I beg you!
You must save us!
It was your name that brought us here... to this.
Your knee is the last altar to which I can run.
You are the only sanctuary I have left.
Here in this place I have no one on my side.
You know all about Agamemnon,
    my husband turned animal.
You see what I am, a woman alone in the camp of men,
    more like a mob than an army,
        blood in their eyes already...
    all very useful and encouraging, I imagine,
        when its on your side.
If you would dare to lift your hand and your sword for us,
    then we will be saved. If not, we are lost.

CHORAL LEADER

Motherhood is a strange, powerful thing,
    a great love charm,
    giving this much in common to all women:
        there is nothing they will not do or endure
            for their children.

AKHILLEUS

Lady, these words of yours, like a brisk wind,
    lift the fire in my soul to full flame.
In grief and in joy, in the worst and in the brightest of times,
    I know all about moderation.
I know what it means to walk a thin righteous line in my life,
    selling my soul to no one.
I know that such a life is possible for any mortal,
    who thinks his way carefully day by day.
There are times, of course, for thinking less,
    when it is sweet to let the mind drift,
        just as there are times for heavy thought,
    when reason is the best rule.
From Kheiron, the most reverent of men,
    my teacher in all things,
        I learned to live these and other simple truths.
Now, as for the sons of Atreus,
    I shall follow them when their commands are just,
        and ignore them when they are not.
I bring to Troy, as to everywhere else, a free spirit;
    and my spear will make the war god proud, always.

Lady, beaten down savagely
    by those who ought to love you most,
        my youth and my strength, such as they are,
    are yours, a wall of compassion thrown around you.
Never, so long as I stand, will your daughter,
    my so-called bride,
        die a victim at her father's hand.
Your father will have to spin his deadly web without me.
No more will my name be the bladeless sword
    that slays your girl.
Let your husband drink the cup he poured.
I would smell the guilt on me forever,
    if your sweet, unsullied girl suffered hideous abuse
    and went to an unthinkable end because of me...
        all because she rushed to be my bride.
How does something, someone, so precious become nothing?
I do wonder about that.

I would be the shabbiest of Greeks, a thin nothing
    like Menelaos...
I would be the son not of Peleus
    but of some nameless outcast,
        if I let my name do your husband's butchery.

By my grandfather Nereus,
>nursed in the arms of the heaving sea,
>>lord Agamemnon will not so much as touch
>the hem of your daughter's robe.
And for the prophet Kalkhas, waiting with his lustral waters,
>there will be a bitter surprise.
What are prophets anyway?
Nothing but liars playing the odds.
When they're lucky, they get a few things right.
When they don't, they disappear.

Let me clarify one thing now, for the record.
I'm not after your daughter.
I have more women after me than Agamemnon has ships.
For me it is a matter of rage, not love.
Lord Agamemnon has done me an outrageous wrong!
If he wants to use my name to trap his daughter,
>he must ask me first.
It was my name more than anything else
>that persuaded Klytemnestra
>>to hand over her daughter to Agamemnon.
If my name were enough
>to send the Greeks on their way to Troy,
>>it would be theirs… for the asking.
I would not deny my fellow men-in-arms
>what is for our common good.
But now, apparently, I am nothing,
>someone for my fellow warlords to humor or abuse
>>at their whim.

Drawing his sword.

You see this sword.
Long before it sees action in Troy,
>it will know the stain and taste of slaughter,
>>if anyone tries to take your daughter.
So, put your heart at rest.
Think of me as a god, capable of anything,
>come to your side.
Of course, at the moment, I am not a god.
It is something I will have to become.

CHORAL LEADER
Child of Peleus, your words are worthy of you,
>worthy too of your mother Thetis,
>>sublime goddess of the seas.

KLYTEMNESTRA
Speechless at first, groping for words.
Where among the words I know
 am I to find the praise you deserve?
Without saying too little and losing your good-will.
 I think few words are best
  for I know that men of your character
 have a way of despising
  those who lavish them with praise.

I am ashamed to parade my afflictions before you.
What I suffer is, after all, my concern.
My pain is not contagious. You cannot catch it from me.
All the same, it is the way of decent, feeling men like you
 to reach out to those in misery
  and to do what can be done for them.
Pity me and my daughter. Surely by now we are pitiable.
I see now that having you as my son-in-law was a mirage,
 wishful thinking, nothing more.
The bright day will come, Akhilleus,
  when you wish to take a wife.
Be careful now.
My daughter's death could cast a long shadow.
You spoke well, just now, from start to finish.
I know that, if you will it, my child shall be saved.

So what now? Would you like my daughter
 to cling to your knees as a suppliant?
Of course that would hardly be fitting at her age.
All the same, if that is what you want,
 she will come to you, all ablush no doubt,
  looking every way but yours.
Yet, if I can win from you what we need,
 without her being here,
  then let her remain inside.
She is very modest,
 something I try as best I can to respect.

AKHILLEUS
Lady, I would rather you didn't bring your daughter
 into my sight.
We would only inspire some mindless scandal.
The vast armies assembled here,
 stranded far from their homes,
  have nothing better to do than to tell sordid stories.

The filthier the better for them.
It makes no difference at all
    whether your daughter comes to supplicate my help.
Only one great issue concerns me now;
    and that is averting your doom.
Now that you've heard that, know one more thing:
    I don't know how to lie.
I would die before I would mock you with a string of lies.
Unless your daughter lives through this,
    my own life is nothing to me.

KLYTEMNESTRA

Bless you for helping us in our need.
May you know lasting happiness.

AKHILLEUS

But for the present, so that it might go well,
    you must listen to me carefully.

KLYTEMNESTRA

What is it? I'm listening.

AKHILLEUS

We must work on your husband... talk him back to sanity.

KLYTEMNESTRA

He may be beyond that. His fear of the army eats him alive.

AKHILLEUS

You can change anyone's mind with the right words.

KLYTEMNESTRA

I hope we don't have to depend on that.
But just tell me what I must do.

AKHILLEUS

First do this. On your knees, beg him not to kill your child.
If that doesn't work, then you must come to me.
But if he listens and does as you ask,
    then there is no need to involve me further;
        for your deliverance is assured.
If your well-being can be achieved with words alone,
    without resort to force, it is all the better for us both.

Besides, once the army turns on me,
    there will be less I can do for you.
So, this is our first plan, in which I play no part.
If it succeeds, you and those you love will know great joy.

KLYTEMNESTRA

It seems a good plan. I am willing to do what you think best.
But if something goes wrong and I fail,
    where will I see you again? Where?
If I am desperate and need your strong arm
    to ward off disaster, where do I go?
Where can I find you?

AKHILLEUS

You won't need to. It is for me to watch over you;
    and that is what I intend to do.
I will be there, at the right place, when you need me.
I would not want anyone to see you in a panic,
    thrashing your way through a mob of men.
Don't do anything like that to shame your father's house.
Tyndareos is a great man in Greece. He deserves better
    than to hear the kind of stories you would provoke.

KLYTEMNESTRA

All right, then. I am yours to command. Tell me what to do.
You are a just man. If the gods exist at all, you will flourish.
If they don't, why should we care... about anything?

Akhilleus exits as Klytemnestra enters the tent. The Chorus enters.

CHORUS

Listen...
Flutes carved from black lotus wood,
Dance-enchanted lyres,
The shrill frenzy of reed pipes...
Imagine the sounds,
The wedding-song
To Peleus and his bride.
With golden sandals strapped to their feet
And their lustrous hair billowing in the breeze,
The divine Muses,
Climbed the slopes of Peleion
To a feast set by gods.
Above the rhythm of their steps
The gracious daughters of Zeus

Lifted their song,
A hymn of praise to Thetis
And to the son of Aiakos,
A hymn that flew over the mountains of the centaurs
And danced through the forests of Pelion.
Then the child of Dardanos,
Phrygian Ganymede,
The bud of joy in Zeus' bed,
Poured a gleaming libation
Into the hollow of a golden bowl,
While down below on the sea's edge
Fifty sparkling daughters of Nereus,
Slipped loose from the waters
And danced in a circle on the salt-white sand,
A wedding-dance for Peleus
And his bride from the sea.

Then of a sudden,
Waving lances of stripped pine
And wearing crowns
Of recklessly woven leaves,
A band of misbehaving centaurs
Hoofed into the feast
And gathered around the bowl of Bakkhos,
Brimming with wine.
In one voice they offered a thunderous toast.
"Hail, daughter of Nereus.
We have it straight from Kheiron, our seer,
On Apollo's word,
That you will bear a son
To be a light to all of Thessaly.
One day he will lead his Myrmidons,
Armed to the teeth,
To the far-famed land of Priam,
Leaving only ashes behind.
He will wear armor
Forged in the flames of Hephaistos,
Armor glinting with hammered gold,
A gift from you, Thetis,
The mother who bore him."
So the gods and their guests
Sang wedding songs to noble Peleus and his bride,
First among the daughters of Nereus,
Proclaiming theirs to be a marriage
Made in the stars, lucky and blessed.

But to you, child,
We sing a different song.
On your soft lovely hair,
Argive warriors will set a crown
Of a different sort,
Suited to the brow of some unblemished calf,
Led by the neck from the mountain cave
To sacrifice.
You too will have your neck cut
Wide and deep,
Child,
You were not raised on some wild mountain slope
To the tune of a herdsman's pipe,
But raised in a palace,
Washed and veiled by your mother,
To be a bride for kings,
What becomes of shame?
When corruption wears the crown?
When mortals turn from decency
And chaos climbs the throne,
When the fellowship of men
In the fear of god
Is a forgotten fancy,
How many more deaths can virtue die?

> *Klytemnestra enters and looks in several directions, scanning*
> *the distance. She addresses the Chorus.*

KLYTEMNESTRA

I've come out to look for my husband.
It's been quite a while now since he left this tent
    and went off somewhere.
In the meantime my poor child has learned
    of the death her father plans for her.
Soaked with her own tears,
    she screams until her voice gives out,
        and then sobs quietly
    until she has the strength to scream again.

> *Klytemnestra sees Agamemnon approaching.*

Speaking of Agamemnon…
I no more than mention his name,
    and he comes running… to his moment of truth.
It is time to cast some light on the atrocity he arranges
    against his daughter.

AGAMEMNON

Daughter of Leda, I'm so glad to find you here,
 outside the tent,
  where I can tell you something,
   away from Iphigenia,
 something a bride-to-be shouldn't hear.

KLYTEMNESTRA

So you've stumbled on the perfect moment
 for saying something.
I wonder what it is.

AGAMEMNON

I want you to go in and send the girl out here,
 to accompany her father.
Everything stands ready for the pre-nuptial sacrifice:
 the purifying waters,
 the barley grains for throwing into the cleansing fire,
 the young, perfect victims, whose dark blood
 will spray the goddess Artemis and make her glad.

KLYTEMNESTRA

When put that way, it sounds so official... so correct.
That's what words can do.
But deeds are different... especially yours.
I have no words at all for them.

Calling into the tent.

Come out here, child; for you already know everything
 about your father and his ambitions for you.
And bring with you your brother Orestes.
Wrap him gently in your robe.

Iphigenia enters with Orestes.

See, here she is, your little girl,
 who doesn't know how to displease you.
So I intend to speak for her... and for myself.

AGAMEMNON
To Iphigenia.

Child, why are you crying?
Why don't you look at me... give me a smile?
Why stare at the ground,
 and cover your eyes with your robe?

KLYTEMNESTRA
One word could tell my story, beginning, middle, and end,
    pain.
Maybe two: betrayal.
So where do I start?

AGAMEMNON
What is this… all of you looking at me the same way,
    with such confusion and anguish in your eyes?

KLYTEMNESTRA
Husband, I'm going to ask you an honest question.
I'd like an honest answer.

AGAMEMNON
There's no need to be confrontational.
I'm happy to answer your question.

KLYTEMNESTRA
It's about my daughter here, yours too…
Are you hoping to kill her?

*Agamemon is, at first, unable to speak. He makes sounds, but
no words.*

AGAMEMNON
What a perverse, reckless thing to say!
You have no right even to think…

KLYTEMNESTRA
Relax… and answer my question.

AGAMEMNON
Ask a reasonable question and you'll get a reasonable answer.

KLYTEMNESTRA
I have only one question. Answer it.

AGAMEMNON
It's fate… destiny… they've come for me.
They are divine, and I am only human.

KLYTEMNESTRA
You mean, they've come for us.
We are lost.

AGAMEMNON
What … what has happened to you?

KLYTEMNESTRA
You can stand there and ask me that?
You must have mislaid your wits.

> *There is a long, tense silence, in which Agamemnon sighs all*
> *but inaudibly.*

AGAMEMNON
To himself.
It's all over. I've been found out.

KLYTEMNESTRA
Look, I know the whole story.
I've learned exactly what you intend to do to me.
Besides, your silence and your sighs are as eloquent
    as any confession you could make.
Still, you might as well say something on your behalf.

AGAMEMNON
I think not. Silence will do.
Telling lies at this point would only add shame
    to my misfortune.

KLYTEMNESTRA
Now you hear me. No more riddles.
I'm going to drag the truth out here where we can see it.
To be orderly about this, I'll begin in the beginning.
First things first… courtship.
You'll remember I was not the most willing bride.
After you murdered my husband, Tantalos,
    and tore our tiny babe from my breast,
        shattering its head against the nearest wall,
    then you took me… not without help.

But then… the unexpected.
My two brothers, the twin sons of Zeus,
    appeared at your door, on horseback.
Even in the midday sun, they glistened like stars.
Behind them marched an army, on my behalf.
It took no time for you to find your knees,
    crawling to my father, Tyndareos,
        who took pity on your neck and saved it.
So once again I was yours.

In time, I came around to you and your house.
In fact—there's not denying it—I became the ideal wife:
    loving, faithful, competent.
I kept the kind of house you could leave with peace of mind
    and return to with joy.
Inane, useless women practically grow on trees.
But the kind of woman you had is a rare catch.
I bore you this son and three daughters,
    of which you are allowing me to keep two.
Somehow I don't feel grateful.
Tell me… if someone, anyone, were to ask you
    why you are murdering this girl,
        what would you say? Tell me.

                    Silence.

Must I put words in your mouth?
"So that Menelaos can get Helen back."
A lovely, perfect girl for a rotten whore…
    no one can accuse you of driving a hard bargain.
So we give what we love most for what we despise!

Let me give you something to think about.
Suppose you do go out on this war of yours,
    leaving me to mind the house,
        and suppose you're away, over there, for a long time,
            what do you think will happen to my… disposition?
For instance, when I see her empty chair, her empty room…
    when everywhere I look, she is gone…
    when I sit alone and weep,
        bleeding from a wound that won't heal…
I can hear myself crying out to the girl who isn't there.
"It was your father, the man who planted your seed.
Your own father killed you, child, with his own hand…
    no one else, no other hand but his."
Do you have a picture yet of what you will leave behind…
    in your own house?
How much of an excuse, a pretext, will we need,
    your remaining children and I,
        to prepare for you
        the kind of homecoming you deserve?
For god's sake, Agamemnon, don't force me
    to become evil… to do evil to you!

    *Klytemnestra breaks momentarily, and then steels herself for
    a second assault.*

After you've sacrificed your girl,
    what are your prayers going to sound like?
What sort of blessing
    does a child-slaughterer like you ask for?
When you go off leaving a trail of shame,
    will you not come home reeking?
And how is it any more fitting for me
    to beg the gods to bless you?
Wouldn't we as much as call the gods idiots,
    if we were to ask blessings
        for those who murder our children?
When you come back to Argos, do you imagine yourself
    falling at the feet of your children... apologizing?
Would the gods permit such a farce?
Or, for that matter, which of your children
    would even look at you, knowing that you
        could just as easily murder one of them?
Do you have thoughts like this on your own?
Or do you only fancy yourself in front of armies,
    flaunting your sceptre?
Why not demand a little fairness from your fellow-Greeks?
Put it to them this way: "Greek warriors,
    do you want to sail to Troy?
    Then cast lots to see whose child must die."
That would be the fair way. But no, you volunteer
    your own child instead, to shed "first blood"
        for this vile war of yours.
Why not Hermione, for her own mother's sake?
Why doesn't Menelaos cut his own girl's throat?
If he's made a mess, let him wipe it up.
I'm the faithful wife, the one who *hasn't* defiled
    her husband's bed. Yet I am the one
    to lose my child, while she—I know it—
        will eventually return to Sparta,
        find her own child flourishing,
    and then live happily ever after.
If anything I've said is off the mark, correct me.
If not, then crawl back to your senses, now.
Change your mind. Don't kill our girl!

CHORAL LEADER
Give way, Agamemnon. Together save your child.
Nothing could be more fair.
No one in the world could disapprove.

IPHIGENIA
Slowly approaching Agamemnon.
Father, if I had the voice of Orpheus and could charm
        even the hearts of stones with my songs,
    I would sing to you now to make you love me.
But, as I am, I have nothing to add to my words but tears.
I will do my best with them.
Like the suppliant's olive branch, torn from its tree,
    I wrap my body around your knees.
I beg for life with the body you once made to live.
Don't make me die before my time.
Don't force me into the world below
    to stare forever at shadows,
        when I love so much the simple light of day.

I was the first to call you "father."
When you called out "child" for the first time,
    you were calling *me*.
I was the first little thing to make its nest on your knees.
I remember how sweetly we held and loved each other, and
        how you used to ask me: "What do think, my little one?
Will you grow up one day and marry?
Will I find you happy in your husband's house,
        flourishing as my daughter deserves?"
And then, gripping your beard
    as tightly as my little fist could, as I do now,
        I used to answer:
    "And do you know what I will do for you then, Father,
        when you are old and gray?
    I will throw wide the doors of my house to you,
        and somehow repay you with my love
        for all that you went through for me
    when I was little and needed you."
All this I remember, and all this you forget.
Instead, you want to kill me.

Don't, Father!
For the sake of Pelops and your father Atreus...
    For my mother's sake... Don't!
My birth was pain enough for her.
Why must she endure my death?
What does the marriage of Helen and Paris have to do with me?
How does what they did add up to my ruin?
Father, look at me. Look me in the eyes. Kiss me.

Give me something sweet to remember as I go to my death,
    something besides your silence to all I say.

To Orestes.

Little brother, wanting to help but so helpless,
    here, go down on your knees with me
        and cry for your father.
With your tears you can beg him not to kill your sister.
You see, when evil and death are near,
    even a tiny child knows it and is afraid.

Father, look at your little boy.
He says nothing, but you can see that he is pleading with you.
Have pity on me. Let me live.
Both of us, together, your oldest and your youngest,
    implore you...
Father, I am running out of words.
A few more will say everything.

To look upon the light of day is for all of us the sweetest joy.
In the dark world below there is nothing.
To pray for death is sheer madness.
To be alive, in whatever lowly condition, is better
    than to die a glorious death.

CHORAL LEADER

O hateful Helen, because of you and your bed,
    the house of Atreus splits open and devours itself,
        one member at a time.

AGAMEMNON

I am not blind.
I can see for myself where pity is appropriate
    and where it is not.
I love my children.
I would be deranged if I did not.

To Klytemnestra.

Woman, it is a strange and dreadful thing to be daring
    what I am about to do.
Yes, but no more strange and dreadful than to refuse.
I must...

To Iphigenia.

You've seen the army, the ships… beyond counting.
You've seen how many kings are assembled here,
 their bronze armor polished for battle.
Yet not one ship, not one warrior, will sail to towering Troy,
 unless I sacrifice you.
The prophecies of Kalkhas are clear on this.
There is no other way for us to mount
 the famed heights of Troy and tear them down.
It is as if Aphrodite has been in every tent, lighting fires.
The army is mad with desire…
  the desire to sail at once against the barbarians,
  the desire to put a final end
   to the plundering of Greek beds.
If I ignore the prophecies and deny Artemis your sacrifice,
 the army will start by killing you and me
 and then go on to Argos to kill your sisters there.

Child, I assure you, what Menelaos wants is irrelevant.
I serve Greece, not him.
And Greece demands that I sacrifice you.
My own wishes count for nothing.
You and I are both pawns in this affair.
Child, Greece yearns to be free,
 free once and for all from barbarians,
  who would do their hunting in our beds.
It is for you and for me to do our part.

Agamemnon exits. The Choral Leader brings Orestes into the tent.

KLYTEMNESTRA

My child… women… it's hopeless.

To Iphigenia.

Your father has already given you away to Hades.
And, being the kind of man he is,
 he walks out on you besides.

IPHIGENIA

O, Mother,
 the same song of fate and loss
  comes to your lips and mine.
The radiance of day gives way to unending night.
I belong now to darkness.

O, Paris,
>one day long ago, in a wintry field, far from here,
>you lay alone, Priam's infant son, abandoned,
>>left to die, sucking the sky for milk,
>>>your mother nowhere near,
>only the cold, silent slopes of Ida watching overhead.
"Paris of Ida" they call you now in Troy.
"Paris of Ida"—named for your fateful mountain.

O, Mother,
>if only the cowherd had never found him there,
never brought him up, never made a herdsman of him,
>>with cattle of his own,
>>grazing by crystal-clear springs,
>>>where the Nymphs dwell,
>>>>in a lush green meadow
>>>>ablaze with hyacinths and roses,
>luring goddesses to come and pick them.

But they did.

Pallas Athena came, and Aphrodite with all her wiles,
>and Hera… Hermes, too, their escort from Zeus.
Tangled in strife, the three came to Ida quarreling,
>to do battle with their beauty.
It was a contest of their charms:
>>Aphrodite offering luxuriance, the sating of desire;
>>Athena offering might, the conquest of enemies;
>>Hera, consort of lord Zeus,
>>>offering the splendor of kingship.
I tell you that day's judgment meant glory for Greece,
>and death for me.
I am to be the price of Troy paid on the altar of Artemis.
O Mother, my father who gave me life has fathered my ruin,
>walked out on me, left me alone with his betrayal.
Helen, hapless Helen, like a hateful spectre you haunt me,
>>embittering each step I take toward my own murder,
>>a victim, not for a wedding, but for a war.
My blood will never wash away, an impious mark
>on an impious man, my own father.

If only Aulis had never opened the haven of its harbor
>>to the bronze-beaked ships,
>>>whose fir-wood hulls will haul an army to Troy.

If only Zeus had never sent the winds that brought them here
    to the banks of Euripos.
What are the winds but the breath of Zeus;
    what drives them but his will?
Mortals long for him to fill their sails and their hearts.
To some he brings fair sailing; on others he breathes doom.
One man sets out and another reaches port,
    while others only wait in stillness.
Unseen, implacable, his breath carries the force of fate.

Mortal life appears to pass in a day,
    until we count our sufferings.
In the shortest life,
    there is always time to endure something more,
        to have one more thing go wrong.
Daughter of Tyndareos, all of Greece labors and suffers
    under the weight of your sin.

CHORAL LEADER
My heart goes out to you in this dark time.
You deserve none of this.

IPHIGENIA
Seeing the army approaching at a distance.
Mother! Mother, I see a mob of men coming.

KLYTEMNESTRA
And I see the son of divine Thetis, Akhilleus,
    for whom you came here.

IPHIGENIA
To the Chorus.
Women, hold open the tent for me,
    so that I can run inside and hide.

KLYTEMNESTRA
Child, why run from Akhilleus?

IPHIGENIA
I am ashamed to meet him.

KLYTEMNESTRA
Why?

IPHIGENIA
Because of the disaster our marriage has become.
I'm embarrassed.

KLYTEMNESTRA
In our situation, embarrassment is a luxury we cannot afford.
Stay here. Modesty can wait.
We have things to do.

Akhilleus enters.

AKHILLEUS
Daughter of Leda, woman of sorrows…

KLYTEMNESTRA
Yes. I am surely that.

AKHILLEUS
The army… you can hear them…
      they've begun to shout and won't stop.

KLYTEMNESTRA
What are they shouting about? Tell me.

AKHILLEUS
About your daughter.

KLYTEMNESTRA
You've said enough for me to think the worst.

AKHILLEUS
They are calling for her sacrifice.

KLYTEMNESTRA
Is there no voice on the other side?

AKHILLEUS
There was mine. I barely escaped.

KLYTEMNESTRA
Barely escaped what?

AKHILLEUS
Being stoned.

KLYTEMNESTRA
For trying to save my girl?

AKHILLEUS
Exactly.

KLYTEMNESTRA
Who would dare lay a hand on you?

AKHILLEUS
The whole Greek army.

KLYTEMNESTRA
Your own army of Myrmidons… aren't they at your side?

AKHILLEUS
No, they are at my throat.

KLYTEMNESTRA
To Iphigenia.
Then we are lost, child.

AKHILLEUS
They mocked me, saying that I was love-sick.

KLYTEMNESTRA
How did you answer them?

AKHILLEUS
I said they would never kill my bride…

KLYTEMNESTRA
Right!

AKHILLEUS
…the bride promised to me by her father.

KLYTEMNESTRA
And brought from Argos by her mother.

AKHILLEUS
But they shouted me down.

KLYTEMNESTRA
A mob is an evil and terrifying thing.

AKHILLEUS
I will protect you.

KLYTEMNESTRA
One against so many?

Two men approach carrying Akhilleus' armor.

AKHILLEUS
See. These men bring my armor.

KLYTEMNESTRA
May you find the strength you need.

AKHILLEUS
I will.

KLYTEMNESTRA
Then my child will not be sacrificed?

AKHILLEUS
Not as long as I am here.

KLYTEMNESTRA
Who is it that will come and try to take her?

AKHILLEUS
Odysseus for one; behind him… thousands.

KLYTEMNESTRA
Odysseus, the son of Sisyphos?

AKHILLEUS
Yes, the same.

KLYTEMNESTRA
Has he taken it to himself to lead the army,
        or did the mob choose him?

AKHILLEUS
He was elected, as he wanted to be.

KLYTEMNESTRA
Elected to murder a child.
It's some office he holds.

AKHILLEUS

I'll stop him.

KLYTEMNESTRA

But he will try to drag her away by force?

AKHILLEUS

By her golden hair. Yes, of course he'll try.

KLYTEMNESTRA

What must I do?

AKHILLEUS

You must not let go of her.

KLYTEMNESTRA

And if I don't, she won't be sacrificed.

AKHILLEUS

It comes down to that.

IPHIGENIA

Mother, listen to me,
    this wild rage of yours against your husband…
        it's pointless. I see that now.

None of us find it easy to be helpless.

Gesturing toward Akhilleus.

This extraordinary man, our new friend,
    deserves our praise and thanks
        for his willingness to help us.
But you must see to it that he does not incur the army's anger.
That would only imperil him and do nothing for us.

Hear me, Mother, hear what has occurred to me
    and what I have in mind to do.
I have imagined my death and all is well.
I want to shine when I die.
I want nothing to do with anything craven or cheap.
Think about it, Mother, and you will see that I am right.
At this very moment, Greece, in all its might and splendor,
    turns to me.

If the fleet is to set sail, if Troy is to fall,
    if Greek women are once and for all to be secure
        in the happiness of their homes,
            never again prey to barbarians,
    if the spoiling of Helen by Paris
        is to be fully avenged,
    then I must die.
For all of these things are in my hands today.
I alone can set Greece free; and, if I do that,
    my story will be told forever.
Mother, I must not clutch my life too tightly.
After all, you bore me for Greece, not just for yourself.
Thousands of our men have taken up their shields
    and gone to sea,
        to right a wrong done to their fatherland.
Each one of those thousands is ready to kill
    or be killed for Greece.
Who am I, with my one life, to stand in their way?
How could that be right? How would I explain it to them?

I have one more thing to say.
It would be a waste for this one man
    to take on the whole Greek army
        and to die for the sake of a woman.
Better that a thousand women should give their lives
    to save one man.
Mother, if Artemis wants my life, can I deny her,
    when she is divine and I am only human?

Besides, I am alone against an army of men.
I am without recourse.
So I give my life to Greece.
Sacrifice me and lay waste to Troy.
Long from now, the memory of these events will make up for
    the marriage and the children I never had.
My life will be summed up and preserved in them.
Mother, it is only right and natural
    for Greeks to rule barbarians,
        never the other way around;
    for all they know is slavery, and we are free.

CHORAL LEADER

Child, your nobility is luminous.
It is your fate and the goddess who decreed it
    that are all wrong.

AKHILLEUS

Child of Agamemnon, if somehow you could be my wife,
  it would reveal that one of the gods
      is eager for my happiness.
As it is, you belong to Greece; and I envy you both.
Your words are a thing of beauty, worthy of the fatherland.
You could never have won the battle
  you were about to wage.
Mortals are no match for the gods; so, instead,
  you've resolved to walk the line of the possible
      with all the dignity you can muster.
And yet, when I stand here, listening to you
  and gazing upon your exquisite nature,
      I can't help myself.
I want you more and more for my wife.
Your nobility is almost more than I can bear.
You see, I want to save you.
I want to take you away to my home.
Thetis, be my witness…
  I don't know if I will be able to live with myself,
      unless I battle the Greek army to save you.
Remember… death is an awful thing.
And it is forever.

IPHIGENIA

What I say now comes from a place beyond all fear.
Let Helen be the one to send men blithely off to battle,
  to kill or be killed for her body and its charms.
From you, dear friend, I ask something different.
Take no one's life on my account;
  and please, please, don't die for me.
Let me save Greece, if it can be saved.

AKHILLEUS

Your resolve is extraordinary.
I have nothing to add to what you've said,
  as your mind is made up.

Your nobility of soul is a simple truth
  no one can deny or diminish.
Nonetheless, you may change your mind.
Don't forget my offer.
I am going now to lay my weapons near the altar.

I want to prevent your death, not take part in it.
Even when you see the blade near your throat,
    I can still make good my promise to you,
        if you permit me.
If you're being impetuous now,
    I won't let it cost your life.
So, I am off, fully-armed, to the altar of Artemis,
    where I will hold my breath
        and wait for you.

Exit Akhilleus.

IPHIGENIA

Mother, you have no words but so many tears.
Why weep for me?

KLYTEMNESTRA

My despair and my pain are reason enough.

IPHIGENIA

O stop.
I need your help to be strong.
Please do as I say.

KLYTEMNESTRA

Child, what could I possibly refuse you?
Tell me what you want.

IPHIGENIA

I want you not to mourn.
Don't cut your hair or wear black for me.

KLYTEMNESTRA

Why do you ask this? Aren't I losing you?

IPHIGENIA

No, not really.
I will be saved not lost.
I will win everlasting fame for us both.

KLYTEMNESTRA

How can you ask me not to grieve for you?

IPHIGENIA

What place is there for grief when there will be no tomb?

KLYTEMNESTRA
You confuse me. No tomb for the dead?
Will that not enrage the gods?

IPHIGENIA
The altar of Artemis, daughter of Zeus,
    will mark my grave forever.

KLYTEMNESTRA
Your words ring true. I will do as you say, child.

IPHIGENIA
I will not be forgotten. Nor will anyone ever forget
    how lucky I was to serve Greece.

KLYTEMNESTRA
Do you have a message for your sisters?

IPHIGENIA
Only that they should not wear black for me.

KLYTEMNESTRA
Do you have some last word for them, from your heart?

IPHIGENIA
Good-bye.
Mother, take care of Orestes for me.
Make a tall, strong man of him.

KLYTEMNESTRA
You must look at him and hold him tight one last time.
*Klytemnestra gestures to one of the Chorus to fetch Orestes
from the tent, which she does.*

IPHIGENIA
To Orestes, as he enters.
O my sweetest, you did your very best to save your sister.
Iphigenia holds tightly, and then lets go of him.

KLYTEMNESTRA
Child, when I go back to Argos, what else can I do for you?

IPHIGENIA
Don't hate him… my father, your husband.

KLYTEMNESTRA
He will pay for your death.
Hell will come as a relief to him.

IPHIGENIA
But he too suffers my loss against his will.
It is all for Greece.

KLYTEMNESTRA
Even his lies?
That man betrayed me and disgraced his own house.

IPHIGENIA
Who will lead me to the altar,
    before they drag me away by my hair?

KLYTEMNESTRA
I will. I will be with you.

IPHIGENIA
No. That's not a good idea.

KLYTEMNESTRA
Just to hold your gown.

IPHIGENIA
Mother, for my sake, listen. Stay here.
It will be better for both of us.
One of father's men can take me to the meadow of Artemis,
    where I will be sacrificed.

KLYTEMNESTRA
Child, are you going now?

IPHIGENIA
Never to return.

KLYTEMNESTRA
Leaving your mother?

IPHIGENIA
All before your eyes.
It feels wrong…

KLYTEMNESTRA
Wait, don't leave me!

Klytemnestra breaks down, weeping.

IPHIGENIA
There will be no tears.
Women, sing with me a hymn of praise
    to Artemis, child of Zeus,
        for me and for my day of destiny.
Let holy silence descend upon the host of men.
Let the sacrifice begin.
The baskets and the barley cakes... someone bring them.
Let the sacred cleansing fire be lit and blaze forth.
Now, Father, go to the altar and walk around it.
I am coming, with victory in my hands,
    a gift for Greece.
I am coming. I bring salvation.

Women, lead me on...
I who will bring down the walls of Phrygian Troy.
Place on my head the wedding crown.
Weave into my hair garlands of victory.
Spatter me with holy waters to make me new and pure.
Around the sacred place of Artemis,
    Artemis, our blessed queen... around her altar...
        lift up your hearts and dance!
For with my blood, spilled out in sacrifice,
    I will answer the gods' demands and set Greece free.

*The Chorus crowns Iphigenia with a wedding crown. They form
a procession with her to the altar of Artemis. The scene changes
to the sacred grove of Artemis, the place of sacrifice.*

CHORAL LEADER
O great mother, mistress of us all,
    we will keep our tears to ourselves.
In your holy place, we must show only joy.

IPHIGENIA
Women, join with me in celebration.
Sing to Artemis, mistress of Aulis,
    whose shrine faces east toward Khalkis,
        across the narrow straits
    where a thousand ships wait.

In my name, they will have their war.
O Argos, mother to me... Mykene, my home!

CHORAL LEADER

Child, is it to the city of Perseus that you cry out,
    the city whose walls the cyclops toiled to build?

IPHIGENIA

You brought me into the light, gave me life, for Greece.
So I die for Greece, with no regret.

CHORAL LEADER

Your name and your story will never die.

IPHIGENIA

O splendorous light of day,
    that gladdens even the heart of god...
        and mine, too... good-bye.
I must begin another life, in another place,
    and let the fates weave something new for me.

CHORUS

See what I see:
The child who would drown Troy in her blood.
Sprinkled with holy water
And crowned for a day,
She walks to the altar of Artemis,
Where she will nod her noble head to the blade
And shower the sacred stones
With her bright blood
For a long, bloody harvest.

Child, your father is waiting
With a last libation,
To make you pure enough to die.
The army too waits on you,
But thinks only of Troy.

Hail, Artemis, daughter of Zeus,
Mistress of the gods,
We sing your praise
And pray for something bright
At the end of this darkness.

Mistress, Lady,
If indeed you have a taste for human blood,
Escort the armies of Greece
To Phrygian shores,
To the treacherous towers of Troy.
There may you one day
Crown the head of Agamemnon
And garland the spears of his men
With glorious victory.
Lady, we ask of you,
Let the story begun today
Live forever.

DRAMATIS PERSONAE

IN ORDER OF APPEARANCE

IPHIGENIA
Daughter of Agamemnon and Klytemnestra,
Priestess of the Temple of Artemis
in the Land of the Taurians

ORESTES
Brother of Iphigenia

PYLADES
Orestes' Cousin and Companion,
Husband to Elektra

CHORUS
Captive Greek Women

CHORAL LEADER
Leader of the Chorus

HERDSMAN
A Taurian

ATTENDANTS
To the Temple and the King

THOAS
King of the Taurians

MESSENGER
One of Thoas' Guards

ATHENA
Daughter of Zeus

IPHIGENIA IN TAURIS

The scene is the temple precinct of Artemis, on the Taurian coast. The steps of the temple lead to a blood-stained altar. Trophies of the dead lie about, propped against the temple walls.

Iphigenia enters from the inner sanctuary of the temple.

IPHIGENIA

I am Iphigenia,
   seed of Agamemnon, flower of Klytemnestra.
My house is the house of Atreus, son of Pelops,
   whose matchless steeds, gifts of Poseidon,
      won him his wife.
Two sons she bore to Atreus,
   Menelaos, my uncle, and Agamemnon,
   who took to his bed the daughter of Tyndareos,
      my mother.
I am Iphigenia,
   for Helen's sake a living sacrifice to Artemis,
   slain, for all my father knows, on the cliffs of Aulis,
   near the dark sea pools spun and whirled white
      in the straits of Euripos.
There in the bay of Aulis
   a thousand sails hung limp,
      the Greek armada,
   the fleet of Agamemnon, King of Kings,
      launched to seize the crown of victory
         and to avenge a spoiled bed.
All this to appease a cuckold's lost pride.
But it came to nothing there, in Aulis,
   where the winds grew still as stone,
      and ships leaned over in the sand.
A proud king resorted to a prouder priest.
Agamemnon bent and knelt and listened,
   while Kalkhas read the sacred flames:
"Lord Agamemnon, you lead this vast Greek force nowhere.
Never will your ships leave their beds of sand
   until you grant Artemis her due—
      your daughter, Iphigenia,
   as victim at my altar.
Your vow of long ago was clear—
   to yield to the goddess of light
      the year's first and loveliest fruit.

That vow is overdue.
The child born in your halls,
    lifted high by your wife
        and proclaimed loveliest of all
    is mine to stain my altars with her blood."

Odysseus spun the tale
    that plied me from my mother's arms.
She bathed me for my husband's bed,
    wove the wedding crown,
        and sang to me.
Bride of Akhilleus,
    ill-starred and marked for slaughter,
        I went to Aulis.
There I was seized and held by many hands.
Flames beneath and blade above,
    death closed in on me.
But goddess Artemis stole me from the knife and fire,
    leaving a deer to bleed and burn in my stead,
        while I was blown through the luminous aether
            here, to Taurica,
        a barbarous land with a barbarous king.
The king's name is Thoas, which means "swift,"
    a name he won with his feet.
Priestess of Artemis is my post here,
    hostess to her altars.
I please her with the rites I keep, prescribed by sacred law,
    festivals in name only.
Fear holds my tongue from saying more than this:
    I make a sacrifice of any hapless Greek
        who stumbles on these shores.
Such is the custom here, long before I came.
I raise no blade, except to cut the victim's hair.
I spill no blood, only water.
Inside, there, in her—the divine one's—inner rooms,
    other hands do the butchering.
I have no words for what they do.

Now, in hope of some release, I face the morning light
    and tell the dark visions come in night.
In sleep I saw myself in Argos.
My exile here was past.
I was sleeping, a virgin among virgins,
    and the earth beneath me quaked.

I fled to the open sky and saw my house fall, stone by stone.
One lone column stood when all else fell,
    the centerpost of my father's house.
This post, it seemed to me, grew golden locks,
    streaming from its capital and flowing down its sides.
It spoke with a human voice.
I paid to it my familiar rites.
As if it were another stranger marked for death,
I spattered it with holy water, bent and wept.

This I tell you, is the meaning of my dream:
    the victim I made ready, the one now dead,
        is Orestes.
For the pillars of a house are its sons.
And my rites mean sure death.
If I could read these phantoms in any other way, I would.
But I cannot.
Instead, I do all that is left me now to do.

Calling out.

Come, women, Greek women like myself,
    gifts of our barbarian king.
Come near and companion me.
I am far from my brother,
    and he is far from me.
I will lift this cup and pour it out
    in sweet memory of him.
Why do they not come?
I must go inside...

Turning and facing the temple.

    the temple of Artemis.
It is where I live.

She re-enters the temple. Enter Orestes and Pylades.

ORESTES

Look, a path!
See if anyone's coming.

PYLADES

I'm looking... and I don't see anyone.

ORESTES

There.

Pointing to the temple.

Pylades, do you think that's it—
    what we've sailed all the way from Argos to find—
        the shrine of Artemis?

PYLADES

Yes, that must be it, Orestes.

ORESTES

And is that the altar
    where they spill the blood of Greeks?

PYLADES

See for yourself the dark stains down its sides.

ORESTES

And there, stacked against the wall...
    the dead men's spoils.

PYLADES

Trophies left by strangers
    long since stacked beneath the ground.
We had best be on our toes.

ORESTES

O Phoibos,
    why do you lay another snare for me
        when I have done your word,
    avenged my father with my mother's blood?
Wave after wave of blood-eyed Furies
    have driven me from my home,
        hounded me down endless paths.
I came to you a suppliant, on my knees,
    asking no more than to see an end to my trials.
I begged release from the whirling wheel of madness
    that spun me throughout Greece like a lost star.
You told me to come here, to Taurica,
    to the altar of your sister Artemis,
        to seize her graven image,
    fallen, they say, from heaven to this very place.

Once I had braved every danger and—
    whether by my own wits or by witless luck—
    had laid my hands upon the holy likeness,
        I was to make of it a gift to Greece.
That was it.
Nothing more was asked of me.
Release from my woes was one last daring deed away.

So here I am, obedient to your words,
    in a land unmapped and unwelcoming.

Pylades, my companion, I need your advice.
What now?
You see the height of that wall.
How could we hope to scale it without being seen?
And we'd be taking quite a risk
    trying to force open those brazen doors,
        when we know nothing of their strength.
And we would be as good as dead, if we're caught up there,
    prying loose the hinges
        and scheming our way into the temple.
I suggest we cheat death,
    and go back where we came from.

PYLADES

Run away? You can't be serious.
We've never run away from anything.
And it is no time to turn coward,
    when we are on god's business.
I suggest we quit the temple now
    and hide in the cliff-side caves
        where the dark tides bathe the gleaming rocks.
We want to be far from our ship for now.
All it would take would be for one wandering eye
    to spot our mast and sound the alarm;
        and they would be down on us like that.
Instead, we wait in the caves for obscuring night to fall.
And then we use whatever nerve and knack we have
    to make off with the temple's glorious relic.
Make note of those projecting beams,
    up there in the temple eaves.
There's space enough between them for the two of us
    to lower ourselves down.
It will be a challenge; but that's what brave men are for.

Cowards come to nothing anyway.
Besides, if all we plan to do is turn around,
    this was a long way to row.

ORESTES
You speak well, the kind of words I can't ignore.
We best go and find our hiding-place.
Phoibos will not stand by and let his word be mocked.
So we must dare to do it.
The fact that it won't be easy is no excuse in youth.

Orestes and Pylades exit.

CHORUS
Silence.
Let holy silence
Shroud this land of hostile seas and clashing rocks.
O goddess of the hunt,
Mountain-wild child of Leto,
We lift our pale feet in ritual steps
To approach your holy place
Roofed in gleaming gold.
Spotless we serve the spotless one,
The keeper of the key,
Locked away in exile here
From all that once brought joy
In the land of our fathers.

To Iphigenia.

What is it?
What draws your face so?
Child of the famed king
Whose scudding ships and bronze-helmed men
Swarmed against the towered walls of Troy
Like a plague of locusts,
Child, why have you summoned us here?

IPHIGENIA
Women, I am lost in my own laments.
Like an unstrung lyre, I make sounds, but never song.
Aiaiaiai. This night has brought dark sights to me.
Banished from the day, they fester in my darkened heart.
I have seen my brother perished.
These tears are for him.

As for me, I am lost.
The last pillar of my father's house
Lies among the ruins.
We are extinct.
Argos, who will sing what you endured?
I curse whatever thieving power
    plunged my only brother into hell.
Sweet brother,
I take this bowl and mix the drink of the dead:
    warm milk of a mountain heifer,
    swirling wine sweet to Bakkhos,
    the flowing toil of tawny bees.
Down through a thirsty earth to hell
    I shall pour this gift to appease the dead
        and to charm their king.

To one of the women.

Give me the purple urn
    and the drink for the god of death.

Scion of Agamemnon, Brother, wherever you lie in darkness,
    these gifts are yours.
Take them from my hands.
I cannot come to your tomb,
    cut my hair and weep over you.
Not that I lie in some miserable grave,
    slaughtered, as men think, long ago.
I am in exile, far from our home.

CHORUS
Lady, our chants echo your grief,
Wild laments,
Litanies learned from barbarians
For times of death and loss.
We sing the dirge of the dead,
Intoned by their king,
A song without a hint of hope.
Lament the house of Atreus.
Lament the house of your fathers.
The brilliant, blinding sceptre of Agamemnon
Is dark as blackest night.
Who is left of all the shining Argive kings
To mount the throne?

Wave after wave of havoc
Crashed against that house
Before it fell.
There was the charioteer,
Whose winged steeds circuited the sky,
Until Pelops toppled him,
As the sacred sun changed course
And turned askance.
The lamb with golden fleece
Brought its own train of horrors,
Each murder and grief
Spawning its successor.
The river of revenge for the slain sons of Tantalos
Crests and quits its banks.
And now the last of the line
Must know a force
Zealous for its ruin.

IPHIGENIA

My evil fate and I were conceived on the same night
    in the same bed.
We were born of the same womb
    and reared to full stature in the same house.
Klytemnestra, ill-starred child of Leto,
    wooed the plumed princes of Greece
        before she lay back in Agamemnon's bed
    and misconceived me, her first fruit,
        for unholy slaughter.
It was for my father's final shame that
I was born and suckled.
Drawn by snow-white mares, I came to sandy Aulis,
    bride of Akhilleus… mockery!
It was a match made in hell.
Now, I live a stern life.
Exiled to the shore of a hostile sea,
    I am unwed, barren, homeless,
        without the solace of a friend.
I have no songs for Argive Hera.
I weave no tales of Titans or Pallas Athena
    in vivid tapestries, on a deep-thrumming loom.
Instead I splash the blood of strangers over grim altars.
Their hideous groans and despairing tears inspire pity
    but not song.

Now my heart eludes their pain and feels its own.
I mourn my brother dead in Argos.
Orestes, I left you clinging to your mother's breast,
    a babe without blemish,
        with a blush in your cheeks.
You were the crown prince of Argos,
    and mother held you close.

CHORAL LEADER
Look. A herdsman comes from the shore.
He seems to have something to tell us.

Enter Herdsman.

HERDSMAN
Child of Agamemnon and Klytemnestra, hear me.
I have strange news for you.

IPHIGENIA
There is panic in your voice. Why?

HERDSMAN
Two young men, with pluck and arms of steel,
    have rowed through the clashing rocks
        and landed on our shore.
They will make a suiting sacrifice,
    a gift to please the goddess.
Quickly, prepare your rites.
Fetch your basin and draw the lustral waters.

IPHIGENIA
These strangers, where do they come from?
Could you tell from their look?

HERDSMAN
They're Greeks, that much I know.
It's hard to say beyond that.

IPHIGENIA
You didn't hear either of their names?

HERDSMAN
I heard the one fellow call the other one "Pylades."

IPHIGENIA
And this Pylades' companion, what of his name?

HERDSMAN
I can't say. We heard nothing more.

IPHIGENIA
How did you happen to come upon them?
Tell me how you took them.

HERDSMAN
Well, we were down at the sea's edge… in the breakers…
    not far from the perilous strait.

IPHIGENIA
Interrupting.
Herdsmen?… in the sea?

HERDSMAN
We went there to wash our cattle in the brine.
It's something we do.
IPHIGENIA
O… well… then let's go back.
Tell me, how did you capture them?
This I want to know.
They have surely taken their time in getting here.
Long has the altar of the goddess
    thirsted for Greek blood.

HERDSMAN
As I was telling you,
    we had driven our cattle down to the sea,
        near where the churning currents
    thread the clashing rocks.
There is a cliff-side cave down there,
        a favorite fishers' haunt,
    carved from the sheer rock face by a determined sea.
That was where one of our company caught sight of the pair,
    and tiptoed back to tell us.
His heart leapt to his mouth as he spoke:
    "Look. Don't you see them? Sitting… there…
        gods for sure… of some sort!"
At the sight of the two, another of us, a god-fearing man,
        lifted his hands in prayer:

"Lord Palamon, guardian of ships," he chanted,
"child of Leukothea, goddess of the seas, be gracious.
Be gracious, too, yonder gods, whoever you are,
            perhaps the holy twins of Zeus,
                    or else two favorites of Nereus,
                    father of the fifty ocean-nymphs."
But another one of us, a rude and reckless fellow,
        was quick to mock this cant.
"Shipwrecked sailors," he taunted,
            "no more, no less...
        cowering among the hollow rocks
        because they know how we welcome strangers here."

These words made sense to almost everyone.
And the two became our quarry,
        victims to be hunted for this altar's rites.
Meanwhile, one of the strangers left the cave
        and stood on a cleft of jagged rock.
His head flew about, up and down, as if on a string.
His hands and arms shook with frenzy
        and he gave out ungodly groans.
Then, with the voice of a hunter on the leash,
        hurled along by dogs who've caught the scent,
            he cried out:
        "Pylades, don't you see them?... There!... There!
        Hellish fiends, craving my death.
            knotted snakes for hair...
        They lick and tear at me...with fangs of fire...
        There!
        Winged scorching demon... sheets of flame!
            Her breath burns my soul.
        In her arms...   Mother!
        She holds you like a giant rock... to hurl...
                splinter me...
            like a pestle to grind me into...
        Where? Where can I flee?"

None of this, nothing of what he said
        was there to be seen by us.
There were cattle and dogs nearby.
And it must have been their lowing and barks
        that he took for the screams of furies.
We drew together and sat close, in silence,
        as if we were the ones whose lives hung by a thread.

But then he drew his sword and leapt among our cattle,
    like a hungry lion.
He thrusted and hacked at the sorry beasts,
      as if to beat back his assailing demons,
    until the curling sea beneath his feet
      bubbled and foamed red with their blood.
This was more than we could sit and watch.
We stood and blew our blaring conch-horns
      to sound the alarm
    and swell our ranks with any who would come.
As we herdsmen stood, we counted ourselves no match
    for bold and brawny foreigners half our age.
But soon we had the numbers that we needed,
    just as the stranger's madness left him.
Drool spewed down his face and beard,
    as his legs wobbled and refused his weight.
One down. It was our chance.
In one barrage after another, we pelted them with rocks,
    hurled with all our might.
The one man did all that lay within him
    to shield his fallen friend.
He wiped the spittle from his chin
    and made a wall of his heavy cloak,
      dodging or warding off our hailing blows
        as best he could.
Then the stricken one regained his wits and sprang to his feet.
He groaned when he saw the battle's tide coming in
    and marked the ruin it carried in its wake.
We closed in, throwing all the harder.
And that same one let out one last cry,
      defiant and despairing:
    "Pylades, we are going to our death. Let's do it right.
    Draw your sword and follow me!"
At the sight of those two brandishing their swords…
      well, we ran… to the nearby woods…
    and tried to look like trees.
Not all at once… Some threw stones while others ran.
And when these were routed,
    the others gathered stones and took their place.
The wonder is that with the sky all but darkened
      with flying rocks, not one struck its mark.

The fact is we took them in the end
      without any daring on our part.

We kept circling them and throwing our rocks,
    until we knocked the swords from their hands
        and they collapsed in sheer exhaustion.

We marched them to the king;
    and he, after one look, sends them to you,
        for the sprinkling of the holy waters
    and the letting of their foreign blood.
Maiden, you used to pray that victims such as these
    might come along.
For when you slaughter them and their kind,
    Hellas begins to pay the price
        for what it would have done to you in Aulis.
Your blood they almost shed cries out for theirs.

CHORAL LEADER
There is something wondrous to your tale
    about this stranger Greek—whoever he is—
        come across the hostile sea.

IPHIGENIA
To the Herdsman.
Well, then, go and fetch these strangers.
And I will see that all is ready for them.

The Herdsman exits.

IPHIGENIA
Wretched heart within me,
You used to be so gentle toward strangers.
Always you showed such pity.
And, when Greeks fell into your hands,
    you wept familial tears.
Now it is all different.
These dread dreams of Orestes dead untame my heart
        and set it wild.
New guests here will find me severe, like slate.
Friends, now I know how true it is that,
        when life turns harsh,
    the heart grows hard, not soft.

Through the twin-rock portals of this land,
        never yet has any god-sent wind or ship
    brought me Helen, my undoing, nor Menelaos.

To them... I have a debt to pay,
    in memory of Aulis.
There, like some bellowing heifer,
I was seized by the Greek chiefs.
My father—my own father—played hierophant.
He would have slain me.
It is a nightmare ten thousand dawns cannot erase.
How I twined myself around my father's knees
    and groped upwards to touch his beard.
I remember my very words:
    "Father, this match you make for me is mockery!
        Imagine it as it will be:
    Mother and the Argive women full with song...
    Festive flutes fill the air...
    You lead me to the altar...
        and give me away... with a knife.
    You marry me to Hades, not the son of Peleus.
    With sheer deceit you coaxed me to a bloody bed."
When I left my home in Argos,
    I hid and blushed behind my wedding veil.
I was too shy to take my brother, now dead, into my arms
    or to give my sister a good-bye kiss.
Farewells were overlooked.
There would be time for them when I returned.
Mine were a bride's thoughts... of Akhilleus...
    and of his bed.

O wretched Orestes, if you are really dead,
    how cheated you are of so much
        that might have been.
Father had such plans for you!

Turning toward the shrine.

Goddess,
    your subtleties elude me.
We mortals are unclean, unworthy of approaching you,
    if we soil our hands with bloodshed,
        touch a corpse
           or assist a woman giving birth.
And yet you yourself revel in human sacrifice.
You find it sweet.
No, this cannot be!
Zeus and Leto his bride
    cannot have spawned anything so spurious.

I don't believe the tale of Tantalos
    and his feast.
I don't believe that gods ever savored
    the flesh of a child.
Here, in this land, men, not gods, are murders.
Men make their own perversions into rituals
      and sacralize their sins.
No god is evil.
That is what I believe.

CHORUS

Dark twin cliffs
Where two seas meet,
And continents converge,
Where Io in her agony,
Driven out of Argos,
Crossed over in flight
From Europe to Asian soil,
Who are these strangers?
Have they come from the fair waters of Eurotas,
Woven thick with reeds?
Or the sweet stream of Dirke?
Who are they come to this savage land
Where the altars of the child of Zeus
And the pillars of her shrine
Are splashed with human blood?
Was it simple greed for gold
That urged these men to hoist their sails
And ride the heaving waves?
Did their heavy fir-wood oars
Plow the angry sea
In quest of foreign spoils?
This dream of distant sparkling plunder
Is sweet beyond the toll of grief it takes.
Insatiate addicts they will become
Who roam the remotest seas
And prowl cities unknown,
Lured beyond the reach of their wits.
Their lust is all they share.
This one strikes it rich,
While that one's luck
Runs out.

How did they thread the clashing rocks
And skirt the sleepless beaches
Of harpy-haunted Phineus,
Scudding across the breakers
To the far beach of Amphitrite,
Where the chorus of fifty sea-nymphs
Weave a circle with their steps,
Chanting and dancing
To the rhythms of the sea?
How did they sail so far across the hostile sea,
As the winds tore at the sails
And the rudder groaned,
To Leuke where the sea-birds flock
And where Akhilleus once
Raced the glistening strand?

If only our mistress' prayers
Might come true,
And Helen, Leda's darling,
Quitting Troy's splendid walls,
Come here,
To have her legendary locks
Splashed with sacrificial waters
Just before our mistress
Slits her soft pale throat
And collects an old debt.
But the sweetest news of all would be
If some Greek seafarer would come to bring an end
To our exile and our bondage.
Our dreams are of home,
To see the walls and the towers of our city,
And to sing with one and all the festal songs.

Temple Attendants enter with Orestes and Pylades.

CHORAL LEADER

See, here they come,
  the two we've heard so much about, tightly trussed,
    the latest catch, fresh for slaughter.
Silence, friends, let us admire the pride of Greece,
  washed up on our shore,
    true to all the herdsman told us.

Goddess, accept this sacrifice,
  if this land's ways suit you.

But in Greece
    our laws give another name
        to what's done here.

Enter Iphigenia.

IPHIGENIA

Let us proceed.
Scrupulously, I must see that all is done
    as the goddess prescribes.
Untie the strangers' hands.
They are hallowed now, and not to be bound.
Go within the temple.
Make all things ready.
And in doing so,
    overlook no observance,
        heed every canon.

*Chorus and Attendants exit into the temple, leaving Iphigenia
alone with Orestes and Pylades.*

IPHIGENIA
Moaning.
Your mother… your father… who are they?
Tell me if you have a sister… and her name.
Her heart will break to lose the two of you.
There is no charting the path of fate.
No one knows who will suffer next, or why.
The gods cast our lots behind our backs.
Fate makes no sound until it catches up with us…
    as it has with you.
Tell me, where have you come from?
It seems to me you have come a long way,
    only to go down below… without hope.

ORESTES
Woman, whoever you are, why all these dark words
    and deep moans?
You are only adding weight to a heavy burden.
Anyone facing death who thinks that tears will bring reprieve,
    I call a fool.
If there is salvation at the gates of hell,
    it doesn't come from groaning.
You double what we endure,
    when you add folly to our fate.

Let these things take their course.
Spare us your pity.
We already know what goes on in there.
You have no news to break slowly to us.

IPHIGENIA
But there is something I want to learn from you.
Which of you is called "Pylades"?

ORESTES
He is. Now aren't you glad you know that!

IPHIGENIA
From what Greek city?

ORESTES
Woman, what difference could it make?

IPHIGENIA
Are you half-brothers… or do you have the same mother?

ORESTES
Neither. Our love makes us one.

IPHIGENIA
To Orestes.
And you, what did your father call you?

ORESTES
My name should be "Accursed."

IPHIGENIA
That wasn't what I asked.
I know the name that Fate has given you.

ORESTES
If I die without a name,
    no one will know how to mock me when I'm gone.

IPHIGENIA
Are you so proud as to begrudge me this?

ORESTES
You may carve up my body. Yes, my name I begrudge you.

IPHIGENIA
Then tell me this much... the name of your city.

ORESTES
Give up... as I have. I'm as good as dead.

IPHIGENIA
Think of it as a favor. Please, why not?

ORESTES
Argos... glorious Argos. I say it proudly.

IPHIGENIA
Stranger, this is the truth? You swear it.
Argos is your home?

ORESTES
I was born in Mykene, when it was flourishing.

IPHIGENIA
Why did you leave? Were you exiled?

ORESTES
You might call it exile, except that I left on my own
    as much as I was driven out.

IPHIGENIA
I'm so glad you've come.
I've longed for someone from Argos.

ORESTES
Then this is your lucky day... not mine.

IPHIGENIA
One more question... Can I ask you one more thing?

ORESTES
I suppose it can't make things much worse.

IPHIGENIA
Famed Troy... do you know of it?

ORESTES
I wish I didn't... not even as a bad dream.

IPHIGENIA
They say it is gone, carried off on the tips of Greek spears.

ORESTES
You heard right.   Troy is no more.

IPHIGENIA
And Helen… did Menelaos take her home?

ORESTES
She came home… doing no good to my house.

IPHIGENIA
She owes me as well. Where is she now?

ORESTES
Sparta… in her old bed.

IPHIGENIA
Bitch! I hate her… and so must all of Greece.

ORESTES
Including me.
Her switching beds did me no good.

IPHIGENIA
And the Greek fleet… are the rumors true?
Are they home?

ORESTES
You expect a "yes" or "no" to that?
I can't tell you everything in one word.

IPHIGENIA
Then tell me all there is to tell… now, before you die.

ORESTES
If that is what you wish, question me
    and I will tell you what I know.

IPHIGENIA
The priest, Kalkhas… did he return?

ORESTES
From what I heard he perished.

IPHIGENIA

Good. Well done, Artemis!
And Odysseus?

ORESTES

They say he is alive… but not yet home.

IPHIGENIA

May he never get there.

ORESTES

I think he's doing badly enough on his own,
    without your curses.

IPHIGENIA

And the child of Nereid Thetis… Akhilleus?
Does he live?

ORESTES

No. In Aulis his wedding came to nothing.

IPHIGENIA

As those who endured it know too well.
Treachery, nothing more!

ORESTES

For someone with no answers,
    you know the questions all too well.
Who are you, anyway?

IPHIGENIA

I too am from Greece, though I died to her long ago,
    when I was a child.

ORESTES

Now it makes sense why you long so for any news of her.

IPHIGENIA

What of her general, the man they call the "blessed king"?

ORESTES

I know of no blessed kings. Whom do you have in mind?

IPHIGENIA

King Agamemnon, son of Atreus.

ORESTES
I know nothing. Woman... stop. No more!

IPHIGENIA
Friend, I beg you. Not until you've answered me,
    and brought me gladness.

ORESTES
The king you think blessed is not.
He is dead... and his death has ruined another.

IPHIGENIA
Reeling and groaning with pain.
Dead? How? No!

ORESTES
Why are you so upset? What was he to you?

IPHIGENIA
The death of such splendor... it is upsetting.

ORESTES
Even more upsetting is how his own wife slew him...
    with an axe.

IPHIGENIA
I weep for them both.

ORESTES
No... no more. We end here.

IPHIGENIA
No, we cannot. I must know more.
Does she live?

ORESTES
No more.
Her son—the one she gave life—took hers.

IPHIGENIA
A house gone mad! Why did he do it?

ORESTES
To avenge his father's death.

IPHIGENIA
How well he crossed perversity with justice.

ORESTES
Not so well does he fare with the gods,
      regardless of his justice.

IPHIGENIA
Then who remains?
Which of Agamemnon's offspring is left at home?

ORESTES
One daughter, Elektra, not yet come of age.

IPHIGENIA
The other daughter, the one they sacrificed…
      what is said of her?

ORESTES
What is there to say?
She's dead and gone to darkness.

IPHIGENIA
She and her murderous father…
      both cursed in what he did.

ORESTES
A shameless deed… for a shameless woman's sake.

IPHIGENIA
The boy, the dead king's son… does he live?
In Argos still?

ORESTES
He lives a wretched life… nowhere and everywhere.

IPHIGENIA
False dreams, I am rid of you.
You meant nothing in the end.

ORESTES
Even the so-called wisdom of the gods
      tells fewer lies
            than do our fleeting dreams.

It is difficult to overestimate the prevailing chaos
    among things human and divine.

But the one real human tragedy
    is when we set aside our common sense
        and put our faith in oracles
            only to be ruined by them.
I know the truth of this firsthand,
    which is the way the truth is learned.

CHORAL LEADER
And what of us... and the parents who bore us?
They may live. They may not.
We will never know.

IPHIGENIA
Listen closely, strangers.
I think I have a scheme to suit us both.
Surely there is no reason to complain
    when the same hammer pounds two nails.
Now this is what I propose.

To Orestes.

Your life I will spare, provided that you go to Argos,
    and take a message to my family there.
I have a letter, written by a man who pitied me.
He was a victim here, who saw my hands too were tied.
He grasped what simply is the case here,
    that murder is the rule of law for a goddess
        who sees sacrifice as her just desserts.
I have had this letter for some time
    but no one to take it back to Argos.
You are a free man, if you will be the one
    to place it in the hands of someone dear to me.
If you are the man you say you are,
    nobly born and no stranger to Mykene,
    likely even to know the one to whom I send you,
        and if I am right you bear me no ill will,
            then save yourself.
It is not a bad swap, your life for a letter.
But as for him, my hands are tied.
You will go your way, and he his... to death,
    in there... on an altar.

ORESTES

Strange woman, your words are music to my ears,
    except for one wrong note.
I don't take lightly your slaughtering my friend.
I steered the ship that brought him here.
He came along on my behalf,
    to lend his shoulder to my burdens.
It would seem a strange form of justice now,
    for me to buy your favor and my freedom
        with his life.
I have a counterplan.
Give him the letter. Send him to Argos.
It would be all the same to you.
Let me be the one to stay behind
    and feed the sacrificial flames.
It is a sad and shameful day
    when, in dark times,
        a man tosses away friendship
            like a bad idea,
        and sells out his friend to save himself.

IPHIGENIA

You are a pure spirit, free of dross.
You must be well-born to give such loyalty to your friends.
How I pray that the one man left in my family
    might resemble you.
For I have a brother, though he is never before my eyes.
Yes, you may have your way.
Your friend will run my errand and you will die.
I wonder at your zeal on his behalf
    and not on your own.

ORESTES

Whose dread calling is it to preside over my sacrifice?

IPHIGENIA

Mine. It is my office to supplicate the goddess.

ORESTES

You are a girl with not a very enviable occupation.
I find you most unfortunate.

IPHIGENIA

I do what I must do.

ORESTES
Does that include wielding the sacrificial knife?

IPHIGENIA
No. I will sprinkle harmless water on your hair.

ORESTES
I don't mean to pry.
But if not you, then who is the local butcher?

IPHIGENIA
They are inside.

ORESTES
Once I'm dead, where will I lie?

IPHIGENIA
Inside, among the sacred flames…
    then scattered into a crevasse.

ORESTES
If only my sister might be here to see to my rites.

IPHIGENIA
Whoever you are, you are cursed,
    and your prayers must fall on deaf ears.
You can see as well as I how far your sister is
    from these uncivilized shores.
But since you and I chance to share in Argos
    a common home,
        I will do all I can to attend to you.
I will strew your bier with bright gifts
    and with golden oil.
I will moisten your remains.
Over the loud licking flames of your pyre
    I will pour sweet lucent honey,
        the proud work of wild mountain bees.

But now I must go inside and fetch the letter.
Please try to think well of me.

To the Guards.

Guards, watch them. But otherwise let them be.

To herself.

Now I will send to Argos, to the one so dear to me,
    words beyond his hopes.
The one he thinks is dead is not.
I live and the news of me will be a sweet rain.

Iphigenia exits.

CHORAL LEADER
To Orestes.
We pity you, marked for the sprinkling of lustral waters
    and for the dark-spattering spray of blood.

ORESTES
Women, I am not to be pitied.
Farewell is enough said.

CHORAL LEADER
To Pylades.
You are the lucky one.
You are the one blessed to see your home again.

PYLADES
Am I to be envied when I lose my friend?

CHORAL LEADER
To Pylades.
True enough, you run a grim errand.
Your life too is spoiled here.
When I ask myself which of you to mourn more,
    you who must perish, or you who must survive,
        my heart wavers and spins in confusion
        like a weathercock in a winter's storm.

ORESTES
Pylades, are you thinking what I'm thinking?

PYLADES
How can I know without your saying more?

ORESTES
I'm thinking and wondering about our young priestess here.
Who can she be?

She knew enough and cared enough
 to ask about the trials we knew in Troy,
  the homecoming of the Greek fleet,
  and the fate of Kalkhas, skilled in augury.
She seemed so Greek when she spoke of Akhilleus
 and grieved to learn from me the unspeakable ends
  of wretched Agamemnon, his wife,
   and their cursed children.
She must indeed be from Argos.
For why else would she have launched
 such a wave of questions
  into the state and fate of Argos,
 as if they were her own?
And why would she be sending this letter of hers to Argos,
 unless Argos were her home?

PYLADES

Your thoughts run ahead of mine.
I guess I would have said everything you've said
 except for one thing.
The calamities of kings are not secrets.
That she or anyone knows of them comes as no surprise.
It was something else she said that concerned me.

ORESTES

What? Share your concern,
 and we might resolve it together.

PYLADES

For me to live on in the light, when you go down to darkness,
 shames me.
We have been companions for this much of the journey,
 and we must be companions the rest of the way...
  to death.
Otherwise, anywhere I go, in Argos,
 or across the countless valleys of Phokis,
  I will be called a coward and a snake.
You know what people are like,
 and you know what they will say:
  that I saved myself and made for home,
  leaving you without a second thought,
 or worse, that I took advantage
   of your family's disarray
  and took your life myself.

You must admit, the pieces of such a scheme lie at hand:
    your demise, your sister's hand,
        and a crown without a head to wear it.
You see what I fear and why I feel shame.
There can be no other way.
Together we must seize our last breaths,
    together slaughtered, together set ablaze.
I am your friend.
I will give no one the pretext
    for saying I was not.

ORESTES

I wish you would say what makes some sense.
Count the fate at hand.
It is one, not two, and it is mine to bear.
And this painful reproach you speak of…
    will it not come down on me
        if I now take your life,
    you who cast your lot with me?

Consider my condition.
How bad can it be to let go of a life
    so plagued by the gods?
With you it is different. You are flourishing.
My house has fallen, crushed by an impious curse.
Your house stands firm, free of offense.
If you save yourself now,
    and give my sister—your wife—sons,
        don't you see, you will let my name live?
Otherwise, my house and the house of my fathers,
    will be childless… blotted out… no more.
Go your way, not mine.
Live in my father's house.
I ask only this… give me your hand as a pledge…

Joining hands with Pylades.

… that when you come to Greece again
and to the plains of horse-breeding Argos,
    you will heap up a burial mound
        and mark it in memory of me.
There my sister will bend over me in painful grief
    and weep and cut her flowing hair.

Tell the story of how I perished,
      at the hands of some Argive woman,
            flattened on an altar and offered up to death.
Never abandon my sister,
      no matter how desolate and despoiled
            you find my father's house.

Goodbye, sweet friend. There has been no one like you.
Companions, we came of age together, fellows in the hunt,
      inseparable even in the darkest of times.

As for me, I was deceived and set upon a false course
      by Phoibos, the "prophet,"
            who should have known better.
He plied his arts and drove me far from Greece,
      to the edges of the earth,
            compliant with his shocking prophecies.
To his words, I gave my total trust.
I've held nothing back,
      taking my mother's life
      and losing my own.

PYLADES

Friend so cursed, you shall have your tomb,
      and never will I betray your sister's bed.
In death you shall know from me
      a loyalty beyond any you've known in life.
But you are not yet in death,
      no matter how near the edge you stand.
And, until you are, the oracle is not confuted.
When the wheel of fate turns,
      there is no night so black
            that it cannot yield the dawn.

ORESTES

No more.
It is too late for Phoibos and his fancy words.
See, she comes for me.

Iphigenia enters, holding the letter in her hand.

IPHIGENIA
To the guards, who exit at her command.
Go and lend a hand inside to those preparing for the sacrifice.

To Orestes and Pylades.

Friends, here it is, my letter, many pages long.
But I am still not at ease with our plans;
    so hear me out.
A man with a noose around his neck
    is not the same without his noose.
He moves all too soon from trembling fear
    to boldness and complacency.

To Pylades.

In short, once you've quit this place,
    I fear how soon you will forget your mission to Argos
      and deliver this letter, instead,
        to the nearest wave.

ORESTES

What more do you want?
What would you need to put your fears to rest?

IPHIGENIA

An oath. Let him swear that he will take this letter to Argos
    and himself place it in the hands
      of him whom I shall name.

ORESTES

And what corresponding pledge
    are you prepared to offer him?

IPHIGENIA

Tell me what you have in mind.
What do you want done or not done?

ORESTES

I want him to leave this barbarous land alive.

IPHIGENIA

So do I. How else could he carry my letter?

ORESTES

But will the king consent to this?

IPHIGENIA

I will persuade the king and myself see your friend off to sea.

ORESTES
To Pylades.

Swear as she asks.

To Iphigenia.

Go ahead, formulate a fitting oath.

IPHIGENIA
To Pylades.
Swear that you will give this letter to my family.

PYLADES
I swear that I will give that letter to your family.

IPHIGENIA
And I, for my part, swear that I will see you safely
    through the clashing rocks.

ORESTES
To what god or goddess do you swear this?

IPHIGENIA
To Artemis… whose temple I attend to.

PYLADES
And I to Zeus… august lord of heaven.

IPHIGENIA
And if you violate your oath and do me wrong?

PYLADES
Then may I never know a homecoming.
And what of you, if you fail to rescue me?

IPHIGENIA
May I too never again set foot alive in Argos.

PYLADES
But there is something that our oaths have overlooked.

IPHIGENIA
It is not too late to include your new concern,
    if it is fair.

PYLADES

I ask one exception to what I've sworn.
If my ship is somehow wrecked at sea,
    and your letter with all else sinks beneath the waves,
      so that I've saved nothing but my very life,
    I ask my oath be null and void.

IPHIGENIA

Don't you know that, with a precaution or two,
    most disasters can be averted?
I will simply tell you now the contents
    of the letter you are to deliver.
Then the message will be safe in any event.
If my letter arrives intact,
    in silence it will tell my tale.
But if it sinks into the sea, you will save my words
    as you save your very life.

PYLADES

What you've said addresses my concerns as well as yours.
So tell me the core of your message
    and who it is in Argos to whom it must be brought.

IPHIGENIA

Go to Orestes, son of Agamemnon,
    and tell him this: "Your sister, the victim of Aulis,
      though dead to Argos, lives
        and sends you greetings, Iphigenia…

ORESTES

Where… where is she?
Has she risen from the dead?

IPHIGENIA

I am she… the one you see now with your own eyes.
But don't interrupt.
Now where was I?
"Dear brother, come and take me back to Argos,
      before I die.
Set me free from this barbarous land…
    and from the sacrificial rites
      in which it is my sacred office to preside
    over the slaughtering of strangers…"

ORESTES

Pylades, what can I say?
Are we dreaming this?

IPHIGENIA

"… or else I will be a curse upon your house, Orestes."

To Pylades.

Twice now you've heard that name,
     so don't forget it.

ORESTES

O gods.

IPHIGENIA

Are you praying?
Why should you?
These are my affairs.

ORESTES

Never mind. Continue.
I was thinking of something else.

Aside.

But I will come back soon enough to these marvels
     with a question of my own.

IPHIGENIA

Tell him: "It was Artemis who saved me,
     substituting the fawn my father sacrificed.
     For all my father knew,
         my breast received his sharpened blade.
     It was the goddess too who brought me here."
In sum this is what the letter says.

PYLADES

Woman, the promises you have made to me
     appear all the more gracious now, when I see
     how easy it will be to keep my pledge to you.
In fact, why should I wait another moment
     to make good my word to you?
Look.

To Orestes.

Orestes, I bring and place in your hand
    this letter from your sister.

Pylades gives the letter to Orestes.

ORESTES
Taking it.
And I receive it from your hand.
I let my fingers taste the pages.
They are sweet even before I read them.

To Iphigenia.

My beloved sister, hearing what I've heard,
    my wits leave me and my mind fades.
Even my arms doubt you. Come…

Approaching Iphigenia.

I want to hold you,
    so that my invalid soul might dance again.

Orestes embraces Iphigenia.

IPHIGENIA
Pulling away.
Stranger, you sin!
I am the virgin priestess of Artemis.
I belong to her.
Your arms… your touch… defile me!

ORESTES
Sister, child of Agamemnon, your father and mine,
    don't turn away now,
        not when you have me, your brother,
            the one you stopped hoping for.

IPHIGENIA
I have… you… my brother?
Won't you stop?
My brother is in Argos… in Nauplia.

ORESTES
Poor unfortunate, that is not where your brother is.

IPHIGENIA

Who bore you?
Was it the Spartan daughter of Tyndareos?

ORESTES

Yes. To the grandson of Pelops.
I am his seed.

IPHIGENIA

What are you saying?
Can you prove any of this?

ORESTES

All of it.
Ask me questions about our father's house.

IPHIGENIA

Just go on talking.
By listening I will learn what I need to know.

ORESTES

First... something Elektra told me.
You know about the feud that flamed
        between Atreus and Thyestes?

IPHIGENIA

Yes. I heard that it began over a golden lamb.

ORESTES

Do you remember weaving that tale upon your loom?

IPHIGENIA

O dearest one,
        you are very close to opening wide my heart.

ORESTES

This too on your loom: the sun turned back.

IPHIGENIA

It made a lovely tapestry.

ORESTES

For your wedding in Aulis,
        your mother drew the lustral water.

IPHIGENIA
Yes. I remember well.
There was no marriage bliss to cloud my memories.

ORESTES
And did you cut your hair and give it to your mother?

IPHIGENIA
I did… as a burial-token, in place of my body.

ORESTES
You asked for proof.
Here is what my own eyes have seen.
In my father's house, I saw the ancient spear of Pelops,
       the one he used to kill Oinomaos at Pisa
              and win the virgin Hippodameia.
This spear lay hidden deep within the palace, in your room.

*Giving way at last, Iphigenia leaps into Orestes' arms and
climbs him like a tree.*

IPHIGENIA
Dearest brother, it is you… no one else. It is you!
Sweet, sweet Orestes, I have you now,
       far from Argos and our home.
I hold you, my dearest treasure.

ORESTES
And I hold you, my sister whom the world thought dead.
These tears I weep… how welcome, like a summer rain.
They fill your eyes too… not tears at all.
Beneath the grief I've known so long,
       my heart begins to leap.

IPHIGENIA
You were still so tiny when I left you.
Such a little one you were when I left home,
       such a darling little one,
              cradled in your nurse's arms.
My dried-up soul drinks you like the sweetest wine.
O, I am so happy.
There are no words for this.
What can I say? What has come to us today…
       is too big for words.

ORESTES

Together... as we are now... never again apart,
    may we find blessing.

IPHIGENIA

Friends, women at my side,
    it feels strange to know such joy.
I am almost afraid to move,
    for fear it will flit away,
        like a phantom or a butterfly.
I call out to our homeland, dear Mykene.
I call out to our hearth, the work of mighty Kyklops.
I give thanks for my brother's life, for his nurture...
    thanks that my brother was reared so tall and shining,
        to be the light of our house.

ORESTES

Sister, we could not have been more blessed in our birth.
But then our fortunes fell from grace
    and blazed us a trail of grief.

IPHIGENIA

Cursed as I am, I know the truth of what you say.
How can I forget the gleaming blade
    my own wretched father lifted...

ORESTES

O god, I can see it, even though I wasn't there.

IPHIGENIA

... near my throat?
Unwed and innocent, I fell into their trap,
    lured by the promise of Akhilleus' bed.
It was a bed of graven stone instead,
    drenched with tears and lustral waters,
        yet thirsting for the first flow of my virgin blood.
Even now I hear the wailing,
    my wedding song gone wrong.

ORESTES

I too wail,
    when I think of what our cursed father dared to do.

IPHIGENIA

My lot assigned to me a father who unlearned his fatherhood.
It was a deadly curse, destined to repeat itself.

ORESTES

Yes, by you and me… on the goddess' grim altar there,
    where a sister came all to close to…

IPHIGENIA

A heinous crime!
Dearest brother, it was unthinkable what I dared to do.
Unthinkable!
How narrow was your escape from these hands, my hands,
    which would have thrown you into hell.
But now, where does all this lead?
What fate now directs my course?
What door can I still open for you in this city of death?
How can I send you back to Argos now,
    before the sharpened blade spills your blood?
God-forsaken soul of mine,
    it is yours to find a way.
By land and not by ship?
Your feet, no matter how swift,
    will only run you to your death.
Barbarous tribes haunt every path
    and the roads in this land go nowhere.
Then by ship?
The seascape, through the clashing rocks,
    is a long way from here.
Lost… lost… I see no way.
What mortal cunning, divine power, or simple miracle
    will now accomplish our escape?
Who will save the last remaining hope
    of the house of Atreus?

CHORAL LEADER

We have seen ourselves, not heard from others,
    this astonishing reunion.
Any telling of this tale must fall short of how it was.

PYLADES

Orestes, nothing is more natural
    than to embrace a long-lost love.

But it is also time to wipe our tears and look at where we are.
If we think our safety is something worth the effort,
    we should be looking for a way out of here.
Anyone with any sense knows that whatever chance we have
    won't wait around for us.
I think the joys of this moment can be stretched out later.

ORESTES

Well said and well taken.
But this time I feel that fate is working with us.
Even so, you are right.
The gods grow stronger on our behalf,
    when we lend a hand.

IPHIGENIA

But first one more question,
    no matter what the present urgency.
Please do not deny me this.
I must know my sister's lot in life.
Any news of her is precious to me.

ORESTES
Pointing to Pylades.

Married to this man,
    her life is blessed.

IPHIGENIA

And this man... where is he from? Who is his father?

ORESTES

His father's name is Strophios... of Phokis.

IPHIGENIA

I see... Atreus' daughter's son.
That makes us kin.

ORESTES

Pylades is your cousin and my one true friend.

IPHIGENIA

Was he not yet born when father tried to kill me?

ORESTES

Not yet. Strophios was childless for quite some time.

IPHIGENIA
To Pylades.
Welcome, my sister's husband.

ORESTES
To me he has been a savior, as well as kinsman.

IPHIGENIA
Orestes, tell me. How did you dare do it?
How could you kill our mother?

ORESTES
Please… shh… not that, Iphigenia…
    to avenge father… that is enough.

IPHIGENIA
But why would she have killed her husband?

ORESTES
Let mother rest.
It doesn't make a pretty story.

IPHIGENIA
All right… but tell me, does Argos now await you?

ORESTES
No. I am in exile. Menelaos rules.

IPHIGENIA
Our uncle… he affronts our stricken house?
He exiled you?

ORESTES
No, not he. The dreadful furies drove me out of Argos.

IPHIGENIA
Was that the seizure they described, along the shore?

ORESTES
Yes… not the first time I've provided
    such a wretched spectacle.

IPHIGENIA
I understand. They haunt you in mother's name.

ORESTES

They force a bloody bit between my teeth.

IPHIGENIA

But what brought you here?

ORESTES

The oracle.
Phoibos commanded me to come.

IPHIGENIA

To do what?
Are you free to tell me?

ORESTES

I will tell you all there is to tell.
First, the root of all my woes.
As soon as my hands avenged our mother's sin—
         the sin we left in silence—
      the furies harassed and hounded me into exile.
It was Loxias who guided my steps to Athens
      where I might appease those nameless fiends.
For in Athens there is a sacred court of law,
         established by Zeus
      to wash the blood-stained hands of Ares.
So I went there.

But so abhorrent to the gods was I
      that no one reached a hand to me.
I was without welcome.
Then some few pitied me
      and set for me a separate place.
I ate my meal under their roof,
      but not at their table.
They raised a wall of silence round me;
      so I ate and drank alone,
While they lifted their brimming cups
      and enjoyed themselves.
I had no harsh words for my hosts.
In silence I endured their slights
      as if I failed to notice them at all.
I moaned, instead, in grief over my mother,
      and what I had done to her.

Then I went to trial atop the mound of Ares.
Platformed on a slab of stone I stood and faced
    the eldest of the furies, stationed on a matching stone.
I answered the grim charges filed against me,
    indicting me with my mother's blood.
It was Phoibos who won my case for me.
His testimony saved me.
Pallas gave the tally of the votes, a verdict split in two,
    good enough for me to win the day
        and leave unscathed.
Those furies who consented to the court's decree
    set up a sacred residence nearby,
        while the rest resumed their tireless tormenting of me,
            in complete contempt of law.

And so it went until I came again to Apollo's holy ground.
I threw myself down before his sanctuary.
Flattened in the dust and fasting from all food,
    I vowed to cut all ties with life
        and expire on Phoibos' very steps
    unless he would undo what he had done to me
        and save me from his own destroying hand.

Then he spoke down to me,
    Phoibos from his golden tripod.
Here, to this place, he missioned me
    to seize the graven sky-dropped goddess
        and establish it on Attic soil.

Sister, be my accomplice now in winning that deliverance
    the god defined for me.
If we can but seize the holy likeness from the shrine,
    my madness will be gone… like that!
And I will speed you home again, to Mykene,
    in our swift-oared ship.
Dear sister, beloved sister, save me.
Save the house of our fathers.
I am lost and the line of Pelops blotted out,
    unless we get that little goddess dropped from heaven.

CHORAL LEADER

Some strange demonic wrath
    storms against the seed of Tantalos
        and drives them through a gauntlet of pain.

IPHIGENIA

How I longed, Orestes, before you came,
    to stand again on Argive soil,
        and to look upon you, my long-lost brother.
My will is to echo yours, to lift from you your affliction
    and to heal a stricken house.
I will tame the wildness I reared within me
    toward a father who would murder me.
I will do my part to put his house in order.
And so I will be spared your polluting sacrifice
    and rescue my own family.

But how do I elude a watchful goddess?
And the king is not to be discounted.
I fear what he will do when he finds an empty pedestal.
How will I then sidestep death? What could be my defense?
Yet the risk would be sweet and so well-taken,
        if only, in one availing act,
    you could sweep up me and the stolen image
        into your well-trimmed ship.

Either I escape or die, I know that much.
But I also know that, with or without me, you may succeed
    and win a safe journey home.
Not one inch will I shy back from saving you,
    even if I must pay for it with my life.
When a man dies, his house is forever empty.
But when a woman dies, she is forgotten.

ORESTES

Already I have murdered my mother.
I am not about to murder you.
Mother's blood is enough to stain my hands.
From now on I want to live at one with you,
    or else die as one with you.
If there is a way out of here, a way home, I lead you down it.
If there is not, we shall both remain and face a common death.
Listen to what I am thinking.
Is it likely that Loxias would have bidden me
    to bring the holy image to the city of Athena,
        or even arranged for me to see your face again,
            if the whole scheme
    were sheer effrontery to Artemis?
No, I think there is a conspiring here in our favor,
    and so I am hopeful, Sister, for our homecoming.

IPHIGENIA
But how are we going to carry off the statue
    and both escape?
This is where our homecoming runs aground.
I think what we need is a plan.

ORESTES
Couldn't we just kill the king?

IPHIGENIA
You propose something dreadful:
    for a guest to slay a host.

ORESTES
Dreadful or not, it must be dared
    if you and I are going to escape.

IPHIGENIA
I admire your zeal, brother. But that I couldn't do.

ORESTES
What if you hid me away deep within the temple?

IPHIGENIA
So that we might escape later, cloaked in the darkness?

ORESTES
Of course.
Daylight is fine, when you've nothing to hide.
But night suits thieves best.

IPHIGENIA
The temple has many guards.
We can't just walk past them.

ORESTES
Then we're ruined.
I see no escape, do you?

IPHIGENIA
I think I have a new trick we haven't thought to try.

ORESTES
What kind of trick? Tell me, so I may know.

IPHIGENIA
We shall turn your famed affliction to our own advantage…
with a little guile.

ORESTES
Women hatch schemes like they do children,
with very little prompting.

IPHIGENIA
I will say you are a matricide from Argos.

ORESTES
Use my wretchedness for what it is worth to us.

IPHIGENIA
I will say you are unfit for sacrifice.

ORESTES
To what end? I think I may know.

IPHIGENIA
Unclean. You are unclean.
I give only pure victims up to slaughter.

ORESTES
What does any of this have to do with stealing the statue?

IPHIGENIA
I will propose to cleanse you at sea,
with waters drawn from pure sea-springs.

ORESTES
But I sailed here for the statue, and it's still in the temple.

IPHIGENIA
Then it too must be cleansed. I will say you touched it.

ORESTES
Where will this take place?
In the breakers off the nearby cape?

IPHIGENIA
Where your ship lies moored, tied fast with lines of hemp.

ORESTES
Will you or someone else carry the statue?

IPHIGENIA
I will. I alone may touch it sinlessly.

ORESTES
What of Pylades? What part does he play in all of this?

IPHIGENIA
I will say his hands bear the same polluting stain as yours.

ORESTES
And the king?
Will he know what you plan to do,
    or will you keep it from him?

IPHIGENIA
I see no way to keep him in the dark.
I will sway him to the sense of what I do.

ORESTES
Well, my ship lies ready,
    its oars poised to plow the seas.

IPHIGENIA
That part and whatever follows I leave to you.

ORESTES
One more thing we will need,
    the silence of these girls who wait on you.
Find whatever words will win or beg them to our side.
Ply the special power you women have
    for wringing pity from a rock,
        much less from other women.
Then we'll hope the rest goes well for us.

IPHIGENIA
Turning to the Chorus.
Dearest women, I look at you and see
    that everything depends on you.
Whether I succeed or fail,
    whether I win or lose my dear homeland,
        all this is in your hands.

Let me begin my appeal to you here,
    on our most common ground.
We are all women.
The good will we bear each other
    runs as deeply in us as our blood.
We are the most watchful guardians of our common trust.
Keep silence and help secure our flight.
A well-kept tongue is cause for no slight praise.
You see the three of us, yoked in love
    and set upon a daring venture.
Either we shall reach the home of our fathers
    or we shall die in the attempt.

And if I escape,
    I will return and see to your escape as well.
My good fortune shall be a cup
    from which we all shall drink our fill.
Take my hand and swear... you... and you...

> *Iphigenia passes among the women, grasping their hands,
> touching their faces and falling to her knees, a suppliant.*

I beg you... by your dear cheek... by your knees...
    by all those you love and treasure at home.
What do you say?
Who is with me?
Who is unwilling?
Say something!
Without you, without some approving word from you,
    my hapless brother and I are as good as dead.

CHORAL LEADER

Take cheer, dear lady, and see to your escape.
Our lips will say no more than stones would
    about your plans.
Great Zeus above will witness to this pledge of ours.

IPHIGENIA

May the gods reward you for these words...
    with great happiness.
Good-bye, my friends.

> *Iphigenia embraces the Chorus one at a time.*

Turning to Orestes and Pylades.

The next step is yours.
Go inside the temple.
The king will be along any moment now.
He will want to know if the strangers' sacrifice
    has been accomplished.

*Orestes and Pylades enter the temple, and Iphigenia lifts her
hands in prayer.*

O goddess,
    once atop the cliffs of Aulis you saved me
        from my father's dread murderous hand.
Save me again now… and those I love.
Otherwise you will carry the burden of blame,
    if never again men heed the words of Loxias.
Be gracious and abandon this barbarous land for Athens.
This country far from suits you,
    while in Athens a city blessed by gods awaits you.

CHORUS

Halcyon,
Denizen of sea-carved cliffs,
Bird of a darkest song.
Keen hearts rend at your mourning
Laments for a mate long lost.
Without the grace of winged flight,
A grave heart within me
Echoes the saddest of your songs.
For the noisy fellowship of the market,
For blessed Artemis worshipped with joy
By the Kynthian hill,
I cry out with longing.
As a bird craves the open sky,
I crave the once familiar palm and laurel,
The sacred silvered olive boughs,
Kind to Leto in her labor,
The glistening pool slowly spun in circles
By a swan singing service
To the Muses.

When my city fell,
My tears ran like angry rivers
Until my face was rutted with my pain.
Dragged through the ruins of all I loved,
I was cast aboard the conqueror's ship,
A prize stowed among the oars and spears.
Sold for someone's price, they shipped me here
To do barbarous service in a barbarous land.
My office is to wait upon the child of Agamemnon
And hers to offer sacrifice not of sheep but men
To deer-slaying Artemis on an altar soaked with death.
How I envy those whose lives of pain are seamless,
Innocent of joy.
They have formed the habits that I need.
And their doom may lift like a passing storm.
But when ruin visits the unexpecting house,
Its companion is despair.

You, lady, are homeward bound,
Aboard a gallant Argive ship
Fitted with fifty oaken oars,
Tilling the untamed seas with rhythmic force,
Quickened and cadenced by the shrill piping
Of a reed and waxen flute,
Sweet to the ears of mountain-leaping Pan.
Phoibos, prolific in his prophecies,
Plucks his seven-stringed lyre and
Lifts a joyous song to hearten and direct
Your journey home to Argos' fertile plains.
Lifted through the churning sea
By straining arms on salt-soaked oars,
You will feel the spray across your face
And watch the raving winds blast the open sail.
But the prow that points and cuts your course
Turns from me
Forsaken.

How I would soar to the luminous course
Where the sun's flaming steeds
Lift the day from night.
I would not rest from winged flight
Until I hovered over the walls and the roofs
That once sheltered my youth.

There I would join the festive company,
As once, a blushing girl beside the splendid bride,
I danced amidst a whirling maze of friends,
And watched my mother smiling wistfully.
Wakened to the rivalry of youth and beauty,
I strew my charms for all to wonder at,
Resplendent robes and a child's soft hair
That blew across my face and glistened
Like a spray of gold.

Thoas enters, attended.

THOAS
Where is the keeper of the temple, the Greek woman?
Has she seen to the strangers' sacrifice?
Are they ablaze yet in the sanctuary?

CHORAL LEADER
King, she is here to tell you clearly all that needs telling.

Iphigenia enters, carrying in her arms the image of Artemis.

THOAS
What is this? Child of Agamemnon,
    why do you carry in your arms the holy image?
Why have you removed it from its sacred pedestal?

IPHIGENIA
King, stay where you are in the portico.
Don't move.

THOAS
Iphigenia, what happened in there?

IPHIGENIA
Spitting, to avert an evil omen.
Silence!
This is prescribed.

Chanting.

O awesome spirit…

THOAS
Wait! Why this strange invocation?
Explain yourself.

IPHIGENIA
Defilement, King. Unclean. Unclean.
The victims you snared for me are unfit.

THOAS
Is this some feeling that you have?
Or do you have some proof?

IPHIGENIA
On her holy pedestal
    the goddess turned and faced the other way.

THOAS
On her own?
Or did the earth quake and rattle her around?

IPHIGENIA
On her own.
She also shut her eyes.

THOAS
And the reason, you say,
    is some pollution from the strangers?

IPHIGENIA
Yes, nothing else.
They are guilty of a heinous crime.

THOAS
Did they murder one of my people on the beach?

IPHIGENIA
They came with murder on their hands,
    murder in their own home.

THOAS
Now you've given me an appetite
    to know these things.
Tell me. Who was their victim?

IPHIGENIA
It was their mother they cut down.
Like two woodsmen,
    they shared the bloody labor.

THOAS

Apollo!
No barbarian would be as bold as that.

IPHIGENIA

They've been hounded out
    of every city and cave in Hellas.

THOAS

Then they are the reason
    why you carry the goddess outside here?

IPHIGENIA

Yes, into the pure and hallowed air,
    for its chastening.

THOAS

How did you learn the source of their defilement?

IPHIGENIA

When the goddess turned her back on them,
    I began to ask them questions.

THOAS

Well done.
They make smart girls in Greece.

IPHIGENIA

Clever boys as well.
These Greeks have already cast sweet bait before me
    in hopes of hooking my heart.

THOAS

What do they use to lure you with?
Bits of news from Argos?

IPHIGENIA

They say my only brother, Orestes, is alive and well.

THOAS

Hoping you will spare them out of gladness at their news?

IPHIGENIA

They say my father lives and prospers.

THOAS
Of course you turned your back on them,
    in allegiance to the goddess.

IPHIGENIA
Of course I did. Greece ruined me and I hate her for it.

THOAS
Then tell me, what do we do with these strangers?

IPHIGENIA
We must do what is prescribed by sacred ordinance.

THOAS
Then we just put to use your lustral waters and your knife,
    don't we?

IPHIGENIA
No, we don't.
I must purify them first with cleansing ablutions.

THOAS
Does that mean spring water or salt water?

IPHIGENIA
It is the sea that washes off the sins of men.

THOAS
All the more suitable they will be for slaughter.

IPHIGENIA
And all the more suitable for my purposes.

THOAS
Well, the waves wash up very near the shrine, yes?

IPHIGENIA
Yes. But we require seclusion;
    for there is more that needs to be done.

THOAS
You see to it.
I am not one to pry into matters not intended for my eyes.

IPHIGENIA
The goddess must, too, be cleansed.

THOAS
If the mother-slayers sullied her.

IPHIGENIA
If they had not, I never
    would have moved the goddess from her pedestal.

THOAS
I commend your piety and your care.

IPHIGENIA
There are things I need done.

THOAS
You need only tell me what they are.

IPHIGENIA
The strangers must be bound.

THOAS
Where could they flee?

IPHIGENIA
No matter. They are Greeks, and Greeks cannot be trusted.

THOAS
To his Attendants.
Men, go and bind the strangers.

IPHIGENIA
And I want them brought here.

THOAS
As you say.

IPHIGENIA
With their heads covered.

THOAS
I see… in case they might pollute the light of day.

Several Attendants go off into the temple.

IPHIGENIA
I will need some of your henchmen with me.

THOAS
Indicating several of his Attendants.
These will go with you.

IPHIGENIA
And you must send word throughout the city…

THOAS
Word of what?

IPHIGENIA
That everyone must stay indoors.

THOAS
Lest anyone meet eyes with the murderers…

IPHIGENIA
And contract their dread stain.

THOAS
Dispatching one of his Attendants.
Go and do as the priestess has said.

IPHIGENIA
I am most concerned for those I love.

THOAS
Including me.

IPHIGENIA
No one must be near enough to see them.

THOAS
You overlook nothing in your care for me and my city.

IPHIGENIA
I hope you are right.

THOAS
I know I am right in saying
    that the whole city wonders at you.

IPHIGENIA
King, it is for you to remain here before her shrine.

THOAS
Doing what?

IPHIGENIA
Cleansing it with fire.

THOAS
For your return, so that you may find it pure.

IPHIGENIA
But before that…
    when the strangers come out here…

THOAS
What do I do then?

IPHIGENIA
Pull your cloak over your eyes.

THOAS
Against their contagion?

IPHIGENIA
And if I seem to be away too long…

THOAS
How long would be too long?

IPHIGENIA
Let's not wonder about that.

THOAS
All in good time, you will do your sacred duty.

IPHIGENIA
Let us pray for this ritual,
    that it may go as planned.

THOAS
Let us pray.

*The temple doors open. Several Guards and Attendants lead
out Orestes and Pylades, whose hands are bound and heads
covered. Thoas throws his cloak over his head as instructed.*

IPHIGENIA

See, the strangers come from the shrine.
With them are carried my sacred robes
    and the two newborn lambs.
Blood for blood, untainted for tainted,
    the one will wash away the other's stain.

To the Attendants.

Good, you have brought the burning lamps
      and all else I ordered
    for the cleansing of the strangers and the goddess.

*Iphigenia raises high the image of the goddess and the procession
forms behind her.*

All people of this city, hear me.
Stand back and avoid defilement.
All ye servants of the sanctuary,
    whose hands are pure for the service of Artemis;
All ye espoused ones, come to make your wedding vows;
All ye mothers heavy with child,
Away! Flee, lest the pollution spread to you.

O mistress, virgin daughter of Zeus and Leto,
    if I cleanse these victims of all stain
      and make of them a fitting sacrifice,
    once more your home shall be free of taint
      and we shall be glad.
Of the rest I say nothing.
In silence I commend my heart's desire
    to you, goddess and your fellow-gods,
    who read our hearts and know all we fail to say.

CHORUS

On Delos once,
Sheltered by gracious boughs bright with fruit,
Leto bore a splendid son, a god with golden hair,
Whose fingers make the lyre sing;
A daughter too, goddess of the bow and quiver,
Whose arrows find their mark.

Then Leto left the site of their famed birth,
And from a ridge girt by glistening sea
Brought her son to towering Parnassos,
Mount of thunderous torrents,
Mount of bakkhant revels.
There the giant serpent,
Livid-eyed and scaly-backed,
Lay coiled among the shading laurel.
Dread and massive beyond report,
The monstrous Python kept grim guard
Over the ancient chthonic oracle.

But you, Phoibos, still a tiny babe,
A lively armful for your dearest mother,
You, Phoibos, slew the great serpent
And seized the sacred oracle.
Seated now upon your golden tripod,
Your throne immune from error,
Beside the pure Kastalian springs,
You make your home at the center of the world,
And from your secret sanctuary,
You send upon us mortals
The sweet dew of your divine decrees.
Now when Apollo drove out Themis, daughter of Earth,
From the seat of holy oracles,
Then Earth spawned dreams instead.
These fluctuating phantoms, born in dead of night,
Visit cities as they sleep
And fashion vague accounts of what once was
And of what is yet to be.
This was Earth's revenge,
For what her sister suffered.
Soon enough her dreams would steal
Apollo's pride and place.
But lord Apollo fell into a fitful rage at this,
And up the steep Olympian slopes
Ran with winged feet
To the very throne of Zeus,
And clung there with an infant's needy grip,
Pleading for an end to Earth's avenging dreams.
Then Zeus smiled on his beloved son,
Amused at his frenzy and his haste
In claiming the golden spoils of piety.
Zeus nodded his assent,
And silenced night's revealing voices.

He banished any truth from visions dreamed in sleep,
And restored to his son every honor lost.
Zeus gave his word to ground the trust
Borne by all who throng the seat of truth
For words of purest light.

The Messenger enters.

MESSENGER

Guards… attendants!
Where is King Thoas? Where can I find the king?
Throw open the temple doors and summon out here
    the ruler of this land.

CHORAL LEADER

What's wrong?
If you can tell us, what is it?

MESSENGER

Gone! The two strangers are gone.
The child of Agamemnon schemed their escape.
They've run off and taken the holy goddess with them.
Stashed her in the hold of their ship,
    bound for Greece.

CHORAL LEADER

I don't believe my ears!
But you want to see the king. He isn't here.
He left the temple in a hurry, not long ago.

MESSENGER

He must be told what's happened. Where did he go?

CHORAL LEADER

How would we know?
Now run off and look for him.
And when you find him, tell him your news.

MESSENGER

Wait.
Where there is one contriving woman,
    there may be many more.
You women breed among yourselves.
All of you have had a share in this.

CHORUS

Have you lost your wits?
What does the strangers' escape have to do with us?
Now, get lost.
You would do well to run your fastest to the palace gates.

MESSENGER

Not so fast. I'm not leaving until I get an answer
    to my question… from behind those doors.
Is the king in there or not?
Unbolt the doors!

Pounding on the doors.

Open up in there!
Tell your king that someone waits out here for him
    with the worst of news.

The temple doors swing open and Thoas enters.

THOAS

Who are you, making such an uproar
    on the goddess' very threshold?
Why were you pounding at the doors
    and throwing your noisy voice inside?

MESSENGER

These women lied to me.
They told me you had left,
    even though you were still inside.
They were trying to get rid of me.

THOAS

But why?
What would they hope to gain from doing that?

MESSENGER

I will get to them later.
But listen now to what is more urgent.
The girl… the one who served here at the altar…
    Iphigenia.
She's run away with the strangers.
And they've taken the holy image of the goddess.
That cleansing business was a trick.

THOAS

What are you saying?
What possessed her to do that?
I don't understand.

MESSENGER

Well, this will make it worse;
    but she did it to save Orestes.

THOAS

Orestes, the son of Klytemnestra?

MESSENGER

He was the one prepared for sacrifice.

THOAS

A miracle. I know no other name for it.

MESSENGER

Never mind its name.
Listen to me.
Once you've heard and pondered all I have to tell,
    we'll need a plan from you,
        some strategy for our pursuit of them.

THOAS

You're making sense. Go on.
If they are hoping to outrun my spear,
    they have a long road ahead of them.

MESSENGER

As soon as we had come to the shore,
        near where Orestes' ship lay in secret mooring,
    the child of Agamemnon shouted to us,
        the men you sent along to guard the strangers.
    and waved us back with her arms.
"Back... stand back," she ordered us, "all of you stand off."
Then she lit the sacrificial flame and began the cleansing rites
    for which we'd come.
She took in her hands the rope that held the two men bound
    and walked off with them alone,
        they in front and she behind them.
I, for one, began to grow suspicious, king,
    but your servants found everything in order.

Time was passing and the priestess saw the need to assure us
    that something was, in fact, taking place.
So she let out a piercing cry and began to chant
    some wild mystical mutterings,
        suited, we supposed, for washing blood.
But then a long time passed... too long.
We waited and we thought at last
    that the strangers may have gotten loose,
    killed the priestess, fled, and sailed away.
But still we sat in silence,
    fearing to see what was forbidden to our eyes.

At last we set aside all that we'd been told
    and agreed to go and find them.
Soon we spied a Greek galley, fitted out with fifty oars,
    like a hawk with fifty wings,
        each oar held poised above the pitching sea
            by a Greek seaman ready at his bench.
Then we saw the two strangers,
    standing free near the galley's stern.
With long poles several seamen steadied the ship's prow,
    while others hoisted anchor, pulled up cables,
    and dropped a ladder for the strangers
        into the churning sea.
We were undaunted when we saw their wiles at work.
We fell on them at once and seized the girl.
We grabbed the mooring cables.
We reached through the stern ports
    and tried to drag out the rudder-oars.
We mixed shouts with our struggles:
"Tell us what right you think you have
    to steal from this land,
    running off with our priestess and our sacred image?
Who do you think you are to kidnap this girl?"
This was his reply:
"I am that girl's brother.
I am Orestes, son of Agamemnon.
I am taking home the sister that I lost."1
But his words weakened not at all the grip we had on the girl,
    nor our resolve to drag her back to you.
You see from my face the battering that we took
    to do just that.
Neither they nor we had weapons at our sides;
    and so it was a battle of fists and feet.

The two strangers flew at us with such frenzied force,
    pounding and kicking us front and back
        no matter where we turned,
    that it was as brief as it was brutal
        before our legs gave way.
Bruised and bloodied, we made a sorry sight
    as we scrambled up the nearest crag,
        with heads aching and eyes swelling closed.
Yet once we reached a vantage point
        above them on the rocks,
    we took up the war again
        and sent down a hail of stones on them.
But soon they put an end to this, with a line of archers
    standing on the galley's stern.
Their whizzing arrows soon sent us on our way.

Just then a crashing wave broke against the Greek ship's hull
    and lifted it towards shore.
Iphigenia shuddered at the swirling foam
    as Orestes lifted her from the threatening sea
        and placed her on his left shoulder.
Then he strode through the surf,
        mounted the swaying sea-ladder,
    and set down on the ship's deck his sister and
        the heaven-fallen image of the child of Zeus.
From mid-ships came a sudden cry:
"Greeks, seamen, grip your oars and plow white the sea.
We have what we came for.
We have done what we crossed the hostile sea
    and risked the clashing rocks to do."
From the belly of the ship thundered their response,
    one rending shout of triumph,
    as they shouldered their oars
        against the unwelcoming sea.
While still within the bay, their way was easy,
    and they skimmed over the gentle breakers.
But when they cleared the bay's mouth and struck
    the untamed sea, the struggle began.
A wild blast of wind spun the ship around
    and hurled it back against its course.
But the Greeks met the challenge
    and fought the sea straight on.
All the same the ship was being driven back to land
        by a contrary sea.

Then the daughter of Agamemnon rose
    and stood upon the deck.
She lifted her arms in prayer:
"O child of Leto, I am your priestess. Save me.
From this land of barbarians bring me home to Greece.
Forgive my theft.
Goddess, you know how you love your brother.
See how I too love my brother and my family."
In concert with the girl's prayers,
    the seamen hymned their own plea,
        while their bare shoulders flexed
        and their ready hands plied the oars,
    keeping the coxswain's time.

Each moment now brought them closer to the rocks.
One of us splashed into the sea and waded towards the ship
    while others made nooses out of rope
        to snare the ship and drag it to the rocks.
I, for my part, came back here at once to you, my king,
    to let you know what's happening there.

Now come at once. Bring ropes and nooses!
For unless the sea calms,
    the strangers' hope of deliverance is a stale dream.
Dread Poseidon, lord of seas, is still watchful over Troy
    and set against the house of Pelops.
And now he prepares to hand over to you and to your people
    the son of Agamemnon, and the daughter,
        who forgot the death she nearly died on Aulis
        and betrayed the one who saved her.

CHORAL LEADER

Ill-starred Iphigenia, you and our brother
    will soon slip back in our master's hands,
        this time to die.

THOAS

Listen to me... everyone!
I want every man in this barbarian land
    to bridle and mount his horse.
Now! Gallop to the shore
    and intercept the Greek ship as it runs aground.
Let the goddess lead you in the hunt
    as you ferret out your wretched prey.

Now, sailors,
>drag your swift-oared ships down into the waves.
We shall run them down by land and sea,
>and fling their bodies from the cliffs
>>or spit them on our spears alive.
As for you women who had your share in all of this,
>>your punishment will have to wait
>until I have a moment free.
For now my hands are full,
>and I haven't time to waste on you.

ATHENA
Appearing overhead.

King Thoas, just where do you think you're off to?
What sort of hunt is this?
Listen to what I, Athena, tell you.
Cease this mad pursuit of yours.
Call in your troops.
It was decreed by Loxias himself
>that Orestes should come here
>>to escape the furies' rage
>and to take his sister home to Argos.
When he removes the sacred image to my land
>>and wins release from his present agony,
>he does Apollo's bidding.
This is what I say to you:
This design you have—
>to seize Orestes in the surf
>>and relieve him of his life—
>it shall not be.
For even now on my behalf,
>>Poseidon lulls the sea to sleep
>to make light work for Greek oars.

And now, Orestes, consider my command to you.
For even from afar you hear the voice of Artemis.
Go now, with your sister and the graven image.
Go to Athens, the city crafted by the gods.
From there seek out a sacred place, a place we call Halas,
>on the Attic border, near the Karustian hills.
There construct a temple to house the holy image
>and bestow on it a name reminiscent of this place
>>and of the agony that was yours
>as you moaned your way through Greece,
>a wretched vagrant stunned by the furies' rage.

In time to come that temple will resound
    with hymns to Taurian Artemis.
And this will be the law you will establish there,
      at the yearly festival:
    in completion of the sacrifice left unfinished here,
    the priest shall press his blade
      against a young man's neck,
      until his bright blood flows
in ritual praise of Artemis and to keep intact her pride.

You, Iphigenia, shall preside over the temple of the goddess
      on the terraces of Brauron,
    and keep her holy keys again.
There you shall die and be laid to rest.
And as tokens on your honor,
    women shall drape your tomb with lovely gowns,
      woven of the finest threads,
    and left behind by women in their beds,
      who gave their lives in giving life,
    exhausted in their labor.
Now you, Thoas, I charge
    to send these Greek women home,
      where their righteous hearts deserve to be.

Orestes, already I saved you once on the Areopagos,
    tipping the balanced scales to your side.
And what I did then shall now be law.
When the jury's votes are tied,
      the verdict shall be innocence,
    as it was for you.
Now, I saved you a second time.
Go, son of Agamemnon,
    take your sister out of this land.

One last time I tell you, Thoas,
    put out your rage now,
      as you would an unwelcome fire.

THOAS

Lady Athena,
    anyone who hears the words from the gods above
      and heedless goes his own way,
    lets his mind run loose like a wild horse.
I bear no malice towards Orestes and his sister.

Let them take the holy image and go.
My fire is out.
What sort of prize could I win,
    wrestling with the gods who have all the power?
Let the two of them take the graven goddess
    to your land and to the pedestal prepared for it.
In all of this, they have my blessing.

As for these Greek women,
    I send them home to happiness.
That was what you said. That is what I do.
There shall be no attack on the strangers.
I shall stay every spear
    and see our ships dragged back on land.
All this in keeping with your will, goddess.

ATHENA

Well done, Thoas. You are no fool.
You, no less, than the god themselves,
    must bend to fate or break.
Winds, rise from sleep,
        fill the sails of the son of Agamemnon,
    and lift him to Athens in the palm of your hand.
In this journey—to watch over the image of my sister—
    I too will companion him.

CHORUS

Go your way with all good fortune.
You are blessed to have your fates reversed,
    and to win deliverance from exile and from death.
O splendid goddess, Pallas Athena,
        wonder to men and gods alike,
    what you say is what we do.
Our hearts aspire to no joy nor hope
    beyond the words you give us.

B A K K H A I

PREFACE

◇◇◇◇◇

This translation of the *Bakkhai* was commissioned by the Shared Experience Theatre Company in London; and, shortly afterwards, I directed its American premier at the Center for the Performing Arts in Kansas City, Missouri. From the beginning, then, it was a translation written specifically for the theater.

As I see it, the first rule in translating a play is that the result should be a play, not a poem fit only for recitation, still less a treatise fit only for study. Accordingly, the definitive aim of this translation has been to provide a playable script, which not only lends itself to but cries out for production, not as a museum piece but as viable contemporary drama. Anything less, as an aim, would be a betrayal of the author, who spent his life not in libraries nor in classrooms but in the theater.

Translating a play into a play, in this case an ancient play into a modern play, requires that the translator address not only two distinct spoken languages—here Attic Greek and modern English—but two distinct theatrical languages, as well. In short, the conventions of Attic tragedy are, in some respects, as foreign to contemporary theater as is the language in which the tragedies were written. Both require translation. What I have in mind are such conventions as the wearing of masks, the use of only three actors to play all speaking roles, the usual omnipresence and centrality of the Chorus, the restrictions to a single set, and so on. The translation of a play written for these conventions into a play that will stand on its own and be compelling in a theater accustomed to quite different conventions is primarily the task of the director together with his or her artistic and technical team. That task, however, inevitably begins with the translator; for every translation of a play, like every original play itself, must be staged in the mind before it can be written on the page. It has its first production in the imagination of its author. For example, questions of tone and pacing are, like a cud, chewed constantly by any director, but not until they have left the mouth of the translator. And, in the case of ancient tragedies, there is the additionally compromising fact that the original scripts were never fully written down; for they contained no stage directions whatsoever. The implications of this fact may appear minor only until, text in hand, one nears the stage.

For my part, as a translator, I have kept my stage directions to a minimum, indicating with them the direction which a production of the *Bakkhai* might, but need not, take. I have not, for example, decided which choral lines are to be assigned to the Chorus as a whole and which are to be assigned individually to the choral leader or to other members of the Chorus. I have, however, provided suggestions for how the Chorus might be moved on and off stage in the course of the play. Both modern audiences and modern dancers, for different reasons, often find the continuous presence of the Chorus on stage to be problematic, if not intolerable. Further, since neither the original music nor the original choreography of the choral odes is known to us and must be composed afresh on our terms, I have appended to this translation radically abridged choral texts, suitable, I hope, to the needs of contemporary composers and choreographers. The fact is that the original choral odes are, for our purposes, mostly too long and unwieldy. If set to music, they constitute oratorios in themselves, all but dwarfing the drama of which they are only an ingredient. The frequent and unfortunate consequence of their disproportionate size and scope is their omission, which does violence to any Greek tragedy, more to some than to others. As for the *Bakkhai*, without its Chorus it is in no better a state than is Pentheus, carried in from Kithairon. Unlike Pentheus, however, the Chorus can and must be reinstated.

Finally, in this translation I have followed, all but unswervingly, E.R. Dodds's critical edition of the Greek text, reconstructing as any translator must, from available fragments and secondary sources, both the gaping lacuna beginning with line 1330 and other lesser lacunae. In several instances [286–297, 1330–1339, 1354–1360, 1371–1372], for a complex of reasons, textual and dramatic, I have taken the liberty of omitting lines. Since the sum of these sections comprise less than two percent of the whole, the possible caprice in these omissions would seem venial. Throughout this translation, I have endeavored to be no less zealous on Euripides' behalf than was Dionysos on his own. If, in any part due to this translation, theaters become "vibrant with his voice," that will be enough to excuse the inevitable measure by which this translation has fallen short of the original.

DRAMATIS PERSONAE
◇◇◇◇◇◇◇◇◇◇◇

In Order of Appearance

Dionysos
Son of Semele, Child of Zeus

Chorus
Women of Thebes, Bakkhants

Teiresias
Blind Seer of Thebes

Kadmos
Father of Semele and Agave,
Grandfather of Pentheus

Pentheus
King of Thebes,
First-cousin of Dionysos

Guard

1st Messenger

2nd Messenger

Agave
Mother of Pentheus,
Sister of Semele

◇◇◇◇◇◇◇◇

BAKKHAI

The scene is Thebes, early in the reign of Pentheus, the grandson of Kadmos. Before the gates of the royal palace there is a monument marking the spot of Semele's incineration.

Enter Dionysos.

DIONYSOS
Land of Thebes, I am back,
   Dionysos, the boy-child of Zeus.
My mother was Semele, daughter of Kadmos.
She was a mere girl, when from her womb
   I was blasted into birth by a bolt of blazing fire.
God though I am, I have taken mortal form
    to stand here beside the River Dirke
    and the waters of Ismenos.
There, I see a stone raised in memory of my mother,
   consumed by a clap of jagged fire.
And there, what remains of my mother's house,
    rubble wrapped in sinuous smoke,
    smoldering with a divine fire that won't go out,
    a token to Hera's unwearying rage against my mother.
But as for Kadmos, I praise him for his piety
    in making this place a sacred precinct,
    a shrine to his daughter,
    holy ground.
The vines you see everywhere, encircling this spot,
    encrusted with grapes…
    this crown is my handiwork.
I have taken leave of Lydia and Phrygia,
    lands lined with glinting gold.
I have crossed the sun-scorched steppes of Persia,
    surveyed the battlements of Baktria,
    survived the grim nowhere of the Medes,
    witnessed Arabian grandeur.
I have traced every curve in the salt-soaked Asian coast,
    where Greeks and barbarians swarm
    and settle in cities topped with splendid towers,
    mingling their lives and their lineages.
On my way, before I reached Greek soil,
    I planted my rituals as I went,
    set my dreams in motion,
    so that I might stand revealed to mortals
    as what I truly am—a god.

Now, in Greece,
   I make Thebes the first city vibrant with my voice.
I wrap its women in fawn-skins.
I arm them with my thyrsos, my wand tangled with ivy.
Years ago, my mother's sisters outdid themselves in shame.
They denied that Dionysos was the seed of Zeus.
This, they said, was a tale sown by Kadmos and told by Semele
   to conceal the truth:
      that she had lost her innocence to a quite ordinary man,
      and then had hoped to deify a common mistake made in bed.
For this lie—her false claim to nuptials with Zeus—
   they said that he himself slew her in a fit of rage and pride.
It is for this I have stung them with my frenzy,
   driven them from their homes and their wits.
They are quite mad now,
making new homes among the mountains.
In fact, I have driven from their homes
   the female half of the race of Kadmos,
      every housewife in Thebes, possessed them,
      made them dress for my sacred rites.
The wives of Thebes
   have joined company with the daughters of Kadmos.
Together they assemble among the rocks,
   under a pallid silver-green roof of towering pines.
As for this city, it is ignorant of my mysteries.
Thebes must learn of me and of my rites,
   whether it wishes to or not.
Thebes must watch me vindicate my mother's honor
   and reveal myself to mortals
   as the true god Semele bore to Zeus.
In Thebes, Kadmos is no longer king.
He has given the prize and the power of his crown
   to Pentheus, his grandson.
Even now this new king wages war, war against a god,
   against me!
He pours libations with one hand,
   and shoves me away with the other.
When he recites his prayers,
   my name never comes up.
Therefore, I will show him, I will show every man in Thebes,
   that I was born a god.
Later, once my worship is well-established here,
   I will take to the road again, visit some other land,
   reveal myself.

But here, now, if this city of Thebes, in a fool's fit,
    sends its troops after my Bakkhai,
    to drive them from the mountains,
    I will take to the field with them,
    lead them into the thick of battle.
For this I have taken human form, cloaked my godhead,
    costumed myself with humanity.
Women, wending behind me in revelry,
    you scaled the heights of Mount Tmolos, Lydia's aged rampart.
From the far lands of the barbarians I have led you here.
Always you are at my side, to do my bidding,
    to dance my dance.
Take up your Phrygian drums that beat to the earth's pulse,
    the drums I have given you.
Dance to the royal doorstep.
Pound on the palace doors of Pentheus.
As for the city of Kadmos and its people,
    make them open their eyes!
Now, I make my way back to the seclusion
    of Kithairon's rocky slopes, where my Bakkhai wait for me,
    to join with them in the dance.

Exit Dionysos. Enter Chorus.

CHORUS

I come from the East.
On holy Mount Tmolos
I have turned my back
To leap from Asia,
To do the sweet bidding of Bromios.
Light is the labor in his service
So long as he screams in the ears of my soul.
Who is it? Whose steps do I hear?
Who goes this way... or that?
Who lurks behind those walls,
Removed... remote?
Let him hold his tongue.
Let one and all keep the holy silence.
Always and forever on my lips,
One song, one name: Dionysos.
Glad is the soul that sees the mysteries of the gods.
Blessed is the life lived in tune with the divine.
Blessed are the Bakkhai,
Who swarm in the mountains,
Cleansing their souls with sacred revelry.

Blessed are those who keep the rites of Kybele,
The Great Mother.
Blessed are those who wave the holy thyrsos,
Who crown themselves with ivy,
And dote on Dionysos.
Rise up, Bakkhai!
Bakkhai, rise up!
Escort your god.
Bring back the boy-child Bromios
From the wild, distant reaches of Phrygia
To the sprawling cities of Greece,
Bromios, God from god.
Long ago,
Semele his mother,
Bursting with child,
Began her bitter labor,
When winged, jagged fire
Clawed the sky in two
And blasted the babe from her loins.
In that fraction of a moment,
No longer than the thunder's clap,
Semele miscarried her child
And her life.
But Zeus himself was there
For her last fiery contraction
And lifted his son away
To a cave more secret and secure
Than his mother's womb.

With surgical dispatch
Zeus inserted his half-born son
Into the fatty folds of his upper thigh
And closed the incision
With sutures of fibrous gold.
The boy lay hidden now.
Hera would not hate
What she would not see.
The Fates chose the moment of his birth,
When Zeus spread wide his thighs
And delivered the bull-horned god.
He then garlanded his son's head
With a seething crown of snakes.
We his maenads wear the same crown,
Plaits of serpents
We catch with our own hands.

City of Thebes,
From whose breasts
Semele once sucked her life,
Crown your head with ivy.
Like a yew tree in springtime,
Unfurl to the sun your timorous shoots
Until they burst into bryony.
Swathe yourselves in the soft skins of dappled fawns,
Tasseled with tufts of plaited snow-white wool.
Tear from trees
Boughs of oak and fir,
Bleeding with sap.
Let all the furious force within you
Erupt into frenzy.
Hold in awe the holy wands,
Gripped in your hands,
Wands not yet tame,
Wild with a life of their own.
Let all the earth
Rise from its foundation
To the dance of our god.
It is Bromios who leads the way,
A wending column of Bakkhants
In his steps.
To the mountain!

To the mountain,
Where a throng of women wait,
Women pried loose
From their looms and their shuttles,
Stung by Dionysos,
Until his frenzy mixes with their blood.
Blind-dark cave of the Kouretes,
Deep in distant Krete,
In you was born our Father Zeus,
God of earth and sky.
There, in your holy womb of stone,
The three-plumed servants of Kybele,
Over a circle of seasoned wood,
Stretched the skin of a goat
And beat the first drum.
Blending its rhythmic Bakkhic force
With the sweet, fluid frenzy of Phrygian pipes,
And shouting to our god.

Then the Korybantes
Passed on the pounding drum
To Rhea, Holy Mother Earth.
In time a band of raving satyrs
Stole the pounding drum
And with its rhythms raised the feet
Of our choruses,
Dancing to Dionysos,
In the festivals that make him glad.
There in the mountains,
How sweet is our god,
Wrapped in the skin of a fawn,
Our sacred vestment.
He breaks from the loping pack of maenads
And pounces on his prey,
Craving the blood of goats,
Ripped open in frenzy,
Eager to sate himself
On their raw flesh.
His heart longs
For the mountains of Phrygia,
For Lydia's rocky slopes.
He is Bromios.
He leads us.
Evohe! Hail Bromios!
The earth opens and flows with milk.
Rivulets of wine trickle from cracks in the earth.
Honey pours from the rocks.

Like the strange, sweet, curling fumes
Of incense from the East,
So are the trails of smoke
Left by the noisy, resinous flames
Of his fir-tree wand,
Waved over his head
As he runs his wild course,
Leading the dance,
Rousing stragglers to a new pitch
Of delirious possession
With his wails and screams,
Tossing his long tawny curls
Back and forth
Over his bare shoulders,
Raising the cry,
Leading the chant.

Evohe!
On, you Bakkhai!
Faster, Bakkhai!
Sing to the slopes of Mount Tmolos,
Running with gold.
Sing of Dionysos.
Pound the drums in his praise.
With joyous shouts,
Shout to the god of joy.
Fill the air with Phrygian screams,
As the sacred flute
Sends its notes swirling overhead,
Notes sweet and holy,
Music to the maenads' feet
As they swarm to the mountain,
To the mountain of their madness.
Like the filly,
Prancing at its mother's side,
Its joy uncontained
In the ecstasy of youth,
So the Bakkhant
Leaps in delirious delight,
Her limbs as light as air.

Exit Chorus. Enter Teiresias.

TEIRESIAS
Who is at the gates?
Go, call Kadmos, son of Agenor, from the palace,
   Kadmos who long ago left distant Sidon
   and built towering Thebes.
Get going, someone!
I say, tell Kadmos that Teiresias wants him.
He knows why I'm here.
The two of us— a relic and a fossil—have made a little pact.
We're going to raise the thyrsos, wear fawn-skins,
   and do up our hair with crowns of fresh ivy.

Enter Kadmos.

KADMOS
O dearest friend, from all the way inside I heard your voice,
   the wise voice of a wise man,
   and I knew it was you.

Well, here I am, all decked out for the occasion
   in the god's garb.
After all, he's my own daughter's boy, Dionysos.
And he's shown himself to be a god.
So it's up to us to do whatever we can
   to help him establish himself.
Now, where should we dance off to?
Where do we go to kick up our feet and let our hair down?
One old codger might as well help another find his way.
So, you lead the way, Teiresias.
You're loaded with wisdom.
You know,
   when it comes to beating the ground with my thyrsos,
   I can do it day and night... and feel nothing!
What could be sweeter, for you and me, than this:
   to have lost track of how old we are!

TEIRESIAS

The same thing! It's happening to me!
I feel like a boy again,
   ready to dance my heart out.

KADMOS

So why don't we hop into my chariot
   and drive up into the mountains!

TEIRESIAS

I think this god might be less than flattered,
   if we arrived in a chariot.

KADMOS

Then I will lead you.
I know we're both ancient;
   but take my hand, as if you were only a child
   and I were teaching you to walk.

TEIRESIAS

The god will lead us both to himself,
   and our feet will barely know they're walking.

KADMOS

Are we the only men in Thebes
   who are going to dance for Bakkhos?

TEIRESIAS

We are the only ones who are thinking straight.
The others use their minds to make nonsense.

KADMOS

Meanwhile, we're taking a long time to launch this procession.
Here, take my hand.

TEIRESIAS

Look, put your hand out. Yoke it to mine.

KADMOS

I am a mere mortal.
I am in no position to ignore gods.

TEIRESIAS

No, we are not about to dissolve the divine
    with agile wit and smooth talk.
What we know we have learned from our fathers.
Our truths have come a long way down to us.
No one is going to reason them away,
    no matter how many subtleties this generation
    manages to skim off the surface of its brain.
Someone may well come along and ask me:
    "Aren't you just a little ashamed of yourself,
    standing there with ivy tangled in your hair,
    waiting to dance… at your age?"
My answer is "no."
What shame can there be in dancing to my god at my age,
    when he draws no line between young and old?
He expects the same honor from all.
In his demand for recognition,
    he does not split hairs.

KADMOS

Teiresias, you do not see the light of day,
    so let me be your eyes and tell you what I see.
Pentheus, the son of Ekhion,
    the boy to whom I have given rule over this land…
    he is making his way toward the palace.
And he is clearly in a hurry.
He looks bothered.
What do you think he's going to say?

Enter Pentheus, accompanied by Guard and Attendants.

PENTHEUS

I happened to be away from the city
  when I heard distressing news...
    something about our city's wives and mothers
    abandoning their homes for so-called "Bakkhic" revels,
    thrashing around in the shaded thickets of nearby mountains.
I was told all their dancing and carry-on
  is in honor of some blow-in god,
  "Dionysos," whoever that is.
I'm told that these women swarm around earthen bowls,
  brimming with wine,
    that they go off into the woods, one here, one there,
    where they lie down and wrap themselves around men,
    doing a duty that belongs at home, in their marriage beds.
They think of themselves as priests at their altars,
  performing sacrifice, frenzied in worship.
No doubt.
But their frenzy and their worship have more to do
  with Aphrodite than with Bakkhos.
The ones I've caught so far have been bound and put away.
The city wardens will keep them safe in the public jails.
As for the others, still loose in the mountains,
  I will hunt them down.
Yes, that includes Ino and Autonoe, the mother of Aktaion,
  as well as Agave, my own mother, who bore me to Ekhion.
I will herd them into iron cages,
  and put a quick end to their lurid liturgies.
Then there are those rumors
  about a stranger come to Thebes.
They say he is a sorcerer from Lydia,
  who warbles and howls enchantments of some sort.
I hear that his hair hangs down in long loose curls
  and reeks of perfumes,
  and that his cheeks are red as wine.
His eyes, they say, are large and luring.
All a bit too much like Aphrodite.
This stranger spends long frivolous days with young girls, seducing them with his mysteries.
If I manage to drag him under that roof,
  he'll wave his magic wand for the last time,
  and his curls will lose their bounce!
In fact, I'll cut at his throat... until I get to the other side.
This same stranger preaches the divinity of Dionysos...
  something about his being sewn up
  in the fatty thigh of Zeus.

But Dionysos was, as everyone knows,
   cremated with his mother by a thunderous bolt of fire,
   because she made up stories of nuptials with Zeus.
Whoever this stranger is, what he's saying and doing,
   his lewd and lawless behavior are enough,
   I think you'll agree,
   to put his head in a dreaded noose.

Noticing Teiresias and Kadmos for the first time.

But wait, here is something else to make my eyes balk.
I see the ever-prophetic Teiresias,
   decked out in a dappled fawn-skin,
   and Grandfather—what a joke!—playing the Bakkhant,
   with his own little wand!
I am so ashamed of you, Grandfather,
   to see you so old, and so mindless.
Shake off that ivy, won't you?
Come on, Grandfather,
   just open your hand and drop that thing.
Teiresias, I see your persuasive powers at work here.
This is your doing.
You want to put a new god on the market,
   another god to be kept happy,
   more birds to watch and offerings to burn,
   more silver in your pocket.
If it weren't for your gray old age,
I'd have you shackled and sent off
   to rot among your recreant Bakkhai,
   just for peddling these perversions,
   these shabby little rituals of yours.
It comes down to this:
   no matter what the meal,
   put wine and women together,
   and you've got an orgy.

CHORUS
Omitted if the Chorus is off-stage.

Blasphemy!
Stranger, where is your fear of the gods?
Where is your respect for Kadmos
Who sowed the dragons teeth
And reaped a race of earth-born men?
Child of Ekhion, why are you so bent
On disgracing your own house?

TEIRESIAS

It is no great feat for a clever man to be eloquent,
   provided he has something worth saying.
Your fancy words, however, drain from your mouth
   the way sap drips from a tree,
   with very little proof of intelligence,
   whatever pretense you mount to the contrary.
A man whose only boast is a bold tongue,
   can only do his city harm with the mind he doesn't have.
Now, regarding this new god you like to ridicule,
   I have no words so great as he will be throughout all of Greece.

Young man, consider this:
   among all the blessed forces gracious to humankind,
   two stand out.

First there is Demeter, or Goddess Earth.
Call her whichever name you wish.
She rears the race of men on what the dry soil throws up.
Next there is the son of Semele,
   who brought to the dry lips of mortals
   a bright, flowing cure,
   the juice of the grape, the miracle of wine,
   that puts broken mortals a few steps from their pain.
For when the cup is drained.
   and the blood of the grape rushes in the veins,
   sleep is sure to come, and with it sweet oblivion.
All the day's woes are forgotten.
It is the only way they leave.
This very god we pour out in libation to other gods,
   to win from them the hopes nursed in our hearts.
What is more, ours is a god of prophecy and vision.
When he possesses us and banishes our wits,
   he brings a third eye.
When he inhabits our bodies,
   he forms words with our lips that tell what is to be.
Even the powers of Ares, god of war, are partly his to wield.
Picture a host of men in heavy arms,
   already in the field, positioned for battle.
Now, even before a single spear is thrown, or even raised,
   terror blows through their ranks
   and scatters them like dry leaves.
This terror is our god's doing.
It is one form of his madness.

One day you will see our god ensconced
  even among the jagged rocks of Delphi.
From peak to peak, and across the cloud-swept plateau,
  he will leap and dance amidst a sea of sparkling torches,
  whirling and shaking his Bakkhic wand.
In Greece great will be his power, everywhere.

Now you listen to me, Pentheus.
Don't flatter yourself as a powerful man,
  just because you can wield a little force.
And don't mistake for wisdom
  the figments of your sick, feverish mind.
Instead, welcome our god to Thebes.
Pour out libations in his honor.
Wear his crown. Join his revels.
As for your concern over the sex-lives of women,
  if anything will restrain them it will be their own nature.
It is not for Dionysos
  to bully the women of Thebes into chastity.
His Bakkhants leave his revels
  no less chaste than they entered them.
Think how glad it makes you, Pentheus,
  when a crowd throngs your gates,
  and the whole city, it seems, with a single voice
  sings your praise.
I do not doubt that he finds praise and recognition
  as sweet as you do.
This is why I and Kadmos, the butt of your laughter,
  wear ivy crowns and dance to our god.
How old and gray we two are misses the point.
The dance is for all.
Your words blow past me.
I shall not resist my god.
You are mad, Pentheus, raving mad.
For the poison in your soul, there is no antidote, no cure.

CHORUS
Omitted if the Chorus is off-stage.
Old man, be assured
Apollo would approve your words.
When you honor Bromios,
Your mind steers a true course;
For this god is great.

KADMOS

Oh child, Teiresias has given you good counsel.
Don't take your stand somewhere beyond where you belong.
Make your home with us.
Your mind has lost it bearings.
You imagine you make sense, when you don't.
But even if the truth is just what you say it is,
   and Dionysos is not divine, say he is anyway.
Think he is.
It makes a lovely lie.
Semele becomes the mother of a god,
   and the entire family profits from her prestige.
You remember Akteon and his undoing,
    how his savage hounds, who as pups ate from his hand,
    worried his flesh from his bones.
His only error had been his boast,
    that he knew more than Artemis
    about dogs and the chase and the kill.
Don't re-enact his fate.
Come here,
   let me put this ivy in your hair, wrap it in a crown.
Join us in giving honor to our god.

PENTHEUS

Don't touch me!
Go! Go off to your Bakkhant revelry.
Just don't let any of your foolishness rub off on me!
As for the one who taught you to take leave of your mind,
   my justice is already on his trail.

To Guard and Attendants.

Someone, anyone, go this instant,
   find the haunts of this priest, where he conducts his rituals.
Take up a crowbar and dig up his shrines,
   flip them upside down.
Let him drink chaos.
Fling his ribbons and fillets to the winds.
A storm will scatter them eventually.
Go, do as I've said.
I want to sting him,
   where he won't forget he's been stung.

Exit several Attendants.

To Guard and remaining Attendants.

Now, I want the rest of you to comb the city
   until you find the effeminate foreigner,
   who infects our women with a strange fever
   and outrages every marriage-bed in Thebes.
And when you find him, bring him here, bound,
   so that he can look justice in the eye… and die.
We'll use stones.
He may even learn to regret his little romp in Thebes.

Exit Guard and remaining Attendants.

TEIRESIAS

You poor rabid fool. You dispatch so many words.
But where do they go? What will come of them?
That far you have not seen.
You walked out on your wits long ago.
Now you're a lunatic.
Come, Kadmos, let's be off.
And on our way we'll say some prayers for this lad,
   even if he has turned beast on us,
   and some prayers for our city too,
   in case there is still time to dissuade our god
   from doing vengeance on them both.
Take up your thyrsos and follow me.
Be my staff and I will be yours.
It's a sorry sight when two old men go down in a heap together.
All the same, we must go.
Bakkhos, son of Zeus, must be served.
Kadmos, beware of this grandson of yours,
   who was named after grief.
I fear he may bring grief to your house.
It requires no psychic powers to say this.
The future is already written in what he is doing.
A fool must swallow his own folly.

Exit Teiresias, Kadmos, and Pentheus. Enter Chorus.

CHORUS

Spirit of holiness,
Revered of the gods,
On golden wing you glide to earth.
Lady,
Do you hear the words of Pentheus?

Do you hear his insolence, his blasphemy
Against Bromios, son of Semele,
Against our god, lord of the blessed,
God of merriment and festal crowns?
He lightens our feet and our hearts
To honor him in the dance.
The music of our laughter
And the wild piping of flutes
Are a portion of his largesse.
Sweetest of all... the oblivion he brings,
The respite from all care,
When the bright blood of the grape
Bursts over the table of the gods,
And ivy-crowned revelers
Lift and tip the brimming bowl
To drink warm, sweet sleep.
Unruly tongues,
And fools enamored of iniquity
Chart a course to certain doom,
While the genial, quiet life,
Ruddered by right-thinking,
Knows calm security.

Our lives are closely watched
By the lords of heaven,
Who make their homes
In the bright luminous air
Far far away.
Here among men,
Wit would pass for wisdom,
But cannot.
It is mortal folly
To think immortal thoughts.
Life is each time brief.
We may dream great dreams
And in the long tomorrow they may come true,
But today is all we have.
The mind swollen beyond mortality
Seems quite mad to me.
Its words are weeds
Fit for the fire.
How I long for Cyprus,
Island of Aphrodite.

Oh to be a pilgrim there,
Where the spirits of love
Bewitch the hearts of mortals
Doomed to brevity.
To be suppliant in Paphos,
Where sea-born Aphrodite washed ashore,
And where the barbarian river of a hundred mouths
Soaks the thirsting soil
Unblessed with rain.
Oh to kneel and drink from the Pieran springs,
Beauteous birthplace of the Muses
On the awesome slopes of Olympos.
Take me, Bromios, lord of the dance.
Bromios, god of bliss,
Take me there,
Where the Graces dwell,
Where desire leaves its banks,
Where the very air
Sanctions our devotions and our dance
To you.
Glad is our great god,
The child of Zeus.
Our festivity feeds him joy.

He is one in love with goddess Peace,
Peace the guardian of prosperity,
Who gives long years to our sons.
With an even hand,
To rich and poor alike,
Our god extends the sweet, swirling cup,
The antidote to life's agony.
But those who refuse to pass their time in peace,
Those who scoff at the happiness
Of simple days and sweet nights,
Our god hates.
It is ordinary wisdom to keep the heart and mind
Away from extraordinary men and their excesses.
Common sense and common decency…
I aspire to nothing more.

> *Exit Chorus. Pentheus enters only a moment before the Guard
> leads in Dionysos, captive in the grip of two Attendants.*

GUARD

Pentheus, we've wasted no time in accomplishing your wishes.
Here we are with our catch, the wild one you sent us after.
But look, he's actually tame.
He doesn't cower when we come near, much less bolt.
The truth is he just gave himself up to us without a fight.
If he's afraid, he doesn't show it.
He just stood there, as he is now, cheeks aglow
    and that wide grin across his face,
    letting us bind him up and lead him away.
He waited patiently on our efforts to truss him up properly.
The whole thing made me ashamed and I had to say so.
"Look, stranger," I said to him. "This isn't my idea.
Pentheus gave the command for your capture
    and sent me off to do it."
As for your captive maenads,
    the ones you rounded up and herded into the public jails,
    manacled to the walls,
    well, they're gone, set free somehow.
They're out beyond the city walls now,
    prancing in the meadows,
    calling to Bromios, their god.
The iron cuffs, like mouths opening themselves,
    released the women's legs.
On the jail house door, the key turned;
    but no hand turned it...
    no mortal hand, at least.
This fellow comes here to Thebes with a bag full of tricks,
    amazing tricks.
The next move seems to be yours, Pentheus.

PENTHEUS

Untie his hands. He's in my net.
He'll need more than feet to flee from here.

To Dionysos.

You are beautiful, stranger.
Women, no doubt, find you attractive,
    which explains what you're doing here in Thebes.
This long plait curling down over your shoulder...
    not for wrestling, I assume. Or is it?
Regardless, the way it brushes against your soft cheek...
    rather exciting.

And your skin, so soft, you must work on it;
   so pallid, you must avoid the sun.
Of course you do.
With Aphrodite as your quarry, and your beauty as your net,
   you do most of your hunting indoors.
Now, tell me this much.
Who are you and where are you from?

DIONYSOS

I can easily answer that without any ado.
I suppose you've heard of the flowering slopes of Mt. Tmolos
   and know where that is.

PENTHEUS

Yes, I know where Mt. Tmolos is
   and how it rings the city of Sardis.

DIONYSOS

Well, I come from there.
Lydia is my homeland.

PENTHEUS

These mysteries you've imported to Greece…
   where do they come from?

DIONYSOS

They come from Dionysos,
   who himself initiated us into them.
And Dionysos comes from Zeus.

PENTHEUS

Now just what "Zeus" is that, spawning new gods?

DIONYSOS

The same Zeus who lay with Semele, *your* Semele.

PENTHEUS

When this god took you over,
   did you dream it or see it happen?

DIONYSOS

We stood face to face, he and I;
   and he bestowed on me his rituals.

PENTHEUS
These rituals of yours…
  if I were to see them, what would I see?

DIONYSOS
Until one is initiated, one is forbidden to see anything.

PENTHEUS
But for those who are initiated,
  what reward or pleasure is there?

DIONYSOS
The answer to that is well worth knowing;
  but you have no right to hear it.

PENTHEUS
You are clever.
The more you deflect my questions,
  the more I want answers to them.

DIONYSOS
In that case our rituals work in strange ways,
  attracting those they hate most, the impious.

PENTHEUS
This god you say you saw with your own eyes…
  describe him to me. What form did he take?

DIONYSOS
Whatever form he wished.
I was in no position to dictate to him.

PENTHEUS
You bypass everything I ask.
You are quite skilled at saying nothing.

DIONYSOS
Tell a fool everything,
  and he'll still think you've told him nothing.

PENTHEUS
Tell me this.
Is Thebes the first stop for your mysteries?

DIONYSOS
Barbarians everywhere already dance and revel in his name.

PENTHEUS
Not surprising.
Barbarians are more dim than Greeks.

DIONYSOS
On the contrary, in these matters barbarians see more clearly.
Let's just say that people differ.

PENTHEUS
These "sacred" rites of yours…
   do you conduct them at night or during the day?

DIONYSOS
Mostly at night. Darkness is better suited to solemnity.

PENTHEUS
To seduction, you mean. Perversion likes to hide.

DIONYSOS
Not always, obviously.

PENTHEUS
You will pay for your wit.

DIONYSOS
As will you, for your ignorant insolence toward our god.

PENTHEUS
What a feisty Bakkhant you are!
Someone taught you how to use words.

DIONYSOS
You're planning some punishment for me.
What is it? What atrocity would you inflict on me?

PENTHEUS
For a start, I'm going to cut off your soft, luxuriant curls.

DIONYSOS
My hair is sacred. I let it grow for my god.

PENTHEUS

Next you will surrender your wand.

DIONYSOS

I carry it for Dionysos.
Come and take it from me.

PENTHEUS

Then, we will lock you away in a dungeon.

DIONYSOS

My god will set me free, whenever I ask it.

PENTHEUS

Be my guest.
Join your Bakkhants in our jail
    and summon your god to your side.

DIONYSOS

But he is here already.
He sees quite clearly for himself what I endure.

PENTHEUS

Where is he? My eyes see nothing of him.

DIONYSOS

He is here, with me. Your own blasphemy blinds you.

PENTHEUS

Seize him! He mocks me and Thebes!

DIONYSOS

I warn you. Do not touch me. Fools obey fools.

PENTHEUS

I say seize him! I am master here!

DIONYSOS

You don't know what you're asking for.
You have no idea what you're doing.
You don't even know who you are.

PENTHEUS

I am Pentheus, son of Agave.
Ekhion was my father.

DIONYSOS

"Pentheus"—"full of grief"—your name suits you.
But it will not bring you luck.

PENTHEUS

Enough of this!
Get him out of my sight.
Chain him in the stables, next to the horse stalls.
It will be good and dark, the way he likes it.

To Dionysos.

Do your dancing there.
As for the women, your followers and companions in mischief,
    either I will sell them on the open market,
    or I will keep them myself.
Once they're at the loom again, where women belong,
    their drums will fall as still as stones.

DIONYSOS

I shall go where you send me.
But nothing, nothing shall befall me that is not meant to be.
And as for you, Pentheus,
    Dionysos himself—the god you deny—will come
    to collect from you the price of your insolence.
You offend us.
You are sending him to the stables,
    to these would-be jails of yours.

*After Dionysos is taken off into the palace under guard,
Pentheus too exits. Enter Chorus.*

CHORUS

Dirke,
Holy one,
Sweet virgin spring,
Happy daughter of the great River Akhelous,
Once you held in your lucent arms
The inchoate son of Zeus.
In your pure crystal stream
You bathed the divine life,
Snatched by its father Zeus
From the jagged, searing teeth
Of insatiable fire
And enwombed in his thigh.

"Come, my son," cried the father of gods,
"One day the chorus of fifty
Will dance in your name.

But now you must enter
The silent seclusion
Of this male womb of mine.
In good time,
Bakkhos, my son,
I will raise you up
And make you shine
Before all of Thebes,
Where your name will resound."
And yet,
Dirke,
Blessed one,
When I, Bakkhos, now bring to your banks
My festive chorus,
Crowned with ivy,
You cast us off.
Why do you disown me now?
Why do you shun me?
I swear by the clustered grapes,
Bursting on the vine.
I swear by the gleaming cup,
Gift of Dionysos,
That you shall learn your duty.
Your neglect of Bromios
Will be brief.
What blind fury
Consumes the son of Ekhion,
Pentheus,
Earth-spawned seed of the dragon,
Sown and reaped in a field of blood,
Savage and wild,
Not yet tamed to mortality,
Murderous throwback
To the race of giants,
Waging reckless war
Even on gods.
Soon he will snare me too,
An intimate of Bromios,
In his awful net.

Already he has my fellows,
My companions in the chorus,
Caged somewhere in his house,
Chained to darkness.

O child of Zeus,
Lord Dionysos,
Open your eyes to our plight.
See what we suffer,
Who proclaim your name.
Come down from Olympos,
Wielding your golden thyrsos,
And be for us a wall
Against the wanton rage
Of a man fast on the scent of blood.
Oh Dionysos,
Where is it
That you muster your army
Of reveling maenads?
Somewhere on the slopes of Mt. Nysa,
Haven to wild beasts,
Or high amidst the crags of Korykia?
Or do you make your lair
Beneath the shading pines
On Mt. Olympos,
Where Orpheus once charmed the trees,
And bemused the wildest beasts
To gather and dance
To the gaiety of his lyre?
Oh blessed Pieria,
Bakkhos, the god of gladness
Honors you.
He will come with his chorus,
Dancing his way to you.
Vaulting the rapids of Axios,
He will wend his way,
He and his twirling maenads,
Across the swift waters of Lydias,
Father of rivers,
Who rewards toil-worn mortals with bliss
And soaks with the purest of streams
Verdant plains
Where glorious horses thrive.

DIONYSOS

Io! Hear me! Hear my cry!
Io Bakkhai! Io Bakkhai!

CHORUS

Who is it?
Who is it crying out to us from somewhere in the palace?
It is the voice of a storm breaking.
It is the voice of god.

DIONYSOS

Io, Io! I cry out to you again.
I am the son of Zeus, the child of Semele.

CHORUS

Io, Io! Lord and master,
    come to us now!
Come, Bromios!
Bromios, come and be one with us.

DIONYSOS

Almighty forces that move the earth,
    I summon you.
Seize the earthen floor beneath our feet
    and send it into spasm.

CHORUS

Ah, ah!
All at once the palace of Pentheus shudders.
Look, it rattles on its foundation
    and begins to come apart!
Dionysos is within.
Kneel and worship him.
Yes, we adore him.
Do you see it?
Do you see how the fissure
    rushes like a torrent through solid stone
    and splits pillars in two?
Listen, deep within the palace.
It is the war-cry of Bromios.

DIONYSOS

Hurl the blinding, blazing bolt of fire!
Swallow the house of Pentheus in flames.

CHORUS

Ah, ah! Do you see it?
Do you see how fire mounts the holy tomb of Semele?
The bolt of Olympian fire that once blasted her is back.
It lunges up from its own deathless embers.
Maenads, down!
Hurl your trembling bodies to the ground.
Your lord is coming.
The son of Zeus treads underfoot the fallen house
    and comes to you.

The Chorus falls to the earth and Dionysos enters.

DIONYSOS

Women of Asia,
    so stricken with fear that you've misplaced your feet?
You must have seen it all,
    how Bakkhos dismantled Pentheus's palace.
But here, lift yourselves from the ground.
Cheer up and stop trembling.

CHORUS

O most radiant light, joyous source and object of our worship!
How glad we are to see you.
Without you, our world became a wilderness.

DIONYSOS

When they took me away, to plunge me
    into some dark pit of a place in the house of Pentheus,
    did you slide all the way to despair?

CHORUS

How could we avoid it?
Once something awful happens to you,
    who is left to protect us?
But how did this happen?
Once you were in the clutches of that godless man,
    how is it that you were set free?

DIONYSOS

I set myself free. It was easily done. No effort at all.

CHORUS

But didn't he bind your hands?

DIONYSOS

That was where I made a fool of him.
He bound me only in his thoughts.
He never laid a hand on me, never touched me.
All he did was to feast on a phantasy, somewhere in his mind.
But in the stalls to which I had been taken, my would-be prison,
    Pentheus found a bull, which he tried to rope.
Drenched in sweat, Pentheus struggled
    to secure a rope around the bull's knees and hooves.
Soon he was out of breath, clawing for air.
In his desperation, he bit through his lip.
I sat nearby, on the very rim of this wildness and watched,
    in perfect calm.
It was in that moment that Bakkhos came.
He convulsed the house of Pentheus,
    and summoned fire to the tomb of Semele, his mother.
Pentheus saw flames everywhere he looked,
    but they burned mostly in his mind.
His house ablaze before his eyes, Pentheus thrashed about,
    screaming for someone to haul the River Akhelous
    from its banks, and heave it on the flames,
    one pot-full at a time.
Every slave in the house answered his cry.
Their efforts could not have been more futile.

Then Pentheus remembered me.
The thought of my escape made him forget the flames
    and quit his efforts to put them out.
He reached instead for his grim sword
    and raced through the palace.
I only think I know what happened next.
Bromios, it seems, fashioned an effigy of me,
    a mere phantom, and put it in his path.
Pentheus charged thin air, hacking and hewing,
    as though I were the victim of his blows.
And even with this Bakkhos had only begun the beating,
    only begun the breaking of the insolent king.

There was more.
Bakkhos brought the whole house down.
And Pentheus, his home in a heap, saw all at once
    the cost to him of my confinement.
A bitter sight.
He dropped his sword in defeat.
It is safe to say that he is exhausted.

He is a common man, nothing more.
Yet he played bold, and gave battle to a god.
As for me, I casually made my way out of the palace
   and came here to join you.
What has become of Pentheus is not my concern.

But wait, listen to that clatter of footsteps inside.
If I were to guess, I would say he is coming,
   and will be out here any moment now.
After all this, I wonder what he will say.
Let him rant and puff all he wants.
I shall be the picture of calm.
It is the mark and measure of a wise man
to guard the stillness of his soul.

*The Chorus exits as Pentheus enters. He is followed by the 2nd.
Messenger.*

PENTHEUS

O god what I have endured!
The stranger, the one I just put away for good,
   got away from me!
Oh! Agh!

Seeing Dionysos.

What? He's here! You! What is going on?
How did you get out here?

DIONYSOS

Just stay where you are, and control your temper.

PENTHEUS

How is it possible?
You were bound hand and foot.
How did you get loose, and just walk out?

DIONYSOS

I thought I already told you that I would be set free.
Did you fail to hear me say that the first time?

PENTHEUS

Set free by whom?
You have a habit of saying something and nothing
   in the same breath.

DIONYSOS

The one who set me free begets for mortals
    the wine-red grape, clustered on the vine.

PENTHEUS

He begets more than grapes.

DIONYSOS

You insult the largesse of the god Dionysos.

PENTHEUS

I order every gate in and out of Thebes closed at once.
I want this city sealed off.

DIONYSOS

Whatever for?
Unless I'm mistaken, gods pass *over* gates, not *through* them.

PENTHEUS

Clever. You are always so clever, except when it counts.

DIONYSOS

Oh but I am at my cleverest when it counts.
Look, one of your errand-boys comes running to you
    with the latest from the mountains.
I suggest you hear him out,
    and try to learn something from his words.
You needn't worry about my running off.
We intend to stay right here.

Enter lst. Messenger.

1st MESSENGER

Pentheus, lord and ruler of the land of Thebes,
    I come to you direct from Kithairon,
    glistening mountain of endless snows, pure, unsullied...

PENTHEUS

If you've come with something urgent to say, say it!

1st MESSENGER

I've just seen with my own eyes the raving Bakkhant women,
    the ones who ran off from the city on soft, bare feet,
    in a wave of frenzy.

I come, lord, bursting to tell my story to you and to the city,
  to tell what wild and wondrous things these women do.
No, they surpass wonder!
But first, I would like to hear from your mouth… something…
  whether… about everything out there…
  whether I can talk freely.
Or would I be wise to "trim my sails," as it were?
The truth is, lord, that I fear getting caught in a tempest.
Your *excessive*—I mean your *royal*—temper
  could easily swamp a boat as small as mine.

PENTHEUS

Speak freely.
You will suffer nothing from me.
To abuse a man whose only fault is telling the truth
  serves no one's purpose.
But I will promise you this as well:
  the more shocking your account of the Bakkhai,
  the more severe will be my justice
  on the one who taught those women their new tricks.

1st MESSENGER

It was just after dawn, when the sun's rays
  first begin to warm the earth after the night's chill.
Our grazing herds of cattle sluggishly climbed the mountain
  toward an upper pasture, near the ridge.
It was then that I caught sight of the women revelers.
They were arranged for their dances in three separate packs:
  one led by Autonoe, a second led by your mother Agave,
  and a third led by Ino.
But by now they all lay asleep,
  each lying where she had dropped from the dance
  in sweet exhaustion.
Some lay stretched across beds of soft pine boughs,
  while mounds of oak leaves served others,
  as pillows for their heads.
All these women, strewn over the ground…
  it was not as you picture it, king,
  not the aftermath of drunkenness or of lust let loose.
No flute had with its wild notes whirled these women
  into dark delirium.
No, it was a scene of modesty and moderation
  that lay before my eyes.
Then, up from a circle of sleeping maenads,
  your mother leapt to her feet.

I can only guess she heard the lowing of our cattle.
She let out a long scream of joy
   to rouse her companions from their dreams.
The field-full of women rubbed the soft dew of sleep
   from their eyes, as they rose straight to their feet,
   forming instant ranks, perfectly in order.
There were young girls and old women in the ranks,
   and virgins too, ripe but not yet taken.
The women shook their heads, letting their hair
   fall loose and free down over their shoulders.
Those whose fawn skins had come loose in the night
   fastened them up again.
Then, over the dappled skins, they wrapped writhing vipers
   that coiled and climbed until they licked the women's cheeks
   with their flashing tongues.
Some of the women cradled in their arms new-born gazelles
   and wild wolf cubs, nursing them from swollen breasts,
   whose warm, sweet milk dripped for their own babes,
   forsaken in their homes.
Then they wove for themselves crowns of ivy and oak
   and flowering bryony.
One of them raised her thyrsos and struck a rock,
   sending up into the air a bright jet of water.
When another drove her fennel wand into the ground,
   her god made the dark soil ooze and bubble
   until a spray of crimson wine burst forth near her feet.
Still others thirsted for fresh white milk
   and found it with their fingers,
   clawing at the earth until it nursed them.
Then they sucked and licked pure, sweet honey,
   trickling from the tips of their ivy wands.
Oh, king, if you had been there yourself and seen all this,
   you would have fallen to your knees
   and mumbled every prayer you know
   to the very god you now despise.
Anyhow, at this point we cowherds and shepherds
   drew into a close circle to confer.
Soon we were quarreling among ourselves over the situation,
   over all the strange, wild, and wondrous things
   we had seen these women do.
It was then that some fellow who had no business being there,
   some slick city-fellow, clever with words, spoke up.
"All of you," he said, looking around at us,
   "you men who make your homes in the mountains,
   in these serene glens, I have a proposition for you.

What do you say we snatch up the mother of Pentheus, Agave,
   from her Bakkhic revelries?
It's a sure road to the king's good side."
Well, he seemed to us to talk sense;
   so we hid ourselves in the undergrowth.
Covered with leaves and brush, we lay in wait.

Meanwhile, the maenads, at the appointed moment in their day,
   lifted and whirled their wands in the air,
   the signal for their revels to begin.
As if from a single mouth came their cry:
"Hail, Iakkhos. Hail Bromios, son of Zeus."
At this, the whole mountain and every beast on its slopes
   went wild.
There was nothing that was not swept into it.
Now it happened that one of Agave's leaps
   landed her for an instant near me,
   where I crouched in concealment.
Hoping to seize her, I lunged from my safe lair.
The only result was that she howled out to the others:
"My wild, swift hounds, there are men stalking us.
Arm yourselves with your wands, and follow me."
Well, we ran for it and managed to escape being dismembered
   by a pack of Bakkhai who fell instead on our cattle,
   grazing nearby in the stillness of a fresh green meadow.
The women went at the cattle
   with only their fingers as flaying-knives.
If you had been there, this is what you would have seen:
A young heifer, lowing in dull terror,
   came apart in their hands.
Calves were torn into many pieces and scattered,
   their hooves hurled in one direction, their ribs in another.
The boughs of nearby pine trees were strewn
   with scraps of hide and flesh, shiny and dripping with gore.
Bulls, beside themselves with fury, lowered their heads
   and glared down their horns at the women.
Moments later the bulls crashed to the ground,
   tripped and toppled by a horde of mere girls,
   who ripped away flesh from bone
   faster than you could wink your royal eyes, king.
Then, like a squadron of birds swept into formation,
   the maenads closed ranks and swooped down
   over the open fields below, along Asopos's stream,
   where the soil is dark and rich,
   generous to Thebes in its harvests.

Like an invading army, the maenads descended on the villages
   of Hysiai and Erythrai, in the foothills of Kithairon,
   turning everything upside down,
   leaving nothing but debris behind them.
They even snatched up babies from houses they passed by.
Their loot they simply piled up on their shoulders,
   where it stayed in place, without a single strap to keep it there.
Nothing, however unwieldy, not even bronze or iron,
   clattered to the ground.
Flames leapt up in their hair, crackling amidst their curls;
   yet nothing burned.
Roused to rage by the havoc these women brought,
   the townsmen took to arms.

Now we come, king, to a sight appalling beyond words.
The men's razor-sharp spears refused to draw blood,
   while the women's blunt wands, once hurled from their hands,
   inflicted deep wounds.
In short, women routed men.
They must have had a god on their side.
The women then retraced their steps back into the mountains
   to the same pure streams
   which their god had made flow for them.
There they washed their hands of blood, while coiling serpents
   licked white again their soft delicate faces, spattered with gore.

My lord, open the city gates to this god.
Whoever he is, welcome him.
In ways beyond anything I've said, he is great and powerful.
I've heard him proclaimed to be the god who gave to mortals
   the vine and its grape,
   our only cure for grief that will not go away.
Besides, without wine to ease its approach,
   how often would love come to us?
When our cup is empty, life is just too harsh.

CHORUS
Omitted if the Chorus is absent.
The thought of speaking freely to a tyrant
   makes me shake with fear.
All the same, the truth must be told.
No child of any god was ever greater than this one:
   Dionysos, son of Zeus.

Exit 1st. Messenger.

PENTHEUS

This Bakkhic outrage already burns out of control.
It is no distant threat.
Before our fellow Greeks, this scandal blackens our name.
The time for scruples is behind us.

To 2nd. Messenger.

Go at once to the Elektran gate.
Muster the heavy and light infantry.
Have my cavalry saddle their fastest steeds.
Call up my archers and have them string their bows.
I want every available man armed and ready
    to follow me into the field.
We shall take these Bakkhai on.
There is a limit to what we need endure.
These women go too far.
We have given enough ground as it is.

*The 2nd. Messenger begins to exit, hesitates, and remains in
place to witness the ensuing encounter between Dionysos and
Pentheus.*

DIONYSOS

Pentheus, nothing I say moves you in the slightest.
Even so, even after all I have endured from you,
    I offer you one more chance,
    one more piece of advice.
Don't go to war against a god.
It doesn't pay.
You would do better to do nothing.
If you try to drive out the Bakkhants
    from the mountains of their joy,
    Bromios will not stand back and watch.

PENTHEUS

I won't have you preaching to me!
Don't throw away the freedom you've just won.
Or do you want another taste of my justice?

DIONYSOS

If I were you, confronted by a god,
    I would be offering sacrifices, not insults.
And I wouldn't try to kick fate from my path with a mortal foot.

PENTHEUS

Oh but a sacrifice is just what I have in mind,
   one to suit your god, a female victim, victims.
Up there, in the shaded glens of Kithairon,
   I plan to unleash chaos.

DIONYSOS

You will run for your lives, every one of you.
It is a shameful sight when women with ivy wands
   make men drop their bronze shields and run.

PENTHEUS

Wrestling with this stranger is a losing game.
Nothing will shut him up.

DIONYSOS

Friend, there is one way left to make everything come out right.

PENTHEUS

What do I have to do… wait on my own slaves?

DIONYSOS

I will lead the women back here.
There will be no bloodshed.

PENTHEUS

Ha! You are setting a trap for me.

DIONYSOS

What kind of a trap is it, if I want to use my powers to save you?

PENTHEUS

What you want is a never-ending revel.
You and those women have a pact on that.

DIONYSOS

My pact is with our god.   The rest I grant you.

PENTHEUS
To 2nd. Messenger.

Fetch me my arms!

To Dionysos.

Meanwhile, not another word from you.

Once again, the 2nd. Messenger begins to exit and doesn't.

DIONYSOS

But... you would like to see them, wouldn't you...
   all lying about together in the mountains?

PENTHEUS

Oh yes. Very much.
I would pay a fortune for that sight.

DIONYSOS

Really? Now how did *you* come upon a desire like that?

PENTHEUS

Of course it would be upsetting to see them
   if they had drunk too much.

DIONYSOS

Yes. The very thing you hate.
Yet, just to look... wouldn't it be somehow sweet to the eyes?

PENTHEUS

You're very wise.
I could crouch beneath the pines and not make a sound.

DIONYSOS

If you try to hide, won't they find you out?

PENTHEUS

You're right. I'll go openly.

DIONYSOS

Shall we go, then?
Are you prepared to set out?

PENTHEUS

At once, if possible.
You're stalling and I don't like it.

DIONYSOS

Then you should get dressed now,
   slip into a gown of fine Asiatic linen.

PENTHEUS
What's this about a "gown"?
Am I going to change sex? Go from man to woman?

DIONYSOS
As a precaution.
If you're recognized as a man, the women will kill you.

PENTHEUS
You're talking sense again.
You're a wise fellow, of the "old school."

DIONYSOS
Dionysos taught me everything I know.

PENTHEUS
You have a good plan.
How do we make it happen?

DIONYSOS
We go together into your house and I dress you.

PENTHEUS
In what? Things women wear?
No, I would be too ashamed.

DIONYSOS
I see.
You no longer really want to see them… gaze at them…
    the wild women.

PENTHEUS
This outfit you have in mind for me… what is it, exactly?

DIONYSOS
First, a wig, a long one.

PENTHEUS
And then? What is the second touch?

DIONYSOS
A gown, long enough to cover your feet.
And, in your hair, a ribbon or two.

PENTHEUS

Yes, and what else?

DIONYSOS

A thyrsos, something to hold.
And, to go along with the rest, a dappled fawn skin.

PENTHEUS

I can't do it. I couldn't bring myself to dress like a woman.

DIONYSOS

But if you do battle with the Bakkhants instead,
    there will be a lot of blood on your hands.

PENTHEUS

Exactly, in which case it makes sense for me to go ahead first,
    and do a little reconnoitering.

DIONYSOS

Much wiser on all counts. Why look for trouble?

PENTHEUS

But how do I walk through Thebes without being seen?

DIONYSOS

On paths no one takes. I will lead the way.

PENTHEUS

Anything, so long as I have the last laugh
    on the Bakkhant madwomen.
But now I must go into my house, think over what you've said,
    and make my own decisions.

DIONYSOS

Good. I'm ready, whatever you decide.

PENTHEUS

Then I'm off.
When I return, either I will wage war in the mountains,
    or I will go along with your scheme.

*As soon as Pentheus exits with the 2nd. Messenger, the Chorus
enters.*

DIONYSOS

Women, this man crawls into my net on his own.
He will go to the Bakkhai and balance the scales with his death.
Dionysos, now it is your turn.
I know how near you are. Give us revenge on this man.
First, unweave his mind.
Drive him gently mad.
His sound mind would make him unwilling
    to wear women's dress; so walk him slowly from his mind,
    into his gown.
I want to see him made a joke.
I want to hear Thebes laugh at him,
    a would-be woman led through the city on my arm.
Yes, that is how I want to see this man,
    who once struck such terror with his big bad words.
Now, I will go in and help him with his outfit;
    help him dress for hell.
His mother, with son-slaughtering hands, will send him there.
Yes, Pentheus, you shall soon lose your ignorance of Dionysos,
    son of Zeus, born a god, consummate in power, of all gods
    the most dangerous and the most endearing.

Dionysos enters the palace.

CHORUS

When shall I ever
In god-wild frenzy
Dance night into dawn,
Pounding earth's drum
With white, winged feet,
Flinging my head back
To drink dark dew
From the pure night air,
Like a fawn,
In the festival of its youth,
Gamboling in the fresh green joy
of the forest,
No longer trembling quarry
For the dread hunt,
Once she leaps to freedom
Beyond the beaters' closing noose,
Over the tight-woven nets,
As the raving huntsman
Shouts his savage hounds
Into deafening pursuit;

And, with fear-blind fury,
The fawn flies across the marshy plain,
Like a sudden burst of wind,
To find in the shaded forest,
Exorcised of men,
A feast of stillness
And fresh life.

What is wisdom?
Of all god-given gifts,
What do men want more
Than to have their enemies
Under their thumb?
It is always sweet
To have one's way.
The might of the gods
Moves slowly.
But its path is sure.
It sobers and straightens
Men drunk on their own ideas,
Would-be rivals of the gods,
Connoisseurs of ignorance.
When the gods hunt the godless,
They lie in wait
And bide their time.
To know and observe the ancient ways
Is best.
It costs very little to acknowledge
The power of the divine,
And to accept as nature's fruit
What has weathered
The long storm of time.
What is wisdom?
Of all god-given gifts,
What do men want more
Than to have their enemies
Under their thumb?
It is always sweet
To have one's way.

Blessed is the man who slips free
Of the storm's mouth,
And rides the sea
To safe harbor.
Blessed is the man who sheds his grief
Like a heavy shell.

In their race for wealth and power,
One way or another someone takes the lead,
While someone slips behind.
There are as many dreams as there are lives.
Some ripen into happiness;
The rest lose their way.
The life I call blessed
Is lived for the joy of living,
One day at a time.

Enter Dionysos.

DIONYSOS
Pentheus, if you are as eager as ever
   to see sights not meant for your eyes,
   then come out of your house.
Pentheus, I am calling you. Come here.
Let me see how you look as a woman.
Model for me your Bakkhant's disguise.
Come out here as the maenad
   ready to spy on his mother and her cohort.

> *Summoned by Dionysos, Pentheus enters, robed and wigged
> as a maenad. Thyrsos in hand, he is already crazed, already
> possessed by Dionysos. The 2nd. Messenger follows behind him.*

Oh yes, yes. You definitely have the look.
You could easily be one of the daughters of Kadmos.

PENTHEUS
I see what seem to be two suns and two Thebes,
   two cities, each with seven gates.
And you, my leader and guide,
   have sprouted horns from your head.
You look to me like a bull.
Were you wild from the beginning?
You are wild now. Your savage leering eyes leave no doubts.
You are a wild bull.

DIONYSOS
It is the god who confronts you.
Before now, he was well-disposed.
But we are allied with him from now on. He walks with us.
Your eyes, once blind, now see what eyes are made for.

PENTHEUS

How do I really look?
Do I carry myself properly?
Could I truly pass for Ino or for my mother Agave?

DIONYSOS

Looking at you, I have to tell myself I am not seeing one of them.
But look. One of your curls has come loose
    from under your net where I tucked it.

PENTHEUS

It must have shaken loose when I was inside,
    doing my Bakkhic dance.
It's no wonder, the way I was whirling.

DIONYSOS

Let me be your handmaid.
Hold still, and I will tuck it back into place.

PENTHEUS

Fine. You fix it.
What would I do without you?

Dionysos fusses over Pentheus's curls.

DIONYSOS

Now look.
Your belt's come loose,
    and your gown is hanging all wrong.
It's all uneven.

PENTHEUS

Oh yes.
I see what you mean there on the right side.
But it seems fine here on the left.

DIONYSOS

You're going to think of me soon as your finest friend,
    just as soon as you see how chaste and sober
    the Bakkhants are… not at all what you're expecting.

PENTHEUS

Tell me, do I hold my thyrsos in my right hand or my left,
    if I want to be a *real* Bakkhant?

DIONYSOS

In your right hand.
And you raise it every time you take a step with your right foot.
What a change of heart you're having! Bravo!

PENTHEUS

Do you think I could heave the rocky dens of Kithairon,
   Bakkhai and all, onto my shoulders and haul them away?

DIONYSOS

You could, if you wanted to. The way you think now, it's so apt.
To think you used to be insane!

PENTHEUS

Then should we bring crowbars? Or shall I use my bare hands?
I'll lean against the summit, lock my arms around it,
   and break it off in one piece.
Yes, I'll carry home Kithairon balanced on my shoulder.

DIONYSOS

But, in doing so,
   you would destroy the haunts of the forest nymphs,
   to say nothing of Pan's holy woods, alive with his piping.

PENTHEUS

You're so right.
Besides, brute strength is no way to conquer women.
I'll hide, instead, among the pines.

DIONYSOS

Just remember to hide the fact that you're hidden;
   for only from a secret place of hiding
   will you be able to spy safely on the maenads.

PENTHEUS

I can see them already, lying in their leafy beds,
   locked in love, twitching like mating birds.

DIONYSOS

Yes, and your assignment is to be their watchman.
Perhaps you may even snare them,
   provided they don't snare you first.

PENTHEUS

Now, conduct me through the center of Thebes.
In all the land, there is no other man daring what I do.

DIONYSOS
Indeed, you are alone.
You take on your solitary shoulders the burden of your city.
The ordeal that awaits you is ordained. It suits you.
Follow me, now. I shall get you there in perfect safety.
Someone else will bring you home.

PENTHEUS
Mother!

DIONYSOS
You will be held up as a symbol to all.

PENTHEUS
It is for that that I am going.

DIONYSOS
You will be carried home…

PENTHEUS
What luxury!

DIONYSOS
In your mother's arms.

PENTHEUS
You insist on spoiling me.

DIONYSOS
Oh, but spoiling…

PENTHEUS
I know. It is only what I have coming to me.

DIONYSOS
You are a strange extraordinary fellow,
   and you walk to a strange extraordinary fate.
You are going to make a name for yourself,
   one that rides high, scraping the sky.
Agave, daughters of Kadmos,
hold out your hands for this young man.
I lead him to the final test of strength,
   a contest Bromios and I shall win.
Time will soon tell the whole story.

Dionysos, Pentheus, and the 2nd. Messenger exit in procession.

CHORUS

To the mountains,
Hell-hounds of Lyssa,
Queen of madness,
Run! Leap to the mountain glens,
Where the daughters of Kadmos
Dance in joy.
Tear loose from his senses
This raving fool,
Who primps himself into position
To spy on maenad revelry.
The voyeur's own mother
Will be the first to find him out,
Ensconced among the smooth rocks
Or poised in a treetop high overhead.
Her cries will rouse the others to her rage:
"Bakkhai, who is this intruder on our mountain?
Who is this mountain-climbing Theban snoop,
Who trespasses on our mountain?
What kind of womb dropped him into life?
Not one of ours.
His mother could be a lioness,
Or even a monstrous, snake-haired Gorgon,
Laired in far-off Libya.

Let justice walk for once in open sight,
And make her work a spectacle,
As her blade cuts deep and clean
The throat of this godless man,
The lawless, ruthless son of Ekhion.
Blind to justice,
Blown beyond every scruple by his own fury,
This man rages against your revels,
Bakkhos,
And scorns your mother's rites.
His mind is adrift.
His plan is no plan at all.
He hopes to use force against force itself.
Only death can cool his fury.
Never question what comes from the gods.
Acceptance is wisdom,
The only chance we mortals have

To live without ruin.
How can I harden my heart against wisdom,
When in its pursuit,
I find such joy?
The world is full of great and simple truths
Right before our eyes.
If only life would flow toward fairness.
If only men would pass their days and nights
In simplest piety,
Honoring the gods in all things,
And weeding from their lives
Whatever habits and customs
Poison justice in their souls.

Let justice walk for once in open sight,
And make her work a spectacle,
As her blade cuts deep and clean
The throat of this godless man,
The lawless, ruthless son of Ekhion.

Dionysos, reveal yourself to us.
Come before our eyes as a wild bull...
As a serpent sprouting heads...
As a lion spitting balls of fire.
Come, Bakkhos,
Masked behind your divinely distant grin,
And smile on the hunter of Bakkhants,
As you tighten your noose
And bring him down
To have his life crushed from him
By a horde of women
Wild for the harvest.

Enter 2nd. Messenger.

2nd MESSENGER

House of Kadmos,
   to think that once you were the envy of Greece!
So many years ago that our old king still felt his youth,
   he sowed the serpent's field with a new crop,
    and a new race of men sprouted from the slain dragon's teeth.
Thebes was born; and for a time it shone.
House of Kadmos, once so blessed,
   even I, a slave, must mourn you now.

CHORUS

What is it?
You have news of the Bakkhai. Tell me.

2nd MESSENGER

Pentheus, the child of Ekhion, is dead.

CHORUS

Lord Bromios, unmasked at last! You are a great god.

2nd MESSENGER

What was that? What did you say, woman?
So you revel in my master's misery?

CHORUS

I was praying.
I am a foreigner and I'm going to pray and sing as I please.
We don't have to fear you or your jails any longer.

2nd MESSENGER

So you think Thebes has run out of men,
   just because we've lost our king?

CHORUS

Dionysos, and Dionysos alone, is our king.

2nd MESSENGER

Which explains your joy, but does not excuse it.
Women, don't gloat over someone else's grief.
It's an ugly thing to do.

CHORUS

Tell me something, man.
Tell me how his lawless mind went blank.
How did the fool find his fate?

2nd MESSENGER

Imagine a procession, to a spectacle.
The stranger led the way, Pentheus and I close behind.
My concern was to be at my master's side.
Before we knew it we were crossing the streams of Asopos
   and beginning our ascent of Kithairon.
Thebes was well behind us now,
   as we picked our way over the rocky scrub land.

When we came to our first glen, we said nothing,
  and tried to walk without a sound,
  so as to see what we had come for without being seen.
Encircled by cliffs, shaded by a canopy of towering pines,
  and veined with trickling brooks,
  the glen made a lush home for the maenads,
  who sat in the soft grass busy at work they found sweet.
Some of the women rewound their frayed wands with fresh ivy,
  while others, as glad as fillies free of bit and bridle,
  formed separate choruses and sang songs of Bakkhos,
  back and forth to each other.
Meanwhile, poor, wretched Pentheus
  couldn't get the view he wanted of the female throng,
  and complained to our guide.
"Stranger," he said, "standing where we are,
  I can't get a decent look at those maenad fakes;
  but if I could mount that lofty pine up there on the ridge,
  then I would be peering straight down on their perversity.
The stranger answered with a miracle. I saw him do it.
The cloud-scraping tip of the tallest pine came under his power,
  and he drew it down, down, down
  until it scratched the dark earth.
Like a bowman stringing his bow
  or a wheelwright shaping a wheel,
  the stranger bent the giant mountain pine with his bare hands
  and brought it down.
What he did no mortal man can do.
Once he had Pentheus straddling the uppermost bough,
  he let the pine slip slowly from his grasp, easing it skywards,
  lest it suddenly bolt and throw its rider.
A moment passed and the pine stood lofty and firm again,
  just as before, only mounted by my master.
He, not the maenads, was now the spectacle.
No sooner was Pentheus perched in open sight,
  then the stranger disappeared,
  and a voice broke through the upper air like a bolt of light.
It seemed to me the cry of Dionysos.
"Women, I bring to you the blasphemer,
  the one who mocked you, laughed at me and my mysteries.
Now make him pay for it."
Even as he spoke, a flash of unearthly fire
  spanned heaven and earth and made them briefly one.
All was still…
  the air, the trees, the leaves, the birds, the beasts.

Lifted to their feet by the piercing cry,
    the women looked everywhere for its meaning.
Again Dionysos issued his command; and this time
    the daughters of Kadmos knew well their master's voice.
Like a thousand doves startled into sudden flight,
    the Bakkhai horde—Agave, her sisters, and the rest—
    swarmed and, on winged feet, swept through the glen,
overleaping torrents, bounding from one jagged rock
    to another, crazed and driven,
    as if the god were blowing fire through their brains.
And when their raving eyes finally found my master
    roosting overhead, some of the women flung stones at him,
while others, climbing a rocky pinnacle opposite the pine,
    hurled makeshift spears torn from nearby trees.
Still others showered the air with their wands;
    but their aim was off and it all came to nothing.
Stranded in the sky above their heads,
    Pentheus sat wretched but safe.
It seemed he was higher than they were wild.
Finally, as if their fingers were shafts of lightning,
    the women splintered nearby saplings into oaken levers,
    to dig up and pry loose the roots of Pentheus's perch.
But, when they failed, Agave cried out:
"Women, encircle the tree and grip it low, around the trunk.
We must unseat its wild rider and make sure he carries home
    no stories of our god's secret rites."
At once a circle of women gripped the giant pine and ripped
it from its roots, while Pentheus, seated high overhead,
    began to plummet to the earth,
    screaming every foot of the way.
He was learning how very little divided him from doom.
The first to pounce on him was his mother,
    the wretched priestess of his slaughter.
In hopes that she might see him as her son and spare his life,
    he tore off his wig and touched her cheeks in supplication.
"Mother," he sobbed, "it's me, Pentheus, your boy.
At home, in the house of Ekhion, you gave me life.
Don't kill me just because I've made a mistake.
Mother, have pity. Don't kill your own son."
But foam dripped down on him from her frothing mouth,
    while her eyes spun randomly in their sockets.
She was inhabited by her god ,
    who ran loose and wild in her mind.
She could not think, much less listen to her son.

Gripping his left arm just below the wrist,
  and planting her foot on his chest,
    she ripped her wretched son's limb loose from its socket,
    with an awful strength not her own, but the god's gift to her.
Meanwhile Ino was at work on the rest of him, flaying him alive,
  as Autonoe and the whole horde of Bakkhai closed in for the kill.
Below the women's shrieks and screams of joy,
  Pentheus's agony could be heard,
    as he gasped and groaned his final breaths away.
Together, with a single cry, they announced the end.
Afterwards, one of the women carried away a part of an arm,
  while another scurried off with a foot, still in its hunting boot.
Once his ribs had been clawed and picked clean of meat,
  the women rose, with dripping hands,
    and began tossing back and forth bits of Pentheus's flesh,
    making up the game as they went.
His body lies out there now, in pieces, scattered everywhere,
  some of it on the desolate rocks, some deep in the woods.
It won't be easy to find it all.
As for the head, his mother has it.
Stuck on the end of her thyrsos, it makes a grim trophy.
She holds it high, thinking it's the head of a wild mountain lion.
Leaving her sisters and the others to their maenad dances,
Agave parades through the forests of Kithairon,
  exulting in her hapless catch.
This is how even now she makes her way back here to the city,
  hailing Bakkhos as her fellow-huntsman,
    her comrade in the chase.
She sings of triumph, but all she's won is tears.
I'm getting out.
I want to be far away from all of this when Agave arrives.
Keeping our hearts humble, and revering all that is sacred…
  I know of nothing lovelier.
This is for mortals the most useful prize and the highest wisdom.

Exit 2nd. Messenger.

CHORUS
Dance, Bakkhai, dance to our god.
Sing out the sufferings of Pentheus.
Proclaim the doom of the dragon-child,
Who in women's robes, and holy wand in hand
Walked to his own sure death,
Lured into lasting darkness
By the bull.

Women of Thebes,
What fame is yours today!
Bakkhai, you have won a great victory,
Though it leads to grief and tears.
How sweet the labor and the pain,
When at last your hands glisten
With your own child's blood.
But look.
I see Agave, mother of Pentheus, rushing towards the palace.
From the look in her eyes, the god is with her.
Women, the festival goes on.
Hail the god of joy.

Enter Agave, holding aloft the head of Pentheus.

AGAVE
Women from the East, Bakkhai!

CHORUS
Yes? What is it? Why do you call us?

AGAVE
Look! Look what I bring home from the mountains.
See how freshly cut it is.
The god smiled on our hunt.

CHORUS
Yes, I can see. Welcome, sister.
We are one in joy.

AGAVE
Look at him. He's the whelp of a ferocious lion.
I caught him without a snare or net. Feast your eyes on him!

CHORUS
In what wilderness did you find it?

AGAVE
On Kithairon.

CHORUS
Kithairon?

AGAVE
Yes. That's where I carved him up.

CHORUS

But who struck the first blow?

AGAVE

I did. That's why he's all mine!
"Agave the blest!" That's what they call me now in the ranks.

CHORUS

Who else had a part in this?

AGAVE

Kadmeans.

CHORUS

Which Kadmeans?

AGAVE

My own blood sisters... they were next to pounce on the prey.
They came second, after me! I was first!
O what a lucky, lucky catch! Now, share the feast with me.

CHORUS

Share what, poor woman?

AGAVE

Look, the little wild thing is so young.
Beneath his soft mane, on his cheeks, nothing but down.

CHORUS

It looks so wild.

AGAVE

Bakkhos was brilliant.
He ran with us maenads in the hunt, keeping us on the scent.
Our speed and cunning came from him.

CHORUS

He is lord of the hunt.

AGAVE

So you applaud our catch?

CHORUS

Oh yes.

AGAVE

Maybe the men of Thebes…

CHORUS

And your son, Pentheus…

AGAVE

Yes… my son… how he will clap his hands
   when he sees his mother carrying the lion she caught.

CHORUS

A most unusual catch.

AGAVE

A most unusual hunt.

CHORUS

You must be proud.

AGAVE

Proud and pleased.
I come from the hunt with something to show for it,
   something great, something unforgettable.

CHORUS

Then let the city see it, poor woman.
Come. Hold high your prize.
Show your fellow-Thebans this savage trophy of yours.

AGAVE

Citizens of Thebes, all you
   who call this land and this city of splendid towers your home,
   come out and see our catch.
Behold the beast brought down by the daughters of Kadmos,
   felled without spears or arrows or nets,
   cut down and flayed with our hands' pale knives.
After what we have done, catching our prey and tearing it apart
   with nothing but our bare hands,
   won't men sound silly, when they bluster on,
   weighed down with their foolish weapons?
But where is my aged father?
I want him here near me.
And my boy, Pentheus… where is he?
Someone go get him.

His mother wants him to lean a ladder against the palace wall
   so that he can climb up with her lion's head
     —this one, the one she just caught—
and nail it up there to the front of her house, as her trophy.

*Enter Kadmos, followed by Attendants carrying on a litter the
remains of Pentheus.*

KADMOS

Follow me, men.
Bring the awful weight of Pentheus here to me.
Set it down before the walls of his house.
How do I describe the labor it has taken
   to bring home the body of my boy?
How we had to scour the glens of Kithairon for him,
   strewn for miles, no two pieces in the same place,
   bits lying here and there, hard to find in a dense wood.
Old Teiresias and I had left the revels behind
   and returned to Thebes.
We were already back inside the city walls
   when I was told the hideous things my daughters had done.
So I turned back at once towards Kithairon
   to collect what was left of my son, savaged by maenads.
There, among the oaks, cursed and still crazed,
   sat Autonoe, mother of Akteon and wife of Aristaios. Ino too.
From them I learned that Agave was making her way back here,
   wild as the wind.

Seeing Agave.

I see they spoke the truth. There she is. Not a happy sight.

AGAVE

Oh Father, you should be bursting with pride; for you have
   by far the best and bravest daughters in all the world.
I mean all three of us. But most of all me.
I have left my shuttle at the loom
   and moved on to greater things...
     to catching savage beasts with my bare hands.
You can see what I mean.
Here in my hands I hold the prize, proof of my daring,
   and now a trophy to hang on the front of our house.
Here, Father, you take it.
Boast all you want of your daughter's pluck,
   and of the booty she brings home.

Invite your friends to the feast.
For you are so blest, blest with daughters
  who do such great things!

KADMOS

It is my misery that has no limit.
Yes, I see in your wretched hands
  the "great thing" you have done.
I see your sweet offering lifted to the gods.
And to such a feast as this you invite me and the rest of Thebes!
Oh how I pity you, my child... you first, and then myself.
Lord Bromios, by blood one of us, has been thorough.
His case was just; but he went too far with it.

AGAVE

Old age is so grudging, so full of sour looks.
I just wish my son would take after me,
  show a little glimmer of his mother's prowess,
  the next time he goes out hunting with his mates.
But the only thing he's good for is waging war... against gods!
He needs a good talking-to, Father.
Now who is going to call him out here into my sight,
  so that he can see me in all of my glory?

KADMOS

Oh my god, what a fearful wound will open,
  when you understand what you have done.
If only you could cling to where you are now,
  for the rest of your life, so accursed and so oblivious.

AGAVE

What's wrong. Why are you so upset?

KADMOS

Never mind. Just look straight up, into the sky.

AGAVE

Yes. I'm looking; but what am I looking for?

KADMOS

Is everything the same, or has anything changed?

AGAVE

It seems brighter and clearer than before.

KADMOS
And the frenzy inside you... is that still there?

AGAVE
I don't know what you mean.
But I do feel like something's changed, as if I've just awakened
    or come to my senses somehow.

KADMOS
Then you hear me?
You think you can answer me with a clear head?

AGAVE
I've forgotten what we were talking about, Father.

KADMOS
On your wedding night,
    whose house did you become a part of?

AGAVE
You gave me away, Father, into the arms of Ekhion,
    the man they say was spawned by a dragon.

KADMOS
And in his house, you gave your husband a son.
What was his name?

AGAVE
Pentheus. He belonged to both of us.

KADMOS
And whose head are you cradling in your arms?

AGAVE
The head of a lion, or so the hunters told me.

KADMOS
Take a close look now. What harm will looking do?

AGAVE
Oh! What am I seeing? What am I holding in my hands?

KADMOS
Keep looking. Study it carefully.

AGAVE
I see a grief in which I will drown.

KADMOS
Then it doesn't look like a lion anymore?

AGAVE
No. It looks like the head... of Pentheus.

KADMOS
Why I was weeping... before you understood.

AGAVE
But who killed him?
How did his head get in my arms?

KADMOS
This truth comes too late and too soon. It is like a knife.

AGAVE
Already the pounding in my heart nearly deafens me.
Have pity. Tell me quickly.

KADMOS
You killed him, you and your sisters.

AGAVE
Where did it happen? At home? Where?

KADMOS
You know where wild dogs tore Akteon to pieces... it was there.
The same place.

AGAVE
Kithairon? What was my poor boy doing on Kithairon?

KADMOS
He went there in mockery of the god, to spy on your revelry.

AGAVE
But what were we doing out there?

KADMOS
You were mad.
The whole city was mad, possessed by Bakkhos.

AGAVE

Dionysos destroyed us. Now I see it all.

KADMOS

He was enraged. You affronted him, denied his divinity.

AGAVE

My darling boy's body... where is it, Father?

KADMOS

It was not easy to find, but I did. Here it is.

AGAVE

It's all back together? It's all here?

KADMOS

So to speak. I did all I could.

AGAVE

I was the fool. Why should Pentheus pay for that?

KADMOS

Because he grew into your foolishness on his own.
He too blasphemed the god.
And so, with a single swipe of his hand,
    the god cut us all down—you, me, him—
    and laid waste my house,
    leaving me with no one to carry on my name.
There lies the corpse of my last hope, hideously spoiled.
What a wicked waste of life!
Your son, wretched daughter, flesh of your flesh.
Oh child, how we all looked up to you.
You were the pillar of your grandfather's house.
Thebes knew well to fear you.
No one who once set eyes on you ever dreamed of affronting me;
    for you paid back wrongs with a swift and steady hand.
But no more.
Naked of all the honor I once had, I will be flung now
    from my own house—I, Kadmos the Great—who once
    sowed a race of warriors and reaped a glorious harvest.
O child, I still love you best.
Somehow, this love hasn't gone away with you.
Never again your hand on my face.
Never again your arms around me.

I've heard you say "Grandfather" for the last time.
No more: "But Grandfather, has someone done you wrong?
Someone dishonored you? Who is it?
Who has upset you and caused you pain?
Tell me, Grandfather, so that he can feel the fist of my justice."
No more.
Now a vast misery engulfs us all:
    me, you, your mother, her sisters.
If there is anyone left who mocks the gods,
    let him have a look at this boy.
Tell him how he died, and let him find faith, fast.

CHORUS

I feel sorry for you, Kadmos.
Your grandson deserved his pain; but you do not.

AGAVE

Oh Father, look what a long way I have been dragged,
    in a moment of time, from triumph to this.
Only a moment ago I was a great hunter exulting in the kill.
Now I am a mother, a murderer.
And this was my prize, my trophy, my sweet son's head.
I wonder, can a mother mourn a son she's killed?
What prayers, what songs are hers?
Can the same hands that... touch him now... make him ready?
My baby, I once kept you so safe, so close,
    cupping your tiny head in my hand,
    while you sucked and made me glad.
And then I set you down... to sleep.
Here. You are one again, whole, nearly.
Yours arms. They grew so strong.
How I loved them around me.
Your legs... Like a deer you ran, so ungainly at first,
    but then so beautiful.
And your feet, your toes... my baby, sweetest of all.
You were so perfect! What monster made such a mess of you?

KADMOS

My poor wretched girl, cover him up.
Let him lie in peace.

AGAVE

I thought I would one day dress you for your bride, not this.
How can this be?

Enter Dionysos.

DIONYSOS

I am Dionysos, son of Semele, child of Zeus,
   revealed at last as the god that I am.
My homecoming here has been spoiled by slander and abuse.
I was blasphemed, my divinity denied...
   my sacred body bound and handled with contempt.
Stupid little threats were hurled at me!
All this I suffered.
Now this is what they shall suffer,
   those who ignored and affronted me.
They shall know indignities that will never end.
Their exile will last as long as they do.
They will drown in wretchedness.
As for this man, Pentheus, he lived up to his name.
He found the grief he deserved.
You were witnesses to his folly.
Now witness his reward.
He so wanted a spectacle, and now he is one.
Gaze at my justice, at how perfect it is.
You, Agave, you and your sisters,
   shall leave Thebes never to return.
Your son's blood will claw your soul forever.
No sea can wash away its stain.
Kadmos, you too shall go into exile.
I have plans for you, demands to make.
Your way will be hard.
But in the end, god Ares shall pity you
   and give you respite in the land of the blessed.
These are my decrees.
I, son not of man but of god, child of Zeus, have spoken.
If only you had known better and shown some sense,
   listened to my will not yours,
      you would find yourselves championed by the child of god,
      and you would this very moment be astonished
      by your blessings.

KADMOS

Dionysos, have pity. We know we have done wrong.

DIONYSOS

But your knowledge comes too late.
When seeing would have made some difference, you were blind.

KADMOS

We grant you all of this. Your case against us is seamless.
But you press it too far.

DIONYSOS

Too far? I, a god, blasphemed by you!

KADMOS

It is unseemly for gods to mimic human rage and revenge.

DIONYSOS

Zeus himself, my father, approved all of this long ago.

AGAVE

Father, we are condemned to exile.
Nothing can change that now.

DIONYSOS

Exactly. So why delay the inevitable?

KADMOS

Oh child, you and I and your sisters, are eclipsed in misery.
We face a dreadful fate. I know my pain will never end.
Not even in death shall I find peace.

AGAVE

And I, in my exile, will not even have you, Father.

KADMOS

Oh my poor girl, why do you wrap your soft arms around me,
    as if, like some giant swan,
    you could shelter this old wreck of a man?

AGAVE

Hurled from my own house, where do I turn?

KADMOS

I don't know, child. Your father is no help to you.

AGAVE

Farewell, Thebes, my homeland, my house, my bed,
    where I once lay long ago as a young bride.
Banished, I leave you now, for nothing but misery.
My heart breaks for you, Father.

KADMOS

And mine for you, child. I weep too for your sisters.

AGAVE

What Lord Dionysos has done to your house
  makes a shocking sight.

DIONYSOS

No more shocking than what I suffered at your hands,
  when Thebes snubbed me.

AGAVE

Good-bye, Father.

KADMOS

Good-bye, poor child.
"Farewell," but I fear you will not.

Kadmos exits with Attendants.

AGAVE

To the Chorus.
Friends, lead the way.
Take me to my sisters, my sad companions in exile.
I go defiled by my own son's blood.
As for where I go,
  I ask only that it be far from the sight of Kithairon,
  in a land without revels and Bakkhic wands,
  a land without memory.
If the dance begins again, I leave it to others.

CHORUS

As they exit, leading Agave.
The gods have many faces.
What we expect least
They bring to pass,
While what seemed sure to us
Never is.
And for what we never dreamed could be
God finds a way;
And so it happened here today.

CHORAL ODES

◇◇◇◇◇◇◇◇◇◇◇

ADAPTED FOR PERFORMANCE

CHORUS 465–469

Blessed are the Bakkhai,
Who swarm in the mountains,
Cleansing their souls
With holy revelry.
Blessed are the Bakkhai,
Who wave the sacred thyrsos,
Treading the earth
Like a drum.

Glad is the soul
Seeing the mysteries
Of our god.
Blessed the life
Lived in tune
With the divine.
Always and forever
We sing his names.

Dionysos! Bakkhos! Bromios!

Light our labor
In your service,
Sweet to follow
Your holy path.
No music like yours,
The scream of god,
A voice of fire
Searing our souls.

Rise up, Bakkhai!
Bakkhai, rise up!
Escort your god.
Raise the cry.
Pound the drums
In his praise.
Sing of Dionysos.
Shout to the god of joy.

CHORUS 477–479

Insolence and blasphemy
Come easily to kings.
The unruly tongues of rulers
Steer a course to certain doom.
Our king's words are weeds
Fit for the fire.

Bakkhos, god of merriment,
Lightens our feet and hearts.
Simple days and sweet nights,
His gifts and his demands.
Sweetest of all
The oblivion he brings.

Take me, Bromios,
Lord of the dance.
Take me there
Where the grape's bright blood
Bursts on the altars and beds
Of the gods.

Take me, Bromios,
Lord of bliss,
Take me there,
Where desire leaves its banks,
And the swirling joy of god
Drowns us in peace.

CHORUS 485–487

Dirke,
Sweet virgin spring,
Once you held in your lucent arms
The inchoate son of god.
With your pure crystal streams
You bathed the divine life,
Snatched by its father Zeus
From the jagged, searing teeth
Of insatiable fire.

Dirke,
Why disown him now?
I swear by the clustered grape,
Bursting on the vine.
I swear by the gleaming cup,
Lifted by our god.
You shall learn your place.
Your neglect of Dionysos
Will be brief.

What blind fury
Consumes the son of Ekhion,
Savage and wild,
Not yet tamed
To his mortality?
Wars against gods
Are never won,
Only lost, like the kings
Who wage them.

Lord Dionysos,
Child of Zeus,
Caged in this house,
Chained to darkness,
See what we suffer,
Who proclaim your name.
Let us hear your voice.
Sing to us
A song of rage.

CHORUS 502–504

In god-wild frenzy
I will dance night into dawn,
Pounding earth's drum
With white, winged feet,
Flinging my head back
To drink dark dew
From the pure air,
Like a fawn,
In the festival of youth,
Leaping in the fresh green joy
Of the shaded forest
Exorcised of men,
Feasting on the stillness
Of the night.

Fools dance to a music
No one else hears.
They mock only themselves.
The might of the gods
Moves slowly.
But its path is sure.
It sobers men drunk
On their own ideas,
Revelers in ignorance.
When the gods
Hunt the godless,
They lie in wait
For a moment
Ripe with truth.

CHORUS 508–509

To the mountains,
Run, hell hounds,
Leap to the mountain glens,
Where the daughters of Kadmos
Dance in joy.
Tear loose from his senses
This raving fool,
Who primps himself
To spy on maenad revelry.

Blind to justice,
Blown beyond scruple
By his own fury,
This man rages
Against your revels, Bakkhos,
Scorns your mother's rites.
His mind is adrift.
Only death
Can put his madness out.

Who can this man be
Who fouls our holy place
With drooling curiosity?
What kind of womb
Dropped him into life?
Not one of ours.
His mother is a lioness,
A monster, a Gorgon
Spawned in hell.

Dionysos,
Reveal yourself to us.
Come before our eyes
As a wild bull,
As a serpent sprouting heads,
As a lion spitting balls of fire.
Come, Bakkhos,
Smile on the hunt.
Run with us.

Bakkhai, lift your feet,
Pound the earth
Until it bleeds.
It is harvest time.
The grapes burst
Beneath our feet.
Their blood makes us glad.
Dance, Bakkhai,
Dance with our god.

◇◇◇◇◇◇◇

REVEL & REVELATION

THE POETICS OF EURIPIDES

REVEL & REVELATION
◇◇◇◇◇◇◇◇◇◇◇

Some works of art, under scrutiny, confess their finitude, while others do not. True to Dionysos, its divine protagonist, the *Bakkhai* is fluid, elusive, and contemptuous of any effort to pin it to a board like a butterfly spread for labeling. The *Bakkhai* is all about "possession," not our possessing it but its possessing us, its translators, directors, critics, and students. Consequently, in the ensuing reflections, I propose no more than a perspective on the *Bakkhai*, one way of looking at the play and of seeing a measured portion of what is there. I do not claim that what I have to say about the *Bakkhai* is what the *Bakkhai* is "about" or is what the *Bakkhai* "says." Like a living organism, which any great work of art is, the *Bakkhai* simply "is" before and beyond its meaning or saying anything. Now, unexpectedly, I wish to begin my approach to the *Bakkhai* at an oblique angle, by looking momentarily to another play, another playwright, and their most famous critic.

THE POETICS OF EURIPIDES

Few would quibble with Bernard Knox when he begins his introduction to Robert Fagles's fine translation of *Oedipus the King* with the following statement: "This play is universally recognized as the dramatic masterpiece of the Greek theater." He goes on to say how Aristotle, in his *Poetics*, cited *Oedipus the King* as the "model for all to follow." There is no denying the universal recognition awarded this play, nor the influence of Aristotle on that recognition. Indeed, if Sophokles had not died twenty years before Aristotle was born, one might suspect a conspiracy. If not conspiracy, surely congeniality. The work, particularly this work, of Sophokles suits the theories of Aristotle; and the theories of Aristotle have certainly done no harm to the long-term career of Sophoklean drama. On the other hand, this creative-critical consortium of Sophokles and Aristotle has unwittingly done a profound disservice to ancient Greek drama by ushering *Oedipus the King* to the center of attention and acclaim and by making it a template and measure of sorts for the rest of ancient tragic drama. In this light, the exciting turbulence and diversity of ancient drama may be seen as qualitative discrepancy, as if the full stable of ancient Athenian playwrights were all running at once, though at different speeds, for the same mark. As in any race, only the first several to cross the line receive notice. To mention a few of the stragglers, whatever happened to Aiskhylos's *Persians*, to Euripides' *Herakles*, *Hekabe*, and *Helen*, or, for that matter, to Sophokles' own *Philoktetes*? The near oblivion they endure is due not to their being inferior but to their being different. The finish line which Sophokles crossed with *Oedipus the King*, thereby winning the prize and crown as consummate master of Attic tragedy, was drawn perhaps seventy-five years after the victorious foot, as it were, stepped across it. In short, Sophokles won a contest which neither he nor his peers thought to enter, a contest in which we have been the real losers.

The aesthetic principles set forth in the *Poetics* of Aristotle are finally the principles not of Attic tragedy but of Aristotelian tragedy, which is a troubling thought, for Aristotle didn't write tragedy. So far as we know, the only ancient tragic playwright who wrote directly, in critical prose, about his art was Sophokles; and his work, *On the Chorus*, is sadly lost, so lost that we have no sure grounds for imagining what it said. What, then, did the playwrights themselves, those who created the genre in which they excelled, think about the theater and its works? In penultimate response to this ultimately unanswerable question, I wish to suggest that in the *Bakkhai* we have as close as we may ever come to the "Poetics" of Euripides.

Written at the close of his career and produced posthumously for him, Euripides' *Bakkhai* may be seen as looking back over a lifetime in the theater, a lifetime in the service of Dionysos. It may, in short, be seen as Euripides' last testament and consummate testimony concerning the theater he knew so well. The *Bakkhai* is, among other things, a play about the theater and its god. Drama is not only the genre but also the subject matter of the *Bakkhai*. It is a play about plays, a drama about drama, a tragedy in which the essence of all tragedy is distilled and disclosed. It contains, we might say, the poetics, the poetic theories and principles, of Euripides in the form of a play, the form we might expect from a playwright. As such, the *Bakkhai* offers a remarkably appropriate and revealing introduction to ancient Greek tragedy, as well as a badly needed corrective to the monoscopic vision of Aristotle.

What is there, we might ask, about Aristotle's vision that requires correction? The full response to that question outstrips the modest ambitions of this essay; but a first, partial response, such as this is, might point to a blind spot in Aristotle's work. Where, we might ask, in the *Poetics* of Aristotle is Dionysos? After all, the two Athenian festivals, for which every ancient play we possess was written, were the City Dionysia and the Lenaea, both festivals of Dionysos. The Athenian theater itself belonged to Dionysos, lay in his sacred precinct, and touched his early temple. The altar or *thymele* of Dionysos occupied the center of the orchestra and held, during the performances, the cult statue of the god, before whom and to whom the plays were performed. The cultic entanglement of Dionysos and drama was indeed close and complex, which surely suggests some relevance of the god to the art. The god of theater must reveal something to us about the art of theater; and yet Aristotle in his *Poetics* is silent on this point. Not so Euripides in his *Bakkhai*.

As truly as Dionysos is eclipsed in the *Poetics*, he is revealed in the *Bakkhai*. In Euripides' *Bakkhai* we witness both the revel [*bakkheusis*] and the revelation [*emphasis*] of Dionysos; and in these two we discover the essence of what we might call Dionysian drama, not as Nietzsche conceptualized it but as Euripides practiced it.

THE GOD OF THEATER

In the first moments of the *Bakkhai*, when Dionysos enters and delivers the prologue, he announces to his home city of Thebes that he is back. He has returned to reveal himself and to receive at last the recognition that is his due. He has returned to take possession of what belongs to him: Thebes. The precise place of his return, the place of his revelation, is a sacred precinct, where long ago his mother Semele was first impregnated and later incinerated by her lover Zeus. It was here, in one luminous, convulsive blast, that divinity and humanity touched. Here is the Dionysian *omphalos*, the center of revel and revelation in the *Bakkhai*, the focus of Dionysos's presence and power, the point of fission. Encircling this spot, marking it out as a sacred *temenos*, and claiming it for Dionysos, are vines, encrusted with grapes, "my handiwork," boasts Dionysos. Clearly, in claiming this place, Dionysos is repossessing what is already his. For, quite unmistakably, this place is the theater. The "stone raised in memory of my mother" to which Dionysos points is, we may assume, the *thymele*, the platform of his theatrical, his real, presence. What Dionysos, the twice-born, has in mind for his homecoming is to reveal his divinity in the place of his first birth, here in his "Thebes," here in his theater. What he has in mind might be described in Aristotelian categories such as imitation, spectacle, reversal, recognition, and katharsis; for what he has in mind is a play. But this is the theater of Dionysos, not that of Aristotle; so we would do better to speak of revel and revelation. In fact, we must know better the nature of this god if we are to know better the nature of his theater. Who, then, is this Dionysos, who in the first words of the *Bakkhai* says "I am back"?

Dionysos, the god of theater, is also a god of nature, metamorphosis, revelry, illusion, possession, mania, masks, vision, and truth. This list of epithets is, admittedly, more suggestive than exhaustive; but once we have examined, even quite briefly, each of these dimensions of Dionysian life, we will find ourselves closer to the core of the *Bakkhai* and, perhaps, closer to an understanding of those aspects of ancient Greek drama on which Aristotle is understandably silent.

Plutarch's turn of phrase for the "natural" domain of Dionysos puts us on the right track, "on the scent" as it were. He assigns to Dionysos not simply nature [*physis*] but "fluid nature" [*hygra physis*]. Clearly, what Plutarch has in mind by this phrase are all of the flowing, dripping, throbbing, sluicing, gurgling forms which the force of life takes in nature, as water, milk, semen, blood, amniotic fluid, honey, saliva, sap, and the special gift from Dionysos himself, wine. The first thing to notice here is that wine is but one form among many of fluid nature, one form of the intoxicating, mind-altering force of life, crushed, distilled, and decanted by Bakkhos. Dionysian revelry is not drunken rowdiness, multiplied by divinity. In the *Bakkhai*, a cowherd, who has chanced to witness the Bakkhai's revels on the slopes of Mount Kithairon, is the first to correct this misconception. "It was not as you picture it, king," he explains to Pentheus, "not the aftermath of drunkenness or of lust let loose." Part of what we learn from the cowherd in the *Bakkhai* is that the followers of Dionysos, those who commune in him, are drunk not with wine but with nature or life, life crushed like grapes beneath the feet of their dancing god and poured for them, for their frenzy.

The second thing to notice about this *hygra physis*—nature communed in, by, and with Dionysos—is that it is "fluid" and not merely "liquid." Nature in its fluid state is beyond containment and categorization; it leaps its own boundaries. It is alive and wild and deliriously confused. We learn this too from the same cowherd's account. He tells how one Bakkhant "raised her thyrsos and struck a rock, sending up into the air a bright jet of water." He goes on to describe what else he saw:

> When another drove her fennel wand into the ground,
>   her god made the dark earth ooze and bubble
>   until a spray of crimson wine
>   burst forth beneath her feet.
> Still others thirsted for fresh white milk
>   and found it with their fingers,
>   clawing at the earth until it nursed them.
> Then they sucked and licked pure, sweet honey,
>   trickling from the tips of their ivy wands.

Water struck from a rock, wine and milk scratched from the soil, honey sucked from a dead stick. This is the *hygra physis* over which Dionysos presides. Nowhere are the familiar words of Heraklitos more telling then here, in the precinct of Dionysos, where "everything flows" [*panta rhei*].

Yes everything. There is more to the world-in-revel than milk or wine welling up from the earth. What the cowherd saw is only the beginning. When Pentheus, in an effort to seal off his city from Dionysian chaos, orders every gate closed, Dionysos only laughs. "Whatever for? Unless I'm mistaken," he taunts Pentheus, "gods pass *over* gates, not *through* them." Dionysos, who leaps easily every boundary in the cosmos, will not have his stride broken by the walls of Thebes. He is the god of metamorphosis, naturally fluid, capable of rapid and radical self-alteration. One moment he is human, the next bestial, and in the end divine. Dionysos changes natures like an actor changing costumes. Effeminate stranger, steaming bull, avenging godhead: all these and countless more are in his repertoire. And for those who commune in his life and power, his Bakkhai, there is a share in his fluidity. They mirror and mimic his metamorphoses.

The followers of Dionysos change appearance not essence, however, behavior not nature. In part, it is a matter of costume: men wearing the robes of women, women wearing the skins of animals, and so on. Beneath these appearances, however, profound changes take place. Old men, relics and fossils like Kadmos and Teiresias, feel and act like boys again. Instead of giving over their weight and weariness to their walking-staves, they receive levity and vigor from their Bakkhant wands. After Kadmos says how sweet this is, this late-blossoming youth, Teiresias joins in. "The same thing! It's happening to me," he says. "I feel like a boy again, ready to dance my heart out." Of course, even stranger things are happening in the mountains. Mothers leave the babes they bore and nurse "new-born gazelles and wild wolf cubs," while writhing vipers climb the women's shoulders and faces and lick their cheeks. Startled from their bucolic bliss by the menacing presence of men, the same women turn bestial. They suddenly possess the speed, agility, and strength of savage predators. Again, from the cowherd's account of what he saw:

> The women went at the cattle
>   with only their fingers as flaying-knives…
> A young heifer, lowing with dull terror,
>   came apart in their hands.

Next, in a scene familiar except for its reversal of the sexes, the women close ranks and descend like an invading army on the countryside and nearby villages, leaving havoc and pain behind them. The Bakkhants, women armed only with ivy wands, turn back the town's defenders and inflict heavy casualties. Summing up the event, the cowherd says that "in short, women routed men." Women did not become men and men did not become women; rather, women inflicted pain the way men often do, and men endured pain the way women often must. Similarly, Kadmos and Teiresias did not become young; they only felt and acted as if they were young again. This "as if" is critical. It suggests that only for Dionysos and not for his followers is nature altogether fluid. Dionysos passes from one nature to another, while his followers pass only from one appearance or state or state of mind to another.

Revel [bakkheusis], communion in Bakkhos or Dionysos, means, therefore, that revelers merely taste the powers and prerogatives of their god. The reveler's cup is shallow. A sip of divinity does not go far or last long. Often, revelry is no more than a state of mind in which nothing is altered beyond the mind itself and its perceptions. Dionysos, as the god of illusion, need not work wonders in the world when he can work them in the mind instead. He makes this clear in his description of what occurred in the Theban dungeons, where he had been taken away to rot. Dionysos tells his Bakkhant Chorus how easy it was for him to escape. Asked about his bonds, Dionysos explains:

> That was where I made a fool of him.
> He bound me only in his thoughts.
> He never laid a hand on me, never touched me.
> All he did was to feast on a phantasy,
>   somewhere in his mind.

In the ensuing account of Dionysos's devastating escape from Pentheus's dungeons, the line between illusion and reality becomes more and more difficult to trace. The Asiatic stranger steps beyond the wildness, finds a place of calm, and merely watches as Bakkhos himself arrives to unleash chaos. This bit of bilocation is only the beginning. Bakkhos sends the house of Pentheus into convulsions. "Everywhere he looked," relates Dionysos, "Pentheus saw flames; but they burned mostly in his mind." Pentheus finds his sword and runs dementedly through his crumbling palace searching for Dionysos, who himself admits: "I only think I know what happened next."

> Bromios, it seems, fashioned an effigy of me,
>   a mere phantom, and put it in his path.
> Pentheus charged thin air, hacking and hewing,
>   as though I were the victim of his blows.

At this point it is anyone's guess what is actually occurring as distinct from what is occurring in the minds of Pentheus and the Asiatic stranger. According to the latter witness's account, "Bakkhos brought the whole house down. And Pentheus, his home in a heap, saw all at once the cost to him of my [Dionysos's] confinement. A bitter sight." Yes, a bitter sight; but, *where* was Pentheus seeing it? After all, the audience pre-sumably has seen no change in the palace facade, no sign that the palace is no more; and Pentheus will shortly re-enter his apparently intact palace and retire to his quarters to robe and wig himself for his voy-euristic sortie into the mountains. One moment the palace is rubble, or appears to be rubble; and the next it is restored, or appears to be restored. Dionysiac metamorphosis and confusion need not touch the world when it can touch the mind. Such is the power of the god of illusion.

The mind-altering power of Dionysos is not always, however, excessive and sadistic. The commonplace devotees of Dionysos find all the illusion they need or want in a cup of wine. Wine is Dionysos's everyday gift to humankind, against whom he bears no grudge. True enough, wine changes nothing in the end; but, in the brief intoxicated interim, reality matters less than it did. When lucidity is pure pain, wine brings distance and distance permits sleep, and sleep is sweet. Admittedly, oblivion can be a curse; but often it is a gift. Teiresias, whose wisdom is legend, claims that "among all the blessed forces gracious to humankind, two stand out." The first, by his account, is Demeter or Goddess Earth, who feeds us with the fruit, the grains, thrown up in the soil's harvest.

> Next there is the son of Semele,
> who brought to the dry lips of mortals
> a bright, flowing cure,
> the juice of the grape, the miracle of wine,
> that puts broken mortals a few steps from their pain.
> For when the cup is drained
> and the blood of the grape rushes in the veins,
> sleep is sure to come,
> and with it sweet oblivion.
> All the day's woes are forgotten.
> It is the only way they leave.

Dionysos himself, in more than one legend, enjoys resurrection after dying a rather grisly death. His followers do not enjoy the same privileged renewal. For them, there is no return from death. Among mortals, however, there are minor deaths and minor renewals, which is to say that new days dawn when yesterday's ruin and loss have already mercifully entered the past, a process in which Dionysos plays his part. Without wine, sleep often will not come; and without sleep we cannot begin again. In the words of the cowherd, "the vine and its grape" are "our only cure for grief that will not go away. Besides," he adds, "without wine to ease its approach, how often would love come to us? When our cup is empty, life is just too harsh." With or without the cup of Dionysos, of course, life remains harsh; and Dionysos, who occasionally convinces us otherwise, remains the god of illusion.

Respite from care, the oblivion of sleep, the unself-consciousness of love, and hysterical communion with the god in his rites: these are among the many forms of Dionysiac possession. Teiresias mentions another. "Picture a host of men," he says, "in heavy arms,

already in the field, positioned for battle.
Now, even before a single spear is thrown,
or even raised, terror blows through their ranks
and scatters them like dry leaves.
This terror [*mania*] is our god's doing.
It is one form of his madness.

Dionysos possesses men, it seems, not only to make them forget their fears and to fall into the arms of women, but also to remember their fears and to run from the arms of battle. Teiresias links Dionysiac *mania* also to prophecy and vision, activities, or more accurately passivities, which he knows well. "When he [Dionysos] possesses us," explains Teiresias, "and banishes our wits, he brings a third eye. When he inhabits our bodies, he forms words with our lips that tell what is to be." It is a commonplace in Greek literature that outer blindness often accompanies, perhaps even occasions, inner sight; and that madness often means entry into truths well beyond the reach of reason. Dionysiac possession, with all of the swirling confusion it brings, only clears the mind to see the truth. Dionysos is also a god of vision.

What, we might ask, does the god of metamorphosis, illusion, manic possession, and masks have to do with vision? This question points us to the theater, the "seeing-place;" for it is in the theater that Dionysos's many aspects come into sharp focus. And, in turning now to masks, we are almost there. Masks, after all, have everything to do with metamorphosis, illusion, and possession. They also have everything to do with vision. But what do they have to do with Dionysos?

Masks assuredly did not originate in the cult of Dionysos, much less in his theater; neither did they originate in Greece. There is evidence of the ritual use of masks throughout the ancient Near East, from as early as the Neolithic period. Whether as an instrument of ritual or play, a mask makes possible the surrendering of one's own identity to a new identity bestowed by the mask. Anthropologists and children know this well. In ritual use, masks possess those who wear them. In the mask of a god or demon, the god or demon is present, alive and powerful. The wearer of the mask may summon that power to heal or to destroy, to utter blessings or curses, to say or to do what the god or demon wants said or done. As for Dionysos, his simplest and oldest known cultic representation is that of a bearded mask, or sometimes two bearded masks facing opposite directions, hung upon a pillar draped with fabric. In the Mycenaean period, gods were commonly represented and worshipped in the form of pillars, masks, beasts, or monsters, as well as in human form. In the classical period, however, when the human form had become canonical for the gods, only two Olympians retained close cultic ties with masks and mummery: Dionysos and Artemis. Both of these gods preside over boundaries, marginal spaces and times, and transitions, the significance of which will become clear.

In short, masks make possible the surrendering of one identity to another; in cult, the surrendering of the human to the divine. Masks are instruments of possession and empowerment, enabling a god not only to be visibly present but also, when his mask is donned, to be personified. The god's mask permits the god to be seen; and, when the wearer of the mask speaks what the god bids him to speak, the mask permits the god to be heard. In short, the mask is an instrument of revelation.

Ordinarily, drawing more from holdups and Halloween than from ancient drama, we think of masks as instruments of concealment. To "mask" something or someone is to hide it or him or her. The ultimate mask would be invisibility. The Greek word for "mask" [*prosopon*], however, suggests the opposite; for a *prosopon* is, literally, a countenance, a visage, a vision. A mask, instead of preventing recognition, provides it. Thus the mask of the god manifests him, presents him to the eyes of his followers. Admittedly any mask worn by an individual conceals that indi-vidual, i.e., calls for the surrender of his identity; but that surrender is for the sake of vision, the vision of the person or power manifest in the mask. On Halloween, the children in our neighborhoods, depending upon the ingenuity of their costumes, become unrecognizable to us; but at the same time ghouls and ghosts, two-legged leopards and pigs, miniature kings and rock stars walk our sidewalks. What we ordinarily see is cloaked so that we might see extraordinary sights. So too, when members of Dionysos's dithyrambic chorus, in a moment lost to historical understanding but not to our imaginations, first stepped out from that chorus, their faces painted or masked, to personify the heroes and gods whose deeds they had previously only sung and danced, in that moment the likes of Agamemnon, Odysseus, Helen, Orestes, Apollo, and Dionysos became visible to the eye. Their words were re-embodied, their deeds re-enacted. Like the lost souls who walk our streets on All Hallows' Eve, the figures of Greek myth and legend walked the stage or orchestra of the theater of Dionysos. They were reborn in the actors who surrendered for the festival time their own identities, their faces, their bodies, their voices, their souls to those whose masks they wore. In sum, the theater of Dionysos, god of masks, is best understood as a place not where actors are hidden but where heroes and gods are revealed.

From the *thymele*, his podium, in the center of the orchestra, Dionysos, present in his cult image, presides over the myriad revelations that occur in his theater. Every drama is performed before him and to him as the god of metamorphosis and masks, the god of revelry and revelation. In the *Bakkhai*, however, he comes down from his *thymele* and becomes a living, walking mask, a *prosopon* or character in his own drama. Oddly, he comes here, to Thebes and to his theater, as a stranger, unknown and unwelcome. Yet both are his native soil. Often, in the many stories told of him, Dionysos is both indigenous and foreign, insider and outsider. Although he is an Olympian and as Greek as any of his peers, Dionysos comes nearly always as a *xenos*, a stranger, a foreigner, whose identity is a mystery and whose exotic Asiatic ways threaten rigid regimes held in place by ignorance and fear.

In the *Bakkhai*, Dionysos is consummately concerned with his own revelation. In his drama he will provide, as every drama does, a spectacle; and that spectacle is ultimately himself. It is a sight which Thebes must witness "whether it wishes to or not." "Thebes," announces Dionysos, "must watch me vindicate my mother's honor and reveal myself to mortals as the true god Semele bore to Zeus." Dionysos is a god obsessed with the slights and slanders he has long endured at the hands of Thebes, whose callow king now wages virtual war on him. "I will show him," promises Dionysos,

> I will show every man in Thebes,
>   that I was born a god.
> Later, once my worship is well-established here,
>   I will take to the road again,
>   visit some other land, reveal myself.

For the time being, however, Dionysos, the god of meta-morphosis and illusion, takes human form, cloaks his godhead, costumes himself with humanity. "God though I am," he says, "I have taken mortal form." Although Dionysos is single-minded in his resolve to reveal himself, his first act is concealment. Revelation is a process. It must occur in stages. No light can dawn except on darkness. Resurrection requires death, just as spring requires winter. Only that which has been concealed can reveal itself; and so Dionysos must be denied, if he is to deny that denial, demanding and finally winning recognition. Dionysos, in short, requires Pentheus. In the *agon*, the contest, between them, the blaspheming king and the blasphemed god, Dionysos finds the occasion he needs to put himself and his power on display. He plays on the brittle inexperience of an adolescent king, provoking him to overstep himself, and then, with no more hesitation than a child pulling apart an insect, Dionysos obliterates him, slowly enough to compromise neither Pentheus's pain nor Dionysos's pleasure. All in good time, Dionysos stands revealed. With divine bad taste, he appears over the pile of stones that is Pentheus's palace and the pile of parts that is Pentheus, and flaunts his ascendancy. "I am Dionysos," he says, as if anyone were unaware of him by now, "son of Semele, child of Zeus, revealed at last as the god that I am."

This is the final spectacle, the final revelation in the *Bakkhai*, wherein the gulf separating humanity and divinity is unveiled. In the next century, Aristotle will argue that never can there be *philia*—friendship, love or fellowship—between god and man, so great is the gulf between them. In the *Bakkhai* we see why. It is stamped into the masks of Pentheus and Dionysos, the one full of pain and the other smiling indifferently. These masks, we may conjecture, never change expression in the course of the drama. From the outset, the masks of Pentheus and Dionysos reveal their characters; and "character," we know from Heraklitos, "is destiny." In the *Bakkhai*, Pentheus and Dionysos simply grow into their masks and so realize their irreconcilable destinies. The truth of Pentheus and the truth of Dionysos are visible in their masks from the moment of their entries into the theater. Greek masks do not lie. They tell the whole story of human tragedy and divine comedy and how the former provides the latter. Modern audiences, who mostly arrive at theaters in search of entertainment, dislike being told in the beginning what will happen in the end. Surprise seems to be an ingredient of enjoyment; knowing too much too soon only spoils things. Pentheus, presumably, would disagree. One cannot know the truth too soon.

Truth is, after all, what is revealed in the theater of Dionysos. It is the last cup offered by the god, the ultimate decoction drawn from existence once it has been crushed beneath his feet. It is a bitter cup, made momentarily sweet by the honey, the dramatic poetry, smeared around its rim. The very word for truth in Greek [*aletheia*], if we consider its root, seems to mean "that which we manage to un-forget." Truth, it seems, is that which we already know but do everything in our power, consciously or uncon-sciously, to overlook. Truth must be mined like ore, pried loose from oblivion. "Nature is inclined to hide," claims Heraklitos. And so, we might add, are we. Like Pentheus, we must be lured out of our ignorant securities into vision, into the spectacle. But how?

Seduction is a personal art for Dionysos. If he can walk through walls and make iron manacles yawn open as if they were alive and obedient to him, then he can break down the defenses of the likes of Pentheus or the audience. The voyeurism of Pentheus is hardly idiosyncratic. Like him, we are willing, even anxious, to stare into the chaos at the core of things, provided we may do so from a safe distance, untouched, untouchable. Who would resist the offer made to Pentheus by Dionysos, the offer of the highest pine in the forest, the best seat in the house? For one brief, oblivious moment, Pentheus feasts his eyes, imagining himself invisible and invulnerable. What he has overlooked is that the pine tree is sacred to Dionysos. Perched on the tip of the tallest pine, he is already in the god's grip. "He not the maenads," writes Euripides, "was now the spectacle." Pentheus plummets into the wildness he wanted only to watch. In fact he excites it and becomes its plaything.

Pentheus is not the only one, however, inclined to forget where he is. The theater of Dionysos is no less sacred to the god than was the pine tree which Pentheus eagerly mounted for the sight of his life. Those who come to the theater to watch a spectacle are no less likely than Pentheus to become one. Here, in the precinct of the god of revelry and revelation, there is no safe distance from his power. There is no ready escape from the truth. His devotees, his Chorus in the orchestra will, at the sound of his voice, tear up by its roots whatever illusions we have perched ourselves on. Then, as we find ourselves in free fall into the drama we came to watch, we, like Pentheus, will learn how very little divides us from our doom. Unlike Pentheus, however, we are permitted to reassemble ourselves and walk away. The play ends before we do. For us, there is still some space left between the illusion of the theater and the reality of the world. We may, like Agave—or we may not—learn from what we have seen and act on what we have learned. Agave, I suppose, stands somewhere between Pentheus and the audience, an illusory survivor, when she says only this: "If the dance begins again, I leave it to others." To us.

The Theater of Dionysos

In reflecting upon Dionysos, the god of theater, as revealed in the *Bakkhai*, we have had occasion to consider a span of ideas and realities, from fluid nature to intransigent truth. Although these considerations have been focused on the *Bakkhai*, they have uncovered elements essential to ancient Greek drama and, perhaps, to all serious drama. Admittedly, these elements and any dramatic principles or theories developed from them are decidedly Dionysian and, for that matter, Euripidean. Dionysos, however, is no intruder in his own theater; and Euripides, in giving Dionysos his due, is no usurper. The *Bakkhai* celebrates Dionysos's homecoming, not only to his Thebes but also to his theater; and it is Euripides' last and only explicit word on the subject. Beyond that word lies conjecture, the precarious endeavor to articulate what is only implicit in the *Bakkhai*. In effect, what I propose next is to conduct a brief philosophical commentary on a missing text, the *Poetics* of Euripides, a text missing because it never was. The subject of that text, and so of this commentary, is the theater of Dionysos, the elements and principles of Dionysian drama.

The taproot, as it were, of Dionysian drama is metamorphosis, the experience of radical change, the crossing of natural boundaries. Dionysos, we know, passes easily from divinity to humanity to bestiality and back again. Ordinarily, if one is not Dionysos, the lines dividing these three natures—divine, bestial, and human—are found to be impassable. I focus on these three *phuseis* or natures because together they constitute the moral cosmos spanned by and mirrored in the ancient Greek theater. They represent, at the same time, the metaphysical community delineated and confirmed in ritual sacrifice, which lay at the core of ancient Greek religion. Whether we consult Greek religion, drama, or philosophy, the ordering of these three natures or modes of being remains always the same: human beings stand midway between the gods above and the beasts below. On this fundamental ordering [*taxis*] of existence, not only the ancient Greeks but the peoples of the entire ancient East Mediterranean world were of one mind.

What, we may ask, in simplest terms distinguishes each of these modes of being? Beginning at the top, with the gods, what does it mean to be divine? Distilled to one word, as it can be, the gods are "the deathless ones" [*oi athanatoi*]. Their lives span "aeons" or virtual eternities. They do not know death, nor can they tolerate its presence. Their wounds, should they suffer any, heal like children's cuts and scratches, overnight. Furthermore, the gods are profoundly conscious of their privileges and prerogatives. They know who they are. It is no surprise to them when they fail to age beyond a certain point and when death fails to come at all for them. In fact, it is the consciousness of their essential immunity from diminishment that shapes utterly their character and the quality of the lives they live and live and live.

At the other end of the natural spectrum from the gods are beasts, who possess neither the deathlessness nor the consciousness of the gods. The life-spans of beasts are brief; but there is no evidence of their being preoccupied with this brevity throughout their lives. Young, healthy beasts presumably do not brood over the fact that they are doomed by their natures to eventual death. They live and then they die. Life and death are, as it were, separate events; separate too are the awarenesses that accompany each. And, since the awareness of death coincides with death, which brings an end to all awareness, beasts would seem to be spared or denied mortality.

Mortality, after all, is not to be confused with morbidity. Being doomed to death is not the same as being mortal; otherwise beasts would be mortal, which they are not. Human beings alone are called *thnetoi*, just as gods alone are called *athanatoi*. This one word, *thnetoi*, like a husk, houses the germ of all that is uniquely human. It means, quite simply, "deathful." Human beings, defined somewhere between gods and beasts, have something essential in common with each. Human beings share in the morbidity of beasts and in the consciousness of gods. Like animals, their deaths are certain; like gods they know who they are. They know that they are doomed; and that knowledge pervades and shapes their lives. Instead of living and then dying, mortals live and die at the same time; for they know that as they are living they are also dying. The unfolding of life and the approach of death are one event, not two. Mortal existence is not Being followed by Non-being but Being and Non-being fused into one: deathful being or "Being-towards-death," as Heidegger put it.

At this point we must add a complication. Ancient Greek poets, playwrights, and philosophers, from Homer to Aristotle, recognized that would-be humans are not born into the consciousness of death, wherein their uniqueness resides; rather, they must grow into it. Humanity, that curious hybrid of Being and Non-being, is best described as a state of Becoming. Gods are born gods. Beasts are born beasts. Humans, on the other hand, must become human. They must come to the consciousness of death. The obligation of morbidity and the obligation of consciousness weigh differently upon human beings. There is no avoiding death, in the end. Its claim is absolute. Mortal consciousness, however, is another matter. Its claim is merely a moral claim; and moral claims are easily denied, though not without paying a price for their denial.

How is it, then, that would-be humans come to the consciousness of their death without having come to the moment of their death? The answer lies in a peculiarly human faculty and activity, which Plato calls *eikasia*, from which we have received the word icon. *Eikasia* is, in Plato's account of the "Divided Line" in Book VI of the *Republic*, what enables human beings to ascend from illusory sensation to intellectual knowledge, from perception to contemplation. *Eikasia* is, for Plato, the foundation of understanding. It is, at the same time, a power and activity altogether familiar to us; for, with some slight hesitancy, we may translate *eikasia* as, simply, "imagination." More awkwardly but more accurately, we may speak of it as "imaging" and intend by that "the seeing of an image as an image." Now, in order to understand what this peculiarly human mode of seeing is, we must reflect pointedly on the word *eikon*, "icon" or "image," from which the act of "imaging" proceeds.

The key to the meaning of *eikon* lies in the curious fact that an *eikon* always both is and is not what it is, which is to say that every *eikon* participates, as it were, in Being and in Non-being.

An everyday example will draw this abstruse discussion closer to hand. If I look at a childhood photograph of a friend and ask the friend "Is that you?" and receive the answer "Yes," I continue to make a distinction between my friend and his photograph; for the photograph is not my friend any more than my friend is the photograph. Similarly, I never hesitate to answer "Yes" to any-one who, noticing a favorite portrait in my home, asks if it is my grandmother, although I know that my grandmother died over forty years ago. That image both is and is not my grandmother. When I look at it, I both see her and don't see her; for I see her both present and absent in the image. In simplest terms, this is what *eikasia* means: to see one thing in another, to see something in what it is not.

How, then, do human beings come to the consciousness of death without themselves yet dying? They die others' deaths from which they are privileged to return. They die imaginatively, vicariously. They see their own deaths in the deaths of others. Prior to and apart from Greek drama, ancient Greek literature is replete with moments of *eikasia*, when one person or death or grief is seen as the image of another. Nowhere is this more evident or poignant than in the *Iliad*. When Patroklos, in Book XVI, enters the thick of the battle in Akhilles' armor, the Trojans see at first not Patroklos but Akhilles; for Patroklos has become an icon of Akhilles. When Patroklos dies, so does Akhilles with him. Even after the Trojans have stripped the armor of Akhilles from the body of Patroklos, Akhilles sees himself in Patroklos. Indeed, the death of Patroklos and that of Akhilles are one, separated only by time, a brief interval, in which Akhilles survives deathfully. Next, in Book XXII, when Akhilles and Hektor meet, it is now Hektor who is clad in Akhilles' armor. He has become a second icon of Akhilles; and, to all appearances, when Akhilles chases Hektor three times around the walls of Troy to his death, it is fleet-footed Akhilles who catches up with himself and consigns himself to Hades. Indeed, Akhilles knows that in taking Hektor's life he is relinquishing his own. In point of fact, Akhilles does not die in the *Iliad*; and yet we see him, as he sees himself, die already twice, once in Patroklos and once in Hektor. Even Priam, the father of Hektor, in Book XXIV, looks at his son's murderer and sees his murdered son, just as Akhilles looks at Priam grieving for Hektor and sees his own father grieving for him.

The truth that reveals itself in these moments of *eikasia* is that individual human beings are images, reflecting each other and refracting for a time a portion of what it means to be human. As an image, each individual human being both is and is not what he or she is, i.e., human. Only a part of what it means to be human is visible in this or that life or moment of life; the rest must be seen elsewhere, in other lives and other moments. Full humanity is available only communally, only through others, only imaginatively or vicariously. This, in simplest terms, is the meaning of the ancient Greek conviction that the nature of human beings requires that they live together in community. In other words, it is possible to realize one's humanity only in and with others, imaging and imagining the fullness of human life together, openly, in a place of common vision. That place in the ancient city of Athens was the theater—the *theatron* or "seeing place"—of Dionysos.

What is it, we might ask, that is seen in the theater? There is, of course, the spectacle of the chorus and actors, robed and masked, moving and dancing before a painted scene. This sight must have been at times quite splendid. Here, before the eyes of thousands, the great figures of legend — Agamemnon, Helen, Herakles, and others — appeared in open sight. For centuries they had been visible only to the mind's eye, as audiences closed their eyes and listened to the songs of poets. Once they had been visible only in words, spoken words, sound-icons, as it were. Now, in the theater, having suffered the *sparagmos* of time, they were, like Dionysos, reassembled and returned to life. For this they required their surrogates, actors, who became "other selves" for the figures of times past and of times out of time, walking, speaking, breathing, living, dying icons. The *theatron*, the house of vision, is a home for images and for the imagination, where sights lost to the everyday, literal eye reveal themselves to heightened sight.

The theater is, as well, the place of metamorphosis; for actors must become Agamemnon, Helen, Herakles, or Athena before they can be seen as such. In donning the robes and mask of a king, a hero, a god, or a woman, actors become what they are not. In the theater they cross lines which, in ordinary life, are crossed only rarely or reluctantly or with the slow passage of time, if they are crossed at all. Actors become kings and slaves, women and barbarians, seers and warriors, peasants and exiles, whatever forms human life (or even divine life imagined in human terms) takes. Like Dionysos, to whom they belong, actors even die and return from death in other forms. In the theater, there are no lines which, once crossed, cannot be crossed again. Theater-life and theater-death resemble play, serious in theme but not in consequence. In the theater, it is possible to revel in anything.

The precinct of Dionysos, the realm of his possession, however, encircles more than the orchestra. Not only the spectacle but the would-be spectators too belong to him. Actors become icons not only of the past but of the present as well. Those who come to the theater to peer into the mythic past learn that there is no escape here from the all-too-real present. The masks of Agamemnon or Medea or Pentheus or Oedipus are finally mirrors confronting their would-be spectators with themselves, stripped of all cosmetic evasion, stripped to their humanity. Like Pentheus, perched on the highest pine in the forest, even those in the safest seats life affords must learn how very little separates them from what they witness taking place in the orchestra. Sooner or later, at a signal they may or may not hear, they will begin their fall into the spectacle. In the theater of Dionysos, as in the cosmos it mirrors, there are finally no spectators, only the spectacle. Neither imaginative life nor life itself, in the end, allows for voyeurism.

Dionysos, for whom all of nature is fluid, defies, as do his devotees, all of the boundaries—metaphysical, sexual, political, moral—which divide god from beast and mortal, woman from man, king from slave, saint from sadist. This defiance, however, if not for the god then for his *attaches*, is brief. For a moment the cosmos appears porous, fluid, unstable; and, in the next moment, the old order returns, fixed, intransigent. The myriad boundaries which define and articulate the order of things are never finally dissolved, only for a time suspended. Those who cross over ordinarily impassable lines must return; for both the crossing-over and the crossing-back are equally critical. Each reveals a truth. The first truth is that all living things are somehow one and that only quite precarious, arbitrary lines divide them, one from the other. This truth found frequent expression in ancient Greek writers from Homer to Anaxagoras to Euripides to Aristotle, who claimed that "the nature of each thing is considered to be that which prevails in it." In other words, there is beast in every human, man in every woman, and, in Thales' words, "gods in all things." Even in modern, molecular chemistry, the same truth stares out at us. Consider, for example, a molecule of chlorophyll, composed of 136 atoms of hydrogen, carbon, oxygen, and nitrogen around a single atom of magnesium. Replace that one magnesium atom with one of iron, leaving everything else in place, and chlorophyll becomes hemoglobin. Whether under an electron microscope or under Dionysiac possession, nature is nearly one, fabulously fluid.

Next, a second truth is revealed in the crossing-back, the return to familiar order and boundaries and more or less rigid identities: the fact of multiplicity, of myriad particularity. Being is one, and it is also many. This is the elusive yet unavoidable mystery confronted by the earliest and the latest Greek philosophers, and by the playwrights as well. Gods, beasts, and mortals share a common life, and at times the lines between them seem the thinnest of fibers, all but transparent. Yet, in an instant, those lines can turn to stone and the stone can grow to a wall too thick to allow even the most desperate voices to pass through. Men and women share a common humanity, as do young and old, master and slave, rich and poor. In fact, there are truly resplendent moments when that humanity prevails in them and they are defined by it. There are other moments, however, when the disparate sexes, ages, and classes of humans encounter and treat one another as utterly alien beings, unrecognizable and undeserving of respect. Since reality, in sum, is to its core a paradox, its truth can be grasped only in movement, back and forth between its contradictions. This movement, this leaping of the imagination across a paradoxical universe is the dance of Dionysos, god of boundaries, boundaries which he, in the same theatrical moment, reveals and defies.

The lines, the boundaries, over which Dionysos leaps define humanity. To "de-fine" anything is to know where it begins and where it ends, to know its boundaries, its *fines* or limits. And, in our universe, where one thing ends another predictably begins. In the Greek *taxis* or order of the universe, and arguably in our own, human being is bounded by divine being and by bestial being, and is defined by its proximity to and its disparity from both. Humanity ends where either divinity or bestiality begins. From the human perspective, what both gods and beasts have in common and what defines them both is their inhumanity. Human beings know well this inhumanity, not only because they suffer its incursions but also because they succumb to its attractions. Although human beings cannot literally become either divine or bestial beings, they can and do mimic both. Human beings often act or suffer as if they were beasts or gods, which is to say they violate their own or others' humanity or suffer its violation by others. They contradict, or suffer the contradiction of, their nature, which in the short run has only a moral claim upon them. Human beings are free, after all, to think of themselves or of others as gods or as beasts, though not with final impunity. Every essential line crossed must be crossed back again; every truth denied will have its day. Human truth, the truth of human nature, is no exception.

The theater, it may be said, is where truth and untruth can be explored with relative impunity. Outside the theater, in life, the inescapable circle of habit described by Aristotle holds firm: conduct shapes character and character shapes conduct. We become what we do and we act out who we have become through our actions. In the theater, however, actors do not truly do what they do nor truly say what they say. When they murder or lie or betray their friends they do not become what others become when they do such things. Actors suffer neither the pollution nor the guilt of their deeds; for their deeds are only imaginary. The *mythoi* or story-lines played out in the theater, like the dialogues of Sokrates with his contemporaries, may be thought of as "experiments" with truth and untruth. When they are over and their participants find themselves contradicted, confounded, even to the core of their souls, they may re-trace their steps and return, unscathed, to the beginning; for nothing real, nothing irrevo-cable, has been done. The only occurrences have been those of imagination and of insight. Imaginary deeds, however, yield real insights. The insights reached, the truths grasped in the theater are not nearly so ephemeral as the words and deeds that produced them. They are the real fruit of vicarious actions and sufferings, the largesse of Dionysos, god of vision, "of all gods the most dangerous and the most endearing."

The ultimate spectacle in the theater of Euripides is humanity: humanity denied, humanity deified, humanity bestialized, humanity defiled, humanity restored. The brightest truth here is humanity—human *physis*, human nature—intact and flourishing. Finally, there is no distinguishing between the

ethics and the poetics of Euripides. His aesthetic is essentially moral. For him there is nothing more unsightly than inhumanity, whether bestial or divine, the inhumanity of Eteokles or Odysseus or Kalkhas or Hekabe or Artemis or Dionysos; nothing lovelier to behold than humanity restored or preserved, gripped barely and desperately, in one's teeth as it were, the humanity of Poluxene or Iphigenia or Herakles and Theseus. In the theater of Euripides, man, human being, may or may not be "the measure of all things" but humanity is, indisputably, the measure of morality. Here, in the theater, as in life, there is one fundamental choice: either humanity or inhumanity.

In the last moments of the *Bakkhai*, when the howling void between human tragedy and divine comedy yawns open in the orchestra, Dionysos, resplendent in his divinity, is alone in his own theater, as vulnerable and indefensible as his dismembered victim. Dionysos is in the same disarray, morally, as Pentheus is physically. They have both, in Kadmos's words, "gone too far." For them, there is no going back; for Pentheus, because he is dead, and for Dionysos, because he will never be dead and thus can never know human limits. For the spectators, however, not yet themselves the spectacle, precious moments remain. Dionysos the dangerous proves endearing and offers a reprieve. The space between the imaginary and the real will not close today as it did for Pentheus. Dionysos gives us time and his playwright gives us insight. No one is offered more than this. It must suffice.

WWW.BOLCHAZY.COM

AP-Textbooks

AP Ancillaries

Latin Studies

Greek Studies

Artes Latinae

Classical Bulletin

Website Galleries

Myth

Gilgamesh

WWII

Slavic Studies

Modern History

Order Online Today